ICSEA 2021

The Sixteenth International Conference on Software Engineering Advances

October 3 -7, 2021

Barcelona, Spain

ICSEA 2021 Editors

Lugi Lavazza, University of Insubria at Varese, Italy

Hironori Washizaki, Waseda University / National Institute of Informatics / System Information, Japan

Herwig Mannert, University of Antwerp, Belgium

Printed from e-media with permission by:

Curran Associates, Inc.
57 Morehouse Lane
Red Hook, NY 12571

Some format issues inherent in the e-media version may also appear in this print version.

Printed with permission by Curran Associates, Inc. (2023)

International Academy, Research, and Industry Association (IARIA)
412 Derby Way
Wilmington, DE 19810

Phone: (408) 893-6407
Fax: (408) 527-6351

petre@iaria.org

Additional copies of this publication are available from:

Curran Associates, Inc.
57 Morehouse Lane
Red Hook, NY 12571 USA
Phone: 845-758-0400
Fax: 845-758-2633
Email: curran@proceedings.com
Web: www.proceedings.com

Table of Contents

ICSEA 2021

Forward

The Sixteenth International Conference on Software Engineering Advances (ICSEA 2021), held on October 3 - 7, 2021 in Barcelona, Spain, continued a series of events covering a broad spectrum of software-related topics.

The conference covered fundamentals on designing, implementing, testing, validating and maintaining various kinds of software. The tracks treated the topics from theory to practice, in terms of methodologies, design, implementation, testing, use cases, tools, and lessons learnt. The conference topics covered classical and advanced methodologies, open source, agile software, as well as software deployment and software economics and education.

The conference had the following tracks:

- Advances in fundamentals for software development
- Advanced mechanisms for software development
- Advanced design tools for developing software
- Software engineering for service computing (SOA and Cloud)
- Advanced facilities for accessing software
- Software performance
- Software security, privacy, safeness
- Advances in software testing
- Specialized software advanced applications
- Web Accessibility
- Open source software
- Agile and Lean approaches in software engineering
- Software deployment and maintenance
- Software engineering techniques, metrics, and formalisms
- Software economics, adoption, and education
- Business technology
- Improving productivity in research on software engineering
- Trends and achievements

Similar to the previous edition, this event continued to be very competitive in its selection process and very well perceived by the international software engineering community. As such, it is attracting excellent contributions and active participation from all over the world. We were very pleased to receive a large amount of top quality contributions.

We take here the opportunity to warmly thank all the members of the ICSEA 2021 technical program committee as well as the numerous reviewers. The creation of such a broad and high quality conference program would not have been possible without their involvement. We also kindly thank all the authors that dedicated much of their time and efforts to contribute to the ICSEA 2021. We truly believe that thanks to all these efforts, the final conference program consists of top quality contributions.

This event could also not have been a reality without the support of many individuals, organizations and sponsors. We also gratefully thank the members of the ICSEA 2021 organizing committee for their help in handling the logistics and for their work that is making this professional meeting a success.

We hope the ICSEA 2021 was a successful international forum for the exchange of ideas and results between academia and industry and to promote further progress in software engineering research.

ICSEA 2021 Steering Committee

Herwig Manaert, University of Antwerp, Belgium
Radek Koci, Brno University of Technology, Czech Republic
Sébastien Salva, University of Clermont Auvergne | LIMOS Laboratory | CNRS, France
José Carlos Metrôlho, Polytechnic Institute of Castelo Branco, Portugal
Luigi Lavazza, Università dell'Insubria – Varese, Italy
Hironori Washizaki, Waseda University / National Institute of Informatics / SYSTEM INFORMATION, Japan
Roy Oberhauser, Aalen University, Germany

ICSEA 2021 Publicity Chair

José Miguel Jiménez, Universitat Politecnica de Valencia, Spain
Lorena Parra, Universitat Politecnica de Valencia, Spain

ICSEA 2021

Committee

ICSEA 2021 Steering Committee

Herwig Manaert, University of Antwerp, Belgium
Radek Koci, Brno University of Technology, Czech Republic
Sébastien Salva, University of Clermont Auvergne | LIMOS Laboratory | CNRS, France
José Carlos Metrôlho, Polytechnic Institute of Castelo Branco, Portugal
Luigi Lavazza, Università dell'Insubria – Varese, Italy
Hironori Washizaki, Waseda University / National Institute of Informatics / SYSTEM INFORMATION, Japan
Roy Oberhauser, Aalen University, Germany

ICSEA 2021 Publicity Chair

José Miguel Jiménez, Universitat Politecnica de Valencia, Spain
Lorena Parra, Universitat Politecnica de Valencia, Spain

ICSEA 2021 Technical Program Committee

Tamer Abdou, Ryerson University, Canada
Morayo Adedjouma, CEA Saclay Nano-INNOV - Institut CARNOT CEA LIST, France
Ammar Kareem Obayes Alazzawi, Universiti Teknologi PETRONAS, Malaysia
Washington H. C. Almeida, CESAR School, Brazil
Eman Abdullah AlOmar, Rochester Institute of Technology, USA
Sousuke Amasaki, Okayama Prefectural University, Japan
Talat Ambreen, International Islamic University, Islamabad, Pakistan
Amal Ahmed Anda, University of Ottawa, Canada
Daniel Andresen, Kansas State University, USA
Jean-Paul Arcangeli, UPS - IRIT, France
Francesca Arcelli Fontana, University of Milano Bicocca, Italy
Benjamin Aziz, University of Portsmouth, UK
Takuya Azumi, Saitama University, Japan
Gilbert Babin, HEC Montréal, Canada
Jorge Barreiros, ISEC - Polytechnic of Coimbra / NOVA LINCS, Portugal
Marciele Bergier, Universidade do Minho | Research Center of the Justice and Governance, Portugal
Silvia Bonfanti, University of Bergamo, Italy
Mina Boström Nakicenovic, Paradox Interactive, Sweden
José Carlos Bregieiro Ribeiro, Polytechnic Institute of Leiria, Portugal
Uwe Breitenbücher, University of Stuttgart, Germany
Antonio Brogi, University of Pisa, Italy
Carlos Henrique Cabral Duarte, Brazilian Development Bank (BNDES), Brazil
Carlos A. Casanova Pietroboni, National Technological University - Concepción del Uruguay Regional

Sanjay Misra, Covenant University, Nigeria
Mohammadsadegh Mohagheghi, Vali-e-Asr University of Rafsanjan, Iran
Miguel P. Monteiro, Universidade NOVA de Lisboa, Portugal
Fernando Moreira, Universidade Portucalense, Portugal
Óscar Mortágua Pereira, University of Aveiro, Portugal
Ines Mouakher, University of Tunis El Manar, Tunisia
Kmimech Mourad, Higher Institute for Computer Science and Mathematics of Monastir, Tunisia
Sana Ben Hamida Mrabet, Paris Nanterre University / LAMSADE - Paris Dauphine University, France
Kazi Muheymin-Us-Sakib, Institute of Information Technology (IIT) | University of Dhaka, Bangladesh
Anitha Murugesan, Honeywell Aerospace, USA
Marcellin Nkenlifack, University of Dschang, Cameroon
Marc Novakouski, Carnegie Mellon Software Engineering Institute, USA
Roy Oberhauser, Aalen University, Germany
Shinpei Ogata, Shinshu University, Japan
Thomas Olsson, RISE Research Institutes of Sweden, Sweden
Safa Omri, Daimler AG / Karlsruhe Institute of Technology, Germany
Flavio Oquendo, IRISA (UMR CNRS) - University of South Brittany, France
Marcos Palacios, University of Oviedo, Spain
Harsha Perera, Monash University, Australia
Beatriz Pérez Valle, University of La Rioja, Spain
Monica Pinto, University of Málaga, Spain
Aneta Poniszewska-Maranda, Institute of Information Technology | Lodz University of Technology, Poland
Valeria Pontillo, University of Salerno, Italy
Pasqualina Potena, RISE Research Institutes of Sweden AB, Sweden
Evgeny Pyshkin, University of Aizu, Japan
Claudia Raibulet, University of Milano-Bicocca, Italy
Muthu Ramachandran, Leeds Beckett University, UK
Aurora Ramírez, University of Córdoba, Spain
Raman Ramsin, Sharif University of Technology, Iran
Fernando Reinaldo Ribeiro, Polytechnic Institute of Castelo Branco, Portugal
Catarina I. Reis, ciTechCare - Center for Innovative Care and Health Technology | Polytechnic of Leiria, Portugal
Michele Risi, University of Salerno, Italy
Simona Mirela Riurean, University of Petrosani, Romania
António Miguel Rosado da Cruz, Polytechnic Institute of Viana do Castelo, Portugal
Adrian Rutle, Western Norway University of Applied Sciences, Norway
Renaud Rwemalika, SnT - University of Luxembourg, Luxembourg
Ines Bayoudh Saadi, ENSIT - Tunis University, Tunisia
Nyyti Saarimäki, Tampere University, Finland
Bilal Abu Salih, The University of Jordan, Jordan
Sébastien Salva, University of Clermont Auvergne | LIMOS Laboratory | CNRS, France
Hiroyuki Sato, University of Tokyo, Japan
Wieland Schwinger, Johannes Kepler University Linz (JKU) | Inst. f. Telekooperation (TK), Austria
Vesna Šešum-Čavić, TU Wien, Austria
Rifat Ara Shams, Monash University, Australia
István Siket, University of Szeged, Hungary
Karolj Skala, Hungarian Academy of Sciences, Hungary / Ruđer Bošković Institute Zagreb, Croatia

Juan Jesús Soria Quijaite, Universidad Peruana Unión, Lima, Peru
Nissrine Souissi, MINES-RABAT School (ENSMR), Morocco
Maria Spichkova, RMIT University, Australia
Fausto Spoto, Università di Verona, Italy
Alin Stefanescu, University of Bucharest, Romania
Sidra Sultana, National University of Sciences and Technology, Pakistan
Yingcheng Sun, Columbia University in New York City, USA
Jose Manuel Torres, Universidade Fernando Pessoa, Porto, Portugal
Christos Troussas, University of West Attica, Greece
Mariusz Trzaska, Polish-Japanese Academy of Information Technology, Poland
Masateru Tsunoda, Kindai University, Japan
Sylvain Vauttier, LGI2P - Ecole des Mines d'Alès, France
Rohith Yanambaka Venkata, University of North Texas, USA
Colin Venters, University of Huddersfield, UK
Laszlo Vidacs, Hungarian Academy of Sciences / University of Szeged, Hungary
Hironori Washizaki, Waseda University / National Institute of Informatics / SYSTEM INFORMATION, Japan
Bingyang Wei, Texas Christian University, USA
Mohamed Wiem Mkaouer, Rochester Institute of Technology, USA
Dietmar Winkler, Institute for Information Systems Engineering | TU Wien, Austria
Xusheng Xiao, Case Western Reserve University, USA
Simon Xu, Algoma University, Canada
Rihito Yaegashi, Kagawa University, Japan
Yilong Yang, University of Macau, Macau
Haibo Yu, Kyushu Sangyo University, Japan
Mário Zenha-Rela, University of Coimbra, Portugal
Qiang Zhu, University of Michigan - Dearborn, USA
Martin Zinner, Technische Universität Dresden, Germany
Kamil Żyła, Lublin University of Technology, Poland

Copyright Information

An Empirical Study of the Correlation of Cognitive Complexity-related Code Measures

Luigi Lavazza
Dipartimento di Scienze Teoriche e Applicate
Università degli Studi dell'Insubria
Varese, Italy
email:luigi.lavazza@uninsubria.it

***Abstract*—Several measures have been proposed to represent various characteristics of code, such as size, complexity, cohesion, coupling, etc. These measures are deemed interesting because the "internal" characteristics they measure (which are not interesting *per se*) are believed to be correlated with "external" software qualities (like reliability, maintainability, etc.) that are definitely interesting for developers or users. Although many measures have been proposed for software code, new measures are continuously proposed. However, before starting using a new measure, we would like to ascertain that it is actually useful and that it provides some improvement with respect to well established measures that have been in use for a long time and whose merits have been widely evaluated. In 2018, a new code measure, named "Cognitive Complexity" was proposed. According to the proposers, this measure should correlate to code understandability much better than 'traditional' code measures, such as McCabe Complexity, for instance. However, hardly any experimentation proved whether the "Cognitive Complexity" measure is better than other measures or not. Actually, it was not even verified whether the new measure provides different knowledge concerning code with respect to 'traditional' measures. In this paper, we aim at evaluating experimentally to what extent the new measure is correlated with traditional measures. To this end, we measured the code from a set of open-source Java projects and derived models of "Cognitive Complexity" based on the traditional code measures yielded by a state-of-the-art code measurement tool. We found that fairly accurate models of "Cognitive Complexity" can be obtained using just a few traditional code measures. In this sense, the "Cognitive Complexity" measure does not appear to provide additional knowledge with respect to previously proposed measures.**

Keywords–Cognitive complexity; software code measures; McCabe complexity; cyclomatic complexity; Halstead measures; static code measures

I. Introduction

Many measures have been proposed to represent the internal characteristics of code, such as size, complexity, cohesion or coupling. Several empirical studies have correlated these measures with external software qualities of interest, such as faultiness or maintainability.

Quite often, new measures are proposed. Some aim at representing specific features of code that had not been considered previously: for instance, Chidamber and Kemerer proposed the Number of Children (NOC) and Depth of Inheritance (DIT) [1] when object-oriented programming languages started to become popular.

Some other measures are proposed with the specific aim of predicting interesting external qualities. A new measure was proposed in 2018 with the aim of representing the complexity of understanding code [2]. This new measure was named "Cognitive Complexity," however, in the remainder of this paper we shall refer to this measure as "CoCo," to avoid confusion with the concept of cognitive complexity, i.e., the property that CoCo is expected to measure.

Some initial work has been done to evaluate whether CoCo is actually correlated with code understandability [3]. The initial results yielded by this research do not support the claim that CoCo is better correlated to code understandability than previously proposed measures.

At any rate, whatever the goal that a new measure is supposed to help achieving, the new measure should provide some "knowledge" that existing measures are not able to capture. If a new measure is so strongly correlated with other measures that the latter can be used to to build models that allow predicting the new measure with reasonable accuracy, it is unlikely that the new measure actually conveys any knew knowledge.

CoCo is receiving some attention, probably because it is provided by `SonarQube`, which is a quite popular tool. Therefore, it is time to look for evidence that CoCo provides additional knowledge with respect to well established code measures. To this end, in this paper we consider the following two research questions:

- RQ1 How strongly is CoCo correlated with each of the code measures that are commonly used in software development?
- RQ2 Is it possible to build models that predict the value of CoCo based on the values of commonly used code measures? If so, how accurate are the predictions that can be achieved?

The paper is structured as follows. Section II provides some background, by introducing CoCo and describing the traditional code measures used in this study. Section III describes the empirical study that was carried out to answer the research questions. Section IV discusses the results obtained by the study and answers the research questions. Section V discusses the threats to the validity of the study. Section VI accounts for related work. Finally, in Section VII some conclusions are drawn, and future work is outlined.

II. Code Measures

In this paper we deal with measures of the internal attributes of code. Internal attributes of code can be measured by looking at code alone, without considering software qualities (like faultiness, robustness, maintainability, etc.) that are externally perceivable.

Several measures for internal software attributes (e.g., size, structural complexity, cohesion, coupling) were proposed [4] to quantify the qualities of software modules. These measures are interesting because they concern code qualities that are believed to affect external software qualities (like faultiness or maintainability), which are the properties that are interesting for developers and users.

Since CoCo is computed at the method level, in what follows, we consider only measures at the same granulatrity level, i.e., measures that are applicable to methods.

A. *"Traditional" Code Measures*

Since the first high-level programming languages were introduced, several measures were proposed, to represent the possibly relevant characteristics of code. For instance, the Lines Of Code (LOC) measure the size of a software module, while McCabe Complexity (also known as Cyclomatic Complexity) [5] was proposed to represent the "complexity" of code, with the idea that high levels of complexity characterize code that is difficult to test and maintain. The object-oriented measures by Chidamber and Kemerer [1] were proposed to recognize poor software design. For instance, modules with high levels of coupling are supposed to be associated with difficult maintenance.

In this paper, we are interested in evaluating the correlation between CoCo and traditional measures. Since CoCo is defined at the method level, here we consider only traditional measures addressing methods; measures defined to represent the properties of classes or other code structures are ignored.

SourceMeter [6] was used to collect code measures. The method-level measures we used are listed in Table I. Because of space constraints, we cannot give here the detailed definition of each measure. Instead, we provide a very brief description; interested readers can find additional information in the documentation of SourceMeter.

Among the measures listed in Table I we have: Halstead measures [7], several maintainability indexes, including the original one [8], McCabe complexity, measures of the nesting level (i.e., how deeply are code control structured included in each other), logical lines of code (which are counted excluding blank lines, comment-only lines, etc.).

B. *The "Cognitive Complexity" Measure*

In 2017, SonarSource introduced Cognitive Complexity [2] as a new measure for the understandability of any given piece of code. This new measure was named "Cognitive Complexity" because its authors assumed that the measure was suitable to represent the cognitive complexity of understanding code. To this end, CoCo was proposed with the aim *"to remedy Cyclomatic Complexity's shortcomings and produce a measurement that more accurately reflects the relative difficulty of understanding, and therefore of maintaining methods, classes, and applications"* [2].

TABLE I
THE MEASURES COLLECTED VIA SOURCEMETER.

Metric name	Abbreviation
Halstead Calculated Program Length	HCPL
Halstead Difficulty	HDIF
Halstead Effort	HEFF
Halstead Number of Delivered Bugs	HNDB
Halstead Program Length	HPL
Halstead Program Vocabulary	HPV
Halstead Time Required to Program	HTRP
Halstead Volume	HVOL
Maintainability Index (Microsoft version)	MIMS
Maintainability Index (Original version)	MI
Maintainability Index (SEI version)	MISEI
Maintainability Index (SourceMeter version)	MISM
McCabe's Cyclomatic Complexity	McCC
Nesting Level	NL
Nesting Level Else-If	NLE
Logical Lines of Code	LLOC
Number of Statements	NOS

Rather than a real measure, CoCo is an indicator, which takes into account several aspects of code. Like McCabe's complexity, it takes into account decision points (conditional statements, loops, switch statements, etc.), but, unlike McCabe's complexity, gives them a weight equal to their nesting level plus 1. So, for instance, the following code fragment

```
void firstMethod() {
  if (condition1)
    for (int i = 0; i < 10; i++)
      while (condition2) { ... }
}
```

the `if` statement at nesting level 0 has weight 1, the `for` statement at nesting level 1 has weight 2, and the `while` statement at nesting level 2 has weight 3, thus CoCo= 1+2+3 = 6. The same code has McCabe complexity = 4 (3 decision points plus one).

Consider instead the following code fragment, in which the control structures are not nested.

```
void secondMethod() {
  if (condition1) { ... }
  for (int i = 0; i < 10; i++) { ... }
  while (condition2) { ... }
}
```

This code has CoCo = 3, while its McCabe complexity is still 4. It is thus apparent that nested structures increase CoCo, while they have no effect on McCabe complexity.

CoCo also accounts for Boolean predicates: a Boolean predicate contributes to CoCo depending on the number of its sub-sequences of logical operators. For instance, consider the following code fragment, where `a, b, c, d, e, f` are Boolean variables

```
void thirdMethod() {
  if (a && b && c || d || e && f) { ... }
}
```

Predicate `a && b && c || d || e && f` contains three sub-sequences with the same logical operators, i.e., `a && b && c`, `c || d || e`, and `e && f`, so it adds 3 to the value of CoCo.

Other aspects of code contribute to increment CoCo, but they are much less frequent than those described above. For a complete description of CoCo, see the definition [2].

III. The Empirical Study

The empirical study involved a set of open-source Java programs. This code was measured, and the collected data were analyzed via well consolidated statistical methods. The dataset is described in Section III-A, while the measurement and analysis methods are described in Section III-B. The results we obtained are reported in Section III-C.

A. The Dataset

The code to be analyzed within the study was a convenience sample: data whose code was already available from previous studies concerning completely different topics was used. In practice, this amount to a random choice.

The projects that supplied the code for the study are listed in Table II, where some descriptive statistics for the most relevant measures are also given. Methods having CoCo=0 or NOS=0 are clearly uninteresting, therefore their data were excluded, so Table II does not account for such methods. Overall, the initial dataset included data from 13,922 methods. The dataset is available on demand for replication purposes.

TABLE II
DESCRIPTIVE STATISTICS OF THE DATASETS.

Project	n	Measure	mean	st.dev.	median	min	max
hibernate	2532	CoCo	3.1	4.3	2.0	1	79
		HPV	32.3	17.1	28.0	0	211
		MI	100.3	14.7	102.2	0	135
		McCC	3.3	2.4	2.0	1	33
		NLE	1.3	0.8	1.0	0	7
		LLOC	15.2	12.3	12.0	3	201
jcaptcha	317	CoCo	3.3	4.0	2.0	1	34
		HPV	35.0	18.4	29.0	10	120
		MI	100.3	14.0	102.5	56	132
		McCC	3.5	2.2	3.0	2	18
		NLE	1.3	0.8	1.0	0	5
		LLOC	14.6	10.6	11.0	3	80
jjwt	205	CoCo	4.0	7.2	2.0	1	84
		HPV	30.6	22.9	28.0	0	280
		MI	101.7	20.6	104.0	0	135
		McCC	4.3	4.6	3.0	2	46
		NLE	1.3	0.8	1.0	0	4
		LLOC	13.5	14.9	11.0	3	169
json_iterator	379	CoCo	5.6	8.7	3.0	1	73
		HPV	38.3	21.1	32.0	14	145
		MI	96.4	15.3	99.0	45	131
		McCC	4.6	3.9	3.0	1	28
		NLE	1.6	1.0	1.0	0	7
		LLOC	18.0	15.1	13.0	3	110
JSON-java	260	CoCo	5.7	15.8	2.0	1	203
		HPV	41.0	36.9	31.5	11	413
		MI	95.7	18.2	97.4	32	133
		McCC	5.0	5.8	3.0	2	50
		NLE	1.5	1.1	1.0	0	7
		LLOC	21.5	26.5	13.0	3	255
log4j	798	CoCo	4.6	6.4	2.0	1	61
		HPV	36.6	21.4	30.0	8	163
		MI	98.1	15.2	100.4	44	135
		McCC	4.1	3.4	3.0	1	34
		NLE	1.6	1.0	1.0	0	8
		LLOC	16.9	13.4	12.0	3	115
netty-socketio	136	CoCo	4.4	5.5	3.0	1	37
		HPV	33.7	20.0	28.0	0	122
		MI	97.7	20.8	101.4	0	132
		McCC	4.1	2.8	3.0	1	19
		NLE	1.6	0.9	1.0	0	5
		LLOC	15.0	12.3	11.0	3	84
pdfbox	3587	CoCo	5.2	8.2	2.0	1	118
		HPV	39.3	25.7	32.0	0	326
		MI	93.7	17.2	96.4	0	128
		McCC	4.5	4.5	3.0	1	58
		NLE	1.6	1.1	1.0	0	10
		LLOC	22.3	21.8	15.0	3	330
jasperreports	6415	CoCo	5.6	10.1	3.0	1	186
		HPV	38.7	28.5	31.0	0	740
		MI	93.4	18.1	96.5	0	132
		McCC	4.9	5.6	3.0	1	117
		NLE	1.6	1.1	1.0	0	10
		LLOC	23.5	26.0	15.0	3	383

B. The Method

The first phase of the study consisted in measuring the code. We used SourceMeter to obtain the "traditional" measures, and a self-constructed tool to measure CoCo. The data from the two tools were joined, thus obtaining a single dataset with 8,214 data points.

The second step consisted in selecting the data for the study. We excluded from the study all the methods having CoCo < 5, since those methods would bias the results, because of 'built-in' relationships. For instance a piece of code having CoCo $= 0$ also has McCabe complexity $= 1$; similarly, CoCo $= 1$ usually implies that McCabe complexity $= 2$, etc. In addition, low-complexity methods are of little interest: since CoCo is meant to represent the complexity of understanding code, it is hardly useful for methods that are so simple that understanding them is hardly an issue. `SonarQube` [9] sets the threshold for CoCo at 15, i.e., CoCo < 15 is reasonably safe, according to `SonarQube`. Therefore, by excluding only methods having CoCo < 5 we are sure to exclude only 'non-interesting' code.

We also excluded methods having CoCo > 50, because our dataset contains too few methods having CoCo > 50 to support reliable statistical analysis.

After removing the exceedingly simple or complex methods, we got a dataset including 3,610 data points, definitely enough to perform significant statistical analysis. In this dataset the mean value of CoCo is 12, while the median is 9.

The third step consisted in performing statistical analysis. We started by studying the correlation between CoCo and each one of the other code measures. Since the data are not normally distributed, we used non-parametric tests, namely we computed Kendall's rank correlation coefficient τ [10] and Spearman's rank correlation coefficient ρ [11]. Since the correlation analysis gave encouraging results, we proceeded to evaluate correlations via both linear and non-linear correlation analysis. Namely, we performed ordinary least squares (OLS) linear regression analysis and OLS regression analysis after log-log transformation of data. In both cases, we identified and excluded outliers based on Cook's distance [12].

In all the performed analysis, we considered the results

significant at the usual $\alpha = 0.05$ level. In almost all cases, we obtained much smaller p-values, though.

C. Results of the Study

The results of Kendall's and Spearman's correlation tests are given in Table III. All the reported results are statistically significant, with p-values well below 0.001.

TABLE III
RESULTS OF CORRELATION TEST.

Measure	τ	ρ
HCPL	0.45	0.62
HDIF	0.38	0.52
HEFF	0.47	0.63
HNDB	0.47	0.63
HPL	0.50	0.67
HPV	0.46	0.62
HTRP	0.47	0.63
HVOL	0.50	0.66
MI	-0.56	-0.73
MIMS	-0.56	-0.73
MISEI	-0.41	-0.57
MISM	-0.41	-0.57
McCC	0.71	0.85
NL	0.50	0.61
NLE	0.50	0.60
LLOC	0.55	0.72
NOS	0.52	0.68

After the evaluation of correlations between CoCo and other measures, we proceeded to building regression models. We obtained 65 statistically significant models after log-log transformation of measures. Because of space constraints, here we do not report all of these models. Instead we report only the ones that appear most accurate.

Table IV provides a summary of the models we found. For each model, the adjusted R^2 determination coefficient is given (obtained after excluding outliers). We also give a few indicators of the accuracy of the models (computed including outliers): MAR is the mean of absolute residuals (i.e., the average absolute prediction error), MMRE is the mean magnitude of relative errors, while MdMRE is the median magnitude of relative errors. MMRE and MdMRE are considered biased indicators: we report them here only as a complement to MAR, which we considered the indicator of accuracy to be taken into account [13].

Note that in addition to the measures listed in Table I, we used also MCC/LLOC, i.e., McCabe's complexity density.

TABLE IV
MODELS FOUND.

Measures	adjusted R^2	MAR	MMRE	MdMRE
MI, NL	0.81	3.60	0.28	0.20
MIMS, NL	0.81	3.60	0.28	0.20
NLE, LLOC	0.79	3.08	0.25	0.20
HCPL, MI, NLE	0.84	2.96	0.24	0.18
HCPL, MIMS, NLE	0.84	2.96	0.24	0.18
HCPL, NLE, LLOC	0.81	3.04	0.25	0.20
HDIF, MI, NL	0.82	3.65	0.28	0.19
HDIF, MI, NLE	0.84	2.96	0.24	0.19
HDIF, MIMS, NL	0.82	3.65	0.28	0.19
HDIF, MIMS, NLE	0.84	2.96	0.24	0.19
HEFF, MI, NL	0.82	3.72	0.28	0.20
HEFF, MI, NLE	0.84	3.01	0.24	0.19
HEFF, MIMS, NL	0.82	3.72	0.28	0.20
HEFF, MIMS, NLE	0.84	3.01	0.24	0.19
HNDB, MI, NL	0.82	3.72	0.28	0.20
HNDB, MI, NLE	0.84	3.01	0.24	0.19
HNDB, MIMS, NL	0.82	3.72	0.28	0.20
HNDB, MIMS, NLE	0.84	3.01	0.24	0.19
HPL, MI, NLE	0.84	3.03	0.24	0.19
HPL, MIMS, NLE	0.84	3.03	0.24	0.19
HPL, NLE, LLOC	0.82	3.03	0.25	0.20
HPV, MI, NL	0.82	3.77	0.28	0.20
HPV, MI, NLE	0.84	2.95	0.24	0.18
HPV, MIMS, NL	0.82	3.77	0.28	0.20
HPV, MIMS, NLE	0.84	2.95	0.24	0.18
HTRP, MI, NL	0.82	3.72	0.28	0.20
HTRP, MI, NLE	0.84	3.01	0.24	0.19
HTRP, MIMS, NL	0.82	3.72	0.28	0.20
HTRP, MIMS, NLE	0.84	3.01	0.24	0.19
HVOL, MI, NLE	0.84	3.04	0.24	0.19
HVOL, MIMS, NLE	0.84	3.04	0.24	0.19
HVOL, NLE, LLOC	0.82	3.03	0.25	0.20
MI, MIMS, NLE	0.81	3.59	0.26	0.19
MI, NL, NLE	0.81	2.89	0.23	0.18
MI, NLE, LLOC	0.83	3.25	0.25	0.19
MIMS, NL, NLE	0.81	2.89	0.23	0.18
MIMS, NLE, LLOC	0.83	3.25	0.25	0.19
MCCC, NLE, LLOC	0.95	1.77	0.15	0.11
MCCC, NLE, MCC/LLOC	0.95	1.77	0.15	0.11
NL, NLE, LLOC	0.78	2.99	0.24	0.20
NLE, LLOC, MCC/LLOC	0.95	1.77	0.15	0.11

The results given in Table IV let us answer RQ2 as follows: Our study shows that it possible to build models that predict the value of CoCo based on commonly used measures, as well as using Halstead measures and maintainability indexes. Many of the obtained models feature quite good accuracy.

Noticeably, the independent variables that support the most accurate models are McCabe's complexity, the nesting level and the number of logical lines of code. This is hardly surprising, given that elements of MCC and NLE are used in the definition of CoCo. As to LLOC, it is clear that the longer the code, the more decision points it contains (on average), hence we can expect also LLOC to contribute to CoCo. In fact, the relationship between CoCo and lines of code was already observed [14].

In conclusion, our study shows that CoCo does not seem to convey more knowledge than sets of properly chosen traditional code measures, like MCC, NLE and LLOC.

IV. DISCUSSION

The results of the correlation tests given in Table III show that CoCo is correlated with all the traditional code measures we considered. Specifically, CoCo is strongly correlated with McCabe's complexity: this is quite noticeable, considering that CoCo was proposed to improve McCabe's complexity.

We can thus answer RQ1 as follows:
Our study shows medium to strong correlations between CoCo and each of the commonly used code measures that we considered. Specifically, CoCo appears most strongly correlated with McCabe's complexity.

V. THREATS TO VALIDITY

Concerning the application of traditional measures, we used a state-of-the-art tool (SourceMeter), which is widely used and mature, therefore we do not see any threat on this side. CoCo was measured using an ad-hoc tool that was built based on the specifications of CoCo [2]. This tool was thoroughly tested using SonarQube [9] as a reference, therefore we are reasonably sure that it provides correct measures. However, when joining the data from SourceMeter with the data from our tool, we were not able to always match methods identifiers, because the two tools reported slightly different descriptions of methods' names, parameters, etc. We just dropped the methods' data for which no sure match could be found: in this way, we lost less than 2% of the measures. Since the lost measures depend on characteristics that have nothing to do with the properties of code being measured, they can be considered a random subset, which can hardly affect the outcomes of the study

Concerning the external validity of the study, as with most empirical studies in the Software Engineering area, we cannot be sure about the generalizability of results. However, the dataset used was large enough, and the selected software projects represent a reasonable variety of application types.

VI. Related Work

Campbell performed an investigation of the developers' reaction to the introduction of CoCo in the measurement and analysis tool SonarCloud [15]. In an analysis of 22 open-source projects, she assessed whether a development team "accepted" the measure, based on whether they fixed code areas indicated by the tool as characterized by high CoCo. Around 77% of developers expressed acceptance of the measure.

An objective validation of the CoCo measure was performed by Muñoz Barón et al. [3]. They retrieved data sets from published studies that measured the understandability of source code from the perspective of human developers. They collected the data concerning various aspects of understandability, as well as the code snippets used in the experiments. They used SonarQube [9] to obtain the CoCo measure for each source code snippet. Then, they computed the correlation of CoCo with the measures of various aspects of understandability. Muñoz Barón et al. reported the correlation between CoCo and various aspects of understandability for each of the 10 experiments reported in the selected papers, as well as a summary obtained via meta-analysis. Muñoz Barón et al. concluded that CoCo correlates moderately with some of the considered understandability aspects.

The paper mentioned above dealt with evaluating the effectiveness of CoCo (a measure of internal code properties) as an indicator of understandability (an external code property). To our knowledge, nobody performed an analysis dealing with how internal code properties only are correlated with CoCo.

Nonetheless, CoCo has been used in some evaluations. CoCo is provided by SonarQube [9] together with many other measures and indicators, so some researchers that used SonarQube to collect code measures ended up using CoCo together with other measures. Among the papers that have used CoCo are the following.

Kozik et al [14] developed a framework for analyzing software quality dependence on code measures and other data. Using their framework they found that CoCo affects the analyzability and adaptability of code.

Papadopoulos et al. [16] investigated the interrelation between design time quality metrics and runtime quality metrics, such as cache misses, memory accesses, memory footprint and CPU cycles. Papadopoulos et al. observed a trade-off between performance/energy consumption and cognitive complexity. However, having used CoCo as the only design time quality metric, it is unknown whether the same kind of trade-off would be observed with respect to other design-time metrics, like McCabe's complexity, for instance. Our study suggests that this doubt is well funded.

Crespo et al. [17] used both the Cognitive complexity rate (defined as CoCo/LOC) and the Cyclomatic complexity rate (defined as McCabe complexity/LOC) as part of an assessment strategy concerning technical debt in an educational context. The found that the Cognitive complexity rate and the Cyclomatic complexity rate provide the same results, or lack of results, actually. Given the strong correlation that we observed between CoCo and McCabe's complexity, the result by Crespo et al. is not surprising.

VII. Conclusions

The "Cognitive Complexity" measure (CoCo throughout the paper) was introduced with the aim of improving the capabilities of McCabe complexity in indicating code that is difficult to understand and maintain [2]. Rather than a proper measure, CoCo is an indicator, whose definition accounts for a few characteristics of source code. Among these characteristics are the number of decision points (e.g., if, for, while and switch statements) and the level of nesting of control statements.

When CoCo was proposed, no evaluations were published concerning the relationship between CoCo and traditional measures that directly address the aforementioned characteristics of code. In this paper, we have reported about an empirical study aiming at evaluating the correlation between CoCo and several traditional measures, including those addressing the same characteristics of code taken into account by CoCo. To this end, we measured a few open source projects' code, obtaining the measures of 3,610 methods. We then performed statistical analysis using both correlation tests (namely, Kendall's and Spearman's rank correlation coefficients) and regression analysis.

We found that CoCo appears strongly correlated to McCabe's complexity and slightly less strongly correlated to several other code measures. We found several regression models of CoCo as a function of traditional measures. Not surprisingly, one of the most accurate models involves McCabe's complexity, NLE (Nesting Level Else-If) and LLOC (the number of logical lines of code) as independent variables. Considering that the most accurate models have MAR=1.7, while the mean CoCo is 12, we may conclude that—at least for the considered software projects—CoCo does not appear to convey additional information with respect to traditional measures.

In conclusion, the study reported here casts the doubt that CoCo does not provide appreciable new knowledge than the measures of code that are traditionally accociated with the notion of complexity.

We plan to extend this work by 1) analyzing additional code, 2) using different statistical instruments (e.g., Pricipal Components Analysis), 3) using Machine Learning techniques.

ACKNOWLEDGMENT

The work reported here was partly supported by Fondo per la Ricerca di Ateneo, Università degli Studi dell'Insubria. The author thanks Anatoliy Roshka for developing the tool that was used to measure CoCo.

REFERENCES

[1] S. R. Chidamber and C. F. Kemerer, "A metrics suite for object oriented design," IEEE Transactions on software engineering, vol. 20, no. 6, 1994, pp. 476–493.

[2] G. A. Campbell, "Cognitive complexity - a new way of measuring understandability," https://www.sonarsource.com/docs/CognitiveComplexity.pdf, 2018, [Online; accessed 7-September-2021].

[3] M. M. Barón, M. Wyrich, and S. Wagner, "An empirical validation of cognitive complexity as a measure of source code understandability," in Proceedings of the 14th ACM/IEEE International Symposium on Empirical Software Engineering and Measurement (ESEM), 2020, pp. 1–12.

[4] N. Fenton and J. Bieman, Software metrics: a rigorous and practical approach. CRC press, 2014.

[5] T. J. McCabe, "A complexity measure," IEEE Transactions on software Engineering, no. 4, 1976, pp. 308–320.

[6] "SourceMeter," https://www.sourcemeter.com/, [Online; accessed 7-September-2021].

[7] M. H. Halstead, Elements of software science. Elsevier North-Holland, 1977.

[8] P. Oman and J. Hagemeister, "Metrics for assessing a software system's maintainability," in Proceedings Conference on Software Maintenance 1992. IEEE Computer Society, 1992, pp. 337–338.

[9] "SonarQube," https://www.sonarqube.org/, [Online; accessed 7-September-2021].

[10] M. G. Kendall, "Rank and product-moment correlation," Biometrika, 1949, pp. 177–193.

[11] C. Spearman, "The proof and measurement of association between two things," The American journal of psychology, vol. 100, no. 3/4, 1987, pp. 441–471.

[12] R. D. Cook, "Detection of influential observation in linear regression," Technometrics.

[13] M. Shepperd and S. MacDonell, "Evaluating prediction systems in software project estimation," Information and Software Technology, vol. 54, no. 8, 2012, pp. 820–827.

[14] R. Kozik, M. Choraś, D. Puchalski, and R. Renk, "Q-rapids framework for advanced data analysis to improve rapid software development," Journal of Ambient Intelligence and Humanized Computing, vol. 10, no. 5, 2019, pp. 1927–1936.

[15] G. A. Campbell, "Cognitive complexity: An overview and evaluation," in Proceedings of the 2018 International Conference on Technical Debt, 2018, pp. 57–58.

[16] L. Papadopoulos, C. Marantos, G. Digkas, A. Ampatzoglou, A. Chatzigeorgiou, and D. Soudris, "Interrelations between software quality metrics, performance and energy consumption in embedded applications," in Proceedings of the 21st International Workshop on software and compilers for embedded systems, 2018, pp. 62–65.

[17] Y. Crespo, A. Gonzalez-Escribano, and M. Piattini, "Carrot and stick approaches revisited when managing technical debt in an educational context," arXiv preprint arXiv:2104.08993, 2021.

Functional Size Measurement in Agile

A Thought Experiment with Measuring Functional Size in Agile Development

Dr. Thomas Fehlmann
Euro Project Office AG
8032 Zurich, Switzerland
E-mail: thomas.fehlmann@e-p-o.com

Eberhard Kranich
Euro Project Office
47051 Duisburg, Germany
E-mail: eberhard.kranich@e-p-o.com

Abstract — **In Agile Software Development, story points indicate the effort needed to implement a user story up to the Definition of Done. Hence, story points can be applied to track the progress of a software product under development. A major drawback of their use is that they do not allow predicting the number of sprints needed to create or modify a software product, not even for a minimum viable product. A more promising way to measure sprints is to use functional size counts determined by IFPUG or COSMIC. Both methods yield useful results when correctly interpreted. However, the functional size of the product is not simply determined by the total functionality implemented in sprints. Agile teams often touch the same functionality more than once; adding new requirements to existing functionality must be handled adequately, and some already implemented functionality is disregarded. Moreover, refactoring, removing technical debt and software testing adds effort, measured in story points, but adds no functionality.**

Keywords—Agile Software Development; Software Metrics; Software Sizing; Sprint Performance; Product Cost Management; Thought Experiment; Gedankenexperiment.

I. Introduction

A *Software Metric* is a measure of some property of a piece of a software artifact or its specifications. A measure relies on a measurement method that fulfills the definition of the VIM and the GUM:

- The VIM: ISO/IEC Guide 99:2007, 2007. International Vocabulary of Metrology – Basic and general concepts and associated terms (VIM) [1];
- The GUM: ISO/IEC CD Guide 98-3, 2015. Evaluation of measurement data – Part 3: Guide to Uncertainty in Measurement (GUM) [2].

ISO 19761 COSMIC [3] defines a software metric; ISO 20926 IFPUG [4] a size count. Both methods are useful for the purpose of measuring sprint performance in Agile.

A. *Combining Measurements*

One can add, subtract, compare, and multiply measurements for instance to combine part measurements into a measurement of the total. Sometimes, for instance when measuring a distance between two places, trigonometry is needed to combine two section measurements into one measure for the whole distance because of hills, slopes and angles.

Counting function points to characterize functional size, or software development effort, or something, are not necessarily metrics. Counting points does not measure anything else except points unless the points mark some unit on a measurement scale.

B. *Measurement Methods*

ISO 19761 COSMIC [5] measures size by counting data movements. Two measured applications can be combined into one by simply adding their counts. This works because the system boundary does not impact the count; contrary to IFPUG. ISO 20926 IFPUG [6] has five elementary units whose counting value depends on the boundary, because of the *File Types Referenced* (FTR). Adding two applications yields questions: what to do if the *Internal Logical File* (ILF) of one application becomes an *External Interface File* (EIF) of the other? What if a new requirement adds some *Data Element Type* (DET) to an elementary data unit? Does it affect all previous counts? There does not seem to be an easy way to combine two IFPUG counts and get the correct count for the combined application. IFPUG does not comply with the VIM and the GUM, whereas COSMIC does.

However, compliance is needed when counting each sprint and trying to get a valid size estimate of the total product by the sum. Each sprint creates a mini application that – theoretically – should already provide value to the customer and provide some functionality. The next sprint adds new functionality, changes existing functionality, and even might remove some already obsolete functionality. A set of stated requirements often varies because during agile software development some requirements can be removed from the backlog, whereas new requirements are added. In addition, modified requirements remain in the backlog.

In COSMIC, these activities can be modeled, basically by distinguishing data movements created anew from those amended or enhanced. The total of data movements, new developed, enhanced, or re-developed, describes the size of the product at any given moment in time – i.e., at the beginning of a sprint – while the performance of a sprint should be measured by counting all data movements touched, be it the total of newly created, enhanced, re-developed, or deleted. This implies that data movements count every time they are touched for the sprint, but only once for size. Since there are usually different product delivery rates for new development and enhancement [7], one can compare such metrics with performance data from other software development undertakings.

With IFPUG, modeling the elementary data functions and transactions also allow sizing the product, or the sprint. However, these sizes do not add easily but still approximate performance of a sprint.

For detailed information about these measurement methods, consult the manuals (COSMIC [3] and IFPUG [4]) and the ISO standards (COSMIC [5] and IFPUG [6]). Fehlmann [8, p. 130ff] provides a comparison for using these methods. When to use which method depends from the application or business domain. For transactional systems, use IFPUG; for *Internet of Things* (IoT), communication, and service architectures, developers prefer COSMIC; compare with Fehlmann [9].

C. Research Questions

While the term 'project' has disappeared from Agile [10] and DevOps [11], the old lore about projects regarding quality, effort and time constraints remains valid. The same laws hold for agile sprints. *Story Points* [12] are widely in use to predict the content of the next sprint, based on a team's effort prediction. There is no distinction between *Functional User Requirements* (FUR) and *Non-functional Requirements* (NFR) [13]. Consequently, story points are not suitable for benchmarking, even if some sort of standard story points are defined for comparison between different teams.

The question is whether functional sizing conformant to ISO/IEC 14143 [14] provides value to agile teams. Some developers will deny that, with the argument that function point sizing traditionally has been used to predict the size of the final product. But agile development works without a known finished product, therefore no such size can be determined.

Nevertheless, there is a need to assess and predict cost of development, operation, and maintenance for software. Traditionally, measuring functional size and benchmarking has been used for predicting operational and maintenance cost [7]. Why should this not be possible for agile sprints?

To make functional size measurement useful for agile, we need to answer the following research questions, for both COSMIC and IFPUG-based size measurements:

- What exactly to measure?
- When to measure?
- How exactly to measure?
- How does the final product relate to sprints?
- How does functional size relate to story points?
- How many sprints are needed to build a *Minimum Viable Product* (MVP)? [11]

To answer these questions, we conduct a *Gedankenexperiment* addressing mobile app development, closely based on actual experiences.

We introduce the two methods for measuring functional size, then describe the approach and the sprints measured, then do a Retrospective and finally present the findings.

II. THE MEASUREMENT APPROACH

Per sprint we execute two distinct functional size measurements in parallel:

- Functional size of each sprint, corresponding to work performed per sprint, and therefore to the development team performance;
- Total product size, corresponding to the total value of work performed that contribute to the product in use.

The total sum of sizes of all sprints is not equal to the total product size, else it would not be agile development.

This is due to new requirements that change functionality that already had been implemented. Also, some functionality might initially be implemented in a provisional way. Still, such work had been performed in the sprints, and it would not be correct to discard such work as "non-productive". Sometimes, the initial functionality was necessary to uncover the correct requirements; sometimes, such functionality was a stub that made the piece of software valuable to the user in an initial, provisional state. Examples include automated data connectivity that initially was substituted by some manual input facility.

A. Data Movement Maps

For measurement, we use *Data Movement Maps* and *Transaction Maps*. From data movement maps, a COSMIC count can be obtained automatically; from a transaction map, an IFPUG count. The automated counts are reasonably good approximations, enough for the purpose of monitoring agile sprints.

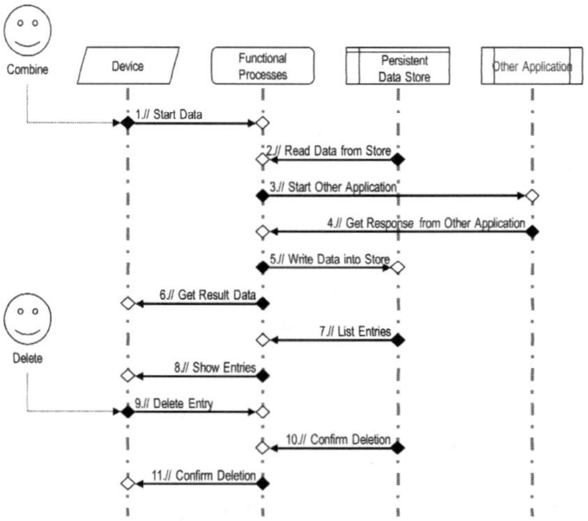

Fig. 1. Data Movement Map with Four Objects of Interest and two Triggers

How to create these maps and its automatic counting, consult Fehlmann [8, p. 130 & 160]. We distinguish four types of *Objects of Interest*:

- Functional Processes: Objects that perform functional processes in the COSMIC sense. One object of interest can perform more than one functional process; thus, it represents for instance one Virtual Machine (VM), or Electronic Control Unit (ECU) performing different calculations rather than a single COSMIC functional process;

- Persistent Store: Objects that persistently hold data. Contrary to the COSMIC definition, they can provide data services to several functional processes;
- Devices: A device can be a system user or anything providing or consuming data;
- Other Applications: other applications use functional processes the same way as devices do, however, they typically represent other software or systems that can be modeled the same way using data movement maps.

As shown in Fig. 1, *Triggers* indicate the starting data movement of one or more COSMIC functional processes. Thus, one object accommodating several functional processes can have multiple triggers. The automatically calculated total count appears on the top.

Data Movements always move a *Data Group*, which can be thought as a data record. Its uniqueness is indicated by color-filled trapezes. A second move of the same data group between the same objects within a COSMIC functional process lets it blank, because it does not add any additional functionality. It is not counted for functional size according the COSMIC method [3].

Data movement maps can automatically be counted for ISO/IEC 19761 COSMIC [3] functional size. Moving the same data group twice between the same objects of interest is counted as one function point only. On the other hand, one can combine as many data movement maps as possible and count the same total of data movements, notwithstanding how the boundaries are drawn.

B. Transaction Maps

The IFPUG model [4] defines a count for functional size by counting model elements that are conceptually familiar to traditional mainframe software: Elementary Data Functions and Elementary Transactions.

The following five functional components of the software evaluate for the count according to the ISO/IEC 20926 IFPUG rules based on the user requirements:

- Internal Logical File (ILF): A user identifiable group of logically related data that resides entirely within the applications boundary and is maintained through External Inputs.
- External Interface File (EIF): A user recognizable group of logically related data or control information referenced by the application being measured; however, maintained within the boundary of another application.
- External Input (EI): An elementary process in which data crosses the boundary from outside to inside. The data can be either control information or business information. If the data is business information, it maintains one or more internal logical files. If the data is control, it does not have to update an internal logical file.
- External Output (EO): An elementary process in which derived data passes across the boundary from inside to outside. The data creates reports or output files sent to other applications. These reports and files originate from one or more internal logical files and external interface file.
- External Inquiry (EQ): An elementary process with both input and output components that result in data retrieval from one or more internal logical files and external interface files. This information crosses the application boundary. The input process does not update any Internal Logical Files and the output side does not contain derived data.

For counting, these five elementary types of data functions or transaction are categorized as either low, medium, or high complexity. This yields its functional size. The complexity depends on the *Data Element Type* (DET) handled by each element, and the number of *File Type Referenced* (FTR). Consequently, ISO/IEC 20926 IFPUG defines a count with jumps, not a metric.

Adding data elements can let the complexity assessment jump from one level into another. Moreover, replacing functionality is sometimes not reflected in the count.

For counting model elements in ISO/IEC 20926, it is necessary to know the boundary for the complete system. The reason is that the total number of FTR – represented as connectors in data transaction maps – impact the size of the transaction-type model elements. Without knowing the whole system, parts cannot be counted, if following the rules of the IFPUG manual [4] exactly.

As already mentioned, the IFPUG count does not conform to the VIM and the GUM. This makes the IFPUG counting method unattractive both for agile software development that needs to count the functional size of sprints, and even more for test metrics. Any such metric relies on the VIM and the GUM when comparing size of sprints, adding sprints to the whole product, or when sizing test cases.

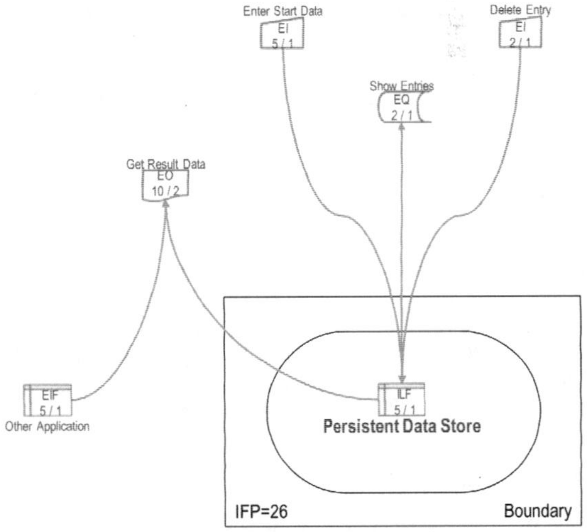

Fig. 2. Transaction Map for the Piece of Software Already Shown in Fig. 1

Transaction Maps, as shown in Fig. 2, are a way to visualize the IFPUG model for a software system. Depending upon the architecture, more than one transaction map is needed for a modern architecture software system. Then, typically, some

ILF has its data managed by one transaction map while others access the same elementary data elements as an EIF. Because of the boundary rules in IFPUG counting rules [4], this leads to double counting. The automatically calculated total count is shown at the bottom.

Both, data movement maps and transaction maps are well suited for use with agile teams, for visualizing which elements of software are touched in each sprint. The model elements can be used for communicating work done in sprints, at the same time providing its functional size. Business people usually prefer the transaction maps; developers the data movement maps.

III. An App Development Example

Software development typically starts with a vision, often described by an initial backlog of user stories – sometimes, rather *Epics*; that are functional user requirements in a granularity way above what is needed for implementation and coding. Usually, epics evolve into user stories during initial sprints. A vision is not what will be implemented at some later time – it is the idea of the vision that it remains a vision but changes while requirements get better understood and change as well. Comparing the initial vision with the product released later, after enough sprints, is nevertheless interesting and helpful for product owners and requirements engineers alike.

A. The Vision

The vision consisted of eight rather simple user stories, based around the introduction of barcodes allowing for scanning paper bills by an ordinary smartphone, creating transaction that a bank can execute.

TABLE I. Initial Backlog User Stories for the Android Mobile App

Label	As a…	I want to…	Such that…	So that…
Login	App User	be sure to access my Giro Account	By using Fingerprint for identification and TAN for authentication	I can be confident for my privacy
Scan QR Code	App User	scan my bills	typing in IBAN and reference information is no longer necessary	paying bills is with one click
Use Giro Account	App User	use my Giro Account	I can access banking services with my Smartphone	to pay bills
Create Transactions	App User	create transactions	it's simple	to pay bills
Edit Transactions	App User	view & edit transactions	I'm informed about what I'll pay	account status remains under control
Schedule Execution	App User	select the date of execution	I can plan for my account balance	account status remains under control
Account Status	App User	review account status	all pending transactions are considered	account status remains under control
Refill	App User	link to a savings account	I can refill my Giro Account	I'm able to pay my bills

In real life, there are a lot more functional users involved – from Compliance Officer to the bank's customer care department – providing additional user stories such that a real set contains rather a hundred stories instead of eight.

Counting the vision for the Android Mobile App with the eight user stories shown in TABLE I only yields 188 IFP; the COSMIC count is 105 CFP. We always start with a vision; thus, product size is approximately known. Sizing the vision allows identifying layers, data functions by IFPUG, respectively objects of interest when using COSMIC.

B. The Architecture

The example shown here is invented; however, it follows as closely as possible real experiences made in practicing size counts in agile development.

The architecture is standard. The smartphone never accesses banking data directly but always uses a middleware – here called *App & Web Server* – to connect to real banking data. Most of the architectural components already exist but need some enhancements for the new Mobile App.

For sizing, the pre-existing parts are tagged as "enhancements", compared with the "new development" needed for the additional features. Product size is the sum of both.

We have functional users for all five application systems; thus, they add to functional size. The functional users are represented by the broad arrows in Fig. 3. TAN, IAM, and CMS services are already existing and will not need any enhancements. The App & Web Server also is standard, but many functions require a server part, for accessing data or storing data that does not belong to the relatively unsafe smartphone. For instance, transactions and access keys are never stored on a smartphone.

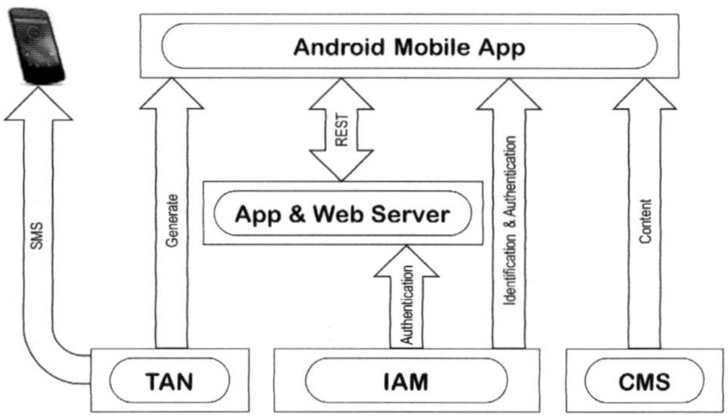

Fig. 3. Architecture Overview

C. The Sprints

Sprint 01 – Allegro. We assume, the development platform for Android was already installed, and thus we do not need an extra sprint to set it up.

Also, the team is experienced and used in cooperation. Accessing a camera on a smartphone is nothing new for nobody. Therefore, the team started without hesitation. The team selected the "View Giro Account Status" user story as its top priority. This user story had been badly implemented before and drawn much criticism. This priority decision allows business to see valuable results within two weeks' time.

In the first sprint, the *View Account Status* user story was selected from backlog – actually, from the vision. Story Point (StP) estimations are in parenthesis:

- As App User, I want to review my Giro Account status such that I can plan for my account balance to keep account status under control (8 StP).

The Product Owner discovered two new user stories, not part of the initial vision, now added to Backlog. The team considered them uttermost important:

- As App User, I want to include my credit cards in the Giro Account statement such that I see the amount necessary to pay my monthly statements, controlling Giro balance (8 StP).
- As App User, I want to connect with my credit card accounts such that I can use the same Giro for credit card payments, keeping account status under control (8 StP).

These two new user stories let the product size grow. Initially, the vision, or initial backlog, can be used to estimate the final product size, but the product size growths with each sprint finally expected when new user stories are discovered and added to the backlog. Therefore, it is safer to measure the real product size, as implemented after each sprint. In our case, the need for linking credit cards affects middleware as well; thus, the App & Web Server also starts growing with the new Android Mobile App product.

Also, the Login procedure was selected for its technical importance. This functionality was reused from a previous Mobile App and thus is not a new development:

- As App User, I want to be sure to access my Giro Account by using fingerprint for identification and TAN for authentication such that I can be confident for my privacy (3 StP).

Involving credit cards from foreign banks has become possible thanks to a new standard ISO 20022, that has been adopted throughout the EU, defining account access interfaces between different banks [15]. This new feature seems to increase customers' acceptance for the new Android Mobile App.

Sprint 02 – Andante. This sprint implements the main functionality, namely scanning a bill and creating a transaction that the Backoffice systems can execute:

- As App User, I want to scan bills received with my smartphone and pay without typing any IBAN or other reference information, with only one click (13 StP).
- As App User, I expect that scanning creates a transaction scheduled for next day to pay my bills (8 StP).
- As App User, I want to use my Giro Account, without a complicated process, to pay my bills (3 StP).

Note that scanning and creating a transaction is only one elementary transaction is IFPUG. We also want a link to Savings Accounts:

- As App User, I want to link my Giro Account to some other Savings Account such that I can refill my Giro for paying my bills with my smartphone (5 StP).

As before, the App & Web Server is also affected and needs some additional functionality. We link the Giro account to some savings accounts in case normal income, e.g., regular salary payments, are not enough to keep the balance in the positive.

Avoiding double counting, we attach a "Not Counted" label to Session Key and Giro Account that was already created in Sprint 01. For IFPUG, the EIF already initiated such as Identity Access Management and Mobile Content are also not counted, since not enhanced.

Sprint 03 – Scherzo. Managing and scheduling transactions means that we somewhat refine two user stories that already were part of the vision:

- As App User, I want to view, edit and delete transactions that I scanned before execution, such that I am informed about what I pay, and my account balance remains under control (8 StP).
- As App User, I want to see pending transactions such that I know what will happen to my account balance (5 StP).
- As App User, I want to reschedule transactions such that I can plan for my account balance and my Giro account is not overdrawn (3 StP).

Now we listen to the voice of the *Private Banking Counselor* and add yet two more user stories:

- As Counselor (or as Compliance Office), I want to be sure that all transactions are traceable such that any misuse or erroneous action can be reversed (5 StP).
- As Counselor, I need the possibility to view the Transaction Log (8 StP).

Thus, the log file becomes a *Transaction Log* and will get enhanced functionality that allows those two functional users to help their customers, respective meet legal requirements, e.g., when scanning transactions for tax fraud.

The transaction log is not something that the user needs, or wishes, but is useful when the bank needs blocking and reopening transactions. Since the App user needs such functionality, and since he or she also wants to see transaction history, this is a FUR that must be counted. The main reason for tracing transaction is compliance. However, we also listened to the voice of the Private Banking Counselor who wants to be able to support its customers effectively.

The need to view the transaction log is logically a part of middleware, the App & Web Server, although it might not exactly belong there, and most probably will be implemented somewhere else.

Sprint 04 – Marche Funèbre. The Security Officer found out that Android posts all images on some Cloud Service as soon as connected to some WLAN. However, this service can be switched off.

The ability to switching off needs additional functionality on the smartphone. It requires saving the user settings that are valid outside of the Mobile Payment App. Therefore, there is another new user story:

- As App User, I want to make sure that my camera scans a bill only for my Mobile App such that nobody can trace my payments, and things keep private (13 StP).

Instantaneous posting of pictures taken with a smartphone to Instagram, Twitter or some cloud service is a standard feature; however, it is not straightforward to consider it. It is not a bug; it is a new feature.

Obviously, a workaround could be to access the camera directly, exclusively. Using the preinstalled camera app increases portability but carries the risk that usually such code is not open. Hidden backdoors might persist even if settings are switched to "No share". For security reasons, the camera settings are kept persistent.

The transaction, or data movement, already counted in Sprint 02 therefore gets changed and replaced by some newly developed software for scanning bills. This sprint provides work on the Android Mobile App only. Because access to internal smartphone camera settings is rather tricky – one must hack around internal privacy protection – total amount of added or enhanced functionality remains low.

Moreover, there is a "Refill Giro" user story implemented in Sprint 04 that complements the link to some savings accounts, and alert functionality:

- As App User, I want to refill my Giro account in case normal funding is late or insufficient, such that I can pay my bills that are scheduled for payment (8 StP).
- As App User, I want an alert in case of missing balance, such that I can pay my scheduled bills (5 StP).

Sprint 05 – Intermezzo. The code quality static tester tool in use by our team, is not very happy with the amount of *Technical Debt* that already has piled up. Source code needs refactoring. This gives rise to a new user story:

- As Developer, I want to make sure that my software is bug free, maintainable, and contains minimal technical debt (13 StP, non-functional).
- Another user story was added to the sprint backlog:
- As Business Owner, I want to make sure that our Mobile Payment App runs on all major smartphone brands and software versions in use (13 StP, non-functional; a suitable test service is commercially available).

This requires software tests:

- Static Tests and fixing of bad code.
- Dynamic compatibility tests with as many popular smartphone brands as possible.

The Intermezzo Sprint does not add or enhance any functionality neither to the Android Mobile App nor to any other applications. Both user stories are nonfunctional.

Sprint 06 – Menuetto. Overall progress is good, thus new ideas find fertile ground with the following new user stories:

- As App User, I like to see my spending history graphically, such that I can distinguish what I spent by payments and credit card, for managing liquidity (13 StP).
- As App User, I want to set the time slot for the graphical spending history, such that I see trends, and I can determine when to refill my Giro Account (3 StP).

A similar new user story also seems important enough for implementation:

- As App User, I like to see spending statistics, such that I can distinguish how much I spent for what, to plan my future spending (8 StP).

Sprint 06 – Menuetto is meant to add better appealing functionality to the Android Mobile App. Graphics are always better than just numbers; the Android library used allows to create graphs with relatively little effort. Thus, the team assigned high priority to these user stories.

This results in rather few new functionality, but some significant enhancements of already implemented functionality.

Sprint 07 – Finale. For the final sprint, we have only one additional user story added, that makes work done previously for the graphical representations partially obsolete, inducing enhancements to the already finished functionality providing graphic settings.

A little late maybe, our product owner might have talked to some user representative and found out that graphics are welcome, but they should be available on the web and – obviously – look the same.

Thus, we must move the graphical settings data function from the smartphone back to the server. This has the additional advantage that users retrieve their settings even after losing or exchanging their smartphone but does not impact the Mobile App. The new functional user story reads as:

- As App User, I like to share my spending history graphics with other platforms, by seeing the same graphics in Web Banking (8 StP).

The necessary finishing touches are represented again as non-functional user stories:

- As a developer, I want everything well documented (13 StP, non-functional).
- As product owner, I want automated tests before release (8 StP, non-functional).

This user story makes the previous solution (keeping graphical settings on the phones) obsolete.

IV. Retrospective

In retrospective, process metrics are analyzed.

A. *Product Size Growth*

Product Size at Start of Sprint according IFPUG

	Android Mobile App				App & Web Server			
	New Dev	Enhanced	Re-Dev	Total	New Dev	Enhanced	Re-Dev	Total
Vision	151 IFP	37 IFP		188 IFP		129 IFP		129 IFP
Sprint 01		27 IFP		27 IFP		129 IFP		129 IFP
Sprint 02	48 IFP	50 IFP		98 IFP	23 IFP	129 IFP		152 IFP
Sprint 03	111 IFP	60 IFP		171 IFP	23 IFP	129 IFP		152 IFP
Sprint 04	153 IFP	65 IFP		218 IFP	36 IFP	129 IFP		165 IFP
Sprint 05	167 IFP	68 IFP	6 IFP	241 IFP	36 IFP	129 IFP		165 IFP
Sprint 06	167 IFP	68 IFP	6 IFP	241 IFP	36 IFP	129 IFP		165 IFP
Sprint 07	199 IFP	68 IFP	6 IFP	273 IFP	36 IFP	129 IFP		165 IFP
Final	**174 IFP**	**86 IFP**	**13 IFP**	**273 IFP**	**52 IFP**	**129 IFP**		**181 IFP**

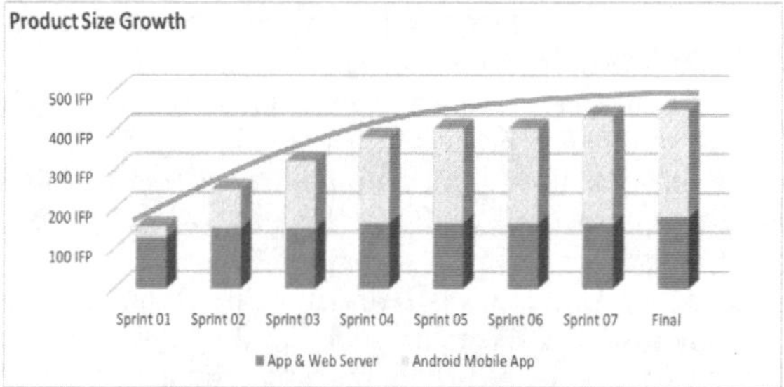

Fig. 4. Application Growth according IFPUG

Product Size at Start of Sprint according COSMIC

	Android Mobile App				App & Web Server			
	New Dev	Enhanced	Re-Dev	Total	New Dev	Enhanced	Re-Dev	Total
Vision	86 CFP	19 CFP		105 CFP		32 CFP		32 CFP
Sprint 01						32 CFP		32 CFP
Sprint 02	20 CFP	19 CFP		39 CFP	8 CFP	32 CFP		40 CFP
Sprint 03	53 CFP	22 CFP		75 CFP	8 CFP	32 CFP		40 CFP
Sprint 04	93 CFP	22 CFP		115 CFP	17 CFP	32 CFP		49 CFP
Sprint 05	110 CFP	24 CFP	1 CFP	135 CFP	17 CFP	32 CFP		49 CFP
Sprint 06	110 CFP	24 CFP	1 CFP	135 CFP	17 CFP	32 CFP		49 CFP
Sprint 07	132 CFP	24 CFP	1 CFP	157 CFP	17 CFP	32 CFP		49 CFP
Final	**120 CFP**	**35 CFP**	**3 CFP**	**158 CFP**	**25 CFP**	**32 CFP**		**57 CFP**

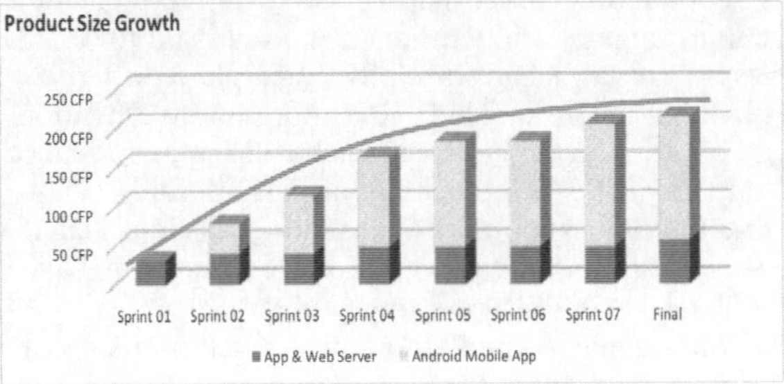

Fig. 5. Application Growth according COSMIC

In COSMIC (Fig. 5), we have less "Enhanced" functionality compared with IFPUG (Fig. 4), because a data movement might be newly developed even if connecting two already existing objects. Therefore, we found no "Enhanced" data movements within the Android Mobile App.

Note that when newly developed functions become enhanced, because of new requirements, they change the status from "New Development" to "Enhanced" for the product size. In fact, it means that these functions have been changed.

B. *Sprint Performance*

The IFPUG sprint sizes sum up to something higher than product size; this is an indication that the vision has been implemented in full. In the Android Mobile App, there is some deleted functionality in Sprint 04 and 07 that does not add to size but to sprint performance. The App & Web Server has no re-developed functionality.

Sprints according IFPUG

	Android Mobile App				App & Web Server			
	New Dev	Enhanced	Re-Dev	Total	New Dev	Enhanced	Re-Dev	Total
Sprint 01	55 IFP	43 IFP		98 IFP	23 IFP	28 IFP		51 IFP
Sprint 02	51 IFP	39 IFP		90 IFP				
Sprint 03	52 IFP	24 IFP		76 IFP	13 IFP	42 IFP		55 IFP
Sprint 04	29 IFP	13 IFP	6 IFP	48 IFP				
Sprint 05								
Sprint 06	32 IFP			32 IFP				
Sprint 07	7 IFP	18 IFP	7 IFP	32 IFP	16 IFP			16 IFP
Total	**226 IFP**	**137 IFP**	**13 IFP**	**376 IFP**	**52 IFP**	**70 IFP**		**122 IFP**

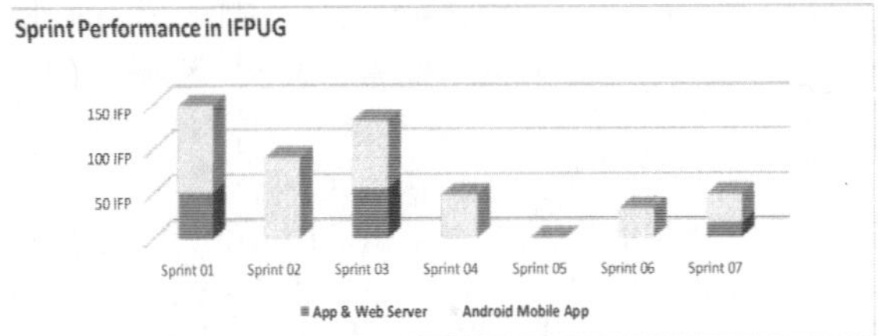

Fig. 6. Sprint Performance measured with IFPUG

Sprint 05 does not add any functionality, for both measurement methods.

Sprints according COSMIC

	Android Mobile App				App & Web Server			
	New Dev	Enhanced	Re-Dev	Total	New Dev	Enhanced	Re-Dev	Total
Sprint 01	20 CFP	19 CFP		39 CFP	8 CFP			8 CFP
Sprint 02	36 CFP	9 CFP		45 CFP				
Sprint 03	39 CFP	9 CFP		48 CFP	9 CFP	4 CFP		13 CFP
Sprint 04	21 CFP	5 CFP	1 CFP	27 CFP				
Sprint 05								
Sprint 06	22 CFP			22 CFP				
Sprint 07	2 CFP	11 CFP	2 CFP	15 CFP	8 CFP			8 CFP
Total	**140 CFP**	**53 CFP**	**3 CFP**	**196 CFP**	**25 CFP**	**4 CFP**		**29 CFP**

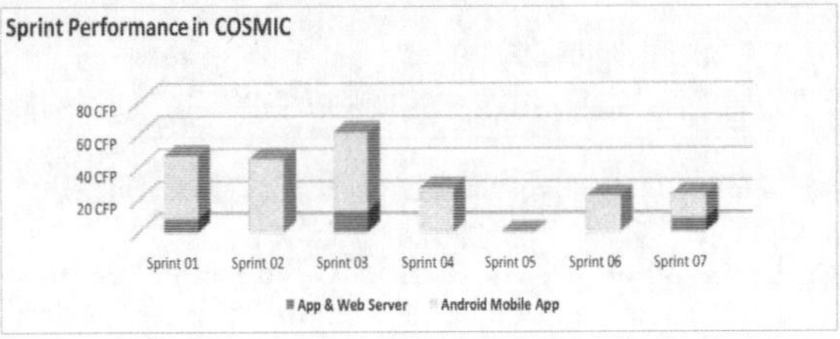

Fig. 7. Sprint Performance measured with COSMIC

Sprint 03 and 04 needed enhancements in existing functionality that was impacted by new, or changed, user requirements. Performance covers both new development and enhancements since both types of work require effort. The increment of product size, in contrary, as shown in Fig. 4 and Fig. 5, deteriorates even more from sprint to sprint.

The team estimated story points as shown in Fig. 8, according to its own habits and rules. The break-in in performance with Sprints 05 and 07 does not appear in Story Points; the team had a lot to do but did not add new functionality.

Story Points

24 User Stories

						Total
Sprint 01	8 StP	8 StP	8 StP	3 StP		27 StP
Sprint 02	13 StP	8 StP	3 StP	5 StP		29 StP
Sprint 03	8 StP	5 StP	3 StP	5 StP	8 StP	29 StP
Sprint 04	13 StP	8 StP	5 StP			26 StP
Sprint 05	13 StP	13 StP				26 StP
Sprint 06	13 StP	5 StP	8 StP			26 StP
Sprint 07	13 StP	8 StP	8 StP			29 StP
Final	**81 StP**	**55 StP**	**35 StP**	**13 StP**	**8 StP**	**192 StP**

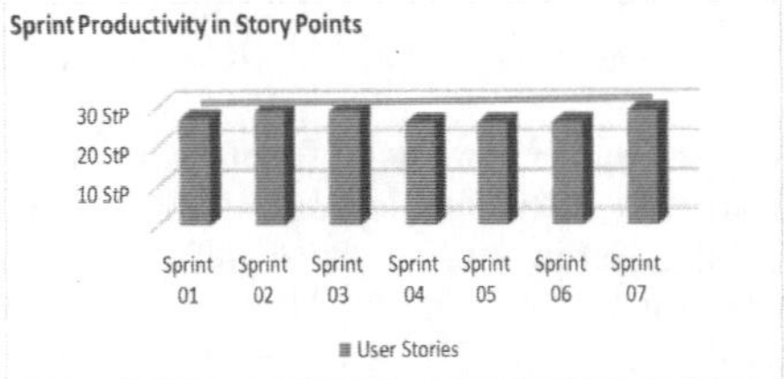

Fig. 8. Story Point Estimates by the Development Team (non-comparable with other teams)

The team estimated a total of 192 StP for the final 24 functional and non-functional user stories, grown from the original eight user stories for the initial vision (Table).

Productivity in IFPUG FP

Total Dev	#Sprints	Length	Hours/Day	Team Size	PDR
498 IFP	7	10 Days	7.2 h	6.8	7 h/IFP

Productivity in COSMIC FP

Total Dev	#Sprints	Length	Hours/Day	Team Size	PDR
225 CFP	7	10 Days	7.2 h	6.8	15 h/CFP

Fig. 9. Overall Productivity, in IFPUG and COSMIC

This yields a *Productivity Delivery Rate* (PDR) of 7 h/IFP, respectively 15 h/CFP. The same calculation can also be done for story points and yields a productivity number.

Productivity in StP

Total StP	#Sprints	Length	Hours/Day	Team Size	Delivery Rate
192 StP	7	10 Days	7.2 h	6.8	18 h/StP

Fig. 10. Overall Productivity, expressed in story points

Agile methodology uses velocity – the number of story points that the team can implement in one sprint – for predicting duration and cost of product development. The respective velocity in our Gedankenexperiment amounts to 18 h/StP. However, velocity does not allow to predict what functionality can be provided at the cost of those sprints.

C. Cost of Agile Software Development

As explained above (section A), cost estimates depend on the sprint productivity; however, it is difficult to predict how many new requirements will be detected during the agile sprints. Nor does the number of sprints planned predict the amount of functionality, and thus size, of the resulting product.

Nevertheless, such predictions are feasible using *Quality Function Deployment* (QFD) [16] by analyzing how well the vision meets the needs of the customer or user [17].

D. Findings

From Fig. 6 and Fig. 7 it becomes apparent that functional size growth diminishes when looking at later sprints. Intuitively this is clear, because tests, refactoring and documentation become more and more dominant later in the product life cycle. The relation between effort and product functional size increment deteriorates over time. The amount of this deterioration is paramount for predicting cost of product development.

Sprint performance in terms of functional size deteriorates from the start value to about one third. Product size increment follows a logarithmic curve whose parameters should be highly interesting to cost estimators. Surprisingly, not much is published in the scientific literature about this curve. It looks like this curve describes some functional growth, without an apparent limit – it is not a saturation curve – even while the effort, expressed in story points, remains stable and constant (Fig. 8). The implemented FUR seem to generate additional FUR like fractals.

This "fractal growth curve" resulting from the shift from FUR to NFR has been observed in all agile development undertakings that the authors have monitored in the last five years. The reasons could be: Teams shift from the focus on developing new functionality to testing, refactoring, and preparing deployment. New, more detailed FUR are uncovered in this process. This seems characteristic for the product under development, and is supported by DevOps. The form of this "fractal growth curve" depend on the amount of shift-lest, and on the details of the DevOps approach. For instance, with *Autonomous Real-time Testing* (ART) [18], testing becomes an ongoing activity. Then, even while effort, and thus cost, is evenly distributed over the full product life cycle, functional growth is not.

Smoothing the curve, the mathematical representation of this curve suggests a logarithm; that would suit to "fractal". However, "fractal" suggests relatively simple growth rules deserving high interest. This needs further investigation. It should become the target when benchmarking performance of software product development methods, and teams.

Our thriving experiment opens more questions than it answers. Nevertheless, for a few research questions we have answers, thanks to our Gedankenexperiment:

- Management should monitor the characteristics of the fractal growth curve.
- We know what to measure when, and how. We need both functional size and story points.
- We prefer the subjective team measure captured by story points over effort measurements by counting hours. Story points better reflect the difficulties encountered and mastered by the team.
- Measuring agile development must address each sprint, not just the final product, an initial vision (or backlog), or the MVP. The reward for these additional measurements is apparent.
- Comparing the size of the product with the effort spent in sprints indicates how much work was spent in getting the requirements right, implementing NFR, refactoring, removing technical debt and other quality improvements.
- While the product can be compared with the vision in terms of size, the implemented features might differ quite a bit. Also, the MVP does not remain stable and undergoes change.
- The question whether IFPUG or COSMIC shall be used for measuring agile depends on the product domain; both methods work for managing development despite the lack of VIM/GUM compliance of IFPUG.

It should be restated that this Gedankenexperiment reflects the practical experiences made when monitoring agile software development, in various industries, over five years now. Also, the tools we use for counting are adapted to agile development, avoiding double counting for sprints and the product. Thus, the effort for measuring sprints is equal to the effort for measuring the final product; only the work is in sprints rather than monolithic.

V. Conclusion

Using story points has the disadvantage that the team must already be available and ready to assign story points to user stories. In contrary, using functional size measurements enables product managers to gauge their vision also in view of product improvement plans and schedules. This works better because the PDRs of Fig. 9 already include the characteristics of agile development. These values can now be used to predict future performance of the same team.

The values presented here with this freely invented simple app product are near to what had been observed in practice in development of mobile applications.

Comparing story points with size metrics is useful on product level but not on the sprint level. The aim of the sprints – expressed by classical musical terms – plays a major role. For predictions, it is safe to assume that the vision covers about half of the product that will be implemented. Often, the initial vision backlog contains user stories or even epics that will become obsolete during development of the product.

COSMIC allows to precisely gauge size in sprints and better sizes NFR that address networking and performance [13]. For technical software, developers find data movement maps useful, see [8]. IFPUG allows for less precision due to the lack of compliance with the VIM and the GUM; however, for transaction-oriented applications such as Web and Mobile development, it is good enough and eases communication with less technical people. From the viewpoint of sizing agile, both methods are equally useful.

The difference between size of the product and total size of all sprints, plus the amount of enhancement works, reflects the effort needed to find the correct requirements by the agile team. A smaller product sometimes better reflects the true needs of its users, and smaller products fit better in DevOps life cycle. Thus, the enhancement effort is not lost.

Functional sizing allows to better understand the percentage of effort that is needed for NFR, refactoring and testing and may vary strongly per sprint. Typically, nonfunctional efforts count for more than half of the total effort; thus, the value of functional sizing for sprint planning is limited. However, for predicting the number of sprints needed to reach a MVP [19], for monitoring progress, and for managing DevOps, functional sizing is without alternative.

Moreover, COSMIC can be used for managing agile development by the Buglione-Trudel Matrix, see [8] and [20]. Finally, COSMIC is the method of choice for sizing tests, especially for Autonomous Real-time Testing (ART) [18]. Combining ART with Agile and DevOps yields particular benefit for large software-intense systems, such as autonomous vehicles, and intelligent things.

ACKNOWLEDGMENT

Thanks to the customers of Euro Project Office and QSMA Switzerland who allowed us to monitor sprint progress in close cooperation with the agile teams and inspired us for this Mobile App Gedankenexperiment.

We are also grateful to the reviewers who provided us with valuable hints how to improve this paper.

REFERENCES

[1] ISO/IEC Guide 99:2007, "International vocabulary of metrology – Basic and general concepts and associated terms (VIM)," TC/SC: ISO/TMBG, Geneva, Switzerland, 2007.

[2] ISO/IEC CD Guide 98-3, "Evaluation of measurement data - Part 3: Guide to uncertainty in measurement (GUM)," TC/SC: ISO/TMBG, Geneva, Switzerland, 2015.

[3] COSMIC Measurement Practices Committee, "COSMIC Measurement Manual for ISO 19761 – Version 5.0 – Part 1-3," COSMIC Measurement Practices Committee, Montréal, 2020.

[4] IFPUG Counting Practice Committee, "Function Point Counting Practices Manual - Version 4.3.1," International Function Point User Group (IFPUG), Princeton Junction, NJ, 2010.

[5] ISO/IEC 19761, "Software engineering - COSMIC: a functional size measurement method," ISO/IEC JTC 1/SC 7, Geneva, Switzerland, 2011.

[6] ISO/IEC 20926, "Software and systems engineering - Software measurement - IFPUG functional size measurement method," ISO/IEC JTC 1/SC 7, Geneva, Switzerland, 2017.

[7] P. Hill, Ed., Practical Software Project Estimation 3rd Edition, New York, NY: McGraw-Hill, 2010.

[8] T. M. Fehlmann, Managing Complexity - Uncover the Mysteries with Six Sigma Transfer Functions, Berlin, Germany: Logos Press, 2016.

[9] T. M. Fehlmann, "When use COSMIC FFP? When use IFPUG FPA? A Six Sigma View," in *COSMIC Function Points - Theory and Advanced Practices*, R. Dumke and A. Abran, Eds., Boca Raton, FL, CRC Press, 2011-3, pp. 260-274.

[10] M. Rehkopf, L. Daly, C. Drumond, D. Radigan, S. Mansour and M. Suntinger, "Atlassian Agile Coach," Atlassian Corporation Plc, Sydney, NSW, Australia, 2020.

[11] F. Erich, C. Amrit and M. Daneva, "A Qualitative Study of DevOps Usage in Practice," *Journal of Software: Evolution and Process,* vol. 29, no. 6, June 2017.

[12] M. Cohn, Agile estimating and planning, New Jersey, NJ: Prentice Hall, 2005.

[13] COSMIC Consortium, "Guideline on Non-Functional & Project Requirements V1.03," November 2015. [Online]. Available: http://cosmic-sizing.org/publications/guideline-on-non-functional-project-requirements/. [Accessed 18 November 2015].

[14] ISO/IEC 14143-1, "Information technology - Software measurement - Functional size measurement - Part 1: Definition of concepts," ISO/IEC JTC 1/SC 7, Geneva, Switzerland, 2007.

[15] The SWIFT Standards Team, ISO 20022 for Dummies, John Wiley & Sons, 2020.

[16] ISO 16355-1, "Applications of Statistical and Related Methods to New Technology and Product Development Process - Part 1: General Principles and Perspectives of Quality Function Deployment (QFD), Geneva, Switzerland: ISO TC 69/SC 8/WG 2 N 14," ISO TC 69/SC 8/WG 2 N 14, Geneva, Switzerland, 2015.

[17] T. M. Fehlmann and E. Kranich, "Early Software Project Estimation the Six Sigma Way," *Lecture Notes in Business Information Processing,* vol. 199, pp. 193-208, 2014-2.

[18] T. M. Fehlmann, Autonomous Real-time Testing - Testing Artificial Intelligence and Other Complex Systems, Berlin, Germany: Logos Press, 2020.

[19] E. Ries, The Lean Startup, New York, NY: Crown Publishing Group, 2011.

[20] T. M. Fehlmann and E. Kranich, "Managing Software Projects by the Buglione-Trudel Matrix," in *11th European Conference on Information Systems Management - ECISM 2017*, Genova, Italy, 2017.

Measuring Coupling in Microservices Using COSMIC Measurement Method

Roberto Pedraza-Coello
Research Institute in Applied Mathematics and Systems
National Autonomous University of Mexico
CDMX, Mexico City, Mexico
Email: rpedrazacoello@gmail.com

Francisco Valdés-Souto
Science Faculty
National Autonomous University of Mexico
CDMX, Mexico City, Mexico
Email: fvaldes@ciencias.unam.mx
ORCID: 0000-0001-6736-0666

Abstract—**The Microservices Architectural Style is one of the latest trends in software development companies. Having highly coupled microservices can lead to latency and network traffic, high interdependency between development teams, among other problems. Being able to measure the coupling between microservices in early phases of the software development life cycle could help the software architects make better decisions when designing. This paper proposes a way of measuring coupling between microservices. This metric is based on the COSMIC measurement method (ISO/IEC 19761). The paper also shows a practical implementation of this metric.**

Keywords-microservices; coupling; measurement; COSMIC; ISO/IEC - 19761.

I. INTRODUCTION

The Microservices Architectural Style (MAS) is one of the latest trends in software development companies. Its main idea is to develop an application as a set of small services. Each one of these services is called a microservice. It is an approach to software and systems architecture that builds on the concept of modularization but emphasizes technical boundaries [13].

Each microservice is implemented and operated as a small and independent system. It offers access to its internal functionality and data through a well-defined network interface. MAS increases the software development process agility because each microservices is an independent unit of development, deployment, operations, versioning, and scaling [13].

The MAS benefits caused companies, including worldwide companies, to migrate their software to this architecture style. However, MAS is not a silver bullet, and it has several challenges in the software development lifecycle phases.

The microservices of an application are interconnected between them to perform the functionality. This intercommunication could imply some coupling between the microservices. Coupling is referred to as the interdependency that exists between different objects. If the microservices depend a lot on each other, then the coupling is high. If the microservices depend little or none on each other, the coupling is low.

One of the MAS problems found in literature is the increment of consumption of network resources. This problem is partially caused because of the coupling that exists between microservices when achieving a particular functionality. Low-level coupling between microservices makes sense to reduce the consumption of network resources. Soldani [15] mentions that, since the microservices in an application intercommunicate through remote API invocations, applications generate higher network traffic with respect to monoliths (where modules interact through memory calls) or service-based applications (composed by a lower number of services, hence reducing the number of remote API Invocations).

Measuring the coupling between microservices in the early stages of the software development cycle could help to quantify the interdependency that exists between different microservices, improving the software architect's decision making in terms of avoiding high interdependency between teams, or high network-traffic areas. Coupling metrics have been proposed over the years. For example, Chidamber and Kemerer [7] have proposed a metric called *Coupling Between Object classes (CBO)*. The CBO of a class is the aggregation of the number of other classes to which it is coupled. It is mentioned that inter-class coupling occurs when methods of one class use methods or instance variables of another class. However, it is never mentioned how to count the usage of methods or instances of another class. It could be counted once by every occurrence in each method, once by every class-type object in each method, etc. The measurement procedure is not clear. Additionally, the use of scales it is not defined. Then, according to the metrology concept "Measurement Foundation" presented by Abran [2], it is not possible to evaluate the validity of this metric.

Other metric called *Weighted Methods Per Class* is proposed in [7]. The idea is to do an aggregation of the complexity of the methods of a class. in [7] the author mentions that "Complexity" is not defined more specifically to allow for the most general application of this metric. The lack of an explicit definition of complexity can result in a same class having very different result measurement values. It can be affirmed that the measurements obtained with this metric are not comparable, which is not good from a metrology point of view, as mentioned by Abran [2].

An additional metric is proposed by Chidamber [7]. It is called *Lack of Cohesion in Methods (LCOM)*. It is the sum of the number of method pairs in a class whose similarity is zero (not similar) minus the count of method whose similarity is not zero (exists some similarity). This means, the lower the measure value the greater the cohesion. The lowest possible LCOM value is zero. The paper mentions that even when LCOM is equal to zero this does not imply maximal cohesiveness, since within the set of classes with LCOM = 0, some may be more cohesive than others or, in other words, some may lack of more cohesion than others. This is a problem, even though multiple classes can have LCOM = 0 some of these classes lack more cohesion than others, therefore we can affirm that this metric is not comparable.

Currently, the only type of software measurement with international standards adopted by the ISO is the measurement of functional size. It is also the only type of software measurement that has a method that complies with the metrology requirements [2]. Up to now, there are five standards of software Functional Size Measurement Methods (FSMM). Of those five standards, the ISO/IEC 19761 COSMIC method is the only standard belonging to the second generation, including several use domains, like Management Information Systems (MIS), real-time infrastructure, Etc. It also solves most of the problems with the FSMM of the 1st generation [16].

This paper presents an approach to measuring coupling between microservices. The coupling metric is based completely on the standard ISO/IEC 197611, the COSMIC method. This approach is proposed to define an objective metric that can improve the knowledge about the coupling between microservices in order to provide to software architects quantitative elements, based in an international standard, to take decisions.

The paper is organized as follows: Section 2 explains the background about microservices and the context about COSMIC. Section 3 presents related work on coupling measurement methods. Section 4 describe the proposed coupling measurement method based on the COSMIC standard, including an example of its application. Section 5 presents the conclusions of the paper and future work.

II. BACKGROUND

This section presents the background of microservices and the COSMIC measurement method.

A. *Microservices*

The Netflix company, like other companies, had a problem a few years ago. They had a monolithic web system that was modified by multiple people every day. The software, with its updates, was deployed once or twice a week. If one of the changes caused a problem, it was hard and time-consuming to diagnose a cause. When a company is trying to compete in the agile environment where the updates must be delivered to the consumer as quick as possible this situation can cause many internal and commercial troubles. Because of these troubles and a few more, Netflix decides to migrate its business software to MAS.

The most repeated MAS definition in literature is from Fowler's and Lewi's blog, where they define that "The microservice architectural style is an approach to developing a single application as a suite of small services, each running in its own process and communicating with lightweight mechanisms, often an HTTP resource API. These services are built around business capabilities and independently deployable by fully automated deployment machinery. There is a bare minimum of centralized management of these services, which may be written in different programming languages and use different data storage technologies [10]."

To better understand this architectural style, it is useful to compare it with the monolithic style. For example, a software that follows a client-server architecture usually consists of three parts: A client-side application, a database, and a server-side application. This server-side application is a monolith, which means a single executable unit. Every change to the server-side app implies building and deploying a new version of the app. However, with MAS, each microservice is implemented and operated as a small and independent system. The microservice offers access to its internal functionality and data via a network interface. This improves the agility of the development process, because every microservices becomes an independent unit of development, deployment, operation, versioning and scaling [10].

The MAS general idea is to develop an application as a set of interconnected services. This interconnection generates a certain coupling between the microservices. It is recognized that if the coupling is high, then technological and management problems can arise.

In most of programming paradigms the software quality characteristics defined as low coupling and high cohesion are ideal. For example, in the Object-Oriented Paradigm a software with low coupling is achieved when each object depends on little or nothing of other objects. The same idea of low coupling applies to MAS. High coupling between microservices could cause latency and network traffic, high interdependency between development teams, among other problems [9][17].

Currently the evaluation of coupling is made with subjective methods, and then there is a need to measure coupling between microservices in a formal and standardized way. With good measures, several problems can be identified and characterized, and decisions can be taken.

B. *COSMIC*

Several ISO/IEC standards have been developed oriented to measure the software functionality in the software engineering field. The ISO/IEC 14143 standard [12] includes a set of rules regarding size measurement in functionality units. For this type of measurement, the standard proposes the following definitions:

"Functional size is defined as the size of the software derived by quantifying the Functional User Requirements" [12]

"Functional User Requirements (FUR) stands for a sub-set of the User Requirements describing what the software does, in terms of tasks and services" [12]

"Functional Size Measurement (FSM) is the process of measuring functional size" [12]

The COSMIC measurement method has been acknowledged by the ISO/IEC as conforming to the rules laid down in the ISO/IEC 14143 and has taken the form of the standard ISO/IEC 19761. There are others FSM that have taken the form of ISO/IEC standards. However, COSMIC is the only one that belongs to the "Second Generation" of FSM methods. The other FSMs belong to the First Generation [3].

COSMIC introduces its own homologated and standardized measure unit called Cosmic Function Point (CFP). 1 CFP represents the size of one data movement (Entry, eXit, Read or Write). Therefore, functional size can be measured by counting the number of data movements. More information about COSMIC and different guidelines to apply COSMIC can be found on the COSMIC website [1].

III. RELATED WORK

Allen and Khoshgoftaar [5] present a way of measuring Coupling and Cohesion in a module-based software. The coupling measurement method starts with a measurement protocol that results in a graph-abstraction representing some aspect of software design. For example, class inheritance, class type, method invocation, class-attribute references. Different abstractions, for a same software, can result in different measures. The metric is based in the software abstracted as a graph and separating the graph into modules. An issue observed for this method is that it is based on a software abstraction generated by humans. Humans have different points of view when abstracting software, and there are no right or wrong abstractions. So, one same software can have multiple abstractions, and each abstraction can have a different coupling measurement, what is not considered correct.

Arisholm et al. [6] propose three different approaches to measure the strength of a coupling relation: number of messages, number of distinct method invocations, and distinct classes. The number of messages refers to the number of different messages that are exchanged between two entities. The other two represent the number of methods called, and classes used by a method in an object. An issue observed in this paper is that there are no standard metric units for messages, method invocations and classes. Also, as the measurement is done at runtime, the measurement can vary a lot depending on when the measurement is being done. So, comparing the coupling of two software becomes problematic. They should be compared at equal conditions for the comparison to be valid. It is not defined how to achieve equal conditions. From a metrology point of view, the measurements should be comparable.

These same situations are observed in Lavazza et al [14]. They propose a theoretical framework based on Axiomatic Approaches for the definition of dynamic software measures. This paper also presents measures based on this framework. These are defined for dynamically quantifying coupling. The coupling measurements are based on counting, at runtime: the number of distinct methods invoked by each method in each object, the count of the total number of distinct messages sent from one object class to other objects, and the count of the distinct number of classes that a method uses. Once again, the measurement obtained for one software is not comparable with the measurement obtained for another software. For instance, the messages send from one object o other object could consider distinct entities, or domain object information, in the same message.

Hassoun et al. [11] propose a relation called DCM (Dynamic Coupling Metric) to formalize the idea of dynamic coupling. That metric works at the object level. It is mentioned that measuring object coupling gives an insight into the system structure and allows the comparison of architectural aspects of a different system relative to reuse and maintenance. This paper uses a complexity measure in its' formulas. However, it is not mentioned how to calculate the complexity nor what complexity means for the context of the paper.

IV. COUPLING METRIC BASED IN COSMIC

One of the main differences between some of the metrics that are usually used to measure software and the COSMIC method is that the COSMIC method complies with the 3 metrology concepts, mentioned by Abran [2] for a "good" design of a software measurement method: Measurement foundation, Quantities and units, and Measurement Standards-Etalons. In one or more of these concepts is where popular software metrics like Function Points, Use Case points, Cyclomatic Complexity, Quality Models, among others fail.

The proposal is to use the concepts of the COSMIC measurement method to measure the coupling between microservices to ensure that, when the coupling between two microservices is measured, the measurement is consistent, repeatable, and comparable. A good measurement method is independent of the person measuring and the measurement environment.

For this paper, microservices coupling refers to the dependency that exists from one microservice MS1 to another microservice MS2. Whenever MS1 makes an HTTP request (or through another protocol) to MS2, it is because MS1 needs to send messages (eXit) or receive messages (Entry) from MS2. In this sense, it is understood that there is a unilateral or a bilateral coupling. By using the COSMIC concepts [8] it can be said that a relationship between two microservices is defined by a correspondence rule that can be hierarchical (exclusively one service uses the services of another), or bidirectional (both services use services of the other service).

For the proposed metric, when said that MS1 is coupled to MS2, it is meant that MS1 depends on MS2 to complete a certain portion of its own functionality. However, it does not necessarily mean the same in inverse mode.

It can be said that MS1 is coupled to MS2 when MS1 starts a request/response communication with MS2. A good analogy is to imagine a client-server architecture where MS1 is the client and MS2 is the server, the client depends on the server, not the other way around.

Keeping the last example, to measure how coupled is MS1 to MS2 we need to count, for each MS1 functional process, the number of data movements that are exchanged between MS1 and MS2 for all the cases where MS1 starts the communication with MS2.

The proposed metric is based on determining the degree of coupling of a particular microservice based on COSMIC method concepts, considering the defined scope of the measurement.

The coupling concept is approached this way because, usually, the microservices offer their services via an HTTP API [10]. These APIs allow the microservices to offer their services to multiple clients. Following the previous example, MS1 is a client of MS2. However, MS2 could have 1000 more clients. It is considered that it does not make sense to think that MS2 is coupled to 1000 clients just because the 1000 clients use MS2's services. It makes even less sense if, from an MS2 perspective, it does not matter what client is using the services.

The COSMIC measurement manual [8] explains how to measure software by counting the data movements in each of the functional processes. There are certain rules of when a certain data movement is considered for the measurement and when not. The coupling metric proposed in this article is based on using the same rules that COSMIC uses and applying them to the metric's context. The coupling measurement between a microservice MS1 and a microservice MS2 can be calculated by counting the Entry and eXit data movements done in each of the functional processes of MS1 when those data movements move data from/to MS2. Also, MS1 must start the communication with MS2 during the functional process that it is being measured.

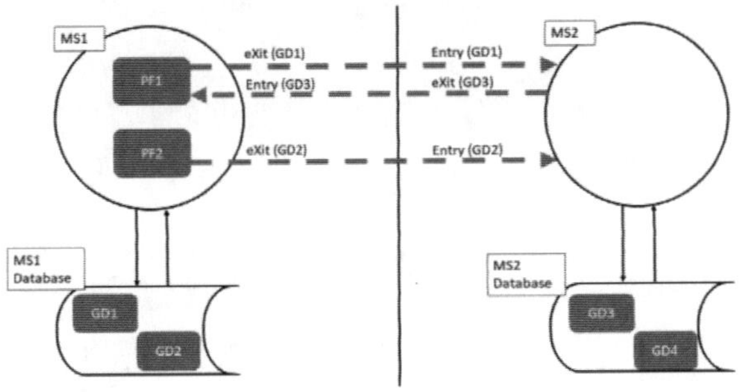

Figure 1. Simple example of MS1 coupled to MS2

For example, Figure 1 shows that functional process 1 (PF1) needs one eXit data movement and one Entry data movement from MS2 to complete its functionality. This means a total of 2 data movements in PF1 from MS1 to MS2. It also can be observed that functional process 2 (PF2) needs to send (eXit) one data group to MS2 to complete its functionality. By adding up the data movements from their two functional processes, the measurement's result is that the coupling level from MS1 to MS2 is 3.

Measuring the coupling between microservices allows one to obtain an objective value of the dependency from one microservice to another microservice. If the dependency is low, then the coupling between microservices is also low, independently how many instances of MS1 or MS2 are generated, the coupling level is measure of dependency between services, not about instances at execution.

V. APPLYING THE METRIC

This section shows an example on how to apply the proposed metric. The example is based on a case study called C-Reg [4]. The case study can be found in the COSMIC web application [1]. The case study shows the whole process of measuring functional size.

To the best of our knowledge, this case study was not thought as MAS software. However, there is communication between the measured software and other pieces of software. This paper assumes that three software pieces mentioned in the case study were built as microservices. This premise does not affect the COSMIC measurement nor the Coupling measurement.

As shown in Figure 2, the C-Reg application has multiple functional users. Some of these functional users are humans and other functional users are software. For this paper, we can ignore human functional users and focus on software functional users.

The C-Reg app [4] counts with 19 functional processes, from which 11 do at least one data movement between C-Reg and one or more software functional users. The rest of the functional processes only communicate with human functional users, so they fall out of the context of this paper. Table I shows the names of the 19 functional processes,) the ones with at least one data movement between C-Reg and external software are marked in green, the external software is considered a functional user (Billing System, Course Catalog System). See Figure 2.

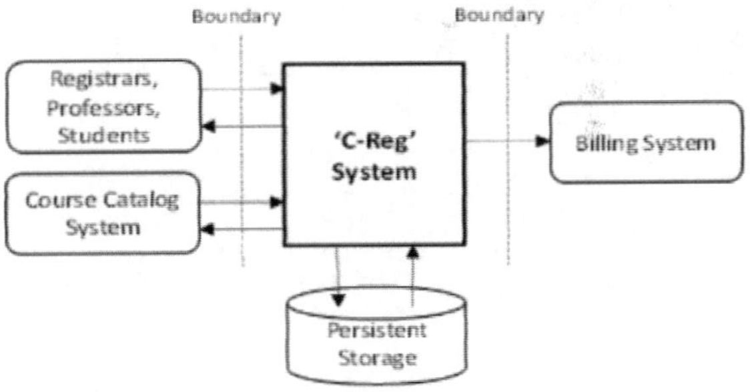

Figure 2. C-Reg Application Context Diagram. Obtained from [4]

Table II and Table III show the detail of 2 of the functional processes to explain how the coupling metric can be applied practically. First, the functional process called "Delete a professor" is presented in Table II. It can be observed that there are 2 data movements between C-Reg and Course Catalog. These 2 data movements are considered with the rest of the data movements between C-Reg and Course Catalog to measure how coupled is C-Reg to the course catalog.

The following functional process that is presented is called "Close Registration". The details of this functional process can be observed in Table III. The table shows that there are 3 data movements between C-Reg and Course Catalog. It also shows that there is one data movement between C-Reg and Billing System. These two results will be considered when calculating how coupled C-Reg is to Course Catalog, and how coupled C-Reg is to Billing System.

By analyzing the tables of each of the functional processes in [4] and applying the proposed coupling metric, we obtain the results presented in Table IV. It can be observed that C-Reg has a level of coupling of 21 CFP with Course Catalog, including 21 data movements between C-Reg and Course Catalog. It also can be observed that C-Reg has a coupling level of 1 CFP with Billing System.

It is easy to observe that the coupling from C-Reg with Billing System is 1 CFP, and with Course catalog System the coupling is 21 CFP, so there is 21 times more coupling with Course catalog Systema than Billing System.

TABLE I. C-REG'S FUNCTIONAL PROCESSES

No	Functional Process
1	Add a Professor
2	Enquire on a Professor
3	Modify a Professor
4	Delete a Professor
5	Enquire on Course Offerings (Professor)
6	Create Course Offering commitments
7	Modify Course Offering commitments
8	Delete Course Offering commitments
9	Add a Student's details
10	Enquire on a Student's details
11	Modify a Student's details
12	Delete a Student's details
13	Enquire on Course Offerings (Student)
14	Create a Student Schedule
15	Modify a Student Schedule
16	Delete a Student Schedule
17	Monitor Course Offering Enrolment progress
18	Monitor Student Schedule Enrolment progress
19	Close Registration

TABLE II. FUNCTIONAL PROCESS "DELETE PROFESSOR" DETAILS. MARKED IN GREEN THE SUBPROCESSES OF COMMUNICATION BETWEEN C-REG AND COURSE CATALOG. ADAPTED FROM [4]

Process descriptions	Functional user	Sub-process Description	Name of Data Group moved	Object of interest of Data Group moved	Data Move -ment Type	CFP
Delete a Professor's details	Registrar	Registrar presses the delete command for the Professor whose details are displayed	Professor ID	Professor	E	1
	Course Catalog	C-Reg asks Course Catalog if Professor has any Course Offering commitments	Professor ID	Professor	X	1
	Course Catalog	Course Catalog replies 'yes' or 'no'	Professor's Course Offering commitment status	Course Offering	E	1
		C-Reg prompts the Registrar to confirm the deletion	Prompt Control Command		-	-
		The Registrar confirms or cancels the deletion	Confirmation Control Command		-	-
		C-Reg deletes the Professor	Professor details	Professor	W	1
	Registrar	Display error messages	Error Messages	Errors	X	1

TABLE III. FUNCTIONAL PROCESS "CLOSE REGISTRATION" DETAILS. MARKED IN GREEN THE SUBPROCESSES OF COMMUNICATION BETWEEN C-REG AND COURSE CATALOG. MARKED IN RED THE SUBPROCESSES OF COMMUNICATION BETWEN C-REG AND BILLING SYSTEM. ADAPTED FROM [4]

Process descriptions	Functional user	Sub-process Description	Name of Data Group moved	Object of interest of Data Group moved	Data Move -ment Type	CFP
Close Registration	Registrar	The Registrar selects sub-option "Close registration"	Date closed	Course Offering	E	1
	Course Catalog	C-Reg requests Course Offering data (with number of students enrolled, etc.) from the Course Catalog	Course Offering Data request	Course Offering	X	1
	Course Catalog	Course Offering data received	Course Offering Data	Course Offering	E	1
		C-Reg checks that at least three students enrolled. If <3, it sets Course Offering status to 'cancelled'	(Data manipulation)		-	-
	Course Catalog	C-Reg sends updated statuses of Course Offerings to the Course Catalog	Course Offering statuses	Course Offering	X	1
		C-Reg retrieves the Student Schedule items for the Students enrolled for each Course Offering	Student Schedule item data	Student Schedule item	R	1
	Billing System	C-Reg sends data to the Billing System for each Student enrolled for each Course Offering that has not been cancelled	Student Schedule item data	Student Schedule item	X	1
		C-Reg retrieves Student name and e-mail address	Student details	Student	R	1
	Student	C-Reg sends info on each cancelled Schedule item to each Student in the form of an e-mail	Student e-mail address.	Student	X	1
	Student		Cancelled Student Schedule item message	Student Schedule item	X	1
		C-Reg updates Student Schedule items for cancelled Course Offerings	Student Schedule item data	Student Schedule item	W	1

TABLE IV. COUPLING MEASUREMENT VALUES FOR C-REG CASE STUDY

No	Functional Process	Number of Data Movements: Course Catalog	Number of Data Movements: Billing System
4	Delete a Professor	2	
5	Enquire on Course Offerings (Professor)	2	
6	Create Course Offering commitments	3	
7	Modify Course Offering commitments	3	
8	Delete Course Offering commitments	1	
13	Enquire on Course Offerings (Student)	2	
14	Create a Student Schedule	1	
15	Modify a Student Schedule	1	
16	Delete a Student Schedule	1	
17	Monitor Course Offering Enrolment progress	2	
19	Close Registration	3	1
	Total	21	1

VI. COUPLING METRICS ANALYSIS

It can be observed in Table V the main differences between the related work and the prosed metric based on COSMIC. Five columns are presented:

- International Standard: Is it based on an International Standard?
- Metrology Requirements: Does it comply with the metrology concepts mentioned by Abran [2]?
- Comparable: Is it valid to compare the measurement results of different software?
- Proved on MAS: Is there a case study where the metric (or an adaptation of it) was used to measure coupling between microservices?

Following with Table V, possible answers to these questions are:

- Yes
- No
- SP: Yes, if and only if the same procedure was used to measure the software
- EC: Yes, if and only if, somehow, equal conditions between the software is achieved.
- NF: No references found

TABLE V. COUPLING METRICS ANALYSIS

Coupling Measurement	International Standard	Metrology Requirements	Comparable	Proved on MAS
Coupling with COSMIC	Yes	Yes	Yes	Yes
Allen and Khoshgoftaar [5]	No	No	No	NF
Arisholm et al. [6]	No	No	SP and EC	NF
Coupling Between Object Classes [7]	No	No	SP	No
Lavazza et al [14]	No	No	SP and EC	NF
Hassoun et al [11]	No	No	No	NF

VII. CONCLUSION

Many companies are developing software based on MAS because of the multiple benefits that come with it. However, MAS is not a silver bullet. Developers face multiple challenges when developing software based on MAS. Some problems could be generated because of the coupling that exists between microservices when achieving a particular functionality, then low-level coupling between microservices could avoid high interdependency between teams, or high network-traffic areas reducing the consumption of network resources, for instance.

When two microservices communicate a lot with each other, it can be said that these two are highly coupled. Finding highly coupled microservices in the design phase of the software development life cycle could lead a software architect to make better decisions about the software design.

In this paper, we propose a way of measuring coupling between microservices. This metric is based on the COSMIC measurement standard to ensure that the measurement obtained is consistent, repeatable, and comparable when the coupling between microservices is measured. The paper also shows a practical example of how to measure coupling between microservices with the proposed metric.

It is observed from the results (Table IV) that the results make sense with the reality that represent the C-Reg system. The C-Reg software is coupled to two external functional users software: Billing System and Course Catalog System. The coupling measurement of C-Reg to: the Billing System is 1 CFP, and for the Course Catalog System the coupling is 21 CFP. There is 21 times more coupling with Course catalog System than with Billing System.

In comparison with the other coupling metrics presented in this paper, the proposed metric complies better with the metrology concepts of a good measurement method. The main advantage of this metric is that it is based on an International Standard.

A. *Future Work*

There can be situations where low-coupled microservices are generating a lot of network traffic, and high-coupled microservices are generating little network traffic. For example, MS1 and MS2, two low-coupled microservices, could generate a lot of network traffic if they include high-usage functionality. Other example is MS3 and MS4, two highly-coupled microservices, that could generate little network traffic if they include low-usage functionality. It could be interesting to look at the correlation that exists between the coupling measurement and network traffic in different kinds of MAS software systems.

Low coupling is a software quality characteristic in all software, not only on microservices, and it could be interesting to find a way to adapt this proposed metric to measure coupling in all kinds of software, not only the ones based on MAS.

It could be interesting to do a comparison of how reliable other coupling metrics against the metric are proposed in this paper. Considering that a good measurement method is independent of the person measuring and the measurement environment. The measurement results must be consistent, repeatable, and comparable

REFERENCES

[1] COSMIC Sizing - The open standard for software size measurement.

[2] A. Abran.Software Metrics and Software Metrology. 2010.

[3] A. Abran and C. Woodward. Guideline on how to convert 'FirstGeneration' Function Point sizes to COSMIC sizes. (November):0–53,2016.

[4] A. Lesterius, A. Abran, C. Symmons. Course Registration ('C - REG ') System Case Study. (December):1–43, 2015.

[5] E. B. Allen, T. M. Khoshgoftaar, and Y. Chen. Measuring couplingand cohesion of software modules: An information-theory approach.International Software Metrics Symposium, Proceedings, pages 124–134, 2001.

[6] E. Arisholm, L, C Briand, and A. Føyen. Dynamic coupling measurement for object-oriented software. IEEE Transactions on Soft-ware Engineering, 30(8):491–506, 2004.

[7] S. R. Chidamber and C. F. Kemerer. A Metrics Suite for Object Oriented Design. IEEE Transactions on Software Engineering,20(6):476–493, 1994.

[8] Common Software Measurement International Consortium (COSMIC).Measurementt Manual v4.0.2. (December):1–115, 2017.

[9] S. S. de Toledo, A. Martini, and Dag I.K. Sjøberg. Identifying architectural technical debt, principal, and interest in microservices: A multiple-case study. Journal of Systems and Software, 177:110968,2021.

[10] M. Fowler and J. Lewis. Microservices - A definition of this new architectural term, 2014.

[11] Y. Hassoun, R. Johnson, and S. Counsell. A dynamic runtime coupling metric for meta-level architectures. Proceedings of the European Conference on Software Maintenance and Reengineering,CSMR, 8:339–346, 2004.

[12] ISO; IEC. Information technology — Software measurement — Functional size measurement — Part 6: Guide for use of ISO/IEC 14143series and related International Standards (ISO/IEC 14143-6:2006(E)),2006.

[13] P. Jamshidi, C. Pahl, N. C. Mendonca, J. Lewis, and S. Tilkov. Microservices: The journey so far and challenges ahead. IEEE Software, 35(3):24–35, 2018.

[14] L. Lavazza, S. Morasca, D. Taibi, and D. Tosi. On the definition of dynamic software measures. International Symposium on Empirical Software Engineering and Measurement, pages 39–48, 2012.

[15] J. Soldani, D. A. Tamburri, and W. J. Van DenHeuvel. The pains and gains of microservices: A Systematic grey literature review.Journal of Systems and Software, 146:215–232, 2018.

[16] F. Valdés-Souto, R. Pedraza-Coello, and F. C. Olguín-Barrón. COSMIC sizing of RPA software: A case study froma proof of concept implementation in a banking organization. CEURWorkshop Proceedings, 2725:1–15, 2020.

[17] R. Subramanyam and M. S. Krishnan. Empirical analysis of CK metrics for object-oriented design complexity: Implications for software defects. IEEE Transactions on Software Engineering, 29(4):297–310,2003.

Software Functional Sizing Automation from Requirements Written as Triplets

Bruel Gérançon, Sylvie Trudel, Roger Kkambou, Serge Robert
Department of Computer Science
Université du Québec à Montréal (UQAM)
Montréal, Canada
e-mail: gerancon.bruel@uqam.ca, trudel.s@uqam.ca, nkambou.roger@uqam.ca, robert.serge@uqam.ca

***Abstract*—The domain of software functional size measurement automation, from software specification documents, has been a research topic over the last years. The literature consulted shows that attempts to automate the process of measuring the software functional size has obtained little success at the industry level. Several tools for automating the measurement of software functional size have been developed according to the Common Software Measurement International Consortium (COSMIC) method (ISO 19761) website and that of International Function Point User Group (IFPUG). However, these tools encountered many flaws, constraints, and limitations. Moreover, the methods, techniques and tools for writing software specification documents used in the industry are far from allowing easily the automation of the measurement of software functional size. In industry, software requirements are often written in natural language, and no technical details are specified. Thus, software requirements are usually incomplete, inconsistent, and prone to ambiguities, and therefore, the analysts can easily make errors of interpretation. Therefore, automating the software functional size measurement is not an easy task. This article introduces a new technique for writing software requirements that could help to automate the functional size measurement process. More precisely, we propose a "triplet approach" for writing software specifications. Furthermore, this procedure is proven, tested, and validated by the development of a new tool for automating the measurement of software functional size, as defined by the COSMIC method. This tool allows to generate triplets (subject, predicate, object) from use cases written in natural language and determines this way the software functional size. Our tool integrates a set of techniques to create a complex artificial intelligence which helps to measure COSMIC function points.**

Keywords-COSMIC; Automation; Functional size; Triplet; Artificial intelligence.

I. INTRODUCTION

The measure of software functional size plays an important role in software engineering, in dealing with new information and in communication technologies (NICT). It is a key factor that allows estimating the effort and the cost of developing software products. Up to now, several estimation methods and approaches have been proposed. As an example, Boehm [5] proposed the COnstructive COst [1] MOdel (COCOMO) method to estimate the cost and duration of software projects. COCOMO is based on the estimation of the number of lines of code to be written for a software. Thus, the number of lines of code corresponds to the physical size of the software. Albrecht [6] proposed a method based on the number of function points, the principle being to identify and quantify user functionalities, thus giving rise to the notion of functional size. Several software measurement methods, such as COSMIC, IFPUG, NESMA, Mark II and FISMA have been proposed and approved by the International Organization for Standardization (ISO). Among the various existing methods and tools, COSMIC is a recent measurement method, developed with the aim of overcoming some limitations of the other methods. A particularity of the COSMIC method is that it can be applied early in the software life cycle and on a set of software components[2].

Although several software measurement methods have been proposed in the literature, the measure of the software functional size is still little used in the industry. The application of software measurement methods remains until now a difficult task [7]. Therefore, the software engineering industry needs tools to automate the functional size measurement process of software [8]. According to the literature consulted, one of the main avenues or research approaches for automating the process of measurement of the functional size of software starts from specifications [1]. In such an approach, the functional size of software is measured from specification documents. However, we can ask: do software requirement writing techniques facilitate the automation of software functional size measurement?

In this article, we will review in section 2 the main techniques and methods for writing software requirements. In section 3, we will describe the limitations of these techniques. Subsequently, we will introduce in section 4, the COSMIC method for sizing software. In section 5, we will introduce our new approach and technique for writing software requirements that could help automate the software functional size measurement process from these specifications, as well as our tool newly developed for supporting the process. Lastly, we will present, in section 6, the results of our research and the future work to be done.

II. TECHNIQUES AND METHODS FOR WRITING SOFTWARE REQUIREMENTS

The automation of the measuring process of software functional size depends necessarily on the mechanism for writing the software requirements, in other words, it depends on the tools, techniques, and methods used to write the specifications. Several techniques and methods for writing requirements have been proposed in the literature, and these techniques are used in industry. For example, Jacobson et al. [9] propose the technique of "Use Cases" to write software requirements. Beck and West [10], on their part, propose "User Stories" as a technique for writing software requirements. These techniques are texts widely used to identify and record the software functional requirements. By definition, Use Cases are textual descriptions used for document software specifications. They influence all the components related to the software development process, including analysis, design, implementation, and testing. Use Cases describe textually how an actor or user will interact with a software system in order to achieve a goal. The purpose of Use Cases is to identify, describe and document the software functionality, specifying how the system can be used to enable different stakeholders and users to achieve their goals. Note that Use Cases are expressed in natural or technically neutral language, without specifying any technical terminology. User Stories consist in a few lines of text that describe a functionality that the software must offer to allow a given actor or user to achieve a specific goal. User Stories are generally written in natural language and do not include technical terms. One of the major advantages of this approach is that it is centered on the system user.

III. Limitations of Approaches, Methods, and Techniques for Writing Requirements

We present, in this section, the definition of software requirement and the limitations of approaches, methods, and techniques for writing requirements.

A. Software Requirements

Requirements engineering is an important phase of the software development life cycle. By definition, a software requirement is a condition that a software or system must be able to meet. In other words, a software requirement is a capability that a system must exhibit to satisfy a contract between a customer and a supplier. In software engineering, the process of requirements engineering, more specifically the activities of elicitating, analyzing, specifying, verifying, and validating requirements are all important for software engineers. Wiegers [3] defines the elicitation of requirements as a process of exploration, discovery, and invention. It helps to uncover the requirements of a software system by communicating with customers, users, and other stakeholders having an interest in the development of the system [3]. The requirements, once discovered, will be analyzed and described in a software requirements specification document. This document will constitute, after the client's verification and validation, the contractual basis between the software engineers and the client. Requirements engineering is an interdisciplinary activity that acts as an intermediary between the supplier and the customer in order to be able to specify and manage the requirements that must be satisfied by the system. It therefore consists in identifying the goals and the scope of the software and in specifying the context in which the software will be used. As for Boehm [5], the requirements engineering process is the upstream part of the software development process. It allows, among other things, the passage of informal needs expressed by stakeholders into abstract requirements until a software requirements specification is obtained [5]. The upstream requirements, once produced, will be described in a specification. This document (the specifications) is the entry point for the software development phases between the customer and the developers.

B. Limitations of Software Requirements Writing Techniques

The techniques used in industry to write software requirements have several limitations. According to Ambler [13], these techniques increase the risk of failure of software development projects, since they describe a large percentage of software specifications that are never implemented. Additionally, the classical approach to requirements writing fails to solve the problem of requirements semantics, since natural language is inherently ambiguous [4]. Indeed, one of the main limitations of the classic or traditional approach to writing software requirements comes from the fact that the techniques, in particular Use Cases and Use Stories used to specify and describe software requirements, are in natural language, with unnecessary details. So, they do not facilitate the automation of the software functional size measurement process. It is necessary to propose a new technique for writing software requirements that could overcome these difficulties.

IV. The COSMIC Method for Sizing Software

Functional size is based on software functionality. The idea is to quantify the amount of functionality provided to a user for a given software product. This implies that the functional size represents the size of the derived software by quantifying the required user functionality (ISO 14143-1). There are different methods for measuring functional size. Within our research, we adopted the COSMIC method. It involves applying a set of principles, rules, and processes to measure the user's functional requirements of a given software. The result is a numerical value as defined by ISO 19761 and which represents the functional size of the software. With COSMIC, we measure the data movements applicable to data groups manipulated by each functional process. A data movement can be of different types (Entry, Exit, Read, or Write). *Figure 1* summarizes the measurement process of the COSMIC method.

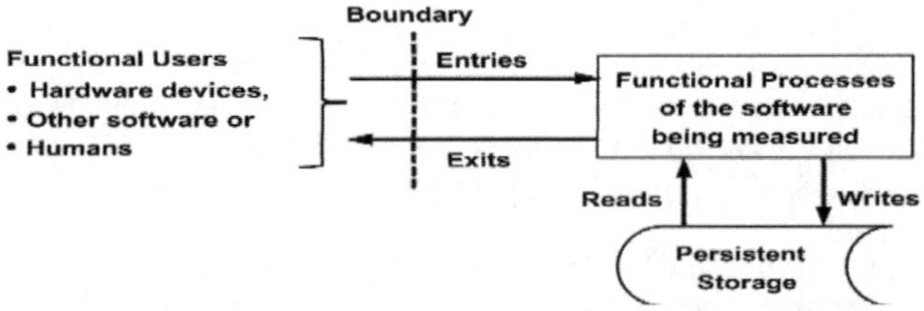

Figure 1. The measurement process of the COSMIC method.

V. Specification of Software Requirements Using our TripletS Structure

We describe, in this section, the software requirements writing technique proposed, and the role of its three (3) components.

A. Triplets Structure

The software requirements writing technique that we propose to facilitate the process of automating the functional sizing of software is a "triplet approach". In other words, each triplet is a single sentence (subject, predicate, object). The subject represents the actor (i.e., the functional user) who interacts with the system. a composite predicate represents the Use case scenario; an atomic predicate represents the methods, transactions or events triggered by the actor (functional, other system, hardware device). Lastly, the object represents a software entity. The goal of the triplet approach is to allow analysts to write or express customers' needs in a simple and effective way with little information. This means that the triplet structure provides an atomic and succinct description of software requirements, expressing the user need with little or no superfluous details. It indeed emphasizes the clarity and brevity of the software requirements. Therefore, the triplet approach could make it easier to perform automatic processing of software requirements, which could automate the software functional size measurement process. Correspondingly, the triplet structure is a requirement writing technique that could complement Use Cases and User Stories. In this case, we developed a tool that automatically extracts triplets from Use Cases, User Stories, or any text written in natural language, and which detects the unnecessary details in the software requirements specification document.

B. Mapping between the Concepts of the Triplet and COSMIC

The triplet structure is a trio of concepts where the subject corresponds to the functional user; the composite predicates correspond to the functional process and the atomic predicates correspond to the data movements. And the objects correspond to the data group manipulated by the functional process. Lastly, the triplet represents a part of the functional process of the software to be measured.

C. Model of Triplet (Triple Store) for Writing Software Requirements

The proposed triplet model is a model that allows to represent the software functional requirements as a triplet, to facilitate the software functional sizing automation. It contains the concepts and knowledge about the COSMIC measurement method, as well as the functional processes of the software to be measured as a triplet. Subsequently, we developed a tool that automatically generates triplets from functional requirements written in the form of a Use Case or a User Story. The structure targeted by the tool is represented as [subject, predicate, object]. The goal is to represent the software requirements as a triplet, consisting of a subject, a predicate and an object. The subject is the functional user of the software; the predicates represent the data movements. As for the object, it corresponds to the data group that is manipulated by the functional process. In addition, the triplet represents a portion of the functional process of the software to be measured. Here is the proposed triplet model for writing software requirements.

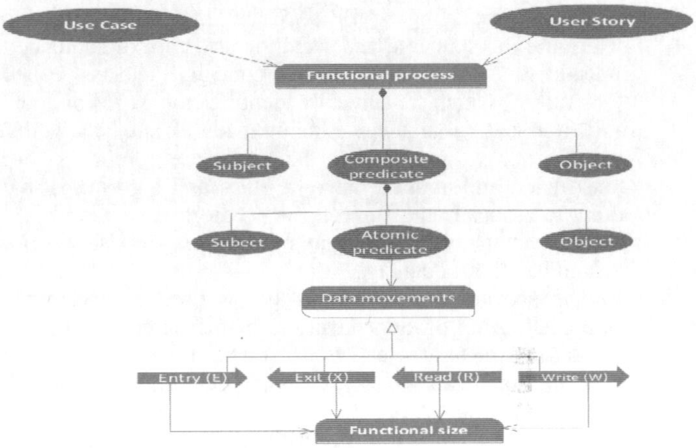

Figure 2. Triplet Model.

Here is a Use Case example written as a triplet:

Description:
Title: Register a new product
The sales manager asks to add a new product. The system displays the product form. The sales manager enters the new product information. The system checks the data. The system records the new product. The system confirms the recording of the new product.

In this example, we described the Use Case using a triplet form (subject, predicate, object). The proposed triplet structure to describe the software functional requirements is simple and effective. It facilitates the process of automating the functional size of the software.

D. Tool for Generating Triplets and Calculating the Functional Size

We have also developed a tool for generating triplets, which contains two modules. The first module is used to automatically generate triplets from Use Cases, User Stories or functional requirements written in natural language. It targets the structure (subject, predicate, object). We assumed that the writing of software requirements is done with dyadic predicates, that is, predicates with two arguments $f(x, y)$. The predicate is expressed by a verb, which is an action to do, and which corresponds to a data movement. The "x" variable is the subject of the action, while the "y" variable is the object of the action. We supposed that in a rule-based system, the rules are based on the idea that writing software requirements is the construction of dyadic functions. In such a perspective, we associate the function **"f"** with the **"x"** and **"y"** variables. We used a descriptive logic to represent the sentences to be splitted into first order predicate formulas. We were inspired by the natural language analyzer offered by Stanford NLP Software Group to generate triplets from functional requirements written in natural language. This language analyzer is a set of libraries in the artificial intelligence domain, more specifically in the field of automatic natural language processing (NLP), which makes possible to determine the syntactic and semantic structure of sentences. Indeed, this language analyzer contains a class called "TagWord", which semantically identifies the words of a text written in natural language as being made of: subjects, verbs, and objects. Inspired by this software program, we constructed and applied our own rules and algorithms that allow to associate the subject, the predicate, and the object, and to generate the triplets from the Use Cases or User Stories written in natural language.

The second module of the tool is used to obtain the functional sizing of the software to be measured. In fact, the generated triplets are seen as processing rules that allow to infer the functional size. This module quantifies the number of atomic predicates (verbs) of each triplet. Subsequently, a set of rules is applied to make each predicate correspond to a type of data movement (Entry, Exit, Read, or Write). Furthermore, we used the repository framework for automation tools for measuring the software functional sizing, proposed by Abran and Paton [15] to ensure that an automation tool could interact with our technique of software requirements writing. This framework describes a set of desirable characteristics for software functional size measurement automation tools. The main characteristics of the reference framework recommended by Abran and Paton [15] can be summarized as follows:

- Automation tools must be associated with recognized standards.
- The tools must offer, for example, the possibility of interacting with the tools for writing software requirements.
- The tools must provide a presentation of the measurement results to facilitate analyzes.

E. Solving Missing Words with Grammatical Ellipse

The ellipse is a rhetorical figure of speech intended to omit one or more elements in order to make a sentence shorter, while promoting comprehension. In the context of the grammatical ellipse, we tend to omit, for example, a verb or an object. Indeed, in the requirements writing domain, analysts, in order to avoid repetition, omit a predicate (verb) or a noun (object). Let's illustrate with an example a Use Case where there is such an omission of an object: the system checks and saves the data. In this Use Case, the system is checking or verifying the data. Subsequently, it will proceed to their recording (to save the data). We suppose that the writing of software requirements is done with dyadic predicates (f (x, y)). The description in formal logic by could be: ∃ object, ∃ subject, such as predicate (object, subject).

Subject:
{x} = The system
Object:
{y} = data
Predicates:
{f1} =checks
{f2} =saves

We obtained the following logical formula:

$$\exists\, x\ [f1(x, y1) \wedge f2\ (x, y2) \tag{1}$$

This Use Case is splitted in two (2) triplets that are respectively:

- The system, checks, the data
- The system, saves, the data

F. Generation of Triplets by Multiple Splittings

In the description of Use Cases, there are sentences containing several objects (complements) and which are connected by logical connectives (AND, OR...), by coordinating conjunctions or by punctuation signs (,). In the automatic text generation literature, there are methods that allow to aggregate structural sentences (subject, predicate, object) using logical connectives. As part of our tool, we were inspired by these methods to proceed by disaggregation. Let's illustrate the following Use Case as an example: "The system verifies the information, saves the data, or returns an error message". We transform each of these actions into a series of predicates of the form: ∃ object, ∃ subject such as predicate (object, subject). We describe use cases in formal logic by variables to represent subjects, predicates, and objects as follows:

Subject:
{x} = The system
Objects:
{y1} = information
{y2} = data
{y3} = error message
Predicates:
{f1} =verifies
{f2} =saves
{f3} =returns

We then obtain the following logical formula:

$$\exists\, x\ [f1(x, y1) \wedge f2\ (x, y2) \wedge f3\ (x, y3)] \tag{2}$$

We give, in the next section, an example of Use Case presenting the manual functional size, as well as the list of triplets generated by the tool and the automatic functional size obtained from the tool.

G. Description of a Use Case and its Manually Measured Functional Size

TABLE I. I illustrates a functional process, for which the data groups are identified, as well as the data movements (EXRW).

The sales manager asks to add a new product. The system verifies the sales manager credentials and displays the new product form or displays a credential error message. The sales manager enters the new product information and asks the system to save the new product. The system verifies the data, records the product, and returns a confirmation message for the addition of the new product or an error message if the product already exists.

TABLE I. EXAMPLE OF MANUALLY MEASURED FUNCTIONAL SIZE

Functional Process Elements	Data Groups	E	X	R	W	Sum of CFP
Asks to add a new product	Credentials	1				1
Verifies the sales manager credentials	Credentials			1		1
Displays a credential error message	Error message		1			1
Displays the new product form	[New product form]					-
Enters the new product information	New Product	1				1
Verifies the data	Data			1		1
Records the product	Product				1	1
Returns a confirmation message	Confirmation message		1			1
Returns an error message	Error message					-
Total:		**2**	**2**	**2**	**1**	**7**

H. *Description of a Use Case and its Automatically Measured Functional Size*

Figure 3. illustrates the same functional process from the previous example, divided by the tool into several triplets. It determines the functional size and identifies the data movement types (Entry, eXit, Read or Write). It is important to mention that the tool obtains the same functional size result as the manual functional size established by the human expert.

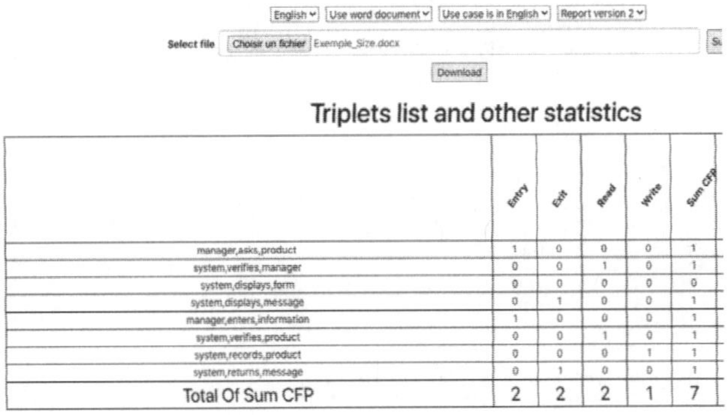

	Entry	Exit	Read	Write	Sum CFP
manager,asks,product	1	0	0	0	1
system,verifies,manager	0	0	1	0	1
system,displays,form	0	0	0	0	0
system,displays,message	0	1	0	0	1
manager,enters,information	1	0	0	0	1
system,verifies,product	0	0	1	0	1
system,records,product	0	0	0	1	1
system,returns,message	0	1	0	0	1
Total Of Sum CFP	2	2	2	1	7

Figure 3. Example of Automaticaly Measured Functional Size.

VI. THE AUTOMATED MEASUREMENT RESULTS OF THE TOOL

We present, in this section, the automated measurement results of our tool developed. The results presented by the tool are compared with those of human experts certified with the COSMIC method.

A. *Rules for Identifying Data Movements Types*

We adjusted the NLP module by applying a set of rules that allow to construct and extract triplets from Use Case or User Stories written in natural language. Our tool integrates a set of techniques to create a complex artificial intelligence which helps to measure COSMIC function points. Then, we implemented a set of rules to identify the types of data movement (Entry, eXit, Read, Write). These rules are applied once the functional sizing (data movements) has been determined. The size of a functional process is equal to the number of its data movements. Each data movement corresponds to an atomic predicate of each triplet and has a size of 1 COSMIC function point (CFP). *Table II* provides a list of the mapping rules that were implemented for identifying the data movement types of each triplet generated by the tool.

TABLE II. DATA MOVEMENT MAPPING RULES

ID	Definition of Mapping Rules (MR)
MR01	Any data movement from the functional user (human, other software, hardware devices) is considered as an Entry (E).
MR02	A data request to the functionality is treated as an Entry(E)
MR03	Any data movement from a functional process to the functional user is considered as an eXit (X).
MR04	All formatting and data presentation manipulations required to send the data attributes to the functional user is treated as an eXit (X).
MR05	Searching of a data group to persistent storage is considered as a Read (R).
MR06	The logical processing and / or mathematical calculation necessary to read the data are considered as a Read (R).
MR07	Any read request functionality is considered as a Read (R).
MR08	Moving a unique data group to persistent storage is considered as a Write (W).
MR09	The logical processing and / or mathematical calculation necessary to create data to be saved are considered as a Write (W).

B. *Software Projects Measured*

We presented the functional size results of three (3) measured projects, which requirement documents written in natural language are publicly available on the COSMIC website as case studies. First, COSMIC experts manually measured the functional size of each project according to the measurement manual definitions and rules. Subsequently, we use our developed tool to automatically determine the functional sizing of these projects from their requirements. We compared the results generated by the tool against those published by experts. Then, we described the observed differences.

C. Automatic Functional Sizing Results from the Tool

We summarized in the *Table III* the automatic functional sizing results of the three (3) projects of software requirements specification documents obtained from the tool. The tool generates the triplets from Use Cases or User Stories described in natural language. Then, it determines the functional size.

D. Evaluation and Validation of Results by COSMIC Experts

Within the framework of this article, we tested the tool with three (3) projects and the results presented were compared with those of human experts certified with the COSMIC method. The manually measured results of these projects are published and available on the COSMIC website. First, our tool generates the triplets from requirements written in natural language, from Use Cases or User Stories written in English or in French. Then, it determines the functional sizing by quantifying the number of atomic predicates (verbs) of each triplet. The research results showed that the generation of triplets from Uses Cases or User Stories can be exploited by measurement automation tools. In fact, our proposed tool presents automated results that are consistent with the manual results validated and published by experts, with an average accuracy of 98.30%, as shown in *TABLE* III, where the accuracy varies between 96.97% and 100%.

TABLE III. AUTOMATIC AND MANUAL FUNCTIONAL SIZE COMPARISONS

Project	Manual Functional Sizing	Automatic Functional Sizing	Accuracy
Resto Sys	119	117	98.32%
ACME Car Hire System	33	32	96.97%
Rice Cooker	24	24	100.00%
Total	**176**	**173**	**98.30%**

E. Threats to Validity

Requirements are generally written with active verbs and not with passive verbs. Nevertheless, it is likely to meet cases where some Use Case scenarios are described in the passive form, i.e., subject and object are swapped. One limitation is that the tool could not generate triplets for sentences written in the passive form. However, the tool detects sentences written with a passive voice and raises the issue as a potential error. Also, the proposed tool is not able to detect format elements of the requirements document, such as headers, footers, titles, etc. Requirements text has to be uploaded from a Word or PDF file into our tool, where this file should contain only requirements text without any format element. Because of manual manipulations to create that file, there is a possibility of human errors, such as some requirement text not copied or copied twice.

VII. CONCLUSION AND FUTURE WORK

We proposed in this article a new method for writing software requirements that could help to automate the functional size measurement process. This technique is a triplet approach. It is proven, tested, and validated by the development of a new tool for automating the measurement of the functional size of software, as defined by the COSMIC method. This tool allows generating triplets from Use Cases or User Stories written in natural language, more specifically in English or in French (Use Cases or User Stories written in English or in French). In addition, it determines the functional sizing of software, in adding the sum of predicates and identifying the types of data movements. The tool approximates the human experts at about 98.30%.

In the future, our perspective will try to integrate a new module which would ensure that the tool could generate triplets for sentences written in the passive form and that would detect the format of the requirements documents. Furthermore, we will work on a machine learning module which would allow that the tool could improve gradually during its implementation. The goal will be to allow the tool to learn to solve problems by itself, without necessarily needing the intervention of human experts.

REFERENCES

[1] V. Bévo, "Analyse et formalisation ontologique des procédures de mesure associées aux méthodes de mesure de la taille fonctionnelle des logiciels: De nouvelles perspectives pour la mesure" (Ontological analysis and formalization of measurement procedures associated with software functional size measurement methods: New perspectives for measurement), Ph.D. thesis, Montreal, Université du Québec à Montréal, 314p, 2005. [Online]. Available from: https://dic.uqam.ca/upload/files/theses/bevo_these.pdf, [Retrieved: April, 2021].

[2] S. Azzouz and A. Abran, "A proposed measurement role in the Rational Unified Process: Automated Measurement of COSMIC-FFP for Rational Rose Real Time", In Information and Software Technology, vol. 47, no. 3, pp. 151-166, 2004.

[3] K. Wiegers, "More About Software Requirements. New York: O'Reilly Media", Inc, 2009.

[4] S. Trudel, "The COSMIC ISO 19761 functional size measurement method as a software requirements improvement mechanism", Ph.D. thesis, École de Technologie Supérieure (ETS), 2012.

[5] B. Boehm, "Software cost estimation with COCOMO II", Upper Saddle River, N.J; London: Prentice Hall International, 2000.

[6] A. Albrecht, and A.J. Gaffney, "Software Function, Source Lines of Code, and Development Effort Prediction: A Software Science Validation", IEEE Transactions on Software Engineering, vol. 9, no. 6, pp. 639-648, 2000.

[7] A. Abran, "Software Metrics and Software Metrology. Hoboken", N.J.: Wiley Los Alamitos, Calif.: IEEE Computer Society, 328 p, 2010.

[8] S. Black and D. Wigg, "X-Ray: A Multi-Language, Industrial Strength Tool", IWSM'99, Lac Supérieur, Canada, vol. 8, no. 10, pp. 39-50, 1999.

[9] I. Jacobson, "The unified Software Development Process", The Journal of Object Technology, vol. 2, no. 4, pp.1-22, 2003.

[10] K. Beck and D. West, "User Stories in Agile Development", In Scenarios, Stories, Use Cases: Through the Systems Developments Life-Cycle, 2004.

[11] A. Cockburn, "Writing effective use cases", Addison-Wesley Longman, 2001.

[12] "IEEE Standard Glossary of Software Engineering Terminology", in IEEE Std 610.12-1990, vol., no., pp.1-84, 31 Dec. 1990, doi: 10.1109/IEEESTD.1990.101064.

[13] S.W. Ambler, "Examining the Big Requirements Up Front (BRUF) Approach", Ambysoft inc., [Online]. Available from: http://agilemodeling.com/essays/examiningBRUF.htm, [Retrieved: April, 2021].

[14] B. Nuseibeh and S. Easterbrook, "Requirements Engineering: A Roadmap", In Proceedings of the Conference on The Future of Software Engineering, New York (USA), pp. 35-46, 2000.

[15] A. Abran and K. Paton, "Automation of Function Points Counting: Feasibility and Accuracy", Université du Québec à Montréal, pp. 1-21, 1997.

[16] A. Abran *et al.*, "The COSMIC Functional Size Measurement Method Version 5.0", [Online]. Available from: www.cosmic-sizing.org, [Retrieved: April, 2021].

[17] K. Manoj, "What is TDD, BDD & ATDD ?", Assert Selenium, Nov. 5th, 2012, [Online]. Available from: http://www.assertselenium.com/atdd/difference-between-tdd-bdd-atdd/, [Retrieved: April, 2021].

[18] M. Downing, M. Eagles, P. Hope, and Ph. James, "ACME Car Hire Case Study v1.0.1", August 2018. [Online]. Available from: https://cosmic-sizing.org/publications/acme-car-hire-case-study-v1-0-1/, [Retrieved: April, 2021].

[19] A. Sellami, M. Haoues, and H. Ben-Abdallah, "Sizing Natural Language/User Stories/UML Use Cases for Web and Mobile Applications using COSMIC FSM", May 2019. [Online]. Available from: https://cosmic-sizing.org/publications/restosys-case-v1-2/, [Retrieved: April, 2021].

Towards a Decision Support System

An Ontology Validation

Raja Hanafi
National School of Computer,
University of Manouba, Manouba, Tunisia
E-mail: rajarajahanafi@yahoo.com

Lassad Mejri
College of Computer and Information Science, Jouf University, Saudi Arabia
E-mail: Mejrilassad@gmail.com

Henda Hajjami Ben Ghezala
National School of Computer,
University of Manouba, Manouba, Tunisia
E-mail: Henda.benghezala@ensi.rnu.tn

Abstract— **In certain complex situations Decision-making takes into account a large number of the so-called knowledge of decision-support. This knowledge is often represented as a set of database definitions, knowledge bases, general information, domain data, statistical data, etc. To make the right decisions and to make good use of this mass of knowledge, it is preferable to formalize, represent and model them. In the literature, several works suggest using the ontology as a adequate solution to represent the decision making and decision support knowledge. Inspired by this work and based on the main objective of our research work, decision ontology was proposed to represent and formalize our decision support system knowledge which is proposed for computer Project Manager. The problem here is that the good practice of a decision-making system or a decision support system is not limited to the structuring and representation of the knowledge used. This knowledge, and given the delicacy of the domain studied (computing) requires to be evaluated and to be validated by domain experts. Accordingly incremental and multi-intervention approaches for the validation of the proposed ontology were proposed. This validation also allowed us to confirm the set of concepts and relationships forming the given ontology. The result of this research is a validated ontology which will allow us to build the memory of our project and to feed a good consistent and rich decision knowledge base.**

Keywords- support decision; decision making; decision ontology; ontology validation; computer project.

I. INTRODUCTION

The main purpose the elaborated ontology [1] is to provide a basis for the proposal decision support system offered to the project managers in the computer field. This system consists essentially of two main modules: The decision-making module which functions as a support system to computer project leaders, to make a decision concerning the onset of their new projects and the decision support modules provides guidance and assistance inspired from historical projects which are already resolved or which have been already dealing with the problematic of their project in question. For the two modules, the need for knowledge, experience, historical information for resolved, unresolved, same context or same class projects, is too important in order to have a right course of the decision support system and especially the decision-making module. To have a broad knowledge of this domain,, we must model and represent it in a structured way. In addition, the newly created ontology must be validated and evaluated thanks to either experts or standard validation tools. Here, we can identify two scenarios [5] which justify the validation of the ontology: an adequate ontology will allow better reuse of the data and oncologists need methods to evaluate and validate their models in order to encourage them to share with confidence their results with the community. In this context, this paper will focus primarily on the problem of validating the content of domain ontology. Besides, an incremental approach for validation approaches was introduced for the proposed ontology which is composed of six steps. In this context, we have studied some ontology validation approaches: those which are questionnaire based, others based on question answering. The problem here that all approaches studied are single actor approaches where a single validation actor can validate the entire ontology and this by applying the semantic and the structural validation definitively with no return. The main novelty of our validation approach consists essentially of three criteria: the incremental validation, the multi-intervention, and the respecting of the –V cycle. In fact, the shift from one validation step to other results in an update of the initial ontology and this occurs-by the intervention of three experts (project management expert, a project computer expert and a specialist in ontology engineering). Our proposal approach requires a resort between all the validation phases and can return to any expert for revalidation if needed.

The paper is organized as the following.. After the introduction, Section 2 describes the application of our ontology in the decision support system. Section 3 is made up of two sub-sections: The first sub-section illustrates some ontology validation approaches and their discussions. The second sub-section describes the proposed validation approach. Finally section 4 reveals the main conclusion and futures works.

II. RELATED WORKS

In the literature, several works have used ontology as a method of modeling and formalizing decision-making knowledge. In the following section, we will describe the most relevant ones.

A. Main Proposals

1) A Decision-Making Ontology for Information System Engineering[2]

The author proposed an ontology for the modeling of Decision-Making knowledge (DM). The proposed DM ontology is a representation of DM concepts and their relationships modeled using a Unified Modeling Language (UML) class diagram. Then an application in the field of Business Process Reengineering (BPR) has been proposed. This proposal is based mainly on the unification of the most important DM concepts within a single model. The suggested Decision-Making-Ontology (DMO) is of a dual use namely: to clarify the DM concepts to formalize the DM situations and to specify the DM requirements and to highlight the components of the DM method.

2) A Productive Credit Decision-Making System Based on the Ontology Model [3]

The author has constructed ontology for the development of Decision Support System (DSS) provoked by reviews of the effects of the pandemic on the global banking system. It emphasizes the relationship and support between companies and banks and the need for response from banks to ensure a reliable business customer experience. It is clear that the decision ontology in banking risk management is a component of the general “Banking” ontology.

3) A Decision Support Ontology for collaborative decision making in engineering design[4]

In this research, a Decision Support Ontology (DSO) is developed to facilitate decision making within the framework of collaborative design. The structure of the developed information model reflects a prior knowledge of decision making and supports the communication of information independent of any specific decision method. As a result, the DSO includes information related to the decision such as the design issue, alternatives, rating, criteria, and preferences. It also includes the rationale and assumptions for the decision, as well as any constraints created by the decision and the outcome of the decision. The DSO is based on the Ontology Web Language (OWL), which facilitates the sharing and integration of decision-making information between multiple collaborators via the Web and description logic.

B. Discusion and synthesis

The study of these different proposals has enabled us to observe that:

- The ontologies used for the proposal of a decision aid or a decision support are a generic ontology of large domain namely the domain of design techniques, the domain of knowledge engineering, the domain of insurance banking , etc.
- Most of these ontologies are not well validated and if this is the case the validation is not complete and suffers from being a support for the formalization and the modeling of knowledge.

It is in this context that we decided to propose decision ontology for the proposal of a decision support on three main levels. In addition and in order to remedy the problem of ontology validation, the following section of this paper is proposed as a validation approach. This approach is an attempt to guarantee an adequate formalization for the knowledge manipulated by the proposed aid system.

III. THE APPLICATION OF THE PROPOSED ONTOLOGY IN THE DECISION SUPPORT SYSTEM

In order to automate the knowledge capitalization approach [1] that we have suggested, we have proposed our decision support system offered mainly to computer project leaders. The main goal of this support system is to guide the manager of a computer project from the start of this new project until the resolution and the illustration of the final results. Our proposed ontology is described in three main concepts: project context, project features and project rational design. The proposed system offered three levels of assistance and for each level of help we will identify, the following: the main role for the proposed support decision ontology.

- The first level of help is "help oriented services". It allows the enrichment, consultation, statistics, framing and contextualization of new projects to be processed. At this stage the conceptualization and definition of concepts and terms describing computer projects are needed. The support decision knowledge recommended in this type of help is given by the instantiation of the concepts and relations defining these two classes "project features" and "project context" as well as their subclasses.
- The second level of help is "help oriented decision making": that presents the main goal of our decision support system. At this level, project leaders (chief or project manager) are into taking a decision of launching their new project. This decision is made by checking whether the problem of their new

project is already addressed or not. Here, the need to define a "problematic" concept for each project is very important. The instantiation of the project feature class that contains the concept "project problematic" forms the answer to the decision-making question.

- The third level of help is "help oriented decision support". For this type of help, the project leader will be inspired by the projects already resolved to complete their new projects. In this case, they will not only be inspired by the suggestions and solutions proposed for old projects, but also they will benefit from the problems and failures encountered during the resolution of these different projects. The instantiation of the project Rational Design (problem, suggestion and solution) forms a basis for decision support knowledge.

Even if the use of the proposed decision ontology plays a key role in determining the knowledge necessary for building a decision-making knowledge base, it is still insufficient. This insufficiency is explained by the fact that this knowledge is not always true and needs to be evaluated and to be validated by experts and specialists. It is in this context that we propose an ontology validation approach which aims to evaluate, to verify and to validate the content of this ontology, the choice of concepts and the relationships between them. The description of this approach is given in the following section.

IV. ONTOLOGY VALIDATION

The ontology validation is considered as a stakeholder of the life cycle of ontology that they can keep their interest related to the applications for which they were built. Then the validation of ontology knowledge has an influence on the evolution and the maintenance of systems using this ontology [6], [7]. In addition, the quality of the knowledge modeled by ontology directly affects the quality of these systems. It is in this context, and to guarantee a good quality of the proposed decision support system, we have decided to validate the content of our proposed ontology and we propose a validation approach for our proposed ontology which is built on a set of criteria.

A. *Main Ontology Validation Approaches*

Several works in the literature have been proposed approaches and validation methods. In what follows, we will present some proposals. To get the Integrity of the Specifications.

a) A validation approach proposed by Rim et al [8] : The authors proposed an ontology validation approach which minimizes the intervention of an expert in the validation of changes through an evolutionary process based on consistency check and quality assessment of the modified ontology. The verification of consistency is employed to ensure that all axioms remain valid after the occurance of the change. The proposed validation process consists in defining weights by the domain expert for each criterion by giving it a weight relative to its importance in relation to the domain and the use of the ontology. Thus, the process will minimize the intervention of an expert in the validation of changes.

2) An approach for validating the content of an ontology proposed by Ben Abacha et al [9]: Authors have proposed a semi-automatic approach called SAVANT based on the generation of questions to validate their ontologies. The first step is to automatically generate a list of Boolean questions from the ontology being validated. These questions are submitted to experts in the field who provide an agreement decision (Yes / No) and then an interpretation of these comments made to validate or modify the ontology. The originality of this approach rests on the fact that the interventions are manual and they are carried out only by health professionals.

3) An interactive method for the validation of ontology proposed by Richard [10]: An ontology validation method called OVIM "Ontology's Validation by Interactive Method" has been proposed. Authors proposed this method for the structural and semantic validation of ontology. This method is be based on five stages. They started with the structural validation that has four stages of validation namely; consistency, validation by OOps, validation by request and validation of the choice of the preferential label. In the fifth step, they realized the semantic validation by collaborating with actors of the modeled domain.

4) An ontology validation Approach by the experts via a questionnaire by Laila et al. [11]: An ontology evaluation and validation approach that has been proposed. This approach starts from an ontology to be evaluated and ends up with an updated ontology according to the evaluators' recommendations. The proposed approach consists essentially of five steps: In the first step, a questionnaire is produced from the components of the ontology. Secondly, results of the survey of the experts will be done. The third step is to analyze and synthesize the results obtained. The update of the questionnaire based on expert feedback as well as the update of the ontology according to the knowledge of the results is realized during the last two stages.

5) A validation approach based on evaluation by Tartir et all[12]: This approach essentially consists of verifying the consistency and measuring the impact of the change on the quality of the ontology. It also allows consistency checking and evaluation of the structure and content of the proposed ontology based on well-defined evaluation criteria and metrics.

B. *Discussion*

Although the validation approach proposed by [9] is a very important approach that allows the validation of concepts, relationships and axiom components of ontology. In fact, it has been evaluated experimentally on three ontologies of different methods of construction but this approach presents some lacuna:

- A bad quality of validated ontology is related to two reasons: the absence of ontology-expert interaction and the absence of interface.
- Wrong time planning of the expert and the reduction of his level of concentration during the answers to the questions.
- The choice of questions is not generic. It also depends on the context of the problem.
- The validation method of [10] like any other method allows the structural and semantic validation.
- The problem here is that during the semantic validation domain actors verify only the existence of the general semantic domain.
- Another limit of this approach is the fact that the domain experts are not allowed to add, modify or update the used concepts.
- Expert, in this approach are simply domain actor and are not necessarily specialists in the field of ontology engineering.

The approach proposed in [11], is a very interesting approach but has some limitations:

- It is an approach not updated in the term of the novelties of the version of the OWL language.
- Uses only English for the generation of questionnaires in natural language.
- The questionnaires are generated using non-specialists in the construction of ontology study which reduces the quality of validated ontology.

The study of these different approaches allows us to notice that:

- A total absence of documentation.
- Absence of multi-expert validation [just one expert involved].

Generally, the major approaches make use simply of an evaluation of their ontology. Effectively, this evaluation could not be considered as a validation permitting to exploit their ontology. In this context, incremental validation approach is introduced which is mainly characterized by multi-intervention, documentation and incrementation. In the next section, we will describe both the process of building ontology and the proposed validation.

V. Incremental & Multi-intervention validation approach

Evaluating ontology means checking and validating two aspects: structural and semantic aspects. The validation of the structural aspect of ontology allows verifying the consistency and the coherence of a model to check. In this way, classes and sub-classes are verified according to the criteria of consistency and coherence between them and to avoid redundancy.

In this way, we proposed a validation approach based on three criteria:

- The first criterion: the Incremental validation of the ontology: the passage from one validation step to another results in an update [modification, deletion or addition] of the initial ontology.
- The second criterion: the Multi-intervention criteria: This approach is characterized by the intervention of several and different experts. Three experts are involved in the validation process:
  - ✓ The project management expert: He is an expert in the field of project management.
  - ✓ The project computer expert: He is an expert who masters all the concepts of computer projects.
  - ✓ The specialist in ontology engineering: This actor has a good command of all the tools and editors of the ontology.

These experts are the main players in the proposed approach; however they are not the only ones. They have the right to bring in other experts and specialists when necessary.

- The third criterion: Our validation approach is respecting the V cycle .We were inspired by the live cycle of software engineering. Effectively our approach like the V cycle requires a feedback between all the validation phases. Hence, in our validation phases, we can return to any expert for revalidation if needed. In contrary to a classic approach which applies semantics and structural validation definitively with no return, we can return at any phase of validation to enhance our ontology.

The proposed validation approach is based mainly on a two-level validation method:

- A technical validation level, which is carried out according to the tools and menus integrated into the "Protégé"(ontology construction environment). During this level, we checked at each phase the consistency and the coherence of the proposed ontology.
- A professional validation carried out by a specialist in the field of computer project and an expert in the field of engineering and ontological construction and a knowledge management expert.

The approach that we proposed is essentially composed of six steps (Fig.1):

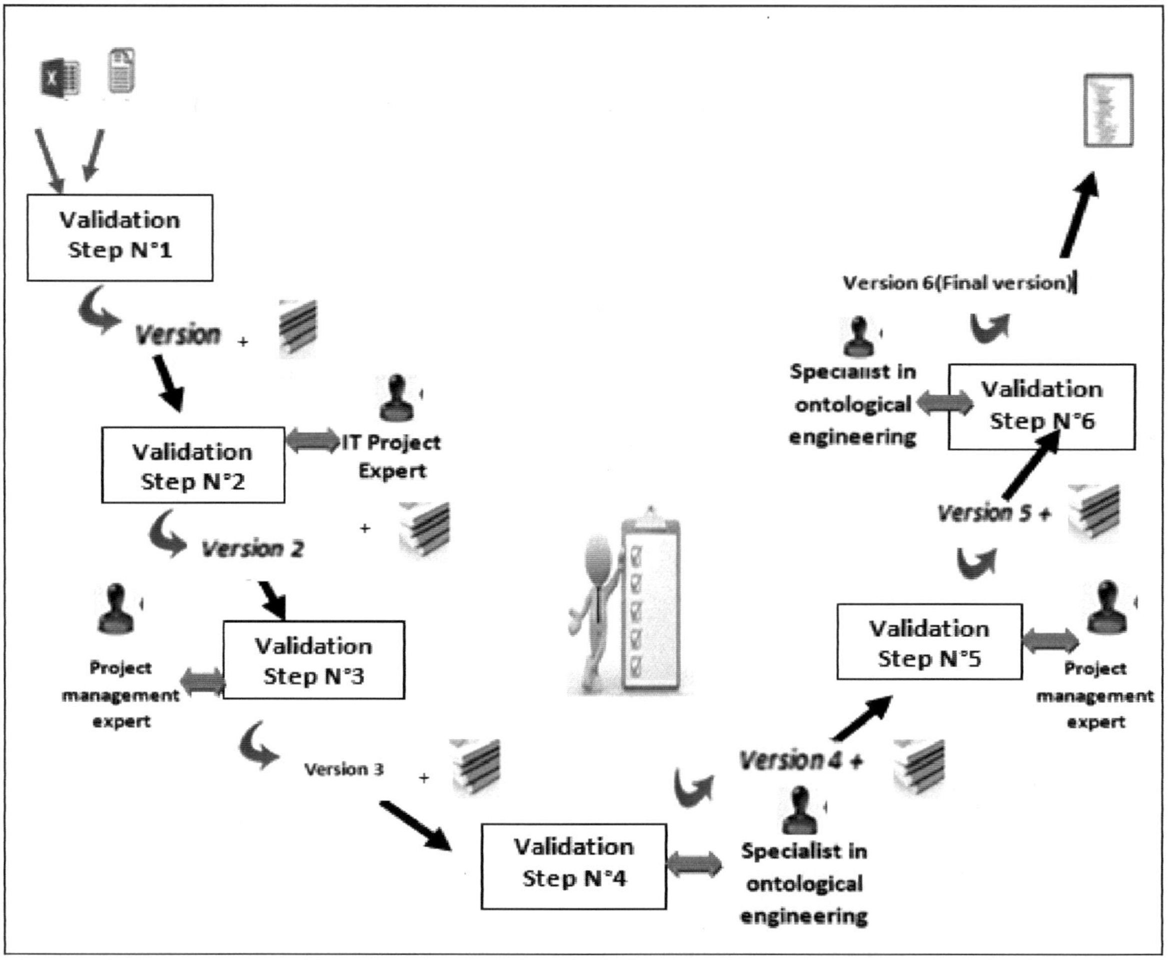

Figure 1. Incremental & Multi-intervention validation approach.

- Step 1: During the first validation step, a descriptive document is presented in a tabular form containing all the concepts and terms as well as their descriptions constituting the first version of the ontology prepared (Fig.2).
- Step 2: In the second step, it is up to us to update our proposal based on the remarks and the assertions given by the computer project expert. This step was considered as a meeting accompanied by discussions. The result of this phase is a second version of ontology that is ready for evaluation by "project computer expert". This version is an amelioration of the version 1 at the level of project features (Fig. 3).

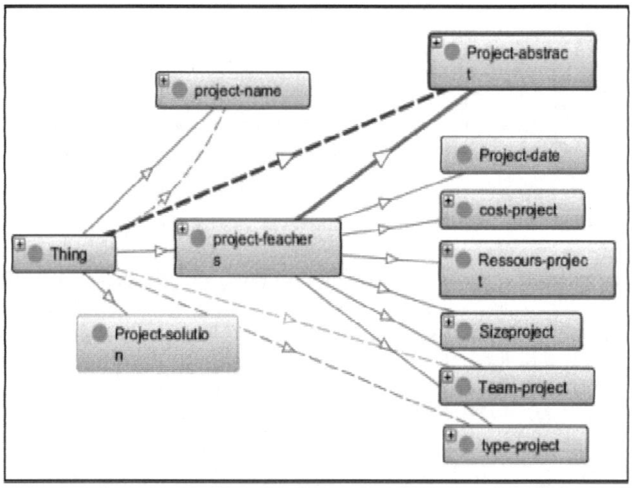

Figure 2. First ontology's version.

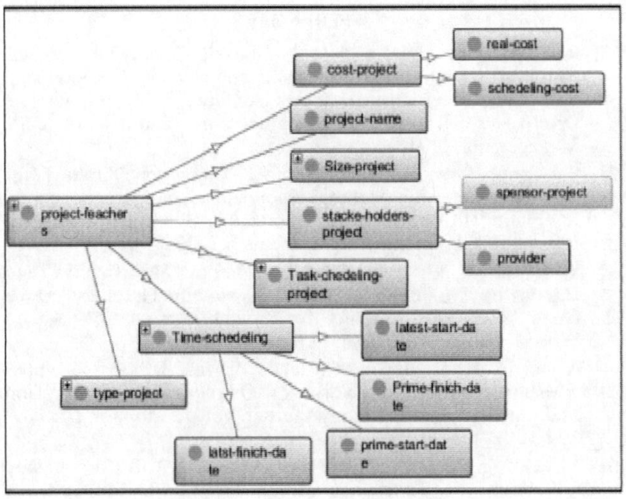

Figure 3. Second ontology's version.

- Step 3. During this step, we prepared a second report: a document describing our objectives and orientations. This report is then submitted to a project management expert for evaluation. This second expert could affirm or refute, add or modify the proposal by adding a textual justification. Effectively, in a version 3, this expert proposes to restrict the ontology by adding a new super class named "project context". This class gives a detailed idea about project deliverables, project abstract‖ and project keywords‖, etc (Fig.4).
- Step 4: After the evaluation done by the project management expert, technical check needs to be done .This check makes use of a software tool in the way to evaluate the consistency and the coherence of the latest version of our ontology. This mission is assured by a specialist in ontology engineering and results in a version 4.

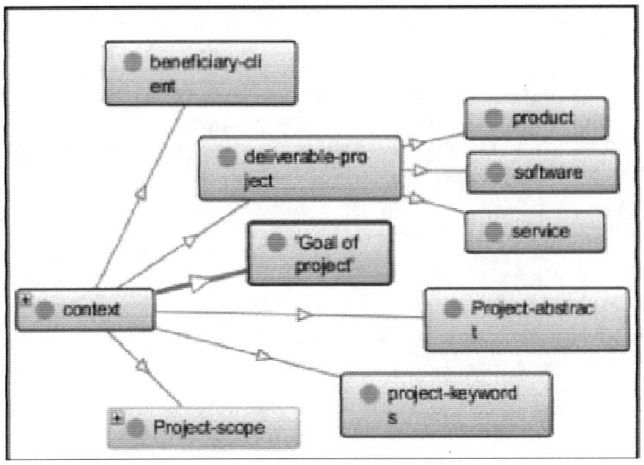

Figure 4. Third ontology's version.

- Step 5: At this step, the fourth version is sent to the project management expert according to our objective which is essentially to discuss projects problem solving. Our goal here is to enrich ontology in the way to facilitate problems solving in a new project by exploiting historical projects. This step leads to a new version of ontology labeled as version 5. At this stage the expert proposes to add a new sub-class baptized "Rational design" (Fig.5).

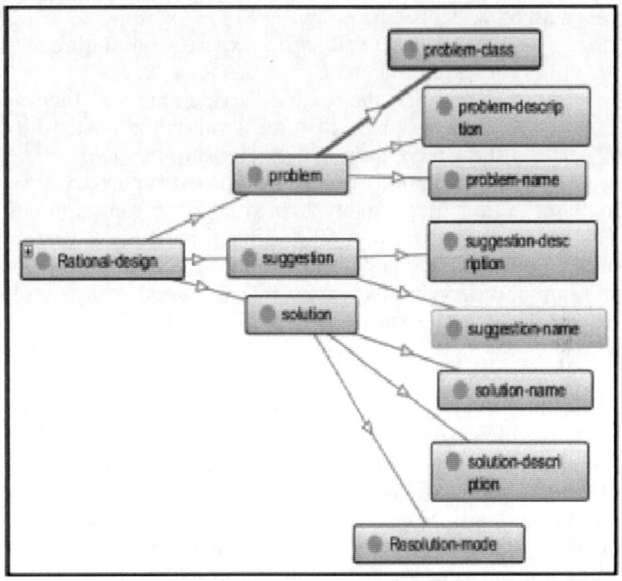

Figure 5. Fifth ontology's version.

- Step 6: For this validation phase the specialist of ontology engineering chooses to use HERMIT [tool integrated in protégé 4.2] to validate the consistency. This step results in a new version 6.

VI. DISCUSSION AND RESULT

The added value of our approach lies mainly in three points:

- The first point is presented by the multi-interventions of experts and specialists who cooperate for the validation of ontology. These will intervene not only when an error has occurred but in each phase where it is necessary to be present.
- The second point is the generic validation goal: a technical validation a semantic validation (contained in the meaning of the concept) and an ergonomic validation.
- The third point consists in favoring a documentation content of each validation step favoring an aspect of reuse and sharing of validation technique for future validation phases and even for future projects.

The validation methodology followed in our validation approach mainly consists in bringing in several experts with different skills and this improves the nature of the corrections and updates proposed each time.

However, this approach has some limitations:

- It is an approach that is limited to computer projects since our experts are restricted to those who are specialists in this field.
- The approach lacks a means of validating the logical aspect of ontology.

For all these reasons we want to improve our proposal with other decisions:

- ✓ We will try to add other experts to strengthen the intervention phase.
- ✓ Carry out the logical validation and this by adding a phase of logical validation ensured by the intervention of a specialist in the field.

For the validation of the proposed approach, the implementation of a prototype proved to be too essential. This prototype will always take as input the current version of the proposed ontology and based on recommendations and human interventions (expert interventions) validation is carried out step by step.

VII. CONCLUSION AND PERSPECTIVES

In this paper, we have presented how we have used our domain ontology for modelling knowledge decision. The proposed ontology decision is a representation of concepts and relationships of computer filed used to create a decision knowledge base. Then we have shown its application in our decision support system. In this context, we proposed a validation approach which is an incremental and a multi-intervention approach that allows a semantic and structural validation of the proposed ontology. After the validation phase, we will validate experimentally this ontology. In this context our future work must focus on the experimentation phase. This phase is carried out by building a knowledge base containing a real computer projects forming the basis of the facts and a set of rules forming the basis of the rules. These rules are of two types: classification rules which help to classify the projects and association rules which provide a help to describe in detail a new project. To do this, we will use the classification data mining techniques and we are going to propose classification and learning algorithms. Although the proposed validation approach seems too important to provide a fluid and reliable environment for the formalization of computer knowledge useful for decision support, it still remains incomplete and inconsistent. To do this an experimental study will prove too essential as a future contribution.

REFERENCES

[1] R. Hanafi, L. Mejri and H.B. Ghezela "Computer-Project-Ontology Construction,Validation and choice of knowledge base",10th International Joint Conference on Knowledge Discovery, Knowledge Engineering and Knowledge Management. (2018).

[2] E. Kornyshova and R.Deneckère, "Using an Ontology for Modeling Decision-Making Knowledge", conference paper, International Conference on Knowledge-Based and Intelligent Information & Engineering Systems , (2012).

[3] A. Bakurova, E. Tereschenko, Y .Filei, M.Pasichnyk and H.Ropalo, "Modeling of Decision Making Ontology", Free Open-Access Proceedings for Scientific Conferences and Workshops /Vol-2362/paper18.pdf (2018).

[4] A. Justin. R. Rockwell, C. Jack, W. Ian, R. Grosse and S .Krishnamurty, "Framework for Ontology-Driven Decision Making", Applied Ontology journal, vol. 12, no. 3-4, pp. 189-194, (2017) .

[5] M. Gruninger and M.S. Fox, "The Role of Competency Questions in Enterprise Engineering", Department of Industrial Engineering, University of Toronto, 4 Taddle Creek Road, Toronto, Ontario M5S IA4, IFIP WG5.7 Workshop on Benchmarking - Theory and Practice, Trondheim, Norway, (1994).

[6] M. Garzallah, "Contributions to Knowledge Engineering: Construction and Validation of Ontology and Semantic Measures", Habilitation to Direct Research (H.D.R.), (2017).

[7] A. Baneyx and J. Charlet, "Evaluation, evolution and maintenance of an ontology in medicine: inventory and experimentation". INSERM, U729, Paris, F-75006 France ;Univ Paris Descartes, F-75006, STIM, DSI, AP-HP, Paris, F-75013 France.

[8] R. Djedidi, H. Abboute and M-A. Aufaure, "Evolution of ontology: Validation of changes based on assessment", projet.liris.cnrs.fr/gom/JFO_2007/4.pdf, (2007).

[9] A.B.Abacha, "Towards Natural Language Question ,Generation for the Validation of Ontologies and Mappings", Marcos Da Silveira and Cédric Pruski, Journal of Biomedical Semantics, (2016).

[10] M. Richard, X. Aimé, M-O. Krebs and J. Charlet, " LOVMI: towards an interactive method for the validation of ontologies", INSERM UMRS 1142, LIMICS, F-75006, (2015).

[11] LZ. Ghomari1, F. Deghmani and A. Meghnous, "Generation of a Questionnaire from a Domain Ontology",conference paper, 28es Journées francophones d'Ingénierie des ConnaissancesAt: Caen, France ,(2017).

[12] S. Tartir, S. Amit,I. and B. Arpinar, "Ontological Evaluation and Validation", from book Theory and Applications of Ontology: Computer Applications,Chapter In book: Theory and Applications of Ontology: Computer Applications (pp.115-130) [pp.115-130] , (2012).

Reverse Engineering Models of Concurrent Communicating Systems From Event Logs

Sébastien Salva
LIMOS - UMR CNRS 6158
University Clermont Auvergne, France
email: sebastien.salva@uca.fr

Abstract—**This paper tackles the problem of extracting design and implementation informations from communicating systems made up of components concurrently interacting with each other, e.g., Web service compositions or IoT (Internet of Things) systems. We present a passive model learning approach, which recovers formal models from event logs, specifically one Input Output Labelled Transition System (IOLTS) for every component of the system under learning. From an event log, our approach is able to automatically recover conversations (a.k.a. sessions), without having any knowledge about the used event correlation mechanisms. It uses correlation pattern definitions and a heuristic based on the quality of the generated conversations to get the most relevant conversation sets. Then, our approach extracts the trace sets of every component and generates IOLTSs. The latter can be used as documentation, for test case generation, or for formal verification.**

Index Terms*—*Reverse engineering; Model learning; Event Log; Communicating systems.

I. Introduction

Software Reverse Engineering gathers numerous techniques specialised in the analysis of software system to extract design and implementation information. Among them, model learning has emerged as a highly effective technique for recovering the models of black-box software systems. Such models, e.g., temporal rules, or finite state machines that encode functional behaviours, offer substantial benefits as they can be employed for security audits [1], [2], real-time anomaly detection [3], or bug detection [4].

This paper addresses passive model learning, for which it is assumed that event logs have been previously collected from a System Under Learning (SUL) and can be mined to learn models. Although numerous passive model learning algorithms and tools are available in the literature, few of them [4], [5], [6], [7] are directly applicable to distributed systems made up of communicating components. These systems indeed raise specific difficulties. Most of them come from the fact that SUL is made up of components that run in parallel and concurrently interact with each other. To recover the behaviours of the components, it is required to extract accurate conversations (a.k.a. sessions), i.e., event sequences of correlated events interchanged among different components that achieve a certain goal. Additionally, traditional model learning algorithms return "flat" models, i.e., one model for a given composition encoding all the event details (parameters) listed in the event logs. With large event logs, it often results in complex and unreadable models.

Contribution: the paper presents another passive model learning approach, which recovers Input Output Labelled Transition Systems (IOLTSs) from event logs. As SUL is a distributed and concurrent communicating system, we assume that correlation mechanisms, e.g., execution trace identifiers, are employed to propagate context IDs and keep track of the process contexts. But, we do not assume knowing how events are correlated in advance. The major contribution of this approach is its capability to automatically retrieve conversations from event logs, without having any knowledge about the used correlation mechanisms. Instead of using a brute-force search over the space of parameter assignments found in events, our algorithm is based upon a formalisation of the notion of correlation patterns and is guided towards the most relevant conversation sets by evaluating conversation quality. As there is no consensus about what a relevant conversation should be, the conversation quality can be adapted to meet user needs and viewpoints. Next, from the retrieved conversations, our approach extracts the trace sets of every component participating in the generation of the event log. And, finally, it generates one IOLTS for every of these components, which captures the behaviours encoded in event logs with inputs and outputs showing the messages received and sent among the components.

The paper is organized as follows: Section II provides some definitions and notations on events, correlations and sessions. Our approach is presented in Section III. Section IV discusses related work. Section V summarises our contributions and draws some perspectives for future work.

II. Events, Correlations and Conversations

A. Preliminary Definitions

We denote by $\mathcal{E}$ the set of events of the form $e(\alpha)$ with e a label and α an assignment of parameters in P sent/received with events, with P the parameter set. The concatenation of two event sequences $\sigma_1, \sigma_2 \in \mathcal{E}^*$ is denoted $\sigma_1.\sigma_2$. By ϵ we denote the empty sequence. For sake of readability, we also write $\sigma_1 \in \sigma_2$ when σ_1 is a (ordered) subsequence of the sequence σ_2. Events are partially ordered in event logs. This is expressed with these partial order relations:

- $<_t \subseteq \mathcal{E} \times \mathcal{E}$, which orders two actions according to their timestamps,

- $<_c \subseteq \mathcal{E} \times \mathcal{E}$, which orders two actions if the occurrence of the first action implies the occurrence of the second one,
- $< := <_t \cup <_c$ is the transitive closure of $<_c$ and $<_t$.

We also use the following notations on events to make our algorithms more readable:

- $from(e(\alpha)) = c$ denotes the source of the event when available; $to(e(\alpha)) = c$ denotes the destination;
- $isReq(e(\alpha))$, $isResp(e(\alpha))$ are boolean expressions expressing the nature of the event;
- $A(\sigma) = \bigcup_{e(\alpha)\in\sigma} \alpha$ is the set of parameter assignments of σ.

In the paper, we use the IOLTS model to express the behaviours of components. This model is defined in terms of states and transitions labelled by input or output events in $\mathcal{E}$.

Definition 1 (IOLTS) *An Input Output Labelled Transition System (IOLTS) is a 4-tuple $\langle Q, q0, \Sigma, \rightarrow \rangle$ where:*

- *Q is a finite set of states; $q0$ is the initial state;*
- *$\Sigma \subseteq \mathcal{E}$ is the finite set of events. $\Sigma_I \subseteq \Sigma$ is the countable set of input events, $\Sigma_O \subseteq \Sigma$ is the countable set of output events, with $\Sigma_O \cap \Sigma_I = \emptyset$;*
- *$\rightarrow \subseteq Q \times \Sigma \times Q$ is a finite set of transitions. A transition (q, a, q') is also denoted $q \xrightarrow{a} q'$.*

B. Event Correlation and Conversations

The correlation mechanisms used from one system to another are seldom the same, but they are often compliant with some patterns. Most of these are introduced in [8]. Given an event sequence $\sigma = e_1(\alpha_1) \dots e_k(\alpha_k) \in \mathcal{E}^*$, we formulate that an event $e(\alpha)$ correlates with σ w.r.t. one of these patterns as follows:

- **Key based correlation:** $e(\alpha)$ correlates with σ if all the events share the same parameter assignment set: $\alpha \cap \alpha_1 \cap \dots \cap \alpha_k \neq \emptyset$;
- **Chained correlation:** $e(\alpha)$ is correlated with σ if $e(\alpha)$ shares some references with $e_k(\alpha_k)$: $\alpha \cap \alpha_k \neq \emptyset$;
- **Function based correlation:** a function $f : \mathcal{E} \rightarrow L$ firstly assigns to each event a label of the form "l:=label" in L according to the event parameter assignments. Then, the event correlation is performed w.r.t. one of the previous patterns;
- **Time-based correlation:** this pattern is somehow a special case of the previous one, in the sense that a label can be injected into an event w.r.t. a condition on time. A function $f : \mathcal{E} \rightarrow L$ assigns labels to events returns a label of the form "t:=l" according to timestamps.

The above patterns can also be combined with conjunctions or disjunctions to formulate correlation expressions. To make our algorithm readable, we write $e(\alpha)$ *correlates* σ if the event $e(\alpha)$ correlates with a sequence σ by such a correlation pattern-based expression.

In reference to [9], a set of parameter assignments used for an event correlation is called *correlation set*. A conversation corresponds to an event sequence interchanged among components, whose events correlate by means of correlation sets:

Definition 2 *Let $\sigma = e_1(\alpha_1) \dots e_k(\alpha_k) \in \mathcal{E}^k$.*

- *σ is a conversation iff $\forall 1 < i \leq k : e_i(\alpha_i)$ correlates $e_1(\alpha_1) \dots e_{i-1}(\alpha_{i-1})$*
- *$corr(\sigma) = \{cs_1, \dots, cs_{k-1}\}$ denotes the set of correlation sets of σ, with $cs_i \subseteq (\alpha_i \cup \alpha_{i+1})$*

III. Model Learning

Given an event log produced by a concurrent and distributed system SUL, our approach aims at analysing an event log collected from SUL and at recovering one IOLTS for every component of SUL, which captures its behaviours.

We assume that the events in the event log are ordered with respect to the $<$ relation. When several log files are given, we assume that they can be assembled with $<_t$ or $<_c$. In particular, the causal order relation $<_c$ may help assemble two log files given by two systems whose internal clock values slightly differ. $<_c$ indeed helps order the actions $a_1(\alpha_1)$ in a first log that imply the occurrence of other actions $a_2(\alpha_2)$ in a second one. The analysis of the pairs $(a_1(\alpha_1), a_2(\alpha_2))$ helps compute the difference of time between these two systems.

Our approach is mainly divided into three main steps: *Conversation extraction*, *Component trace extraction from conversations*, and *IOLTS Generation and Generalisation*. Beforehand, we assume that the event log is formatted into a sequence S of events of the form $e(\alpha)$ by means of regular expressions. The techniques proposed in [4], [10], [11], [12], [13], [14] can assist users in the mining of patterns or expressions from log files, which can be used to quickly derive the appropriate regular expressions.

A. Step 1: Conversation Extraction

The first step of our approach extracts conversations from a sequence S. Our conversation extraction algorithm is devised to explore the possible correlations among the successive events of S, thus in a depth-wise way, while being efficiently guided by the conversation consistencies. This notion of consistency is expressed by means of conversation invariants and conversation quality. Invariants and quality metrics also formulate a heuristic that guides our algorithm towards the most relevant conversation sets.

1) Conversation Invariant and Quality: The correlation patterns implicitly restrict the structure of a conversation according to some properties that are always true, i.e., invariants, over correlation sets. Indeed, an event must correlate with only one conversation σ of a conversation set C with a unique correlation set; a correlation set cs of $corr(\sigma)$ cannot be empty, cs cannot be found in another conversation σ_2 of C. Besides, σ must have parameter assignments for building potential correlation sets, it must include parameter assignments that cannot be found in any other conversation σ_2. These three invariants are formulated in the following proposition. Other invariants can also be added to meet user preferences. For

```
/login(from:="cl", to:="ShopS", id:="tocken",
    account:="1")
ok(from:="ShopS", to:="cl", id:="tocken"
    trans:="t1")
/order(from:="cl", to:="ShopS",
    trans:="t1",item:="a")
/stock(from:="ShopS", to:="StockS",
    trans:="t1", item:="a")
ok(from:="StockS", to:="ShopS", trans:="t1",
    item:="a")
ok(from:="ShopS", to:="cl",
    trans:="t1",content:="stock")
/supply(from:="ShopS", to:="WS", trans:="t1",
    key:="k1",item:="a")
ok(from:="WS", to:="ShopS", trans:="t1",
    key:="k1")
/supplyWS(from:="WS", to:="WS1", key:="k1",
    key2:="k2",item:="a")
/supplyWS(from:="WS", to:="WS2", key:="k1",
    key2:="k3",item:="a")
/supplyWS(from:="WS", to:="WS3", key:="k1",
    key2:="k4",item:="a")
ok(from:=WS1,to:="WS", key:="k1", key2:="k2")
ok(from:=WS2,to:="WS", key:="k1", key2:="k3")
Unavailable(from:="WS3",to:="WS", key:="k1",
    key2:="k4")
/login(from:="cl", to:="ShopS", id:="tocken2",
    account:="12")
ok(from:="ShopS", to:=cl, id:="tocken2",
    trans:="t2")
/order(from:="cl", to:="ShopS",
    trans:="t2",item:="b")
ok(from:="ShopS", to:="cl", trans:="t2"
    content:="no stock")
```

Fig. 1. Formatted part of an event log

instance, the last invariant imposes conversations to start with a request.

Proposition 3 (Conversation Set Invariants) *Let C be a conversation set and $\sigma \in C$. Inv stands for the set of conversation set invariants:*

- $\forall cs \in corr(\sigma) : cs \neq \emptyset$
- $\forall cs \in corr(\sigma), \forall \sigma_2 \in C \setminus \{\sigma\} : cs \cap A(\sigma_2) = \emptyset$
- $A(\sigma) \setminus \bigcup_{\sigma_2 \in C \setminus \{\sigma\}} A(\sigma_2) \neq \emptyset$
- $\forall e_1(\alpha_1) \dots e_k(\alpha_k) \in C : isReq(e_1(\alpha_1))$

For readability, we denote that the conversations of a conversation set C meet conversation invariants with C *satisfies* Inv.

Our algorithm uses quality metrics as another way to limit the conversation set exploration, but also to prioritize this exploration among several conversation set candidates. We formulate a comprehensive quality metric of a conversation set C by means of a utility function for representing user preferences. The following definition refers to quality metrics $M_i(C)$ over conversation sets, themselves calculated by means of metrics $m_i(\sigma)$ over conversations:

Definition 4 (Conversation Set Quality) $0 \leq Q(C) = \sum_{i=1}^{n} M_i(C).w_i \leq 1$ *with* $0 \leq M_i(C) = \frac{\sum_{\sigma \in C} m_i(\sigma)}{|C|} \leq 1$, $w_i \in \mathbb{R}_0^+$ *and* $\sum_{i=1}^{k} w_i = 1$.

The conversation quality metrics can be general or established with regard to a specific system context. Our approach actually does not limit the metric set. We provide four metric examples below. m_1 and m_2 evaluate whether a conversation σ follows the classical request-response exchange pattern (sender sends a request to receiver, ultimately returning a response). m_1 evaluates the ratio of requests in σ associated with some responses with $ReqwResp(\sigma)$. m_2 evaluates the ratio of responses following a prior request with $RespwReq(\sigma)$.

$$0 < m_1(\sigma) = \frac{|ReqwResp(\sigma)| + 1}{|Req(\sigma)| + 1} \leq 1 \qquad (1)$$

$$0 < m_2(\sigma) = \frac{|RespwReq(\sigma)| + 1}{|Resp(\sigma)| + 1} \leq 1 \qquad (2)$$

The metric m_3 examines whether σ is composed of correlated events, in other terms, whether σ has more than one event:

$$m_3(\sigma) = \begin{cases} 1 & \text{if } corr(\sigma) \neq \emptyset \\ 0 & \text{otherwise} \end{cases} \qquad (3)$$

The metric m_4 evaluates the ratio of assignments used to correlate the events of a conversation. The simpler the correlation mechanism is, the closer to 1 the metric is.

$$0 \leq m_4(\sigma) = 1 - \frac{|\bigcup_{cs \in corr(\sigma)} cs|}{|A(\sigma)|} < 1 \qquad (4)$$

Algorithm 1: Conversation and Correlation Set Extraction

```
input : Event sequence S = e_1(α_1) ... e_k(α_k), boolean first
output: Conversation sets C_1, ..., C_n,
C := {e_1(α_1)};
call Find_C&CS(C, 2);
Procedure Find_C&CS(C, i) is
    if i ≤ k then
        foreach σ ∈ C : e_i(α_i) correlates σ do
            CS := P(α_i ∩ last(σ)) \ {∅} ;
            foreach cs ∈ CS do
                σ' := σ.e_i(α_i);
                corr(σ') := corr(σ) ∪ {cs};
                C_2 := C ∪ {σ'} \ {σ};
                if C_2 satisfies Inv and Q(C_2) ≥ T then
                    Find_C&CS(C_2, i + 1);
        C_3 := C ∪ {e_i(α_i)};
        corr(e_i(α_i)) := ;
        if C_3 satifies Inv and Q(C_3) ≥ T then
            Find_C&CS(C_3, i + 1);
    else
        return C;
        if Q(C) ≥ T2 then
            STOP all Find_C&CS instances;
```

2) Conversation Set Extraction Algorithm: The conversation set extraction is implemented in Algorithm 1. It takes as input an event sequence S and returns conversation sets, which are ordered with regard to their respective conversation set quality. It builds a first set C composed of one conversation equal to the first event of S. The events of S are then successively covered by recursively calling a new instance of $Find\_C\&CS(C, i)$. This procedure takes an event $e_i(\alpha_i)$ and

C = {
/login() ok() /order() /stock() ok() ok()/supply() ok() /supplyWS()/supplyWS() /supplyWS() ok() ok() unavailable(),
/login() ok() /order() ok()
}
T(SS)={ ?/login() !ok() ?/order() !/stock() ?ok() !ok() !/supply() ?ok(), ?/login() !ok() ?/order() !ok() }
T(WS)={ ?/supply() !ok() !/supplyWS() !/supplyWS() !/supplyWS() ?ok() ?ok() ?unavailable() }
T(St)={ ?/stock() !ok() }
T(WS1)=T(WS2)={ ?/supplyWS() !ok() }
T(WS3)={ ?/supplyWS() !unavailable() }

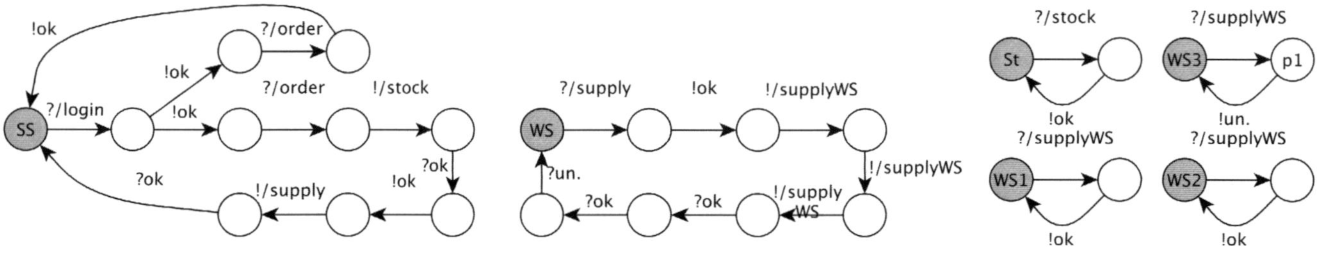

Fig. 2. Conversation set and IOLTSs modelling a composition of 6 Web services

tries to find, in the conversation set C, a conversation σ such that $e_i(\alpha_i)$ $correlates$ σ. If there exists such a conversation, the procedure builds for every possible correlation set (line 7) a new conversation set with the new conversation $\sigma.e_i(\alpha_i)$. Besides (line 13), an additional conversation set C_3 is built to consider that the event $e_i(\alpha_i)$ might also be the beginning of a new conversation. For every new conversation set that meets conversation invariants and quality, $Find\_C\&CS$ is recursively called (lines 12, 16).

Let us consider the event sequence of Figure 1 whose events include varied parameters e.g., $from$, to, key. Algorithm 1 extracts the conversation set C of Figure 2 (the events are given without parameter assignment for readability). We obtain 2 conversations whose events are correlated with the parameters in $\{id, trans, key, key2\}$.

Algorithm 1 may return several conversation sets ordered by quality if different correlations have been detected among successive events of S. In this case, the user has to choose the most appropriate conversation set with regard to its needs and knowledge.

B. Step2: Component Trace Extraction

The second step of our approach now generates as many trace sets as components found in the system SUL. This step, implemented by Algorithm 2, firstly covers the events of every conversation to identify the components of SUL (line 5). A the same time, it converts events by integrating the notions of input and output. In lines 6-8, every request or response is indeed doubled by separating the component source and destination. The component that executes the event is identified by a new assignment on the parameter idc injected to each event. Non-communicating events (neither requests or responses) are marked as outputs. Then, Algorithm 2 segments the resulting sequence σ' into sub-sequences, each capturing the behaviours of one component only of the set $Comp$ (lines 9, 10). The algorithm returns form every component $c \in Comp$ a set T_c that gathers the traces of the component c only.

Algorithm 2: Component Trace Extraction

input : Conversation set C
output: Trace sets $T_{c_1} \dots T_{c_n}$

```
1  T := {};
2  foreach σ = e1(α1) ... ek(αk) ∈ C) do
3      σ' := ε;
4      foreach ei(αi) ∈ σ do
5          Comp := Comp ∪ {from(ei(αi)), to(ei(αi))};
6          σ' := σ'.!ai({idc := from(ei(αi))} ∪ αi);
7          if isReq(ei(αi)) ∨ isResp(ei(αi)) then
8              σ' := σ'.?ei({idc := to(ei(αi))} ∪ αi);
9      foreach c ∈ Comp do
10         Tc := Tc ∪ {σ' \ {e(α) ∈ σ' | (idc := c) ∉ α}}
```

C. Step 3: IOLTS Generation

Every trace set $T_c = \{\sigma_1, \dots, \sigma_n\}$ is now lifted to the level of IOLTS.

A first IOLTS denoted L_c is obtained by transforming the traces of T_c to IOLTS paths. L_c is the IOLTS $L_c = \langle Q, q0, \Sigma, \rightarrow \rangle$ derived from T_c such that:

- $q0$ is the initial state.
- $Q, \Sigma, \rightarrow$ are defined by the following inference rule:

$$\frac{\sigma_i = a_1(\alpha_1) \dots a_k(\alpha_k)}{q0 \xrightarrow{e_1(\alpha_1)} (q_1 i, cl(\sigma_i)) \dots (q_{k-1} i, Cl(\sigma_i)) \xrightarrow{a_k(\alpha_k)} q0}$$

By applying this trace set to IOLTS conversion on every component, we obtain the IOLTSs $L_{c_1}, \dots, L_{c_n}$. Those IOLTSs are finally generalised by merging their equivalent states. The state merging is performed by means of the k-Tail algorithm [15], which is known to be a flexible state merging algorithm in the sense that it assembles the states sharing the same k-future, i.e., the same event sequences having the maximum length k.

Figure 2 depicts the IOLTSs generated from the conversation set given on top of the figure. Our approach has detected 6 components among the events of the two conversations. These have been converted to 6 trace sets, which capture the behaviours of each component. The traces sets have finally been converted to the IOLTSs depicted in the figure. In this example, we call k-Tail with $k := 2$.

With these IOLTSs, it becomes much easier to understand the general functioning of the whole system. In particular, it is now easier to understand that three services allow to interact with wholesalers. Two of them seem to be behavioural equivalent, but the last one is faulty.

IV. Related Work on Passive Model Learning

Event correlation has been widely studied in different kinds of domains, e.g., process mining, or event association mining. In short, many approaches try to recover conversations by mining frequent association rules in event logs, without using correlation mechanisms [16], [17], [18], [19]. Other works propose to recover conversations by using some correlation patterns [20], [21], [22]. In particular, Process spaceship [22] gathers a set of algorithms allowing to scan event logs and retrieve conversation sets. The event correlations are mined by using a sort of breadth search strategy over the parameter assignments found in events. It explores all the possible correlations over the domain of parameter assignments and prunes them with interestingness properties. All the interesting conversation sets are found, at the expense of time complexity. Compared to Process spaceship, algorithm 1 uses another strategy, which aims at finding correlation sets while building conversations. This can be considered as a depth search guided by heuristics based upon invariants and quality metrics. This strategy allows to quicker find a first solution. Our algorithm also has the capability of ordering conversation sets that meet quality requirements.

Passive model learning includes techniques that passively recover models from a given set of samples, e.g., a set of execution traces. These are said passive as there is no direct interaction with the system under learning. Models are often generated by encoding sample sets with state diagrams whose equivalent states are merged. For instance, k-Tail has been later enhanced with Gk-tail to generate Extended Finite State Machines encoding data constraints [23]. Other approaches also enhance k-Tail to build more precise models [24], [25], [26]. kBehavior [27] is another kind of approach that generates models from a set of traces by taking every trace one after the other and by completing a finite-state automaton in such a way that it now accepts the trace. These previous passive algorithms usually yield big models, which may quickly become unreadable.

Some passive approaches dedicated to communicating systems have also been proposed. Mariani et al. proposed in [27] an automatic detection of failures in log files by means of model learning. This work extends kBehavior to support events combined with data. It segments an event log with two strategies: per component or per user. The former, which can be used with communicating systems, generates one model for each component. CSight [6] is another tool specialised in the model learning of communicating systems, where components exchange messages through synchronous channels. It is assumed that both the channels and components are known. Besides, CSight requires specific trace sets, which are segmented with one subset by component. CSight follows five stages: 1) log parsing and mining of invariants 2) generation of a concrete Finite State Machine (FSM) that captures the functioning of the whole system by recomposing the traces of the components; 3) generation of a more concise abstract FSM; 4) model refinement with invariants that must hold in FSMs, and 5) generation of Communicating FSM.

We have proposed in [28] a passive model learning algorithm for recovering models of component-based systems. The requirements considered in this approach are different from those of the above approaches. The main difference lies in the fact that the communications among components are assumed hidden (not available in event logs). The algorithm is hence specific to this assumption. Then, we have proposed the approach Ck-Tail in [7] to generate models of communicating systems from event logs. Compared to CSight, we do not assume that the trace sets are already prepared. The novelty proposed by Ck-Tail lies in its capability of detecting sessions in event logs. Compared to this work, we assume with Ck-Tail that the components follow a strict behaviour: they cannot run multiple instances; requests are processed by a component on a first-come, first served basis. Besides, components follow the request–response exchange pattern

We showed that Ck-Tail builds more precise models than the other approaches by better recognising sessions, but we also concluded that its requirements are too restrictive to be widely used. The approach proposed in the paper relaxes these assumptions and now supports any kind of communicating system.

V. Conclusion and Future Work

This paper has proposed the design of an approach specialised into the recovery of formal models from event logs generated by communicating systems made up of concurrent components. The approach firstly explores the conversation set space that can be derived from an event log and is guided toward the most relevant conversation sets by means of invariants and conversation quality metrics. The latter can be adapted to define user preferences or system contexts. Then, the approach generates one trace set for every component along with one IOLTS expressing its behaviours. These IOLTS can be later used as documentation or for automatics analyses.

There are several issues which require further investigation before evaluating our approach. One of them is to be able to propose a good balance between model size, readability and precision. For instance, the generated IOLTSs may be very large on account of similar event sequences having different parameter values. We hence intend to add further steps to raise the IOLTS abstraction level, while preserving the possibility to analyse of use concrete parameter values.

Acknowledgement

Research supported by the French Project VASOC (Auvergne-Rhône-Alpes Region) https://vasoc.limos.fr/

REFERENCES

[1] S. Majumdar, Y. Jarraya, M. Oqaily, A. Alimohammadifar, M. Pourzandi, L. Wang, and M. Debbabi, "Leaps: Learning-based proactive security auditing for clouds," in *Computer Security – ESORICS 2017*, S. N. Foley, D. Gollmann, and E. Snekkenes, Eds. Cham: Springer International Publishing, 2017, pp. 265–285.

[2] S. Salva and E. Blot, "Verifying the application of security measures in iot software systems with model learning," in *Proceedings of the 15th International Conference on Software Technologies, ICSOFT 2020, Lieusaint, Paris, France, July 7-9, 2020*, M. van Sinderen, H. Fill, and L. A. Maciaszek, Eds. ScitePress, 2020, pp. 350–360.

[3] X. Zhang, Y. Xu, Q. Lin, B. Qiao, H. Zhang, Y. Dang, C. Xie, X. Yang, Q. Cheng, Z. Li, J. Chen, X. He, R. Yao, J.-G. Lou, M. Chintalapati, F. Shen, and D. Zhang, "Robust log-based anomaly detection on unstable log data," in *Proceedings of the 2019 27th ACM Joint Meeting on European Software Engineering Conference and Symposium on the Foundations of Software Engineering*, ser. ESEC/FSE 2019. New York, NY, USA: Association for Computing Machinery, 2019, p. 807–817.

[4] L. Mariani and F. Pastore, "Automated identification of failure causes in system logs," in *Software Reliability Engineering, 2008. ISSRE 2008. 19th International Symposium on*, Nov 2008, pp. 117–126.

[5] A. Petrenko and F. Avellaneda, "Learning communicating state machines," in *Tests and Proofs - 13th International Conference, TAP 2019, Held as Part of the Third World Congress on Formal Methods 2019, Porto, Portugal, October 9-11, 2019, Proceedings*, 2019, pp. 112–128.

[6] I. Beschastnikh, Y. Brun, M. D. Ernst, and A. Krishnamurthy, "Inferring models of concurrent systems from logs of their behavior with csight," in *Proceedings of the 36th International Conference on Software Engineering*, ser. ICSE 2014. New York, NY, USA: ACM, 2014, pp. 468–479. [Online]. Available: http://doi.acm.org/10.1145/2568225.2568246

[7] S. Salva and E. Blot, "Cktail: Model learning of communicating systems," in *Proceedings of the 15th International Conference on Evaluation of Novel Approaches to Software Engineering, ENASE 2020, Prague, Czech Republic, May 5-6, 2020*, R. Ali, H. Kaindl, and L. A. Maciaszek, Eds. SCITEPRESS, 2020, pp. 27–38.

[8] A. Barros, G. Decker, M. Dumas, and F. Weber, "Correlation patterns in service-oriented architectures," in *Fundamental Approaches to Software Engineering*, M. B. Dwyer and A. Lopes, Eds. Berlin, Heidelberg: Springer Berlin Heidelberg, 2007, pp. 245–259.

[9] OASIS Consortium, "Ws-bpel version 2.0," April 2007, http://docs.oasis-open.org/wsbpel/2.0/OS/wsbpel-v2.0-OS.pdf, Accessed on 09.2021.

[10] Q. Fu, J.-G. Lou, Y. Wang, and J. Li, "Execution anomaly detection in distributed systems through unstructured log analysis," *2009 Ninth IEEE International Conference on Data Mining*, pp. 149–158, 2009.

[11] A. Makanju, A. N. Zincir-Heywood, and E. E. Milios, "A lightweight algorithm for message type extraction in system application logs," *IEEE Transactions on Knowledge and Data Engineering*, vol. 24, no. 11, pp. 1921–1936, Nov 2012.

[12] R. Vaarandi and M. Pihelgas, "Logcluster - a data clustering and pattern mining algorithm for event logs," in *2015 11th International Conference on Network and Service Management (CNSM)*, Nov 2015, pp. 1–7.

[13] S. Messaoudi, A. Panichella, D. Bianculli, L. Briand, and R. Sasnauskas, "A search-based approach for accurate identification of log message formats," in *Proceedings of the 26th Conference on Program Comprehension*, ser. ICPC '18. New York, NY, USA: ACM, 2018, pp. 167–177. [Online]. Available: http://doi.acm.org/10.1145/3196321.3196340

[14] J. Zhu, S. He, J. Liu, P. He, Q. Xie, Z. Zheng, and M. R. Lyu, "Tools and benchmarks for automated log parsing," *CoRR*, vol. abs/1811.03509, 2018, accessed on 09.2021. [Online]. Available: http://arxiv.org/abs/1811.03509

[15] A. Biermann and J. Feldman, "On the synthesis of finite-state machines from samples of their behavior," *Computers, IEEE Transactions on*, vol. C-21, no. 6, pp. 592–597, June 1972.

[16] X. Fu, R. Ren, J. Zhan, W. Zhou, Z. Jia, and G. Lu, "Logmaster: Mining event correlations in logs of large-scale cluster systems," in *2012 IEEE 31st Symposium on Reliable Distributed Systems*, 2012, pp. 71–80.

[17] L. Liu and J. Liu, "Mining web log sequential patterns with layer coded breadth-first linked wap-tree," in *2010 International Conference of Information Science and Management Engineering*, vol. 1, 2010, pp. 28–31.

[18] B. Serrour, D. P. Gasparotto, H. Kheddouci, and B. Benatallah, "Message correlation and business protocol discovery in service interaction logs," in *Advanced Information Systems Engineering*, Z. Bellahsène and M. Léonard, Eds. Berlin, Heidelberg: Springer Berlin Heidelberg, 2008, pp. 405–419.

[19] K. Musaraj, T. Yoshida, F. Daniel, M.-S. Hacid, F. Casati, and B. Benatallah, "Message Correlation and Web Service Protocol Mining from Inaccurate Logs," in *IEEE International Conference on Web Services*. Miami, Florida, United States: IEEE Computer Society, Jul. 2010, pp. 259–266. [Online]. Available: https://hal.archives-ouvertes.fr/hal-01381551

[20] S. Dustdar and R. Gombotz, "Discovering web service workflows using web services interaction mining," *Int. J. Bus. Process. Integr. Manag.*, vol. 1, pp. 256–266, 2006.

[21] R. Conforti, M. Dumas, L. García-Bañuelos, and M. La Rosa, "Bpmn miner: Automated discovery of bpmn process models with hierarchical structure," *Information Systems*, vol. 56, pp. 284–303, 2016. [Online]. Available: https://www.sciencedirect.com/science/article/pii/S0306437915001325

[22] H. R. Motahari Nezhad, R. Saint-Paul, F. Casati, and B. Benatallah, "Event correlation for process discovery from web service interaction logs," *VLDB J.*, vol. 20, pp. 417–444, 06 2011.

[23] D. Lorenzoli, L. Mariani, and M. Pezzè, "Automatic generation of software behavioral models," in *Proceedings of the 30th International Conference on Software Engineering*, ser. ICSE'08. New York, NY, USA: ACM, 2008, pp. 501–510.

[24] I. Beschastnikh, Y. Brun, S. Schneider, M. Sloan, and M. D. Ernst, "Leveraging existing instrumentation to automatically infer invariant-constrained models," in *Proceedings of the 19th ACM SIGSOFT Symposium and the 13th European Conference on Foundations of Software Engineering*, ser. ESEC/FSE '11. New York, NY, USA: ACM, 2011, pp. 267–277.

[25] T. Ohmann, M. Herzberg, S. Fiss, A. Halbert, M. Palyart, I. Beschastnikh, and Y. Brun, "Behavioral resource-aware model inference," in *Proceedings of the 29th ACM/IEEE International Conference on Automated Software Engineering*, ser. ASE '14. New York, NY, USA: ACM, 2014, pp. 19–30.

[26] F. Pastore, D. Micucci, and L. Mariani, "Timed k-tail: Automatic inference of timed automata," in *2017 IEEE International Conference on Software Testing, Verification and Validation (ICST)*, March 2017, pp. 401–411.

[27] L. Mariani and M. Pezze, "Dynamic detection of cots component incompatibility," *IEEE Software*, vol. 24, no. 5, pp. 76–85, 2007.

[28] S. Salva and E. Blot, "Confect: An approach to learn models of component-based systems," in *Proceedings of the 13th International Conference on Software Technologies, ICSOFT 2018, Porto, Portugal, July 26-28, 2018.*, 2018, pp. 298–305.

The ISO 27000 Family and its Applicability in LGPD Adaptation Projects for Small and Medium- Sized Enterprises

How the ISO 27000 family standards can help with the challenge of complying with the General Data Protection law for small and medium-sized businesses

André de Freitas Fernandes, Fabiano Camilo Santiago de Brito, Fátima Fernandes Periard, Grazielle A. Viana Matias, Mariana Sbaite Gonçalves, Reinaldo Gomes Baldoino Filho
IESB University Center
andre.fernandes@serpro.gov.br, fabianocamilos@gmail.com, fatima.periard@crmbrasil.com.br, grazielle@m2cloud.com.br, marianasbaite@gmail.com, reinaldo.baldoino@iesb.edu.br

Abstract - This article describes the relationship between the Brazilian Data Protection Law (LGPD) - nº 13.709 / 2018 - with the information security through ISO Standards. The theme is extremely relevant, as it shows the difficulty for small and medium-sized companies to comply with current and applicable legislation on privacy and protection of personal data, as well as the need for security and investment, to protect the privacy of the holders of personal data and not suffer future damage, whether property or reputation. Some companies have already received fines for the irregular processing of personal data. Being adequate is the immediate answer for the evolution of their businesses and the protection of personal data. This article demonstrates the importance of complying with the LGPD and using security frameworks and investment in information security, improving data management and governance of associations.

Keywords- LGPD; Adequacy; ISO; Security; Technology; SMEs.

I. INTRODUCTION

We live in a challenging environment when it comes to protecting personal data. On the one hand, personal data protection and privacy laws take shape, bringing changes in society. On the other hand, there is an epidemic of data exposures and breaches affecting businesses of all sizes and market segments globally. Companies are at the heart of this situation, which depends on technology and data to maintain their business continuity.

A survey conducted by Microsoft between September and October 2020 [1] indicated that for small and medium-sized companies, technology was the best answer to get around the crisis. The study shows that, during the pandemic, 42% of SMEs accelerated the adoption of new technologies, mainly medium-sized companies and, for 83% of respondents, these technologies lead the way towards economic recovery.

While these businesses need to use technology for their reinvention, they must comply with a series of regulations related to their performance, and now, they need to adjust to comply with current and applicable privacy and data protection laws. The matter would be simple if all companies had a vision of processes and budgets defined for the security and compliance areas. However, for most small and medium-sized Brazilian companies, the reality is quite different.

In a survival market, SMEs are focused on producing and delivering, in the famous so-called "turning the wheel." With leaner structures and tight cash, the SME entrepreneur has not defined business processes, and many do not even consider information security necessary. Their concerns are precisely on product or service.

This article aims to demonstrate that one of the ways to achieve compliance with the LGPD – General Data Protection Law is the use of the frameworks of the ISO 27000 standards as well as making room for small and medium businesses to evolve in their management, with information security as one of the pillars of this process.

Some questions that guided the article:

- *What is the need to adapt SMEs to the LGPD?*
- *What difficulties do SMEs face on a day-to-day basis?*
- *How to invest in Technology, Information Security and Compliance?*
- *Are these companies aware of the risks that non-compliance with the Law brings to the continuity of their business?*

In the following sections, we will see the purpose of the article and the questions that guided the work. In section II, we will talk about SMEs and citing examples from Brazil. In section III, we will talk about the General Data Protection Law and its impacts. In section IV, we will talk about the DPO career. In section V, we will talk about the LGPD and ABNT standards. In section VI, we will talk about ISO 27000 standards. In section VII, we explain privacy management. In Section IV, we present our final remarks.

II. WHAT IS SMALL AND MEDIUM SIZE COMPANIES

SME is an acronym for Small and Medium Enterprise. It is an acronym often used to classify the size of a company as a function of the number of workers employed and the annual income earned. This type of company occupies an important place in the economy of countries through the generation of jobs.

The classifications according to the number of workers employed are as follows:

Industry:

- Microenterprise - up to 19 employees
- Small Business - from 20 to 99 employees
- Medium Company - from 100 to 499 employees
- Large Company - 500 or more employees

Trade and Services:

- Microenterprise - up to 9 employees
- Small Business - 10 to 49 employees
- Medium Company - 50 to 99 employees
- Large Company - more than 100 employees

According to Sebrae (Brazilian entrepreneur support service) [2], they can also be divided into four segments by revenue range, except for small rural producers. Briefly, small businesses are divided as follows:

- Individual Microentrepreneur – Annual turnover up to R$ 81 thousand.
- Microenterprise – Annual turnover up to R$360 thousand.
- Small Business - Annual turnover between R$360 thousand and R$4.8 million.
- Small Farmer - Property with up to 4 fiscal modules or annual sales of up to R$ 4.8million

Segmentation by billing follows the criteria of Complementary Law 123/2006, also known as the General Law for Micro and Small Companies.

According to Data Sebrae [2], there are approximately 19 million companies in Brazil, and of this total, about 7.5 million are into the SME categories. In 2020, these companies corresponded to around 29% of GDP. Regarding the volume of jobs, the same Data Sebrae indicates that in 2018 SMEs generated about 17.79 million jobs with a salary volume of around R$ 34.27 billion. Data from the PNAD (National survey by the sample of households) carried out by the IBGE show that between 2003 and 2013, there was a 10% growth in the number of business owners in the country, from 21.4 million to 23.5 million people. In this same period, the number of highly computerized business owners almost quadrupled, from 3.9 million to 14.3 million people (an increase of 10.4 million individuals).

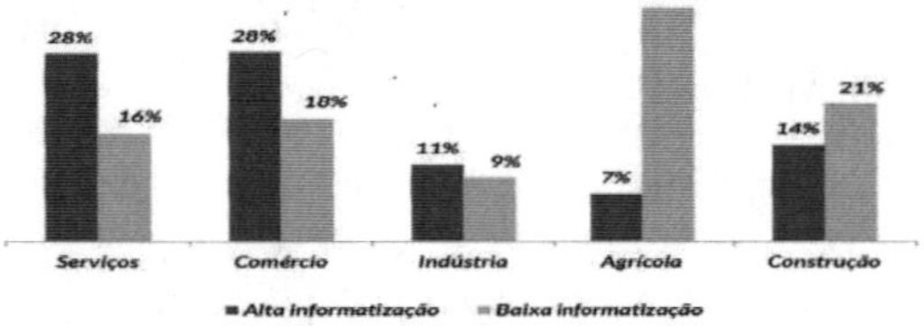

Figure 1. Distribution by sector of activity [3]

This data leads us to a potential market of millions of SMEs seeking to adapt to new data protection legislation and needing support for this task, mainly in the Commerce and Services sectors.

According to consulting firm Price Waterhouse Coopers: "The power of SMEs is evident in their 30% share in the Gross Domestic Product (GDP) of R$4.4 trillion in Brazil. The segment employs more people than any other: 10.1 million employees in small companies and 5.5 million in medium ones"

According to Disterer [20], a 2008 survey of ISO27001 - certificated companies found that 50 percent of the certificated organizations which responded had fewer than 200 employees and were therefore in the SME category. Perhaps more surprisingly, around half of these had fewer than 50 employees. The framework has used the ISO27002 code of practice to define the elements considered within the ISMS. Each component is then developed through a maturity model life cycle to establish an ISO 27001-compliant ISMS process.

III. The General Personal data Protection Law and Small and midsize Enterprises

The Brazilian Law No. 13.709/2018 – General Law for the Protection of Personal Data (LGPD) [4] provides for companies' processing of personal data throughout Brazil, without mentioning differences in the dealings of the small, medium large companies or self-employed professionals. It is clear to establish equal guidelines for all figures.

The administrative sanctions provided for in the Law are effective from August 2021, and with less than two months to go before the scheduled date, few companies are complying.

The purpose of the Law is to organize and structure organizations about privacy, preserve the dignity of the human person and allow holders to be able to exercise their rights.

In addition to bringing principles and new rights to the holders of personal data, it needs to adopt technical and administrative measures to maintain the security and confidentiality of information. Furthermore, it requires a governance plan and the application of good practices to protect and preserve the safety of all personal data involved in business flows and processes. The problem is: it is neither easy nor cheap to adapt to the LGPD. Therefore, companies need to structure themselves to have the budget and human resources to practice everything the law requires. In the case of SMEs, it turns out to be arduous, not only for lack of investment but also for lack of information.

The General Law for the Protection of Personal Data requires internal organization, the definition of roles and responsibilities, and increased budget to invest in training and tools, among other activities that most companies do not have in Brazil. It is essential to point out that the administrative sanctions of the Law started in August 2021, and few companies are in compliance, which can lead to financial and reputational losses. According to Almeida [20], "...we consider it fundamental to think of ways to make the application of the law by small businesses viable so that they can successfully fulfill their obligations." To believe that the

LGPD, to be applied, must treat all companies equally, respecting their characteristics and enabling the actual applicability of its rules.

One of the most important novelties is the need for the person in charge of Data Processing, corresponding to the Data Protection Officer of the General Data Protection Regulation and about which we will discuss below.

IV. Data Protection Officer Figure entry

The General Data Protection Law introduced the figure of Data Protection Officer, the person responsible for the processing of personal data, who, in a simplified way, has the function of conducting the organization's compliance process, in addition to being the point of communication between the holders of personal data, the processing agents and the regulatory body National Data Protection Authority. To perform its role well, the Data Protection Officer needs to know much more than the Law. It must understand compliance, processes, technology, people management, and being familiar with security frameworks. The Data Protection Officer must be involved in all techniques or flows involving personal data to verify gaps and the best security controls to be applied to mitigate or eliminate the risks.

The LGPD [4], in its article 46, brings to treatment agents the need to adopt technical and administrative security measures. However, the Data Protection Officer is responsible for making things happen and developing a culture of privacy within companies. And it is precisely at this point that the need to know and apply the requirements of the ISO 27000 family of standards comes into play. These standards, which address cybersecurity, bring clarity and structure to business processes that need to be revised but are not even known by small and medium companies. These businesses do not have process management and compliance budgets and cannot see value in their adoption. The standard brought by the ISO family adds both in the sense of assisting in information security, as it allows companies to improve their way of managing assets, flows, processes, and people.

The requirement of compliance with the LGPD will bring these companies greater visibility into their processes, previously in the dark, leading to new approaches for all areas and more excellent organization in terms of management, improving the trust relationship with customers and business partners.

V. LGPD, ABNT and the ISO Standards

Chapter VII of the LGPD [4], addresses Security and Good Practices: Section I - Security and Data Secrecy; and Section II: Good Practices and Governance. In this sense, it determines the adoption of security measures and good practices to maintain confidentiality, when necessary, and for better governance; however, it does not clarify how companies can comply with these requirements. Then, the ISO 27000 family standards come into play to help businesses of all sizes to structure their compliance and governance processes, helping to adapt to the LGPD and allowing for a more comprehensive governance performance.

The Brazilian Association of Technical Standards (ABNT) [19] is the National Forum for Standardization. The Brazilian Standards, whose content is the responsibility of the Brazilian Committees (ABNT/CB), Sectoral Standardization Bodies (ABNT/ONS), and Special Study Commissions (ABNT/CEE), are prepared by Study Commissions (CE), formed by the interested parties in the subject-object of the standardization. ABNT Technical Documents and International Standards (ISO and IEC) are voluntary and do not include contractual, legal, or statutory requirements.

These ABNT Technical Documents do not replace Laws, Decrees, or Regulations, which users must comply with, taking precedence over any ABNT Technical Document. Therefore, the ISO standards and the technical documents developed by ABNT serve as a support tool for companies of different sizes to follow best practices and follow the guidelines and guidelines provided in the documentation.

VI. A turn through the ISO 27000 Family Standards

The ISO 27000 set of standards constitutes complete security and privacy framework. Compliance takes place in continuous improvement, which, in addition to promoting improvement in internal processes, brings noticeable results to the end customer. Next, we will talk about each standard.

According to Gillies [21], when companies use the ISO 27000 standard, they can significantly improve information security management.

A. ISO 27001 – Information Security and Management System

This standard covers the concept of information security in an integral way, dealing with various topics, such as protection of the physical environment, telecommunications, application security, human resources, business continuity, licensing, and other items that may vary according to the model business.

As a general principle, it addresses the adoption of a set of requirements, processes, and controls, which aim to correctly identify and manage the Information Security risks present in organizations, helping to adopt an adequate model of establishment, implementation, operation, monitoring, review, and management of an Information Security Management System.

The Information Security Management System (ISMS) is, following the principles of the ISO 27001 standard, a holistic model of approach to Security and independent of technological brands and manufacturers, as it is intended to establish processes and procedures that can be materialized in each organization differently, according to the specificity of each technological and organizational environment [5].

B. ISO 27002 – Information Security - Requirements

ISO 27002 establishes a code of best practices to support implementing the Information Security Management System (ISMS) in organizations, complementing the previous standard. Its main objective is to establish guidelines and general principles to initiate, implement, maintain, and improve information security management in an organization, including selection, implementation, and management of controls, considering the identified risks. The items below make up the standard's approach [5] [6]:

- Information Security Policy
- Information Security Organization
- Asset Management
- Security in human resources
- Physical and environmental security
- Security of operations and communications
- Access control
- Acquisition, development, and maintenance of systems
- Information security incident management
- Business continuity management
- Conformity

The objective of NBR ISO/IEC 27002:2013 is stated as follows [6], "Information security is achieved by implementing an adequate set of controls, including policies, processes, procedures, organizational structure and software and hardware functions. These controls need to be established, implemented, monitored, critically analyzed and improved as necessary to ensure that the organization's business and security objectives are met."

C. ISO 27003 – Guidelines to Implementation the Security Management Information System

While ISO 27001 provides the requirements for implementing the ISMS, ISO 27003 provides guidance on the process and recommendations, possibilities, and possible permissions. According to the standard, there are 5 phases of planning an ISMS project [5] [7]:

1. Obtain approval from senior management (top management) to initiate the ISMS project.
2. Define the scope, limits, and policy of the ISMS.
3. Conduct analysis of information security requirements.
4. Conduct risk analysis/assessment and plan risk treatment.
5. Define the ISMS.

D. ISO27004– Information Security Management

ISO 27004 guides how to assess the performance of ISO 27001, providing a set of standards to guide the development, operation, and measurement of processes to evaluate and report the results of a set of information security metrics [5] [8].

The standard demonstrates how to build an information security measurement program, how to select what to measure and how to operate the necessary measurement processes, it also includes comprehensive examples of different types of measures and how can assess the effectiveness of those measures.

Among the greatest benefits of adopting the law, we highlight:

- Greater responsibility
- Improved performance of information security and ISMS processes
- Evidence of compliance with the requirements of ISO / IEC 27001, as well as applicable laws, rules, and regulations.

E. ISO 27005–Iformation Security Risk Management

To provide guidelines for the management of information security (IS) risks, ISO 27005 supports the concepts specified in ISO 27001, in addition to assisting in the implementation and certification of such management systems[5] [9].

According to the standard, the IS risk management process comprises the following activities:

- Identify and assess risks.
- Decide what to do about risks (how to deal with them)
- Monitor risks, risk treatments etc., identify and respond appropriately to significant changes, problems/concerns, or opportunities for improvement.
- Keeping stakeholders (mainly the organization's management) informed throughout the process.

F. ISO 27007–ISMS Audit Guidelines

The text of ISO 27007 discusses the management of an information security management system (ISMS) audit program, the performance of audits, and the competence of the ISMS auditors. It is an applicable standard for those who need to understand or conduct internal or external audits of an ISMS or to manage an ISMS audit program [10].

According to the standard, they constitute a management and auditing process:

- Audit principles
- Management and audit program
- Conducting an audit
- Competence and assessment of auditors

G. ISO 27014 - Information Security Management

ABNT NBR ISO/IEC 27014 (2013) points out that Information Security Governance should aim to [11]:

- Align business objectives with the Information Security strategy.

- Ensure that information risks are elucidated and forwarded to those responsible.
- Add value to the business, senior management, and stakeholders.

H. ISO 27031 - ICT Preparation (Information and Communication Technology) for business continuity

The ISO 27031 standard guides the concepts and principles behind the role of ICT – Information and Communication Technology in ensuring business continuity [12].

By default, the norm:

- Suggests a structure or structure (a coherent set or set of methods and processes) for any organization - private, governmental, and non-governmental.
- Identifies and specifies all relevant aspects, including performance criteria, design, and implementation details, to improve ICT readiness as part of the organization's ISMS, helping to ensure business continuity.
- Allows an organization to measure its ICT continuity, security and therefore readiness to survive a disaster in a consistent and recognized manner.

I. ISO 27032 – Cyber Security

The ISO 27032 standard addresses basic security practices for stakeholders in cyberspace, providing [13]:

- Cybersecurity overview,
- Relationship between cybersecurity and other types of security,
- Definition of stakeholders and description of their roles in cybersecurity,
- Guidance for addressing common cybersecurity issues, and
- Framework to enable stakeholders to collaborate on solving cybersecurity issues.

J. ISO 27037 – Preservation of Digital Evidence

The content of ISO 27031 [14] makes up a relevant set of information for forensic professionals. It makes up an international standard for identifying, collecting, acquiring, and preserving digital forensic evidence at all stages of the investigation process.

The standard standardizes the specific activities in the treatment of digital evidence, ranging from identifying, collecting, acquiring, and preserving digital evidence that may have evidential value. It assists organizations in their disciplinary procedures in facilitating the exchange of digital evidence between jurisdictions.

ISO 27031 generally considers the following devices or functions that are used in various circumstances [14]:
Digital storage media used in computers, such as HD, floppy disks, CD/DVD, pen-drive, smartphones, tablets, Personal Digital Assistants (PDA), Personal Electronic Devices (PED), Memory Cards, and Mobile navigation systems (GPS).

- Embedded systems.
- Digital video and photo cameras (including CCTV).
- Desktops, Notebooks.
- Networks based on TCP/IP and other digital protocols, and
- Devices with functions like those described above.

K. ISO 27701 – Privacy Management

As mentioned at the beginning of this article, almost all organizations handle personal data, whether employees or customers. In addition, the amount and types of personal data processed is increasing, as is the number of situations in which an organization needs to cooperate with other organizations regarding the processing of personal data. The protection of privacy in the context of the processing of personal data is a societal need and a topic of dedicated legislation and/or regulation around the world.

ISO 27701 is an extension of ISO 27001 and 27002 [5] [6] [15] that specifies the requirements and provides guidance to establish, implement, maintain, and continuously improve an Information Privacy Management System (IPMS), the document specifies in detail the requirements related to the IPMS and the guidelines that must implement in companies that are responsible for the processing of personal data.

The table below presents the mapping of the extension of the term information security for application and use of this document, it is possible to see how both are similar just adding the aspect of privacy in their content.

TABLE I. SECURITY AND PRIVACY APPROACH IN ISO 27001 AND ISO 27701 STANDARDS

ABNT NBR ISO/IEC 27001	ABNT NBR ISO/IEC 27701
Information Security	Information Security and Privacy
Information Security Policies	Privacy and Information Security Policies
Information Security Management	Information Security Management and Information Privacy
Information Security Management System (ISMS)	Privacy Management System
Information Security Objectives	Information Security and Privacy Objectives
Information Security Performance	Information Security and Privacy Performance
Security Information Requirements	Security Information and Privacy Requirements
Information Security Risks	Information Security and Privacy Risks
Information Security Assessment	Security Risk Assessment of Information and Privacy
Treatment of Security Risks of Information	Treatment of Security Risks of the Information and Privacy

VII. Conclusion And Future Work

From risk definition to business continuity and response plan, the ISO 27001 family provides a robust framework that allows understanding and applying the concepts of security and privacy. The standards guide how to identify risks related to the processing of personal data, in addition to reinforcing the need for policies, internal and external contractual agreements, items that are unknown to most small and medium-sized companies. When guided by the requirements of this set of standards, an organization tends to develop secure processes to manage the security of the information it handles. Therefore, privacy tends to be included in the process, becoming part of the business culture.

Considering the recent arrival of the General Data Protection Law in Brazil, small and medium-sized companies should pay attention to information security and the protection of personal data collected and held in custody to comply with regulations and ensure the image and reputation of their businesses. Understanding that small businesses run the same risks as large corporations can be the starting point for a strategic vision regarding privacy and data protection. Small businesses in this regard are even more vulnerable, as the lack of investments in cyber security makes them an easy target for cybercrime.

The biggest cost is the non-investment in information security. According to a recent survey carried out by First Data Corporation, about 90% of intrusions are directed to the systems of small and medium-sized companies. The average cost of vulnerabilities was enough to increase these companies' expenses by around U$D 36,000 annually. In that same survey, identified that the biggest impact is not the financial one. Still, the reputational one and in the scope of public relations, 31% of the clients and consumers said that upon discovering that the company was the target of data leakage due to malicious attacks, they would not return to doing business with the institution.

In another article in the Brazilian magazine Gestão&Negócios PME (Management and Business SME), 128 Edition/ 2019, November, was reiterated that despite investments in security systems, having a partner with vast expertise in the field of information security and data protection to help with this transition coupled with a mapping of personal data throughout the data lifecycle is a key part of greater protection in companies.

As a practical guide on improving the maturity of information security and data protection in companies, the ISO 27000 Family Standards provides a series of tools that help implement Information Security policies, whatever the size and budget of the company. With the recent arrival of the General Data Protection Law (LGPD - Law 13.709) [4], the need for adaptation was even greater as sanctions related to the protection of personal data also need greater attention from now on, where before the arrival of the Law only corporate data had a relevant adequacy need due to trade and trade secrets.

It is also important to highlight that the Law should not be seen as a hindrance or an obstacle in front of the commercial and technological evolution of companies, as many claim to be, as well stated by Leonardo Gondim, executive director of IT2S, in Gestão&Negócios PME Magazine, 128 Ed.: "The Law does not prevent the data from being used for one purpose or another, it only requires the user to be informed of this use and authorize it. It ends up giving back to the user the control of something that has always been his, allowing him to decide whether or not to provide the data and, also, knowing exactly what it will be used for".

In conclusion, the best thing to do going forward, both for the preservation of holders' privacy and for the business, is to have a security mindset in the first place. As explored in this article, not even small and medium-sized companies can assume risk-free, especially when much of the information is in an online environment. Changing the mindset is essential to avoid future losses and maintain the trust of customers and business partners.

For future work, a study will be carried out in companies called SMEs. Still, this study will verify the applicability of the general data protection law and its impact in the information technology sector.

References

[1] Microsof News, "Como as PMEs brasileiras enfrentaram a pandemia de COVID-19" - https://news.microsoft.com/pt-br/82-das-pmes-brasileiras-pretendem-continuar-o-processo-de-adocao-de-novas-tecnologias-apos-a-pandemia-segundo-estudo/- Aug. 17, 2021.

[2] Data Sebrae, https://datasebrae.com.br/ – Aug, 29, 2021

[3] B. A. Marcos, "Os donos de negócio no Brasil: análise por faixa de renda (2003-2013)": Sebrae, 2015.

[4] Presidência da República, Lei Geral de Proteção de Dados - http://www.planalto.gov.br/ccivil_03/_ato2015-2018/2018/lei/l13709.htm - Aug, 25, 2021

[5] International Organization for Standardization, ISO/IEC 27001: 2013, Information Technology--Security Techniques--Information Security Management Systems, 2013.

[6] International Organization for Standardization, ISO/IEC 27002:2013, Information technology-Code of practice for information security management, 2013.

[7] International Organization for Standardization, ISO/IEC 27003:2017 - Information technology — Security techniques — Information security management systems — Guidance, 2017.

[8] International Organization for Standardization, ISO/IEC 27004:2016 - Information technology — Security techniques — Information security management — Monitoring, measurement, analysis and evaluation, 2016.

[9] International Organization for Standardization, ISO/IEC 27005:2018 - Information technology — Security techniques — Information security risk management, 2018.

[10] International Organization for Standardization, ISO/IEC 27007:2020 - Information security, cybersecurity and privacy protection — Guidelines for information security management systems auditing, 2020.

[11] International Organization for Standardization, ISO/IEC 27014:2020 - Information security, cybersecurity and privacy protection — Governance of information security, 2020.

[12] International Organization for Standardization, ISO/IEC 27031:2011 - Information technology — Security techniques — Guidelines for information and communication technology readiness for business continuity, 2011.

[13] International Organization for Standardization, ISO/IEC 27032:2012 - Information technology — Security techniques — Guidelines for cybersecurity, 2012.

[14] International Organization for Standardization, ISO/IEC 27037:2012 - Information technology — Security techniques — Guidelines for identification, collection, acquisition and preservation of digital evidence, 2012.

[15] International Organization for Standardization, ISO/IEC 27701:2019 - Security techniques — Extension to ISO/IEC 27001 and ISO/IEC 27002 for privacy information management — Requirements and guidelines, 2019.

[17] Ministério da Economia, "Especificação de Requisitos de Segurança da Informação em Contratações de Tecnologia da Informação", Secretaria de Governo Digital, 2020.

[16] PriceWaterHouseCoopers, "O poder das PMEs no Brasil", 2013.

[17] Gestão & Negócios PME, "De olho na segurança do seu cliente", Edição 128, 2019.

[18] D. Almeida, Mirante contábil, "Proteção de dados e o papel dos pequenos negócios", 2021.

[19] A. A. Bertini, J. C. Martins and E. Thomaz, "Desempenho de edificações habitacionais: guia orientativo para atendimento à norma ABNT NBR 15575/2013.", 2013.

[20] D. Georg, "ISO/IEC 27000, 27001 and 27002 for information security management.", (2013).

[21] G. Alan, "Improving the quality of information security management systems with ISO27000.", 2011.

Proposed Incident Response Methodology for Data Leakage

Presenting the best processes and procedures tosafeguardyour business while preventing data leakage

Alex Rabello, Junior Goulart, Marcelo Karam, Marcos Pitanga, Reinaldo Gomes Baldoino Filho and Ronaldo Ricioni
IESB University Center
alex.rabello@privamax.com.br, jgoulart@vidalink.com.br, karam@unb.br, marcos.pitanga@talkcomm.com.br, reinaldo.baldoino@iesb.edu.br and ronaldo@r3force.com

Abstract - Most Brazilian companies disregard the national privacy law (LGPD) by not ensuring data governance and well-managed security controls with technical and organizational measures to prevent data leakage. Brazilian LGPD specifies that organizations must report to the national authority (ANPD) and the data subject if any security incident occurs that could cause relevant risk to the data subject. However, this privacy law lacks information on how to respond effectively to data leakage by embracing preventive measures against data breaches. The appropriate approach to handling data leakage is to invest in trained personnel, cutting-edge technology, and processes, enabling a proper incident response methodology. Organizations will be more willing to comply with the privacy law by administering a more approachable and straightforward path for security and privacy best practices. The development of this methodology is based on the international standard (ISO 27035) and some recommendations from the NIST 800-61 publication. The adaptation of these standards provides a more detailed checklist for determining when to perform incident reporting and transparency to the Brazilian authority (ANPD) and data subjects. Other points discussed are related to properly building the security incident response team, using security automation tools and playbook resources to ensure the application of best practices by handling data leakage processes.

Keywords-Data Leakage; Information Security; Incidents; LGPD.

I. INTRODUCTION

The advent of privacy and data protection laws and regulations worldwide raises one of the most relevant questions for most organizations: Has your company ever suffered a data leak? If so, the business impact of responding publicly with transparency can be massive, with the imposition of significant fines and the loss of customer trust affecting the company's reputation. Otherwise, in most cases, if a company has not had leaked data, it is because it has not yet been the target of attacks or because it has invested in strategic and tactical actions to avoid Information Security incidents.

The purpose of this article is to describe a methodology to propose best practices for the Information Security Incident Management, following the definitions and concepts standardized by the International Standards Organization (ISO / IEC 27035) [6] and some procedures described by the National Institute of Standards and Technology(NIST 800-61) [7] publication, with applicability in the context of personal data protection as it is the evolution of the Information Security applied to the current scenarios of data leakage.

In the media, reports of data leaks, cyber-attacks, and selling of information, including disclosure of confidential data, are frequently published by the Ponemon Institute and IBM Security [5], disclosing the cost of a data breach, for example, on average, the time to identify and contain a data breach is 280 days, and 80% of the breaches relate to the leakage of personal customer data.

Examples of security incidents may include system or service malfunctions, cyber-attacks (such as social engineering or denial of service), unauthorized access to confidential/restricted data, sending or receiving malicious code, changes to a system without owner approval, loss, misplacement, theft of data or equipment containing critical/sensitive information. These security vulnerabilities in organizations are among the greatest threats to privacy and data protection in the 21st century.

In this context, it becomes inevitable for any organization to prioritize incident governance and management of Information Security events to deal with breaches involving personal data leakage.

Some questions that guided the article:

- ***What is the proper way to analyze security incidents?***
- ***How to handle a risk analysis to avoid data breaches?***
- ***How can companies adopt a methodology for Security***
- ***Incident Management involving data leakages?***
- ***What is the appropriate communication and notification to the national authority and data subjects?***

The following Section II describes the standard frameworks applied for information security incident management and their phases to handle a lifecycle of the incident related to data leakage. Section III demonstrates the proposed methodology focusing on the key points to be addressed during incident security response. Topics IV, V, and VI provide specific data leakage scenarios and the appropriate solutions available to address the incident response.

II. Standards and Frameworks for Information Security Incident Management

ISO standards and NIST publications are recommended tools that can help organize and manage security incident response for any organization. The NIST 800-61 publication brings crucial insight into the structure of the incident response team, including three models: centralized, distributed, and coordinated. To choose the appropriate model, size and possible locations of the organization must be evaluated, but there are also other vital decisions, such as defining 24/7 availability, being composed of people working either whole or part-time, having in-person or outsourced work, cost of hiring based on experience and level of knowledge and evaluating stress factors. Regarding the incident response lifecycle, NIST recommends four phases: 1. Preparation, 2. Detection and Analysis, 3. Containment, Eradication and Recovery, and 4. Post-Incident Activities.

ISO/IEC 27035 standard is divided into three parts: Incident Management Principles (ISO/IEC 27035-1), Guidelines for Planning and Preparedness for Incident Response (ISO/IEC 27035-2), and Guidelines for Incident Response Operations incidents (ISO/IEC 27035-3). According to ISO/IEC 27035, a fundamental part of an organization's overall information security strategy must establish controls and procedures to prevent or contain the impact of information security incidents, reducing the direct and indirect costs caused by incidents. The main steps to minimize the adverse effects of information security incidents are 1. Plan and Prepare, 2. Detection and Reporting, 3. Evaluation and Decision, 4. Responses and 5. Lessons Learned.

III. Proposal for an Incident Response Methodology for Data Leakage

Our proposed incident response management methodology for personal data leakage scenarios is based on a response framework adapted to the context of personal data protection. An appropriate incident response plan prepares the team to handle threats, notifies incidents, isolates incidents, identifies severity, contains the attack, eradicates the underlying cause, recovers production systems, and conducts a post-mortem analysis to prevent future episodes.

A. *Formation of the incident response team*

The incident response team, also known as Computer Security Incident Response Team(CSIRT) [1], consists mainly of members of the privacy, information security, and legal team, with pre-established roles, objectives, and goals for each member of the team. The team will improve upon implementing procedures and processes to dominate the sector in which it operates, bringing the concepts of the cybersecurity ecosystem closer to the operational reality of the organization. It is essential to recruit and train the members in team building, ensuring they have access to the relevant systems and technologies for the best performance quality.

B. *Defining the roles and responsibilities*

The responsibilities involved are defined in the roles of a Chief Information Security Officer (CISO), Data Protection Officer (DPO) in case of data subject breaches, incident response manager, security analyst, threat researcher, legal representative, corporate communications, risk management, and external forensic security experts.

Among the main objectives of the incident response team, such as incident analysis, documenting the extent, priority, and impact of a breach, to see what assets are affected and whether the incident requires attention. With this, the team must plan and document procedures are containing the description of the incident response plans for different types of occurrences, severity levels, and affected regulatory bodies.

C. *Plan and identify the risks*

Another relevant procedure refers to implementing a risk assessment in case of cyber-attacks, knowing the most valuable assets and possible critical impacts on the organization's business. In addition to establishing a communication plan declaring the situations that require or not the issuance of internal and external notifications, depending on the level of impact and extent of violations of personal data of the holders. This methodology enforces the contextualization and adequacy given to the treatment of infringements containing personal data, not observed in the ISO/IEC 27,035 and NIST 800-61 standards, such as the figure of the DPO and notifications referring to violations containing personal data. In addition, it should be defined which will use tools to record and document incidents and mechanisms for detection and correlation of events and anomalies to obtain predictability and generate evidence records in audits supporting analysis of the incident.

D. *Selecting the proper security tools*

Incident response tools work with applied security measures, obtaining response information via network traffic analysis, system logs, endpoint alerts, and identity systems to detect network security-related anomalies. These tools investigate malware infections, password attacks, phishing, information leakage, privilege abuse, and other internal and external threats.

Information gathered from security tools, and IT systems should be kept in a central location, such as a Security Information Event Management (SIEM) [9], which consolidates events and logs from all types of critical computing resources. As a result, this information should be used to create an incident timeline and conduct an incident investigation with all relevant data points in one place. Technology alone cannot detect security breaches therefore, human perception must be trusted where the security operation team carefully monitoring events and behaviors, highlighting the following action approaches:

- Network traffic anomalies on sensitive internally used connections and servers that typically have a stable and predictable traffic volume;
- Access accounts without elite or administrator permission levels for more information and systems than

regular employees. Since employees tend to be the most accessible entry point into cybercrime, it is relevant to closely monitor accounts with administrator profiles, noting the increase in privileges on standard user accounts.

• Excessive consumption and suspicious files when observing an increase in the performance of the memory or hard disks in the environment could signal someone illegally accessing or leaking data.

• Use modern security tools, such as User and Entity Behavioral Analytics (UEBA) [11], which automatically identify anomalies in user behavior or file access. Provides a much better coverage of potential security incidents and saves time for security teams.

E. Handling incidents and threats

After developing an information security team specializing in monitoring threats and anomalies, it is necessary to detail how the organization will handle the incident. In conjunction with privacy and data protection experts, this information security team must determine what types of data are involved and assess the potential harm caused, evaluating any jurisdictional or industry laws that the company needs to comply with.

The proposed methodology gives the incident response team an accurate analysis of the severity of the breach involving personal data and the need for escalation to the national authority (ANPD), as required by various legislations, including the GDPR and the LGPD.

F. Incident investigation and recording

Investigations are based on two types of incident input to be handled: IT systems gather events from monitoring tools, log files, error messages, firewalls, and intrusion detection systems. This data must be analyzed by automated means and security analysts to decide whether anomalous events represent security incidents. There can be a report of a user from any area of the organization who submits a new happening in the system reporting an occurrence stating the cause of the incident, assets, and suppliers involved. This activation carried out via the incident system must follow a treatment flow. There is a prior assessment by a member of the information security team enabling classification of the type of incident, severity, the risk to the business, and possible impacts on personal data.

All evidence and records must be collected and preserved in case any criminal activity is recorded. Preservation of proof during screening and scope should be considered, especially if it becomes apparent that the incident involves illegal activity or data breaches. This methodology extends the need to preserve evidence and records for violations involving personal data, even if it is not criminal activity, aiming at the defense in possible lawsuits based on privacy filed by the data subjects and administrative data by the national authority (ANPD).

Proper preservation of evidence requires establishing a chain of custody procedures that must properly track any electronic evidence.

G. Incident containment, recovery and remediation

The next step in the process, called containment, aims to isolate the security incident to prevent further damage to the organization. The strategy to limit damage to organizational resources involves activating the information security team that works in management and control of confidentiality detection and protection resources to identify which business process is affected so that it is possible to isolate the problem. The priority is to have short-term containment with an instant response so that the threat no longer causes damage, but also to provide for long-term containment, planning corrective actions on affected systems, taking measures to prevent the incident from recurring or augment, such as installing the latest security patches on affected and associated systems, removing accounts and backdoors created by intruders, changing firewall rules involving the intruder's address, etc.

The information security team working on remediation must isolate the root cause of the attack, removing threats and malware, and identifying ways to mitigate vulnerabilities that have been exploited to prevent future episodes. These steps make configuration updates with a focus on minimizing the negative effect on the organization's operations. Choosing the proper way to accomplish this is to limit the amount of data exposed. In acting to recover affected systems, there must be guidelines to minimize the chance of another related incident.

H. Post Incident activities

Therefore, must validate that another incident does not occur by restoring clean backup systems, replacing compromised files with clean versions, rebuilding systems from scratch, installing patches, changing passwords, and strengthening network perimeter security (router access control lists rules, firewall rule sets, etc.). It would help to consider how long it would take to monitor the network system and verify that the affected systems are functioning normally. Therefore, the cost of the breach and the associated damages are minimized.

I. Comunnication and Data Breach notification

In cases of high risk of data breach and possible impacts on privacy, the flow should include an immediate notification to all members of the communication team and crisis team/committee, data protection officer (DPO), third-party vendors and executives involved, as well as actions to preserve all physical evidence regarding the location of the breach with detailed documentation of the incident to be used in the development of the incident response and forensic investigation process when necessary.

This methodology understands that the DPO must be promptly informed about all the steps in handling incidents involving the breach of personal data, especially about the increased risk. So that it is possible to exercise its role as an interlocutor between the organization, national authority (ANPD), and the data subjects, following the federal privacy law (LGPD). If determined during the previous phases of the incident response plan, the responsible team will communicate following the notification process where strategic communication and dissemination are developed for external audiences and internal staff.

J. Review and Process Improvement (PDCA)

Once critical incidents are addressed, and the systems involved are recovered, the organization should hold a meeting to review the effectiveness of the incident handling process and identify necessary improvements to existing security controls and practices.

Information gathered from these meetings should identify and correct systemic weaknesses and deficiencies in policies and procedures. The security specialist must determine how the incident was managed, revalidating what took action to recover the attacked system, the areas where the response team needed improvement, and the areas where they were effective. Evidence reports provide a clear review of the entire incident and can be used in meetings, as benchmarks for comparison, or as training information for new incident response team members.

K. Development of an incident response playbook

In addition, the root cause analysis must be prepared so that complete documentation is provided with greater accuracy after the incident response process, which also helps to improve the process for prioritizing technical data protection measures aligned with the organization's cyber risks.

Gerard Johansen [3], can elaborate the steps of the incident response plan with a set of instructions and actions described in a playbook process, where the risks of critical threats must be evaluated, indicating the appropriate scenario to be followed.

Due to the large volume of incidents, and the short deadlines present in the legislation for the notification of violations involving personal data, within 48 hours for a response (LGPD) and 72 hours (GDPR), we believe it is necessary that these best predictability practices can be automated with the implementation of a playbook process, building a continuous flow of known approaches to handling recurrent or similar cases. The methods described in this playbook should seek to identify patterns, deeply understanding the TTP (Tactics, Techniques, and Procedures) [8] commonly used by threats, performing governance based on threat scenarios with use cases instead of just rules, and using connected and integrated security platforms using technology such as Security Orchestration, Automation, and Response (SOAR) [12] for a centralized approach with the ability to automate incident response, including personal data breaches.

IV. Scenario Analysis of Data Leakage to Apply DLP Solutions

Technology capabilities for preventing data loss or leakage are defined by a strategic program that detects, monitors, and blocks potential breaches of sensitive data while in use (endpoint actions), in-motion (network traffic), and at rest (storage data).

Following Bose et al. [12], data leakage is an error condition in information systems in which information is destroyed by failures or neglect in storage, transmission, or processing. Information systems implement backup and disaster recovery equipment and processes to prevent data loss or restore lost information. Data leakage is distinguished from data unavailability, such as that arise from a network outage. According to Xi et al. [13], it is also essential to check the data loss in the use of mobile platforms because there has been a significant growth in the usability of mobile equipment with innovative platforms, unintentional loss of sensitive data due to a malicious agent, an inside job, or an unknown employee can lead to significant financial loss and reputational damage for any organization. To avoid these damages and losses, it is imperative to implement solutions for data loss prevention (DLP) [2], which can include:

- DLP Endpoint (end-user device) when the user has a scope of data on desktop, laptop, USB storage, and virtual desktop.
- DLP for data at rest or storage is usually unstructured data that resides on a server or structured data that resides in databases.
- Network DLP is applied to data that transits or leaves the network to the Internet and.
- DLP for cloud is data residing in Google Workspace, Microsoft 365, and other personal cloud providers.

DLP methods [10] are designed to discover and analyze content and context to determine if the presented data matches a pattern or expression of an identification number or a specific keyword. Once the way is reached, a violation or alert can be generated, and it is sent to a management console for review by an incident triage and support analyst.

When evaluating some proposed scenarios, the possible focus of data leakage should be identified, for example, of a fictitious company that processes medical insurance claims for a regulated health care organization. They are aware that sensitive personal data resides on file servers, but they are unsure where the data is located. In this case, we should prioritize the analysis in the resting DLP solution. The strategy would include an unstructured data discovery scan, which will scan the selected storage and find data matching the keyword pattern (health data) as stated in the scan policy. Another common scenario is when a Human Resources (HR) manager learns that some department members have emailed sensitive files to their email address to work on corporate requests overdue over the weekend. To address this situation, we must prioritize the use of DLP for networks and endpoints. Also, can create a network security policy to prevent file uploads to personal email platforms. DLP for Endpoint can also detect HTTP/HTTPS connections as data leaves the Endpoint to the Internet.

V. Conclusion

As a result of applying the proposed methodology, some factors are observed as gaps to be treated about the procedures and recommendations of the NIST and ISO standards. One of these factors is the use of automation in incident processing driven due to the significant increase in recent years and the short deadlines established by legislation for notification of personal data breaches, and the possibility of automating many processing tasks with retransmission to systems and IT tools, reducing the amount of human activity and human decisions required. Suppose the organization already has an incident response team. In that case, it must carefully consider all the team building factors provided in the NIST document, adding professionals with privacy and data protection knowledge, and dual user verification of all processes, except for the DPO. As emphasized by NIST, handling incidents is a complex task, which can customize by implementing security automation.

An important point within this proposal is the massive and in-depth training of information security teams, especially those responsible for handling the response to incidents, so that they prepare adequate documentation for the proper chain of custody, thus tracing the entire timeline along with the proper procedures to safeguard the environment, avoiding the contamination of evidence, which may be necessary for a more in-depth investigation in the civil/criminal scope that can use to prove the truth with the national data protection authorities or in the public judicial spheres for the judgment of the rights of the holders.

In terms of the ISO / IEC 27035 approach, this standard describes and details incident management and allows an organization to apply prevention proactively. However, this approach depends on the effectiveness of the lessons learned and continuous improvement of treating incident management as a linear or cyclical activity.

The adaptation of the incident response methodology also allows for the inclusion of a checklist of actions to decide when it is time to notify the incidents to ANPD, as well as the data subjects, as in the ISO standard and the NIST recommendation, these notification procedures are not as emphasized concerning the importance of this requirement stated in the LGPD law.

References

[1] J.Novak, D. Mcintire, A. Hueca, B. Manley, S. Mudd and T. Bills , Technical Report - The Sector CSIRT Framework, [Online]. June2021,Available from: https://resources.sei.cmu.edu/assetfiles/TechnicalReport/2021_005_001_734796.pdf 2021.08.25

[2] A. Gorecki, "Cyber Breach Response that actually works", Willey 2020.

[3] G. Johansen, "Digital Forensics and Incident Response, 2nd ed." Packt Publishing, Birmingham, UK, 2020.

[4] LGPD: Lei Geral de Proteção de dados 13.709.[Online]. Available from:http://www.planalto.gov.br/ccivil_03/_ato2015-2018/2018/lei/l13709.htm 2021.07.23

[5] Ponemon Institute: The cost of a Data Breach report.[Online]. Available from: https://www.ibm.com/security/data-breach

[6] ISO/IEC 27035:Information technology - Security techniques - Information security incident management.[Online]. Available from: https://www.iso.org/standard/60803.html

[7] NIST 800-61:NIST Special Publication 800-61, Revision 2, Computer Security Incident Handling Guide.[Online]. Available from: https://www.nist.gov/privacy-framework/nist-sp-800-61

[8] Threat Intelligence: Radware. [Online]. Available from: https://www.radware.com/getattachment/Security/Hackers-Corner/2218/HackersCorner-TTPsDDoS-FINAL-V3.pdf.aspx?lang=en-US

[9] Security information and event management (SIEM) technology: Gartner.[Online]. Available from: https://www.gartner.com/en/information-technology/glossary/security-information-and-event-management-siem

[10] The practical executive's guide to Data Loss Prevention:Forcepoint.[Online]. Available from: https://media.bitpipe.com/io_14x/io_147455/item_1939907/whitepaper_practical_executives_guide_data_loss_prevention_en%20%283%29.pdf

[11] User and Entity Behavioral Analytics (UEBA): Forcepoint.[Online]. Available from: https://www.forcepoint.com/pt-br/product/ueba-user-entity-behavior-analytics

[12] Security Orchestration, Automation, and Response (SOAR).[Online]. Available from: https://searchsecurity.techtarget.com/definition/SOAR

[13] Bose, Neetu, and N. Vishwanath. "An Improved Method for Preventing Data Leakage in an Organization."

[14] Xi, Ning, et al. "Information flow based defensive chain for data leakage detection and prevention: a survey." arXiv preprint arXiv:2106.04951 (2021).

Studying Digital Literacy and AI Adoption in Software Engineering & Technology Companies

Marko Jäntti
Centre for Measurement and Information Systems
Kajaani University of Applied Sciences
Ketunpolku 1, 87100 Kajaani, Finland
Email: marko.jantti@cemis.fi

***Abstract*—Traditional IT organizations and software companies are transitioning into digital service companies in order to survive in increasing competition. However, this transformation process is a major change requiring new digital skills, learning new methodologies and ways to work, introduction of new digital technologies as well as introducing new roles and responsibilities within the organization. In this study, we explore how skills, technologies, methods, ways to work and processes are changing in Finnish IT companies due to digital transformation. Our research focused on studying and promoting the adoption of Artificial Intelligence (AI) in IT organizations. The research problem of this study is: How traditional IT companies are approaching AI and advanced digital technologies? The main contribution of this paper is to show preliminary findings from an interview study.**

Keywords*—*Digital literacy; Artificial Intelligence; digital transformation, software company.

I. Introduction

Digital transformation and uprise of advanced digital technologies (Artificial Intelligence, Extended Reality, Internet of Things, Digital Twins) affect not only non-ICT organizations but also ICT companies and software development units. Very likely, most IT companies use at the moment combinations of a software engineering approach (software development, project management and maintenance activities) and a service engineering approach (service design and engineering, cloud engineering, agile service development, service management). However, the role of service engineering is becoming stronger all the time and service management is altering many of the software maintenance activities.

IT companies are continuously updating and modernisizing their key operational processes, such as software release management [1] to service release and configuration management [2], changing the scope of IT architecture from software architectures to enterprise architectures [3] and extending software quality-focused processes, for example, software defect management and failure management [4] to have wider approach (service incident management [5]) that also covers incidents due to poorly implemented processes, knowledge gaps of employees and failures made by third party service providers and seeks permanent solutions by investigating the root cause of service failures with problem management procedures [6].

Additionally, when a software development organization grows and complexity of service provision increases, the toolset of the organization also hanges and evolves. For example, most software development companies provide bug tracking systems (Jira and open source ticket systems) and problem solving communities for their customers since they start operating as a company. When a company decides to start operating in a service business, their toolset shall be expanded and very likely shall include an IT service management tool.

The business growth and digital transformation have a significant impact on organizational structures of software development. Most of Finnish IT companies are very small entities. This means that their development and support teams are small, have relatively limited resources and a richer set of responsibilities compared to those employees of large IT service provider organizations where service design, service transition, service operation, and continual service improvement are typically provided with different resources but certain level of systematic overlapping can be identified.

In a mature service organization, development teams are responsible for Early Life Support (ELS) [7] of new services for a certain time period. After that customer service and support are provided by service desk units that may evolve and mature into omnichannel service centers [8]. The key difference between a multichannel and omnichannel approaches is how integration between customer communication channels has been implemented. The omnichannel approach often involves usage of integrated environment for modern customer experience (CX) and well-integrated communication channels [9].

In addition to structuring organizational resources, companies need to pay attention to competencies required by the digital era. Every employee in the company should understand his/her role during and after the digital transformation process as well as understand the opportunities of digital technologies for the company's business. This is called in general digital literacy [10]. For a software development organization, the transformation might mean that there is less need for traditional Java developers, business analysts creating Unified Modeling Language (UML) diagrams [11] and business case documents [12] and project managers using waterfall and Rational Unified Process approaches; and more need for cloud service specialists, service design engineers and Agile project specialists.

Concerning digital literacy, governments world-wide are investing hundreds of millions for increasing competences of artificial intelligence, such as conversational AI [13], Machine Learning, Machine Vision, predictive analytics and other forms of artificial intelligence. Well-defined AI Application

Programming Interfaces (AI APIs) enable software developers to utilize latest AI functions in their software code without investing huge efforts in creating those functionalities in-house. The large scale use of APIs and related business models and practices together form the basis of API economy [14]. Software companies could use AI not only in information systems they provide to customers but also improve their own processes such as use Machine Learning in defect management to predict defects [15]. Additionally, machine learning could assist project management and project portfolio management to [16] in making better decisions or predict project success.

The goal of the Digital Innovation Hub (DIH) is to act as a one-stop shop that helps companies of the region in tackling digital challenges (our focus is on AI, HPC, data analytics and digital transformation). This study supports directly the objectives of the DIH by producing new knowledge on AI-powered digital transformation in Finnish companies and the status and targets of AI adoption as well as usage of other digital technologies (cloud, digital service management platforms) in service operation.

In this paper, we aim at answering the research problem: How traditional IT companies are approaching AI and advanced digital technologies? The main contribution of this paper is to study

- How evolvement of AI and digital literacy skills is supported by software development/ICT organizations' managers?
- How AI and related technologies are used in software development/ICT organizations?
- How AI affects the daily business operations of a software development/ICT organization?
- How AI is linked to software development/ICT organizations' productivity?

This paper aims at providing research communities of software engineering and service science new knowledge on how managers support increasing AI capabilities related digital technology competences within their organizations.

The results of this study might be useful for digital transformation managers, development managers of SMEs, project managers of the projects where digital technologies are applied as well as HR managers for identifying what digital skills might be needed in IT companies in the future. The remainder of the paper is organized as follows. In Section 2, we present the research methodology of this study. In Section 3, main findings of the interview study are presented. Section 4 is the analysis part of our study. Finally, the conclusions are given in Section 5.

II. Research Problem & Methodology

The research problem of this study is: How traditional IT companies are approaching AI and advanced digital technologies? We selected the research problem because both companies and government (ministries, regional, national and international funding agencies) in Finland are pushing more and more resources for transforming traditional production methods with artificial intelligence. However, small and medium sized companies seem need a lot of help in introduction of these technologies and integrating AI components to their products and services.

The research problem was divided into the following research questions:

1) How evolvement of AI & digital literacy skills is supported by software development/ICT organizations' managers?
2) How AI and related technologies are used in software development/ICT organizations?
3) How AI affects the daily business operations of a software development / ICT organization?
4) How AI is linked to software development/ICT organizations' productivity?

The first research question highlights the management support for digital transformation initiatives and our aim was to receive information that demonstrates the management support for AI projects and increasing competences of AI. The second research question was created to identify popular technologies and services that organizations use in their AI initiatives. This information might give non-AI companies a list of potential starting points for their AI journeys. With the third research question, we wanted to explore the impacts (both short term and long term) of AI programmes and finally the fourth research question aimed at generating a view to what types of benefits AI would result in the organization's productivity.

A. *Data Collection Methods*

The paper writing, selection of research methodology and analysis were performed at CEMIS research centre. However, empirical data for this study was collected during Digital and Intelligent Management of Service Operation project (ESF ELY) from 8 interviewees and their organizations represented various business domains in service provision such as ICT, energy, miscallenous services, marketing and advertisement. Interviewees were selected for this study by using convenience sampling, however, we tried to achieve a rich, balanced set of interviewees with varying work positions, including management and governance (CEOs, senior management), product owners and product managers, customer service employees, service managers and designers. ot The questionnaire included both structured and open-ended interview questions. Due to COVID-19, most of interviews (1 hour) were conducted by using Microsoft Teams video conferencing tool and interviewees were provided an option to receive questions before the actual interview event by email.

B. *Data Analysis*

The data of this interview study were analyzed using a thematic content analysis technique that focuses on identifying common themes while searching the materials organically. The main objective in the analysis is to find common patterns across the data set. For video interviews conducted with Microsoft Teams, we used the recording function of Teams to capture entire interview discussions. This turned out to be an excellent solution because some answers were really long and complicated.

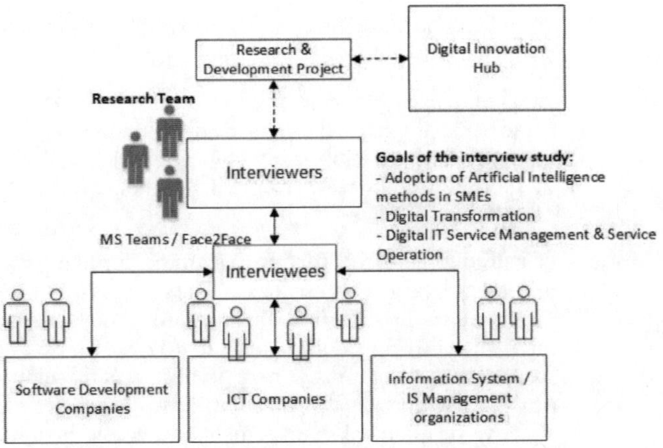

Fig. 1. Context of our interview study

Transcript files were stored as digital files in the project's digital, cloud-based work environment (internal Teams environment) and shared among the research project team. Each interview transcript was numbered and named according to predefined naming conventions: ordernumber, name of the study, status of transcript: rawdata/validated. Transcript files were sent to interviewees for short validation and interviewees were offered an opportunity to remove or change their answers.

III. Findings of the Interview: AI and Digital Literacy

Figure 1 shows the context of our interview study. This paper shows preliminary findings from first eight interviews and from preselected four interview questions that formed our research questions.

Transcripts were coded according to a thematic content analysis technique (a category class was allocated to each answer). During the first round, we did not pay a lot of attention to duplicate categories.

A. How evolvement of AI & digital literacy skills is supported by software development/ICT organizations' managers and employees?

The first topic that we focused in exploring digital literacy was how managers of software and technology firms had supported the development of AI skills and competences. We observed that one answer from an interviewee may result in several category classes.

- "By innovating new services that utilize AI and identifying demand and customer need for AI solutions. Additionally, we have recruited AI specialist to our company."**Class:** Recruitment of AI specialists, Identify customer's AI needs, Service innovation
- "I have not participated myself in AI training events. However, I support aims to do work tasks smarter. I participate in introduction of AI in those parts that are understandable for me. I act more like a coach / inspirator in AI matters."**Class:** Support for smarter work, Coaching
- "I have not been able to support and have not had an opportunity to participate in AI development"**Class:** No support
- "I participated in Elements of AI course and studied AI topics myself. I have also explored AI-powered apps that support our business such as Trello Butler. We have saved quite a lot of efforts with that app (avoided around 6000 UI clicks)."**Class:** Personal AI learning, Exploring AI features
- "I have a 'bad' habit to link all interesting articles and videos to our team's Slack. Thus, information sharing is one way to support. By sharing links and webinar invitations and encourage colleagues to participate in these events."**Class:** Sharing AI-related information
- "I have not supported because AI has not been in our core focus yet. However, if we start purchasing a new application, we need to observe and think whether there are some AI features available (cherries on the cake) and whether it is possible to include those features to that application."**Class:** Exploring AI features
- "We have organized general information sessions to our personnel and encouraged our staff to make their work more visible and we have also rewarderd employees based on it. Developing AI competences is among employees' personal goals."**Class:** Organizing AI information sessions to staff, Rewarding staff on AI work, Linking AI to employee's personal work goals.
- "Not at all yet"**Class:** No support

B. How AI and related technologies are used in software development/ICT organizations?

The second research question focused on identifying AI technologies and targets for AI usage in software development and ICT organizations.

- Machine vision and machine learning as well as Natural Language Processing in our products and services. For example, in care facilities one can listen operational instructions. **Class:** NLP, Machine vision, Machine learning)
- We use data lakes, Azure cloud technologies and maintain user information concerning Office 365 services. I do not know about usage of AI technologies. **Class:** Azure cloud, data lake, O365
- Azure for managing user right information, AWS cloud in server management, we also store information to Dropbox cloud storage, Google Ads for promoting our products and services. **Class:** Azure cloud, AWS cloud, Dropbox, Google Ads
- We have AWS virtual servers, cloud based file management and a web-based support system (a contact form for ordering new items). Some applications we use have AI features. **Class:** AI-powered apps, AWS cloud, cloud file storage
- Facebook and Google ads. We obtain services that utilize these two. Storing information and centralizing

it. We have a chatbot introduction project running. **Class:** Facebook, Google Ads.

- We have a commercial chatbot service, we use Requeste systen for managing support tickets and Azure cloud. **Class:** Commercial chatbot, Requeste support ticket system, Azure cloud.
- We do not use Machine Vision in our own work but for customers we do. We use Machine learning and neural networks a lot. We use cloud services almost for everything. Azure, AWS, Google.. We have a service portal that we have built on ServiceNow. **Class:** Azure cloud, AWS cloud, Google cloud, Machine vision, Machine learning, Service portal
- We have NLP/NLU (an AI-based bot), we use Azure and AWS and self service portal. **Class:** Azure cloud, AWS cloud, NLP, NLU, AI bot, Service portal

C. Impacts of AI to daily business operations?

Concerning the third research question, we captured what types of impact AI may have to software development organizations' and ICT organizations' daily business operations. Interviewees were guided to identify impacts to predefined business processes: Customer service, sales and marketing, financial management, human resources management, logistics, IT and free choice. Additionally they were asked to describe rationale for their choices.

- "In application development, we utilize various AI algorithms and we develop AI solutions to our customers. Regarding sales and marketing, we could use more analytics for marketing purposes, for example, with Facebook's own AI one can target marketing campaigns."
- "In customer service, AI helps in routing tickets automatically over the first support level or with small amendments. In financial management AI helps in processing purchase invoices or routing them to a correct person. In inventory management, AI may trigger alerts automatically when thresholds for inventory saldos are exceeded. AI shall save time in those areas where it is possible to utilize it. "
- "Customer service: when customers send requests, automation can process them smoother and we can reduce / avoid paper notes. AI also helps in monitoring sales and marketing by automating the monitoring. AI can be used to monitor servers if there are a lot of customers using systems (loads can be seen beforehand) "
- "Through AI, one does not need to wait for customer service and level of automation can be increased. AI may also result in personalized service and customer service staff can focus on delighting customers in interactive situations. Self service portals enable employees and customers to do things by themselves. For IT organizations, AI can help improving information security and preparing for Denial of Service attacks. AI can detect potential attacks and route the traffic elsewhere because there is some simple artificial intelligence in routers. "
- "Especially sales and marketing. It is a big challenge for us to analyze the data. I see already now that many organizations develop their own services on the top of Google and these services help them to identify correlations in data."
- "Customer service: for us customer service is the biggest part of our business. Thus, everything that makes it more effective shall improve our business most. It can bring automated recording of cases and workflow automations. These issues free more work time and improve the data validity. From the perspective of financial management, the whole invoicing could be automated and checked that accounts and reference numbers are correct. "
- "Employee satisfaction has increased, customer service process is faster, throughput times are better, AI has had comprehensive effects to customer satisfaction, automation works more effectively and with less errors than a human."
- "We launch increasingly more chatbots in customer service and logistics and inventory management utilizes AI. "

D. How AI is linked to software development/ICT organizations' productivity?

The final research question addressed the linkage between artificial intelligence and the organizational productivity in the interviewee's organization. The original questions in the question form addressed also links between AI and wellbeing at work, however, these answers were excluded from this paper due to space limitations:

- "Concerning productivity, we produce AI services but we do not exploit AI ourselves."
- "Related to financial management AI decreases workload in invoicing. If we can introduce better solutions, we can reduce management's workload."**Class:** Decreased workload
- "Yes of course there is a link if we can get things that makes work faster and actually helps when we do not do unnecessary manual work. AI has to be brought into right targets. We welcome AI. Sure, there are things in various domains where AI can help."**Class:** Eliminates manual work, makes work faster
- "Manual work is not among the most motivating work. Through automation, we have more time for creative work. In our company, automation removes clicks in the UI. Less clicks and more time for drinking coffee."**Class:** Eliminates manual work, more time for creative work
- "There is direct connection if you look at marketing. We have so much data. If we had to perform these tasks ourselvels and with our own brains, it would be impossible. Now, when we can rely on AI provided

by existing platforms, it is a big plus."**Class:** Helps in processing large amounts of data

- "It is very close to all processes where we can use automation and machine learning. These can be utilized for example automated ticketing. It would enable people focusing on more demanding problems or communicating with people. When the basic reporting is ok, we can start creating prediction models of our customers and own finance."**Class:** Automated ticketing, enables focusing on demanding work, creates basis for predictions
- "To a significant extent, AI results in productivity and it should be introduced more and more. It makes work faster and predictive and correlates with profitability and productivity. "**Class:** Makes work faster, affects profitability
- "There is a positive connection. There are processes in the background and we aim at improving them continously in order to make our operations smoother and more effective. "**Class:** Smoother and effective operations

IV. Analysis

The data analysis was performed by using thematic content analysis technique for the interview data. The goal of the analysis was to categorize interview data to classes and identify frequently used classes. Regarding the first research question, we identified the following categories on management commitment to support the organization's AI skills:

- Recruitment of AI specialists,
- Service innovation
- Identify customer's AI needs
- Support for smarter work
- Coaching/inspiring
- Personal AI learning,
- Exploring AI features in products
- Sharing AI-related information
- Organizing AI information sessions to staff
- Rewarding staff on AI work
- Linking AI to employee's personal work goals
- No support

According to our observations, only one of the interviewed organizations demonstrated clear management commitment for supporting AI. In that company, they had increased AI awareness within the organization, introduced rewarding mechanisms for staff and also taken care that AI was visible in employees' personal development path. However, other activities we identified support well the management's work on getting people focused on AI. While used together these activities (classes) provide management a very good start for AI roadmap.

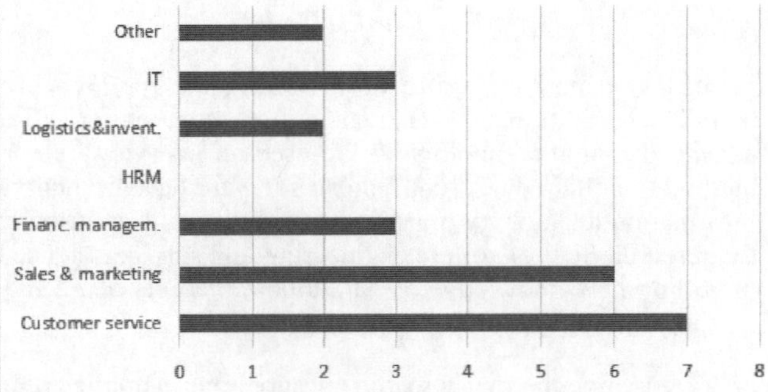

Fig. 2. Impact of AI on organizations' business processes

Related to the second research question, identified classes revealed the use of common AI types (conversational AI (NLP), machine learning, machine vision) and strong existence of cloud service platforms (Azure, AWS) but also AI-powered services such as Google Ads. Regarding the third research question (impact of AI), we analyzed the answers regarding the frequency of business processes mentioned by interviewees. Figure 2 shows our findings. Each interviewee was asked to select three business processes from the list of predefined processes that he/she thinks AI is going to affect in the near future. Predefined process areas were: customer service, sales and marketing, financial management, human resources management, logistics and inventory management, information technology and other (free selection by the interviewee). According to our interview findings, customer service was most frequently mentioned (7/8 interviewees) process to be affected by AI in the near future.

The thematic content analysis of the answers to the fourth research question resulted in the following category classes.

- Decreased workload
- Eliminates manual work
- Makes work faster
- More time for creative work
- Helps in processing large amounts of data
- Automated ticketing
- Enables focusing on demanding work
- Creates basis for predictions
- Affects profitability
- Smoother and effective operations

Our first observations on these findings was that 'Makes work faster' was mentioned several times. The key message in the findings was that AI provides tools for automation and opportunity to eliminate non-valuable, routine and manual, demotivating work tasks while resulting in more time for more meaningful work activities and human to human communications. However, organizations should carefully evaluate where to use artificial intelligence because it does not fit everywhere.

V. Conclusion

In this paper, we aimed at answering the research problem: How traditional IT companies are approaching AI and advanced digital technologies? We used an interview research method to collect data from Finnish software development and information technology organizations. Our results contribute to the research field of softare engineering and service science by providing new knowledge of AI adoption, targets of AI usage and impacts of AI to operational processes.

Concerning the first research question, our thematic content analysis revealed several ways how managers and employees support development of AI skills in their organizations: by personal AI learning, exploring AI features of products they are purchasing, sharing AI-related information (such as web links and AI-related webinar invitations), organizing AI information sessions to staff, rewarding staff members on visible AI work, and linking AI to employee's personal work goals.

Through the second research question, we received information on current AI & digital technologies used by the companies. Cloud technologies were most frequently mentioned technologies, especially Azure. From AI side, both machine learning and NLU/NLP from conversational AI was clearly mentioned in two of the eight interviewees. Some of the companies had ongoing chatbot projects but the interviewees could not provide any details on technologies used in those projects. Furthermore, machine vision was mentioned by two interviewees and one of those stated that they use machine vision in a customer project.

Related to the third research question, our findings showed that customer service is the process area to be most likely affected by AI in the near future followed by sales and marketing. Our study revealed few IT-related AI impacts such as better monitoring of servers and improved information security though better detection of Denial of Service attacks.

Our final research question addressed the relation between AI and productivity. AI provides tools for powerful tools for automation and enables organizations to eliminate non-valuable, routine and manual, demotivating work tasks which at the same time frees more time for more meaningful work activities and communicating with customers and employees.

There are certain limitations related to the interview method that we utilized. First, data were collected from 8 interviewees by using standard interview data collection procedures. Increasing the number of interviewees (especially senior business managers and programmers) could have provided new insights and experiences on applying AI services.

Second, thematic content analysis was used for transcripted data but the analysis and creation of category classes was performed by one person. Inviting more people to assist the data analysis would have very likely result in a richer set of categories. Third, due to space limitations only four questions from the interview questionnaire were selected for this paper. It was very difficult to prioritize content. However, this provides us a fruitful foundation for further research where we can present the rest of the interview results and new emerging categories on AI adoption.

Acknowledgment

We would like to thank interviewees for valuable responses that helped us to perform this study as well as managers of companies enabling this study.

References

[1] S. Jansen and S. Brinkkemper, "Ten misconceptions about product software release management explained using update cost/value functions," in *Proceedings of the International Workshop on Software Product Management*. Washington, DC, USA: IEEE Computer Society, 2006, pp. 44–50.

[2] K. Jokela and M. Jäntti, "Challenges and problems in product portfolio release and deployment management," in *Proceedings of the 9th International Conference on Service Systems and Service Management (ICSSSM12)*. Shanghai, China: IEEE, 2012, pp. 138–141.

[3] J. Korhonen and M. Halen, "Enterprise architecture for digital transformation," in *2017 IEEE 19th Conference on Business Informatics (CBI)*, vol. 01, July 2017, pp. 349–358.

[4] W. Florac, "Software quality measurement a framework for counting problems and defects," Technical Report CMU/SEI-92-TR-22, 1992.

[5] M. Jäntti, "Lessons learnt from the improvement of customer support processes: A case study on incident management," in *Product-Focused Software Process Improvement*, ser. Lecture Notes in Business Information Processing, W. Aalst, J. Mylopoulos, N. M. Sadeh, M. J. Shaw, C. Szyperski, F. Bomarius, M. Oivo, P. Jaring, and P. Abrahamsson, Eds. Springer Berlin Heidelberg, 2009, vol. 32, pp. 317–331.

[6] M. Kajko-Mattsson, "Problem management maturity within corrective maintenance," *Journal of Software Maintenance*, vol. 14, no. 3, pp. 197–227, 2002.

[7] Office of Government Commerce(c), *ITIL Service Transition*. The Stationary Office, UK, 2007.

[8] N. Ilk, M. Brusco, and P. Goes, "Workforce management in omnichannel service centers with heterogeneous channel response urgencies," *Decision Support Systems*, vol. 105, pp. 13 – 23, 2018.

[9] R. Picek, D. Peras, and R. Mekovec, "Opportunities and challenges of applying omnichannel approach to contact center," in *2018 4th International Conference on Information Management (ICIM)*. New York, NY, USA: IEEE Press, 2018, pp. 231–235.

[10] D. Cetindamar, B. Abedin, and K. Shirahada, "The role of employees in digital transformation: A preliminary study on how employees' digital literacy impacts use of digital technologies," *IEEE Transactions on Engineering Management*, pp. 1–12, 2021.

[11] M. Jäntti and T. Toroi, "Uml-based testing: A case study," in *Proceedings of NWUML'2004. 2nd Nordic Workshop on the Unified Modeling Language*. Turku: Turku Centre for Computer Science, August 2004, pp. 33–44.

[12] M. Jäntti, "The rationale for building a business case in software development," in *IRIS 28. Information Systems Research Seminar in Scandinavia (Proceedings of the 28th IRIS)*, Kristiansand, Norway, 2005.

[13] A. Rajagopal and N. Vedamanickam, "New approach to human ai interaction to address digital divide amp; ai divide: Creating an interactive aiplatform to connect teachers amp; students," in *2019 IEEE International Conference on Electrical, Computer and Communication Technologies (ICECCT)*. New York, NY, USA: IEEE, 2019, pp. 1–6.

[14] K. Lee and N. Ha, "Ai platform to accelerate api economy and ecosystem," in *2018 International Conference on Information Networking (ICOIN)*. NY, USA: IBM Press, 2018, pp. 848–852.

[15] S. Pradhan, V. Nanniyur, and P. Vissapragada, "On the defect prediction for large scale software systems – from defect density to machine learning," in *2020 IEEE 20th International Conference on Software Quality, Reliability and Security (QRS)*. New York, NY, USA: IEEE Press, 2020, pp. 374–381.

[16] A. Marchinares and I. Aguilar-Alonso, "Project portfolio management studies based on machine learning and critical success factors," in *2020 IEEE International Conference on Progress in Informatics and Computing (PIC)*. NY, USA: IEEE Press, 2020, pp. 369–374.

SYS2VEC: System-to-Vector Latent Space Mappings

Theo Mahmut Bulut
Computer Science
University of Kaiserslautern
Kaiserslautern, Germany
Email: mahmutbulut0@gmail.com

Vasil L. Tenev
Embedded Systems Engineering
Fraunhofer IESE
Kaiserslautern, Germany
Email: vasil.tenev@iese.fraunhofer.de

Martin Becker
Embedded Systems Engineering
Fraunhofer IESE
Kaiserslautern, Germany
Email: martin.becker@iese.fraunhofer.de

***Abstract*—As a product line evolves, new members emerge and existing ones are maintained – more or less in sync with each other. In the context of long-living software and system product lines, the capability to predict evolution trends within the structure of the various assets is essential. It helps to understand the underlying dependencies between work items now and in the future and helps to make the product line architecture more robust against the predicted trends. With this, unnecessary erosion can be avoided and overall engineering efficiency can be increased. With the increasing complexity of today's systems, approaches that can identify and evaluate commonalities, variabilities, and interdependencies in a large number of complex product variants and versions are gaining importance. In order to increase efficiency, approaches that support an incremental analysis in the space and time dimension are desirable. A promising approach to this end is to map the versions of each variant to points in a vector space. Doing so, two challenges can be efficiently addressed: (i) the similarity measurement becomes the distance between vectors; and (ii) the estimation of evolutionary trends can be reduced to the well-known interpolation problem. In this paper, we present SYS2VEC – an approach for mapping product line variants into a latent vector space by means of machine learning techniques. With our approach, we are able to show an increase in accuracy by a factor of 4 and halve the execution time compared to similar machine-learning-based solutions.**

Keywords*—*System comparison; machine learning; graph similarity; product lines.

I. Introduction

The rapid development in the embedded and IT world demands steady growth of customization flexibility for products and services. To satisfy this need, companies can do two things. On one side, new product variants can be forked and modified from existing ones or be derived using a strategic reuse approach, where a variation model exists [1]. On the other hand, existing product variants continue to develop in new versions. Such systems often evolve over long periods, during which they usually diverge from each other. Each new variant typically addresses new customer requirements, causing it to drift away from the product line' core. At the same time, variants can also grow closer together due to changes in the environment and the emergence of common architectural drivers.

Unfortunately, these tendencies are often not apparent, but it becomes essential to predict such evolution trends within the asset structure in the problem and solution space of a product line. It helps to understand the underlying dependencies between work items now and in the future and helps to make the product line architecture more robust against the predicted trends. With this, unnecessary erosion can be avoided and overall engineering efficiency can be increased. With the increasing complexity of today's systems, approaches that can identify and evaluate commonalities, variabilities, and interdependencies in a large number of complex product variants and versions are gaining importance. In the context of product line engineering, assets of the system architecture are considered. Requirements, architectural models, source code, configuration, and test artifacts could be subject to such analyses. In the following we focus on the analysis of architectural models, although the presented approach can be applied to other engineering artifacts as well.

To cope with the increasing complexity of today's systems, organizations are increasingly using model-based approaches in systems and software engineering. In these models, architecture, requirements, realization and quality assurance work items are tightly connected with each other. The models grow proportionally with the product line size and complexity. In principle, the models are highly interconnected graphs. Estimating the evolutionary trends for the architecture model aids in managing and planning of deviations that emerge between product variants and versions.

In order to increase efficiency of analyses in large-scale product lines, approaches that support an incremental analysis in the space and time dimension are desirable. A promising approach to this end is to map the versions of each variant to points in a vector space. Doing so, two challenges can be efficiently addressed: (i) the similarity measurement becomes the distance between vectors; and (ii) the estimation of evolutionary trends can be reduced to the well-known interpolation problem. This raises the question, of whether there is an efficient way to translate the structure of product line assets into a vector space.

In this paper, we present SYS2VEC – an approach for mapping system variants into a latent vector space by means of machine learning techniques. SYS2VEC approach is based on the Graph2Vec method, which uses Weisfeiler-Lehman hashing [2] to incorporate unified relabels for node features. With SYS2VEC, we are able to show an increase in accuracy by a factor of 4 and halve the execution time compared to similar machine-learning-based solutions. The paper provides the following *contributions*:

- it introduces an innovative approach to analyze system variants by representing them as graph-like structures in

a latent vector space,
- it discusses implementation aspects of the approach,
- presents validation results, and
- provides an overview on related machine learning approaches.

The remainder of the paper is structured as follows: Section II gives an overview on the approaches, techniques and tools related to this work. Section III discusses the main idea of using latent space representation for addressing the aforementioned challenges. In Section IV we present our approach and implementation in details. The validation with respect to our goals is shown in Section V. Section VI concludes the paper.

II. Related Work

In this section, we present the context in the conducted research work and provide an overview on machine-learning approaches, techniques and tools related to our approach.

1) Feature Extraction: In machine learning, feature extraction is a method to create input for ingestion by models. There are various ways to extract features from textual information. One of the most common methods is the Term Frequency-Inverse Document Frequency (TF-IDF) [3]. Some methods extract features to embedding space directly using Bag-of-words (BOW) methods with skip-gram models like WORD2VEC [4]. WORD2VEC extracts features to latent space straight from sentences. For feature extraction at the paragraph level with multiple sentences, DOC2VEC has been proposed. DOC2VEC has two approaches: one of them is Paragraph-Word Distributed Memory (PV-DM), and the other one is the Paragraph Vector-Distributed Bag Of Words (PV-DBOW) approach [5].

Since we do not need to incorporate individual word vectors from the fixed-length sliding window, we discard the PV-DM approach and use the PV-DBOW approach in our work. For our algorithm introduced in Section IV, vector output of WORD2VEC and DOC2VEC prevents preprocessing node attributes with vector input. Muhammad Isa et al. [6] have successfully applied TF-IDF for semantic feature extraction. They use frequency table output for graph representation learning. TF-IDF allows filtering of terms with low occurrence in the whole graph. Thus, a threshold can be used to filter the sparse matrix output of TF-IDF. In Sections IV, IV-B, and IV-C, we have detailed term and inverse document frequency related filtering to supply a better canonical input for the representation learning stages.

2) Unsupervised Machine Learning: Unsupervised machine learning methods learn the representations with minimal or no external intervention [7]–[10]. Unsupervised methods are broader in scope and fit the context of variant analysis better, as they incorporate hierarchies and node contents and features. One of the unsupervised approaches to feature learning over graph descriptions is OhmNet [11]. OhmNet originates from bioinformatics and generates multiple neural network layers for all protein sequences that are similar to each other. To this end, it trains a single machine learning model that maps the layers of protein structures to the corresponding tissue. In the context of variant analysis, each system variant corresponds to a different tissue. The training time depends on the number of system variants and increases linearly. Applied to our context, this method does not provide accurate prediction as it tends to converge to the global minima of all variants. Whereas in a real scenario, the variants may not even be related and should not even be considered and trained together.

Non-Negative Matrix Factorization (NNMF) is one of the Blind Signal Separation (BSS) techniques widely used in unsupervised methods. It learns graph structures while incorporating both graph shape and node content into embedding space. One of the adapted NNMF method is FSCNMF (Fusing Structure and Content via Non-negative Matrix Factorization for Embedding Information Networks) [12], where the model uses attribute context of the nodes to learn node feature representation. This node based embedding generation method works with factorizing both adjacency and feature matrices. Node and feature embeddings are regularized together for create a representation in embedding space. It doesn't embed full graph shape, as it is supposed to be, since this method uses adjacency as main driver for embedding vector generation. The FSCNMF method outputs an N-dimensional representation, where N is the maximum nodes between training graphs. This output needs to be combined with manifold methods like t-distributed Stochastic Neighbor Embedding (t-SNE) [13] to produce a sensible output from the original output with dimensionality reduction techniques. When the methods are adopted in variant analysis context, multiple graphs of the same product line will fit the same model. That said, contextual inference will be high, but the graph shape will not be preserved very well.

Another approach for creating embedding for nodes, which utilizes a random-walk-based approach, is text-associated DeepWalk (TADW) [14]. TADW, like FSCNMF, factorizes textual node attribute matrix with actual representation matrix. Apart from FSCNMF, this method does random walks over the graph and creates matrices from the these walks. These walks are used as similarity measure for the graph's core representation. When adapted to variant analysis context, this method creates a single vector representation from both content and structure together. By default this method assumes that two graphs are different when they have different shapes. TADW doesn't apply to variant analysis domain very well, because content and structure might vary differently and if either one of them is different, they are assumed different by the learning method. Since this method also outputs an N-dimensional representation, it needs to be combined with manifold methods for more sensible outputs for the identification of formed clusters.

In addition to attribute-based graph embedding methods, whole graph embedding methods are most suitable to learn the representation of graphs [15]. They rely on various techniques and incorporate different partial information about the graphs. These methods can enrich an embedding graph structure by embedding edge features [16], by node features only [17], or by permutation preservation [18]. For large datasets, tracing

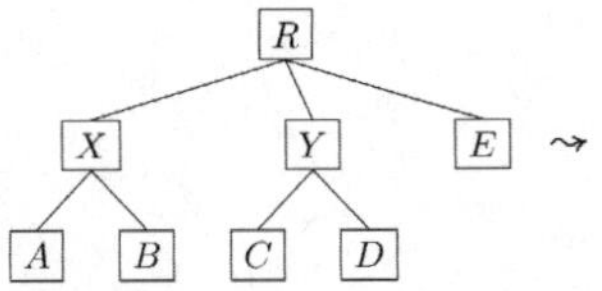

(a) Graph representation of system variant S_1.

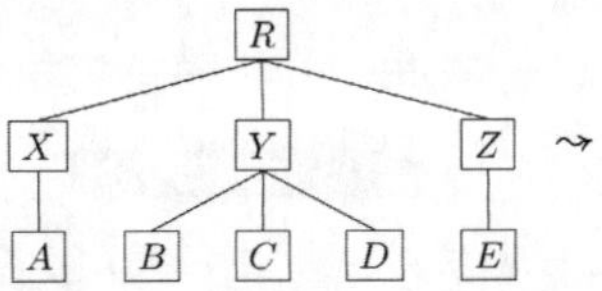

(b) Graph representation of system variant S_2.

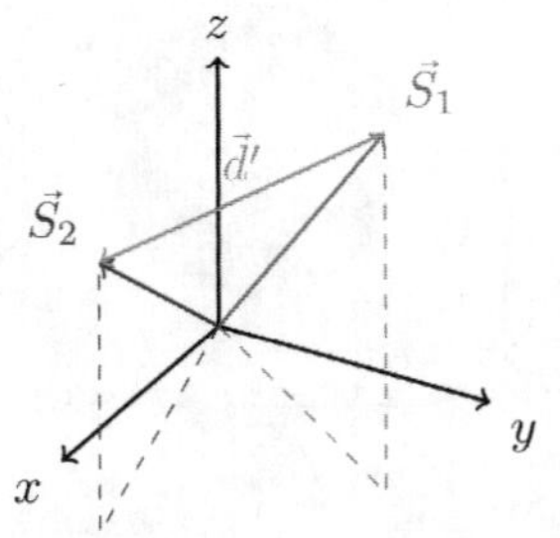

(c) Similarity measurement between S_1 and S_2.

Figure 1: Input system variants and output vector representations of example system S_1 and S_2.

based on Taylor series by eigenvalue decomposition is a hard task. Since first-order terms in Taylor expansions tend to approximate to a local maximum of the distribution, large graph eigenvalue growth rate cannot be estimated for large graphs [19]. These methods fallback is always hit for graphs, i. e., making the method's main optimization discarded for NetLSD.

The Weisfeiler-Lehman Kernel (WLK) can be used to incorporate graph topology information into the nodes and take the vertex neighborhood into consideration. WLK allows the quantization of neighborhood groups to the individual node attributes through hashing. Other than WLK, there are random walk kernels that do random walks with varying lengths over the graphs. DeepWalk is one of the methods that incorporate a random walk approach to learning the graph representation with unbiased, fixed-length, random walks starting from each node. According to Narayanan et al. [17], these methods tend to have low confidence values against the WLK based methods. Graph2Vec [2] is a method, which uses Weisfeiler-Lehman hashing to incorporate unified relabels for node features. Graph2Vec approach is well aligned with the variant problem, due to its graph representation learning. Furthermore, its base accuracy is good enough to deliver meaningful results out of non-linear substructures.

III. Latent Space Representation

Latent space is a multi-dimensional vector space, where representation vectors for variants are used to make correlation for similarity. The similarity between the variants is related to the angles between the vectors, their magnitude, and their orientation. For example, let S_1 and S_2 be two system variants (see Figures 1a and 1b). The similarity between them can be computed in three-dimensional space, as shown in Figure 1c. Here $\vec{S_1}$ is the vector representation of S_1, $\vec{S_2}$ represents S_2, and $\|d'\|$ corresponds to their similarity. In general, we work with finite-dimensional vectors in vector space, also known as finite-dimensional Hilbert space.

Distance measures between vectors enable computing similarities. We can compute the pairwise similarity between two variants in the vector space using the Euclidean norm. In Figure 1c, we can see that $\|d'\|$ is the Euclidean norm between two vector representations. For computing pairwise similarities, SYS2VEC relies on the Euclidean norm of vectors.

For having consistent vector representation for ingested systems coming out from SYS2VEC, variant hierarchies should have a consistent notation. Our algorithm uses PV-DBOW, which doesn't produce word vectors in a fixed window of elements like the other alternative model of DOC2VEC called Paragraph-Word Distributed Memory (PV-DM). But even though the order of the words in the graph's corpus is not essential for us. For this very reason, using a graph traversal notation is crucial to always get a consistent representation of the graph. When given a set of systems, our algorithm runs with Deep First Search (DFS) with vertex ordering notation of preordering. Since this approach can build a topological sort for nodes, it is a natural choice for the SYS2VEC. The underlying DOC2VEC [5] model works by doing subgraph sampling, and this approach can always yield the correct final form for any given subset of the graph.

IV. SYS2VEC Approach

SYS2VECs core processing pipeline and its processing stages can express a single variant with row vector representation. This Section discusses the algorithm's workflow and its stages in depth.

This section explains our main algorithm's stages which are:

- **System Variant Traverser.** Traversing systems structure and preparing a system variant as input for the normalization passes are explained in Section IV-A (cf. stage **1** in Figure 2).
- **Normalization Scheme.** In Section IV-B, we explain how system contents are normalized as input for the Weisfeiler-Lehman kernel and how its output is used by the representation learning (cf. stage **2** in Figure 2).
- **Representation Learning.** Section IV-C explains important arguments for SYS2VEC and its core representation learning model. In addition to that, we will discuss generated embedded space representations and their properties in Section IV-D (cf. stages **3** and **4** in Figure 2).
- **Latent Space Similarity.** Section III describes our approach of computing similarity based on the latent space representation (cf. stage **5** in Figure 2).
- **Method Optimization.** For getting most of the accuracy from our approach, we have developed model optimization. Section IV-E explains how SYS2VECs hyperparameter tuning approach works in detail. In addition to that, we explain how additional optimizations considered and incorporated into SYS2VEC.

A. System Variant Traverser

However the system represented digitally, we traverse through the system, and create variant trees. Our traversal algorithm (stage **1** in Figure 2) uses the Depth-First Search

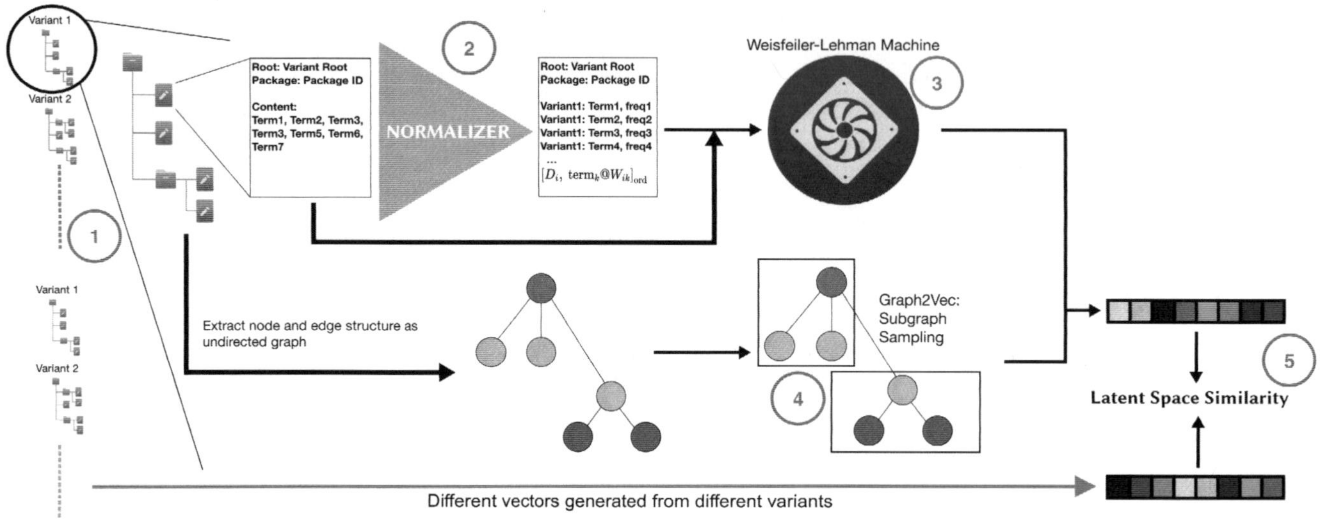

Figure 2: SYS2VEC, Similarity Seeking Variant Analysis Machine Learning Pipeline.

(DFS) to extract the hierarchical structure of the variants. DFS traversal gives us a consistent view between all graph variants and for their subsampling undergoing in DOC2VEC [5]. Since our data model is a generalized model for software variant graphs, our algorithm should also work with large graphs and datasets. Datasets containing elements over one billion nodes should be organized at scan time, which reveals the internal structure of graphs for achieving better results for machine learning models. Finding ordering with optimizing a cost function is solely an NP-hard problem. Since finding optimal ordering relies on vertex locality and can vary between graphs [20], we skip finding vertex ordering for each graph and utilizing DFS for all graphs.

B. Normalization Scheme

In order to do the graph core extraction using Weisfeiler-Lehman Kernel (WLK), [2], data of content filled elements should be normalized. In Section II-2, we explained the necessity of WLK pass for the extraction of graph topology. The content normalization scheme we have defined (stage **2** in Figure 2) will be used for creating Weisfeiler-Lehman hashable features after traversal (see Figure 3). Moreover, through a content-oriented normalization scheme, terms of low importance (aka lonely terms) can be optionally detected and eliminated.

Reduction parses all content definitions and then creates vocabulary with unique terms received after tokenization. Based on this vocabulary, first term frequencies and then graph-wide inverse document frequencies are generated. Learned frequencies produce document-term matrices based on single key-value tuples reduced from their sparse representations held in TF-IDF. By reduction, these corresponding tuple sets are added to ordered feature sets in all nodes of the graph. Normalized contents are generated with this method refills content filled elements to make graphs ready to be processed by WLK in the next stage.

procedure CONTENTNORM(V, c) ▷ Where V - array of vertices' contents, c - count of all content filled elements in variants
  $X = makevectorizer()$ ▷ Create TF-IDF vectorizer
  $D = X(V)$ ▷ Process variants through vectorizer
  Let $L[1 \dots c]$ be new array
  for $j = 1$ to c **do** ▷ Iterate over each content filled element
    $k = len(V[j])$ ▷ Get number of TF-IDF tuples
    $\mathbf{A}_j = create\_ordered\_set\_with\_size(k)$ ▷ Create ordered set for content filled element at index j
    for $b = 1$ to k **do**
      $A_j.append(D[V[b]])$ ▷ Append TF-IDF pairs to ordered set
    end for
    $L[j] = A_j$ ▷ Assign content filled element's ordered set to the aggregation set
  end for
  return L
end procedure

Figure 3: Content Normalization.

After reduction, vertex contents are made into a TF-IDF document matrix. At this state, every vertex content state has filled key-value dictionary item. Before fed into Weisfeiler-Lehman Kernel, normalized inverted index pairs in ordered dictionaries can further be ranked. Moreover, if needed, lonely terms can be filtered by their threshold of occurrence. In addition to all the previous steps, preprocessing can be done [21]. In addition to that, the proposed normalization scheme can work with an ample amount of content (which is bounded by the underlying TF-IDF implementation). Since every normalization run is a one time pass for a single graph, most of the time is taken for building the vocabulary for graphs with a large degree. In [22], authors define "large graphs" as graphs with hundreds to thousand nodes. Our experiments showed that SYS2VEC already works with approximately 2400 and more nodes. We detailed our experiments in Section V-A.

The researcher can configure the tokenization algorithm for the TF-IDF system. Standard structured formats like XML and JSON can easily be converted to dictionaries and then fed into dictionary-based tokenizer. Dictionary-based tokenization allows SYS2VEC to consume different system views like control flows, configuration files, structured binary representations, and various other formats by a simple adaptation of normalizer. For control flow graphs, one can use the original SYS2VEC repetitively for every node's control flow. Since control flows are applying the rule of rooted graphs, they can be usable with SYS2VEC. When it comes to configuration files, text objects can be either translated into record formats like CSV or TSV then fed into the normalization scheme with a comma or tab-separated tokenization. When compared to control flows and file configurations, binary objects are needed to be either parsed into structured plain-text representations or encoded with binary-to-text encoding algorithms. The latter solution decreases TF-IDF confidence in normalization passes since binary data (when directly encoded into text) won't give good term frequency but rather give inverse document frequency. For dealing with binary data, recent bioinformatics papers [23] [24] followed an approach where authors created weighted sparse binary matrices with a predefined aggregation window and then applied TF-IDF for normalization.

C. Representation Learning

Fundamentally, the algorithm creating latent space representation of the system variants should be task agnostic with a row vector output. Task agnosticism needed for whatever input features given, we should be able to produce a row vectors for the given system variants. Since we need to compare whole graphs, we take advantage of the paragraph vector-distributed bag of words (PV-DBOW) [5] representation used in Graph2Vec [17] . Since Graph2Vec is a transductive approach, intrinsically, SYS2VEC is transductive [25]. In SYS2VEC, "transductive" means that vector representations are generated for a given fixed set of graphs to generate vector space lookup matrix.

Since our variant representations are rooted graphs, Graph2Vec does subgraph matching over the given set of system variants (stage **4** in Figure 2). During the normalization of the previous step, feature dictionaries were created for all nodes. These features are hashed for compression with their neighborhood similarities with Weisfeiler-Lehman kernel (stage **3** in Figure 2). Thus at each iteration phase, neighborhoods and features have been stored in nodes. Finally, graphs with aggregated data in their nodes dispensed and can be feed into DOC2VEC [5] to learn the representation with subgraph sampling followed by matrix factorization steps.

Representation learning for graph clustering doesn't incorporate task-specific information from SYS2VECs reduction mechanism. This feature of Graph2Vec allows us to extend or manipulate feature dictionaries in the content nodes to represent relations. Moreover, the separation of SYS2VECs reduction mechanism from the representation learning model provides great flexibility to change the underlying model with other techniques in the field. Example relations like includes excludes at the package level, composition, and aggregation for classes can be appended to content dictionaries and preprocessed with the same workflow that we have described Section IV-B. Graph2Vec performs better generic representation when task-specific information doesn't factorize together with the underlying PV-DBOW model [17]. Via underlying PV-DBOW, DOC2VEC skip-gram training learns the graph representation interpreted as document representation and yields a row vector.

Configuration of SYS2VEC relies on various parameters; these parameters are scattered through the pipeline components seen in Figure 2. Parameters below adjust representation learning from graphs in SYS2VEC. Variant traverser (in Figure 2 marked with **1**) receives these arguments:

Vertex ordering notation: Vertex ordering that nodes placed to form the graph after traversal. Ordering notation can change how row vector values are displaced through representation learning. Indirectly it changes vector orientation and magnitude in Hilbert space.

Tokenization scheme for creating the variant knowledge corpus: Tokenization procedure given to tokenizer for extracting sensible words as input for TF-IDF algorithm underneath. By default, SYS2VEC comes with word tokenization, which allows feature extraction by parsing two or more characters that assemble a word. Tokenization can be changed to adapt to structured data formats like XML, JSON, or blobs. SYS2VEC can create meaningful normalized features from existing variant data when tokenization is adapted. Adaptation can be made by changing the regular expression of tokenizer or supplying a custom function closure.

(Optional) Normalization stage bypass argument for experimenting with untouched vertex features: Optional flag for skipping normalization stages as will. By default, skipping normalization is disabled. If features are not meant to be preprocessed, TF-IDF reverse lookup can be skipped. In that case, Weisfeiler-Lehman will process all of the non-normalized feature set. Our experimentation showed that if the non-normalized feature set is in key-value format, this doesn't change representation learning. Moreover, it doesn't change the pairwise similarity computation. If nodes have heterogenous data scattered among them, it is better to use normalization passes to create homogenous representation for the graph.

Learning rate of the model: A factor that enables how much generalization should be memoized from the previous iteration of the training. Feature slices given to DOC2VEC should incorporate all details of normalized feature sets. For this reason, the learning rate during the training should be controlled for how much generalization memoized from a batch. A higher learning rate lowers the generalization, and a lower learning rate won't incorporate most of the features given in a graph. Finding a good learning rate is an experimental discovery. A good learning rate gives a low loss value but won't prolong the model's training duration. For this exact reason, we have a learning rate as a parameter to optimize at the hyperparameter optimization stage in Section IV-E.

Output vector dimensions: Graph representation's row vector size, in other words, dimension output per variant. In Hilbert space, vector dimensions are essential to represent generalized notions of graphs. The row vector representations should have enough dimensions for variants to achieve better vector space similarity. Increasing dimensions can output better vectors for condensed features in content filled elements. When data is not enough, higher dimensions won't create a difference. Hyperparameter tuning is utilized to detect an optimized dimension count (as explained in Section IV-E).

Frequency threshold for features: Before running Weisfeiler-Lehman hashing, TF-IDF pairs can still have lonely terms that mightn't contribute to overall graph representation learning. This threshold behaves like a high-pass filter for TF-IDF frequencies in the ordered set. SYS2VEC comes with the tuning option of filtering terms with a low term occurrence frequency (see Section II-1). We have explained that option in Section IV-B as lonely term filtering. This option filters learned TF-IDF frequencies below a particular threshold value. SYS2VEC doesn't implement key-specific inverse transform for filtering by specific thresholds. Since filtering specific keys is an expert decision, and we don't want to incorporate another function to increase the time complexity of the processing. Not having additional key-specific filtering doesn't have downsides for SYS2VEC.

Epochs: Defines how many times full dataset batches are fed into the model. Almost all machine learning models have epochs to adjust how many times batches are fed as a complete cycle to a model. When epochs increased, subsampling for PV-DBOW will give different data attention and weights to update vector representations. Increasing epochs for large datasets enables producing more generalized vector representation. If epochs are kept less, the model can underfit and will not generalize enough to make meaningful vector space representations. Since accuracy determines the generalization of the model and generalization directly dependant on epochs, this value is also optimized by our hyperparameter optimization scheme (see Section IV-E).

D. Embedding Space Representation

After system traversing, normalization, and graph kernel extraction, learned graph representations need careful tuning from the machine learning model parameters' perspective. As explained in Section IV-C, subgraph representations are incorporated into embedding space with the influence of both SYS2VECs parameters and underlying Graph2Vec model parameters. The dimension for vector representation wasn't selected arbitrarily. Higher dimension count gives longer training times and sparse graph representations. Thus accuracy for the similarity correlation decreases due to heavy entropy interference and sparsity of generalized model parameters. Mentioned entropy interference prevents convergence of the model for very high output dimensions. In [26], authors noting having more parameters to generalize will increase the error rate of the model inference. When dimensionality increased parallel to model parameters, the model's accuracy will first seem to improve but then decrease drastically. This phenomenon is called Hughes phenomena [27]. In [28], empirical observations showed that after 1000 dimensions, convergence to at most 50% probability of error is relatively slow.

In contrast to that, giving a low dimension to the SYS2VEC prevents capturing all given system variants' features. Similarity metrics don't diverge when no attention is given to the system variants specific properties. For this reason, output embedding dimensions should carefully be picked between multiple systems. Selecting the optimum dimension can be automatized and optimized by various parameter optimization methods, which are explained in section IV-E.

Representation learned from graphs projected from latent space to embedding space and generates row vectors for every system variant individually. SYS2VEC heavily relies on PV-DBOWs embedding projection. Embedding representations for SYS2VEC is unchanged Graph2Vec embeddings. After pairwise similarity computations finished, dimensionality reductions can use embeddings to visualize vectors' density in vector space.

Apart from the embedding generation, there are various improvements suggested for PV-DBOW. PV-DBOWs embedding projection uses dot product similarity for word-paragraph correlation. In SYS2VEC, the mentioned projection corresponds to a random subsample of a graph against the whole graph. For this reason, representations are heavily influenced by the distribution of subsamples over a graph. Though there are suggestions to improve PV-DBOW for better embedding generation for randomly distributed subsamples [29], we didn't consider subsample randomness as a problem in a diverse set of systems and their graphs since they are not relevant to our approach.

E. Method Optimization

Representation vector generation after model training gives output vectors for every variant. Since SYS2VEC is taking parameters mentioned in Section IV-C, accuracy against the validation dataset varies with different model parameters for both SYS2VEC and underlying Graph2Vec implementation.

Successful representation vector and similarity matrix generation don't mean that our system is perfectly working with its full potential. For getting better accuracy from the model, hyperparameter optimization methods exist. For this purpose, we have included an automatic hyperparameter tuning method inside SYS2VEC. Our autotuning optimization strategy is using the Optuna framework, which is a cutting-edge black-box optimization toolbox for machine learning models [30]. We have defined Optuna's optimization goal for its' black-box approach as the maximization of the accuracy scalar defined by pairwise similarity of sampled variants throughout trials of representation learning with different parameter spaces, which the framework has estimated throughout the hyperparameter optimization.

SYS2VECs hyperparameter tuning configures the parameter spaces listed below for maximizing the accuracy with given categorical and range-based parameter space. Parameter spaces are manually selected and tweaked based on the knowledge about our problem. First, we have tested minimum and maximum values of parameters with our approach, then we set them as a parameter range:

- **Weisfeiler-Lehman iterations over the system variants.** Integer parameter space from 2 to 10.
- **Output dimensions.** Categorical parameter space with powers of 2 as in 128, 256, 512, 1024, 2048, 4096.
- **Epochs** Categorical parameter space with multiples of 10 as in 10, 20, 30, 40, 50.
- **Learning rate** Uniform distribution between 0.005 and 1.0.

The aforementioned parameters and their parameter space are explored and tested for the convergence to the global maximum during the hyperparameter optimization. After the hyperparameter optimization trials finish, the framework outputs the best parameter selection and accuracy received with these parameters. If received accuracy is better than our method's initial accuracy, we are accepting this parameter set as the new basis for SYS2VEC. We have observed that after optimizations successfully finished, we see nearly 10% accuracy improvement against the validation dataset.

A tree-structured Parzen estimator [31] does parameter sampling for the hyperparameter optimization. SYS2VEC comes with hardcoded 100 trials for optimization passes, which is seen enough during our optimization trials. Since sampling and objective function seeks the global maximum throughout the optimization, we haven't defined any early termination criteria when no accuracy improvement has been seen during these trials.

With hyperparameter optimization, accuracy levels rise to 64%. When our optimization for hyperparameters runs, it lays out better quality than the out-of-the-box method. These results can be compared with the accuracy of the graph2vec model [17] using the MUTAG dataset. MUTAG is a data set containing graphs of 188 chemical compounds labeled with respect to their mutagenic effect on bacteria. MUTAG dataset can be processed by SYS2VEC since our method's core for learning graph representations is the same as Graph2Vec. Generated representations will be the same as processing data through the Graph2Vec method.

SYS2VEC consists of various runtime optimizations in its stages, which makes representation generation and similarity computation faster compared to unoptimized interpreted code:

Embedding generation: The DOC2VEC implementation we are using has C extensions for parallelizing the computation and working faster with native code. In our experiments, precompiled C implementation brought nearly sixty times faster epochs than pure Python implementation [32].

Similarity calculations: SYS2VECs vector space similarity calculation is using LLVM's vectorization backend for faster similarity computation through the Numba just-in-time (JIT) compiler for Python [33]. Vectorization enables us to use SIMD instructions dedicated to vector processing. Normally this optimization is only possible with a backend dedicated to analyzing loop specialization. LLVM's JIT compilation engine gives code auto-vectorization and enables faster similarity computation for our case [34]. We can compute similarities for the given variant pairs faster with single instruction multiple data (SIMD) instructions. The mentioned JIT compiler only compiles pairwise similarity distance methods for variants to enable compiled bytecode reuse across the whole variant ranges during similarity computation. This compilation happens once at the very beginning when vector space similarity calculation starts; after that, it is cached to reuse across all given systems [33].

Model and vectorizer caching: TF-IDF vectorizer used in the normalization scheme can save the vocabulary and don't need to rebuild between the runs of the SYS2VEC. SYS2VEC can freeze models and load and save dictionaries and embeddings. These actions allow bypassing the traversing stage if needed and enable faster experimentation over the variants. Moreover, it allows running inference tasks on SYS2VEC. These optimizations are incorporated for improving the performance for processing high volume variant data in SYS2VEC.

V. VALIDATION

In this section, we validate the SYS2VEC method and compare it with other approaches in the field, following different approaches to solve the similarity computation for system variants.

The main validation obstacle for the research is having a broader set of graph data to test full accuracy against the approximation-based methods in the field. Graph datasets used for validation in research either lack graph counts (cf. Zitnik et al. [11], where authors use a dataset with 219 graphs describing cellular systems) or the amount of nodes per graph is way less (cf. Bai et al. [7], where authors have at most 100 nodes). Nevertheless, initial observations showed that SYS2VEC performs with good accuracy for the graph-based similarity analysis.

Our method uses the transductive approach of Graph2Vec [17], but it is flexible enough to use another representation learning method. Stages of SYS2VEC can be independently used to feed graph data back into the deep learning techniques like Graph Matching Networks (GMN) [35] [36] for representation learning. In addition to that, our approach's accuracy baseline without hyperparameter tuning is 55%. With hyperparameter tuning, it goes beyond 65%. Additionally, SYS2VEC is flexible for adaptation with various model bases as mentioned in Section IV-C.

A. Correctness

As shown in Table I, SYS2VECs dataset contains five systems by the same tier one supplier with variant count varying from 16 to 91 variants for each system. Each variant corresponds to a software-hardware management system for

TABLE I: SUMMARY OF THE DATASET USED FOR THE EXPERIMENTATION.

System Name	Variant Count	min. Nodes	max. Nodes
System Z	63	1864	3462
System Y	23	952	2458
System X	16	1079	3267
System W	91	1209	2406
System V	51	229	3397

TABLE II: RELATIVE ACCURACY AND ERROR BOUND OF SYS2VEC COMPARED TO OTHER METHODS.

Algorithm	Accuracy (avg. ± std.)	δ - Mean Error Bound	Total Runtime	Algorithm Type
Multiple Alignment	87.2 ± (0.2)	~ 12.8	<1 hour	Deterministic
OhmNet	16.1 ± (0.9)	~ 80.0	~ 3 hours	ML based
SYS2VEC	65.4 ± (2.3)	~ 42.0	<30 minutes	ML based

an automotive facility. More concretely, we analyzed the configuration data structured in hierarchical sets, where each node in the set represents a pair of a configuration item and the associated value. Our approach is validated against the similarity computation method, called Multiple Alignment, developed by Tenev [37] and additionally described by Duszynski [38].

In Table II, we have compared our method with relative success rate against similarity heuristic of multiple alignment method in [37]. The relative accuracy of SYS2VEC against the deterministic Multiple Alignment method [37] is lower than expected. But SYS2VEC can be used as internal heuristics to guide Greedy algorithms to converge to optimal alignment solution as an alternative to the proposed modified Center-Star heuristic [37]. With an error rate of likely 40 percent against the approach mentioned in [37], [39], SYS2VEC can also be used to get an overview of which variants are highly similar and what is possible evolutionary tree can be consolidated from them.

Our next aim to improve SYS2VEC is to incorporate accuracy improvements. The main breakthrough of SYS2VEC is operating on graphs without extra micro-tuning for their content and structure. SYS2VEC creates embedding, which is reusable across various vector space algorithms. Moreover, our method is flexible enough to substitute the embedding generation model with different algorithms. This substitution will be towards improving the accuracy of the representation learning by experimenting with deep neural networks.

B. Comparison to Other Techniques

Experiments ran with various methods showed that our method's transductive approach exploits the representation learning and similarity calculation well over the large graphs. As shown with the dataset specifications in Table I, our method handed out better accuracy than other machine learning methods, which can be observed from Table II. In addition to that, total runtime where the sum of training and inference runtime is way less compared even to deterministic methods. Moreover, since it doesn't need Graph Edit Distance (GED), or Tree Edit Distance (TED) as a supervisory signal for representation learning, it's time complexity is lower than other methods. As shown in Table II, Zhang-Sasha [9] TED approximations are taking ample amount of total runtime on very large graphs. For similarity calculation, we aim for an interactive analysis approach; for this reason, the Zhang-Sasha-based SimGNN method is not suitable with a runtime of 2 days. This timing behavior is too long, and it is not useful for practical use case scenarios. In addition to that, GED calculation is NP-hard [40]. For this reason, we have also experimented with approximate GED methods with error bound [41]. But these methods time complexity increases exponentially with respect to the graph's node count, like in the Zhang-Sasha case in Table II. Above a certain degree of the graphs, machine learning methods execution is dedicated mostly to the edit distance calculation.

Experiments showed that SYS2VEC has an acceptable error rate against the baseline of the greedy alignment in [37]. Unlike edit distance-based approaches, our approach can work with a vast amount of data. Also, SYS2VEC doesn't need to learn for correspondence of certain systems into vector representations like OhmNet. Since our systems are separated, and the learning correspondence doesn't bring value for generalizing representation learning, the OhmNet [11] method does not add extra features to the whole-graph embedding generation procedure.

Apart from Machine Learning methods we have experimented, Clustal [42] has been used on our dataset. Initial experiments showed that Hidden Markov Model (HMM) states are way larger than bioinformatics problems. Multiple sequence alignment tools like Clustal takes node coloring into consideration, which corresponds to nucleobases. For system variant analysis case, this can grow based on the features generated from the normalization scheme, and later combined for neighborhood feature incorporation using Weisfeiler-Lehman hashing. Thus, for large graphs, node coloring can have way more elements than nucleobases. While bioinformatics problems have well-known nucleobases (AGCT) to accept as node coloring, they are less than our dataset's distinct variant count. Thus, HMM-based tools are not working with an arbitrary number of node coloring for fixed ordered graphs.

Nevertheless, we have experimented with this approach by changing the Clustal Omega code to accept UTF-8 table characters to see how it will be done in practice. But this gave us a lot of states which took a long time to process. So we have to terminate our experiment because of this method's time complexity. Even with modified Clustal code, we haven't successfully made it work with systems with 91 variants.

VI. Conclusion and Future Work

In this paper, we introduce SYS2VEC, a new approach that analyzes system variants by combining a novel normalization scheme with unsupervised machine learning for fast graph comparison. Moreover, our method improves the time performance in comparison to other machine-learning approaches and can easily be applied to existing system

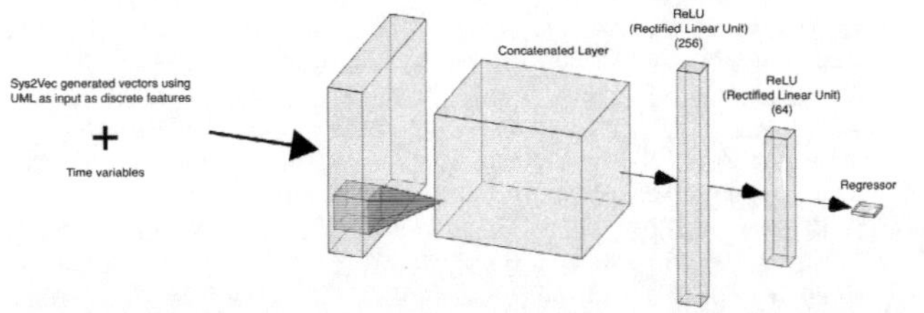

Figure 4: Example evolutionary tree deep learning methodolody using SYS2VEC.

variants. SYS2VEC is exploiting the stochastic nature of the machine learning models to decrease the time taken for pairwise similarity comparison using row vectors in the finite-dimensional vector space. Additionally, our approach enables inference tasks like clustering and trend estimation using supervised methods for variant analysis.

In addition to creating an unsupervised graph comparison method for variant analysis, we have explored various existing machine learning models (e. g., SimGNN [7], FSCNMF [12], OhmNet [11], TADW [14]) for either learning graph structures in a supervised manner to create a heuristic for alignment methods, or learning whole-graph representations to utilize similarity metrics to assemble a comparison heuristic for known graphs.

A. Future Work

SYS2VEC can be used to predict evolution trends with supervised learning methods like LSTM. Supervised methods can be trained with time-series data using our vector representation per time slice to predict the evolution of software and system products. The inference of evolution trends will help to consolidate product lines and will make variant aggregation easier. For this, first using Unified Modeling Language (UML) as variant content input for the SYS2VEC for generating similarity, and then using these similarities and time information to building evolution steps with UML evolutionary notation [43] is possible. As shown in Figure 4, utilizing deep learning and selecting time as a continuous feature in addition to discrete embeddings generated by SYS2VEC is possible to model evolutionary trees.

Our future work will include exploring other similarity measurement methods for variant analysis in SYS2VEC. These include, but are not limited to, Jensen-Shannon distance, first or second Kulczynski coefficients, and Hellinger distance. These methods are promising, since better similarity results can be achieved with them for document learning and classification tasks compared to Euclidean and Manhattan distances [44].

In future research, good exploration can be on Graph Matching Networks [35] as a supervised message passing neural network (MPNN) for embedding generation stage to improve the method's accuracy. Moreover, one of our future explorations will be on unsupervised learning methods like embedding propagation [45]. For improving ordering passes in the normalization scheme, experimenting on token position preserving advanced embedding techniques like Google BERT [46] is another way to improve embedding structure for SYS2VEC. In the long term, we focus on developing time-series-based evolution-prediction (as suggested in Figure 4) with the help of SYS2VEC vector space mapping output, auto-tuning for learning, and the normalization scheme improvements. These improvements will enable aggregating DTIs and allow experimenting on product line consolidation with machine learning methods.

References

[1] D. Faust and C. Verhoef, "Software product line migration and deployment," *Software: Practice and Experience*, vol. 33, no. 10, pp. 933–955, 2003.

[2] N. Shervashidze, P. Schweitzer, E. J. Van Leeuwen, K. Mehlhorn, and K. M. Borgwardt, "Weisfeiler-Lehman graph kernels," *Journal of Machine Learning Research*, vol. 12, pp. 2539–2561, 2011.

[3] Q. Liu, J. Wang, D. Zhang, Y. Yang, and N. Wang, "Text features extraction based on tf-idf associating semantic," *2018 IEEE 4th International Conference on Computer and Communications, ICCC 2018*, pp. 2338–2343, 2018.

[4] T. Demeester, I. Sutskever, K. Chen, J. Dean, and G. Corado, "Distributed Representations of Words and Phrases and their Compositionality," *EMNLP 2016 - Conference on Empirical Methods in Natural Language Processing, Proceedings*, pp. 1389–1399, 2016.

[5] Q. V. Le and T. Mikolov, "Distributed Representations of Sentences and Documents," *31st International Conference on Machine Learning, ICML 2014*, vol. 4, pp. 2931–2939, may 2014.

[6] S. Muhammad Isa, R. Suwandi, and Y. Pricilia Andrean, "Optimizing the Hyperparameter of Feature Extraction and Machine Learning Classification Algorithms," Bina Nusantara University Jakarta, Tech. Rep. 3, 2019.

[7] Y. Bai, H. Ding, S. Bian, T. Chen, Y. Sun, and W. Wang, "SimGNN: A Neural Network Approach to Fast Graph Similarity Computation," *WSDM 2019*, 2020.

[8] C.-L. Lin, "Hardness of approximating graph transformation problem," in *Lecture Notes in Computer Science (including subseries Lecture Notes in Artificial Intelligence and Lecture Notes in Bioinformatics)*, 1994, vol. 834 LNCS, pp. 74–82.

[9] K. Zhang and D. Shasha, "Simple Fast Algorithms for the Editing Distance between Trees and Related Problems," *SIAM Journal on Computing*, vol. 18, no. 6, pp. 1245–1262, dec 1989.

[10] E. D. Demaine, S. Mozes, B. Rossman, and O. Weimann, "An optimal decomposition algorithm for tree edit distance," *ACM Transactions on Algorithms*, vol. 6, no. 1, pp. 1–19, dec 2009.

[11] M. Zitnik and J. Leskovec, "Predicting multicellular function through multi-layer tissue networks," *Bioinformatics*, vol. 33, no. 14, pp. i190–i198, jul 2017.

[12] S. Bandyopadhyay, H. Kara, A. Kannan, and M. N. Murty, "FSCNMF: Fusing Structure and Content via Non-negative Matrix Factorization for Embedding Information Networks," *CoRR*, apr 2018.

[13] L. Van Der Maaten and G. Hinton, "Visualizing data using t-SNE," *Journal of Machine Learning Research*, vol. 9, pp. 2579–2625, 2008.

[14] C. Yang, Z. Liu, D. Zhao, M. Sun, and E. Y. Chang, "Network representation learning with rich text information," Tsinghua University and HTC Beijing Advanced Technology and Research Center, Tech. Rep., 2015.

[15] H. Cai, V. W. Zheng, and K. C. C. Chang, "A Comprehensive Survey of Graph Embedding: Problems, Techniques, and Applications," *IEEE Transactions on Knowledge and Data Engineering*, vol. 30, no. 9, pp. 1616–1637, 2018.

[16] H. Chen and H. Koga, "GL2vec: Graph Embedding Enriched by Line Graphs with Edge Features," in *Neural Information Processing - 26th International Conference, ICONIP 2019, Sydney, NSW, Australia, December 12-15, 2019, Proceedings, Part III*, ser. Lecture Notes in Computer Science, T. Gedeon, K. W. Wong, and M. Lee, Eds. Cham: Springer International Publishing, 2019, vol. 11955, pp. 3–14.

[17] A. Narayanan, M. Chandramohan, R. Venkatesan, L. Chen, Y. Liu, and S. Jaiswal, "graph2vec: Learning Distributed Representations of Graphs," *28th Modern Artificial Intelligence and Cognitive Science Conference, MAICS 2017*, pp. 189–190, jul 2017.

[18] A. Tsitsulin, D. Mottin, P. Karras, A. Bronstein, and E. Müller, "NetLSD: Hearing the Shape of a Graph," in *Proceedings of the 24th ACM SIGKDD International Conference on Knowledge Discovery & Data Mining*. New York, NY, USA: ACM, jul 2018, pp. 2347–2356.

[19] C. Moler and C. Van Loan, "Nineteen dubious ways to compute the exponential of a matrix, twenty-five years later," *SIAM Review*, vol. 45, no. 1, pp. 3–49, 2003.

[20] K. Zhao, Y. Rong, J. X. Yu, J. Huang, and H. Zhang, "Graph Ordering: Towards the Optimal by Learning," *CoRR*, jan 2020.

[21] T. N. Phan, J. Küng, and T. K. Dang, "An Efficient Similarity Search in Large Data Collections with MapReduce," in *Future Data and Security Engineering - First International Conference, FDSE 2014, Ho Chi Minh City, Vietnam, November 19-21, 2014, Proceedings*, ser. Lecture Notes in Computer Science, T. K. Dang, R. Wagner, E. Neuhold, M. Takizawa, J. Küng, and N. Thoai, Eds. Cham: Springer International Publishing, 2014, vol. 8860, no. May 2019, pp. 44–57.

[22] Y. Tian and J. M. Patel, "TALE: A tool for approximate large graph matching," EECS Department, University of Michigan, Tech. Rep., 2008.

[23] D. A. Cusanovich, A. J. Hill, D. Aghamirzaie, R. M. Daza, H. A. Pliner, J. B. Berletch, G. N. Filippova, X. Huang, L. Christiansen, W. S. DeWitt, C. Lee, S. G. Regalado, D. F. Read, F. J. Steemers, C. M. Disteche, C. Trapnell, and J. Shendure, "A Single-Cell Atlas of In Vivo Mammalian Chromatin Accessibility," *Cell*, vol. 174, no. 5, pp. 1309–1324.e18, 2018.

[24] M. Moussa and I. I. Măndoiu, "Single cell RNA-seq data clustering using TF-IDF based methods," *BMC Genomics*, vol. 19, no. Suppl 6, 2018.

[25] M. Grohe, "Word2vec, node2vec, graph2vec, X2vec: Towards a Theory of Vector Embeddings of Structured Data," *Proceedings of the ACM SIGACT-SIGMOD-SIGART Symposium on Principles of Database Systems*, pp. 1–16, 2020.

[26] M. R. B. Clarke, R. O. Duda, and P. E. Hart, "Pattern Classification and Scene Analysis." *Journal of the Royal Statistical Society. Series A (General)*, vol. 137, no. 3, p. 442, 1974.

[27] G. F. Hughes, "On the Mean Accuracy of Statistical Pattern Recognizers," *IEEE Transactions on Information Theory*, vol. 14, no. 1, pp. 55–63, 1968.

[28] G. V. Trunk, "A Problem of Dimensionality: A Simple Example," *IEEE Transactions on Pattern Analysis and Machine Intelligence*, vol. PAMI-1, no. 3, pp. 306–307, jul 1979.

[29] J. H. Lau and T. Baldwin, "An Empirical Evaluation of doc2vec with Practical Insights into Document Embedding Generation," in *Proceedings of the 1st Workshop on Representation Learning for NLP*. Stroudsburg, PA, USA: Association for Computational Linguistics, 2016, pp. 78–86.

[30] T. Akiba, S. Sano, T. Yanase, T. Ohta, and M. Koyama, "Optuna: A Next-generation Hyperparameter Optimization Framework," *Proceedings of the 25th ACM SIGKDD International Conference on Knowledge Discovery & Data Mining*, pp. 2623–2631, jul 2019.

[31] J. Bergstra, R. Bardenet, Y. Bengio, and B. Kégl, "Algorithms for hyper-parameter optimization," in *Proceedings of the 24th International*

[36] X. Ling, L. Wu, S. Wang, T. Ma, F. Xu, A. X. Liu, C. Wu, and S. Ji, "Multilevel Graph Matching Networks for Deep Graph Similarity Learning," *IEEE Transactions on Neural Networks and Learning Systems*, pp. 1–15, jul 2020.

Conference on Neural Information Processing Systems, ser. NIPS'11. Red Hook, NY, USA: Curran Associates Inc., 2011, p. 2546–2554.

[32] R. Řehůřek and P. Sojka, "Software Framework for Topic Modelling with Large Corpora," in *Proceedings of the LREC 2010 Workshop on New Challenges for NLP Frameworks*. Valletta, Malta: ELRA, May 2010, pp. 45–50, %urlhttp://is.muni.cz/publication/884893/en.

[33] S. K. Lam, A. Pitrou, and S. Seibert, "Numba: A LLVM-based Python JIT Compiler," in *Proceedings of the Second Workshop on the LLVM Compiler Infrastructure in HPC - LLVM '15*. New York, New York, USA: ACM Press, 2015, pp. 1–6.

[34] A. H. Ashouri, W. Killian, J. Cavazos, G. Palermo, and C. Silvano, "A Survey on Compiler Autotuning using Machine Learning," *ACM Computing Surveys*, vol. 51, no. 5, pp. 1–42, jan 2019.

[35] Y. Li, C. Gu, T. Dullien, O. Vinyals, and P. Kohli, "Graph Matching Networks for Learning the Similarity of Graph Structured Objects," DeepMind, Google, Tech. Rep., 2019.

[37] V. Tenev, "Directed coloured multigraph alignments for variant analysis of software systems," Bachelor Thesis, University of Kaiserslautern, Germany, 2011.

[38] S. Duszynski, *Analyzing similarity of cloned software variants using hierarchical set models*, ser. PhD theses in experimental software engineering. Stuttgart: Fraunhofer Verlag, 2015, vol. 51.

[39] D. Gusfield, "Efficient methods for multiple sequence alignment with guaranteed error bounds," *Bulletin of Mathematical Biology*, vol. 55, no. 1, pp. 141–154, jan 1993.

[40] L. Chang, X. Feng, X. Lin, L. Qin, W. Zhang, and D. Ouyang, "Speeding Up GED verification for graph similarity search," *Proceedings - International Conference on Data Engineering*, vol. 2020-April, pp. 793–804, 2020.

[41] Z. Abu-Aisheh, R. Raveaux, J. Y. Ramel, and P. Martineau, "An exact graph edit distance algorithm for solving pattern recognition problems," *ICPRAM 2015 - 4th International Conference on Pattern Recognition Applications and Methods, Proceedings*, vol. 1, pp. 271–278, 2015.

[42] F. Sievers, A. Wilm, D. Dineen, T. J. Gibson, K. Karplus, W. Li, R. Lopez, H. McWilliam, M. Remmert, J. Söding, J. D. Thompson, and D. G. Higgins, "Fast, scalable generation of high-quality protein multiple sequence alignments using Clustal Omega," *Molecular Systems Biology*, vol. 7, no. 539, 2011.

[43] R. France and J. Bieman, "Multi-view software evolution: a UML-based framework for evolving object-oriented software," in *Proceedings IEEE International Conference on Software Maintenance. ICSM 2001*, no. Icsm. IEEE Comput. Soc, 2001, pp. 386–395.

[44] K. Rieck KONRADRIECK and F. Pavel Laskov PAVELLASKOV, "Linear-Time Computation of Similarity Measures for Sequential Data," *Journal of Machine Learning Research*, vol. 9, pp. 23–48, 2008.

[45] A. Garcia-Duran and M. Niepert, "Learning Graph Representations with Embedding Propagation," *Advances in Neural Information Processing Systems*, vol. 2017-Decem, no. Nips, pp. 5120–5131, oct 2017.

[46] J. Devlin, M.-W. Chang, K. Lee, and K. Toutanova, "BERT: Pre-training of Deep Bidirectional Transformers for Language Understanding," *NAACL HLT 2019 - 2019 Conference of the North American Chapter of the Association for Computational Linguistics: Human Language Technologies - Proceedings of the Conference*, vol. 1, no. Mlm, pp. 4171–4186, oct 2018.

A Dynamic Threshold Based Approach for Detecting the Test Limits

Cristina Landin†, Jie Liu*§, Sahar Tahvili* ‡
*Product Development Unit, Cloud RAN, Integration and Test, Ericsson AB, Stockholm, Sweden
{sahar.tahvili, anna.a.liu}@ericsson.com
†School of Science and Technology, Örebro University, Örebro, Sweden
cristina.landin@oru.se
‡Mälardalen University, Product Realization, School of Innovation, Design and Engineering, Eskilstuna, Sweden
§Technical University of Berlin, Germany

***Abstract*—Finding a balance between meeting the testing goals and testing resources is always a challenging task. Therefore, employing Machine Learning (ML) techniques for test optimization purposes has received a great deal of attention. However, utilizing ML techniques requires frequently large volumes of data to obtain reliable results. Since the data gathering is hard and also expensive, reducing unnecessary failure or retest in a testing process might end up minimizing the testing resources. Final test yield is a proper performance metric to measure the potential risks influencing certain failure rates. Typically, production determines the yield's minimum threshold based on an empirical value given by the subject matter experts. However, those thresholds cannot monitor the yield's fluctuations beyond the acceptable thresholds, which might cause potential failures in consecutive tests. Furthermore, defining the empirical thresholds as either too tight or too loose in production is one of the main causes of yield dropping in the testing process. In this paper, we propose an ML-based solution that detects the divergent yield points based on the prediction and raises a flag depending on the yield class to the testers when a divergent point is above a data-driven threshold. This flexibility enables engineers to have a quantifiable tool to measure to what extend the different changes in the production process are affecting the product performance and execute actions before they occur. The feasibility of the proposed solution is studied by an empirical evaluation, which has been performed on a Telecom use-case at Ericsson in Sweden and tested in two of the latest radio technologies, 4G and 5G.**

Keywords–Software Testing; Test Optimization; Machine Learning; Regression Analysis; Imbalanced Learning

I. INTRODUCTION

Test optimization is of vital importance for the industry to get better products in quality and also affordability. As the Internet of Things (IoT) is becoming a reality, the demand for faster and cheaper products is increasing. To stay competitive in the market, Telecommunication companies apart to ensure the coverage and the quality of the emerging technologies, also need to optimize the form these products are being tested by reducing waste in the manufacturing process. In 5G (fifth generation) radio technology, the need for faster response, communication speed, capacity, and the number of features has increased remarkably compared to older radio generations. As consequence, the number of tests the new products need to comply with has increased exponentially. Therefore, those innovations demand new optimization methods that need to be applicable to the industry. Data-driven approaches have been shown to be useful in order to predict future trends of continuous data [1]. These trends can be extended to have dynamic thresholds, which give a more realistic approach to the behavior of future points than the currently utilized fixed thresholds. However, fixed thresholds do not give information of behavioral changes of the units tested nor their direction as long as they are within the predefined limits [2]. A method to measure the effectiveness of a production process is to measure its production yield. The yield is one of the major factors directly influencing the manufacturing operational costs [3]. The traditional definition of yield states that yield is proportional to the tested items, which comply with the test specifications or fixed thresholds. As the yield evolves according to the products are being tested, it follows a trend that can be modeled. This model can be useful in fault-localization and fault-prediction by finding the points where the yield diverges from normal production patterns. Furthermore, this model can identify low yield sources at a much earlier production stage compared to current practices and execute preventive actions. Our vision is to use a historical data approach to propose an intelligent framework that defines data-driven thresholds based on the yield predictions and finds abnormal points, thus optimize the test process for future radio generations. Though, this solution work with any kind of product can also be applied as a quality indicator for software testing factories for the similarities of the whole process, as test cases, test suite, and yield. This paper compares different regression methods, after data pre-processing, to predict the final test yield, define dynamic thresholds, and thereby detect the divergences of the characterized trends. Thereafter, the auto labeling process is added to label automatically the data inputs into the following three main labels: Pass, Warning, and Fail by using the Support Vector Machine (SVM) in the yield classification. The new thresholds give insightful information for the execution of future tests and the automatic labeling might also reduce the amount of manual effort in the yield loss analysis. These new thresholds can also be employed to enhance the yield by facilitating the fixed thresholds since they are often determined based on previous experience or by defining some stricter fixed test limits to ensure compliance with the regulators.

TABLE I. TEST REQUIREMENTS EXAMPLE IN THE DIFFERENT STAGES OF TESTING.

Test Requirement according 3GPP	Test Case	Test point
6.6.2 of 3GPP TS36.141 ACLR upper limit $44.2dBc$	Test Case 1: This test case will measure the Adjacent channel leakage power ratio (ACLR) of product A $Configuration$ $Procedure$ $Passcriteria > 45dBc$	$Configuration$ Test point 1.1: Send the right settings to the product Test point 1.2: Set up the carrier Test point 1.3: Send the right settings to the instrument to start measuring the ACLR $Procedure$ Test point 1.4: Measure the ACLR $Passcriteria$ Test point 1.5: Compare the results to the pass criteria

The proposed solution in this paper has a low computational complexity because it is designed to work in an online environment, despite the limitations of the infrastructure. In fact, the chosen ML-based methods have low computational cost, and the complete model is tested using an offline data set, typical of batch production and not access to Cloud compatibility. Moreover, the proposed solution in this study can handle high-dimensional input parameters, therefore it easily can be adapted and utilized in any other domain, e.g., sensors outputs and weather forecast. In order to make the proposed approach more generic and also confirming that transfer learning can be utilized, we trained the model on the 4G data set, and later we tested it on a 5G production data set. Furthermore, the obtained results in this study show a good harmony between the predicted points and the ground truth (the labeled data).

This paper is organized as follows, Section II explains all the theoretical background necessary to understand our approach. Section III the authors aim to compare prior results of similar solutions in close areas of expertise. Section IV explains in a detailed manner each step of the proposed solution to our problem that also can be applied to other research areas. Section V explains more about our data set, characteristics, properties, and types of inputs. The results after applying our solution approach to the given data set: prediction, classification, and validation methods are illustrated in Section VI. Finally, Section VII discusses the limitations, the assumptions, and the great potential of our approach and Section VIII concluded by briefly summarizing the study, results, and the direction of future research.

II. BACKGROUND

This section provides the required academic and industrial concepts and information for understanding the proposed solution in this paper.

A. Testing process of Radio Base Station (RBS)

Radio Base Stations (RBSs) are radio transceivers produced at Ericsson and contain analog and digital components.

To guarantee product quality and coverage, Ericsson follows international Telecommunication standard regulators, e.g., 3GPP for Europe and FCC in North America. The standards are translated into technical documents called test requirements. Each RBS generation has its own test requirements that follow the international regulators. The test requirements contain test cases where each test case is divided into several test points and

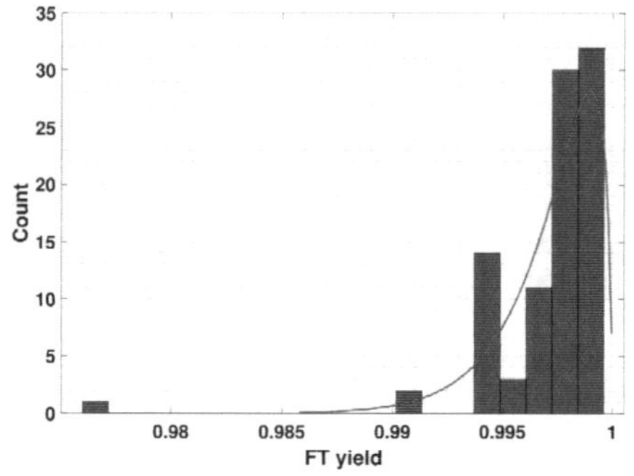

Figure 1. The 4G RBS production final yield (FY) distribution. The FY aims to reach 1 (100%) viz. It is a negatively skewed.

all together make a test suite. The reason for distributing a test case into several test points is the limitations of the product's internal components, the production infrastructures, and also the modularity search. In order to get a better understanding of the analogy between standards, test cases, and test points, Table I provides a hint on how a standard is translated to small units. As we can see in Table I the 3GPP TS36.141 standard requires measuring the power in the adjacent channels of the main transmitting carrier, also Adjacent Channel Leakage Ratio (ACLR). Later, the design team has translated this requirement into the Test Case 1 where it is divided into 5 test points according to the infrastructure limitations (see Table I).

A test case typically tests a specific task to validate certain principles stated in the test requirement and it usually requires input and provides an expected output. The input describes the settings of the products while the output must follow the fixed thresholds given by the test requirements. On the other hand, a test point provides execution details of the different points, which are described in the test case. The test points can be executed in a different sequence, therefore a test suite (which includes several test cases and thereby test points) can be executed in sequential or parallel mode. The sequential execution mode can be beneficial if there is a dependency between test cases, i.e., the success of a test point depends on the success of the previous test points. On the contrary, the parallel execution mode can be useful when test cases are independent. In this paper, we assume that the test cases are independent of each other and can be executed in any order. The analysis of dependency between test cases is outside the scope of this paper and is carried out in an extension paper.

Moreover, in a fixed threshold, the output of the test points

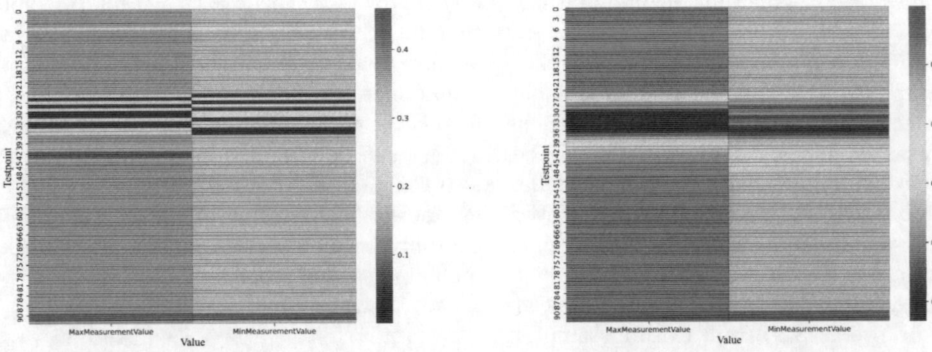

(a) Captured data before smoothing.

(b) Captured data after smoothing.

Figure 2. Heatmap of feature inputs before after smoothing, for a 4G radio product.

depends on compliance with those thresholds. They can be given in form of range (low and high), greater than, equal to, or lower than - of the fixed thresholds, for instance, the Pass criteria $> 45dBc$ in Table I. Furthermore, in this study, only the test points with thresholds within a range are analyzed. However, in any case of having only one threshold, the proposed solution is still valid by assigning both boundaries to the same value.

A production yield is a performance indicator of a product over time, which measures how efficient a manufacturing process is. It also shows how the different changes, e.g., hardware, software, new components -revisions, influence the production process. Figure 1 mirrors the production yield distribution of the data set utilized in this study. As we can see in Figure 1, the production yield in our data set is left-skewed and does not show the Gaussian distribution. The final test yield (FY) is used through this paper, the final test yield is the percentage of good products produced taking into account the reworked products, unlike the First-Time Yield (FTY), which does not consider them. The FY formal definition is given in (2). The FY is chosen as an important feature in the production process of RBS at Ericsson because it gives an insight on how efficient the product is in a determined time slot and can be modeled to predict future patterns based on historical data by using regression methods.

B. Data Smoothing

Data smoothing is a statistical method for eliminating outliers from data to make the important patterns more visible [1]. Another purpose of using smoothing algorithms is to minimize statistical noise from the data set and assist prediction patterns. Some of the most known methods used for data smoothing are the Random method, simple moving average, random walk, simple exponential, and exponential moving average. In this paper, we focus on a single exponential moving average that applies weights to historical data. Those weights make the model focus on the most recent data observations. Therefore, the exponential moving average is more sensitive to the changes if compared to the moving average smoothing method.

Figure 2a shows the heatmap of the original input data before smoothing and Figure 2b after applying exponential moving average. Both figures have the same pattern, though the smoothed version makes the pattern more noticeable.

C. Regression Analysis

In the integration testing level, each test point is a continuous and dependent variable for different independent test configurations. Therefore, the approach to study the FY based on the test results of test points can be considered as a regression problem. The Regression models are being applied for predicting different purposes, they also measure the relationship between the input features and target data. This relationship can be linear or non-linear. There are several kinds of regression models, wherein this paper, linear regression, ridge regression, polynomial regression, and XGboost are applied and compared to each other in order to predict the production yield of RBS.

D. Imbalanced Classification

Once the production yields are predicted (by using the best regression model), then the predicted results need to be classified. The obtained investigations in the domain indicate that this classification suffers from an imbalanced dataset [1]. Therefore, the classification step of the proposed solution can be considered as an imbalanced classification, which is a typical problem in industrial applications. The imbalanced data set refers to a data set that has more labels in one class than the other classes, which makes it difficult to generalize the model. In fact, the problem arises when the important classification lies on the minority represented class. This issue may cause that one class dominates the other classes and that machine learning algorithms have poor performance on the minority class. Furthermore, imbalanced classification has shown to be challenging due to the severely skewed class distribution and also misclassification [1].

Generally, there are two main solutions for imbalanced classification: 1−employing the classification algorithm, which can handle imbalanced data such as IFROWANN (Imbalanced Fuzzy-Rough Ordered Weighted Average Nearest Neighbor Classification [1]) and 2−utilizing some data pre-processing methods to mitigate the imbalanced data sets such as random sampling (in forms of under and oversampling). The random under-sampling randomly removes samples of the over-represented class to match the minority class, while oversampling generates new samples of the under-represented class to match the majority class. However, in the oversampling, since the minority class does not add new information, instead, new samples should be synthesized from existing samples. SMOTE or Synthetic Minority Oversampling Technique, is an over-sampling method that uses the k-Nearest Neighbors (k-NN) to create a synthetic new sample [4]. In fact, the SMOTE model uses the Euclidean distance to calculate every minor point to get the k-nearest points. According to the imbalanced data set X_{origin}, select randomly n sample of the minority class, which will help us to pick up the nearest samples of X and name them X_i. Then randomly generate new samples of the minor class based on these X_{new} as represented in (1), where $i = 1, 2, ...n$. The ratio to generate new samples is $1/IR - 1$, where the Imbalance Ratio (IR) is defined as the ratio of the number of minor class samples to the number of major class samples as stated in [5].

$$X_{new} = X_{origin} + \text{rand}(0, 1) * |X_{origin} - X_i| \quad (1)$$

In this paper, the SMOTE model is used to improve the imbalanced data set for the classification and auto labeling process. On the other hand, SVM is a supervised machine learning algorithm, is used for binary classification by its kernel function, which could transform the data and classify different groups. This margin can be described as a line for two-dimension data and a hyper-plane for multi-dimension data. However, SVM can also be employed for the multi-classification problems by building different SVM models for every two labels. Especially, SVM works more effectively in high dimensional spaces where the feature dimensions are larger than the number of samples. For instance, the tool *One Vs One Classifier* [6] can separate the multiple classes or labels classification task that uses one classifier per class or label, i.e., it breaks down the problem into different binary classifications. In this paper, SVM is used to classify the different levels of acceptance and warning in the monitoring process done in production.

E. Anomaly detection and Fault Prediction

In a complex communication system, such as the production of RBS for 5G and 4G, the production data are collected in form of time series data. Due to the inherent complexity of the test production process of RBSs, the test time must be efficiently minimized, to apply traditional fault diagnosis is limited because it repairs after the fault occurs. In contrast, prognostic health management [7] provides a promising application in production where the variable time is of vital importance. Figure 3 illustrates a block diagram of a data-driven prognostic health management. It monitors relevant data from the process, e.g., production yield, analyzes them, triggers alarms or warnings, and takes actions before the fault appears. Furthermore, by adding failure predictors, it can forecast the fault occurrences [8] before they happened, and then preventing actions can be executed in the monitored system. There are also some other data-driven approaches that can contribute to prognostic health management [2] where the faulty behavior can only be seen when a huge amount of data is viewed in multidimensional space.

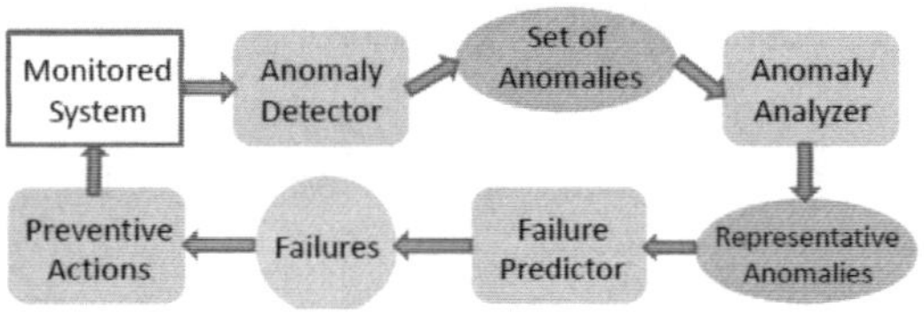

Figure 3. Data-driven prognostic health management (see [7]).

F. Transfer Learning

Many machine learning methods perform better under the assumption that the training and test data have the same distribution or have the same feature space. However, if the mentioned variables change, the algorithms might not perform properly and the methods need to be adjusted based on the changes and further data gathering might be required to update the models. Transfer learning or knowledge transfer can be considered as a potential solution to this problem. In transfer learning, the knowledge obtained in one domain needs to be transferred and applied in another domain. Conversely, another application can be able to train the models using data set from a domain where one has sufficient data and to use the same model in another domain where the data is limited. Transfer learning techniques have been applied to many real-world applications, which show promising results. One of the assumptions of transfer learning is that the source and target domains are related, which otherwise opens the possibility to negative transfer [9]. In this paper, transfer learning is employed by reusing the models found using a 4G (mature product) data set in a 5G radio product. We need to consider that, although 4G and 5G are two different radio generations, however, both products share some similarities.

III. Related Work

In many industrial applications, test cases' limits are still defined by the test requirements as fixed thresholds, and not data-driven modeling of these thresholds is used to optimize the total testing time. Furthermore, there is not enough follow-up of the sources of yield losses. The main goals of this paper are to design a dynamic monitoring tool that supervises critical variables, predicts normal patterns, and sends warning messages to the user when anomalies are observed. One of the methods commonly used in industry is based on sample test measurements such as Process capability index (CPK). CPK is entirely done in offline mode and assumes

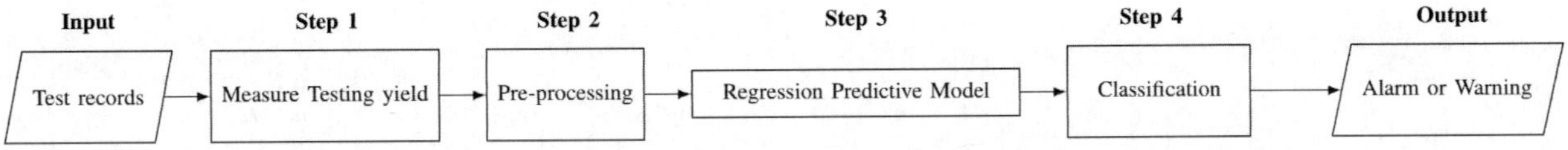

Figure 4. The required input, steps and expected output of the proposed solution in this study.

that the process is consistent over time. Though CPK has worked well in the past in specific samples, it does not give enough information to understand the whole process. For instance, it may perhaps represent only one side of the process when the data distribution is not centered within the specific thresholds [10]. Likewise, most of the methods for anomaly detection found in the literature are based on ruled-based methods, statistic approaches, or a combination of both [11]. Regarding anomaly detection in linear dynamic processes for simple inputs, Cho et al. in [12] studied the behavior of a gas regulator using Multiple output Gaussian Process Regression (MO-GPR) and Extreme Value Theory (EVT) to predict the output and directions of the anomalies. The real-time acquisition and updating of the coefficient are left as future work. Similarly, Chang in [13] uses linear regression to predict the anomalies in mine earthquake and update the counts above a certain threshold in real-time because of the importance of the application. Nevertheless, this method is designed to work online, the author does not use the advantages of machine learning and still uses a fixed threshold, making this solution hard-coded to work with only this application. On the other hand, for multiple inputs, Pang et al. [14] find the anomalies of multiple sensors using Multiple output Gaussian Process (MOGP) and Square Prediction Error (SPE) to find the anomaly score in real monitoring series. In his study, MOGP shows better results than PCA for dimension reduction giving more flexibility and adaptability in the findings of anomalies that otherwise need to be labeled by domain experts or by using fixed thresholds. Those approaches assumed the data set follows a Gaussian distribution, which is not always the case for another kind of application such as the analysis of multi-modal yield distributions. The production yield usually has heavy-tailed distribution as shown in Figure 1. On the data-driven anomaly detection, Chae [15] uses a statistical analysis-based Anomaly-based Detection System (ADS) to set an appropriate anomaly threshold in dynamic environments such as distributed systems. The difficulties the authors faced are multiple due to the inherent problem of dynamic environments and not further comparison between their method and the existing algorithms are explained in the paper. The same authors in [16] find the adaptive thresholds in trust-based detection systems where the anomalies come from known attacks and not 'smart attackers' showing the difficulties this model suffers to adapt to a broader field where there are abrupt changing conditions. Regarding anomaly prediction, Chen et al. [2] study the prediction of system-level test (SLT) failures on system-on-chip (SoC) products where their analog circuits provide space to search faulty behavior by analyzing the outliers. A chip fails when any measured parameter falls outside its specifications, i.e., fixed threshold. However, this is not enough because they might be data points (parameters) that are far away from the nominal values but still comply with the specifications. This approach is the closest we could find to our application due to the similarity of the products, though this approach looks promising, it can not find the root cause of failures. In our case, the yield value of the different test points is analyzed, then whenever we see an abrupt change that does not follow the nominal trend, it will be easy to identify which test point is the source of failure in the whole process. Respecting test yield prediction using machine learning methods, many studies have been done in the last years. Jiang et. al [3] developed a data analysis tool for semiconductor manufacturing that predicts the final test yield in the early stages of production, hence improve the operational efficiency and reduce the production costs. The framework uses Gaussian mixture models (GMM) to identify and cluster the FY, Encoders to manage the difference on categorical or numerical inputs and does not need knowledge of the previous low yield root cause. Furthermore, this paper tries to find the root cause of low yield using the Gini importance. The problem with this approach is that their solution does not take into account the passed values of the important features and does not give importance to how the fixed thresholds can affect the FY. Based on our extensive survey, there are limited studies for FY-related problems in the production of RBS. In general, there are two major common difficulties for RBS FY prediction problems, which are high dimensional input data and complex process variations. For the sake of simplicity, we only use numerical data as inputs, and not feature reduction was used in our solution.

IV. Proposed Solution

This section provides our proposed solution for solving the initial problem stated in Section I. The overall FY for predicting and finding its dynamic thresholds flow framework is illustrated in Figure 4. As can be seen in Figure 4, the required inputs to the proposed solution are the test records, such as the test results recorded after the execution of each test point. As mentioned earlier, the main goal of this paper is to utilize historical test records to predict the normal FY by applying some regression models. The regression models are able to solve the problem with the continuous data, assist the finding of dynamic thresholds, and also the yield classification for optimization purposes. The following paragraphs provide more information regarding the mirrored steps in Figure 4:

- **Step 1. Measure Testing Yield**: the test results of each test point can mainly be divided into *Pass* or *Fail*. For employing the proposed solution in Figure 4, we utilize

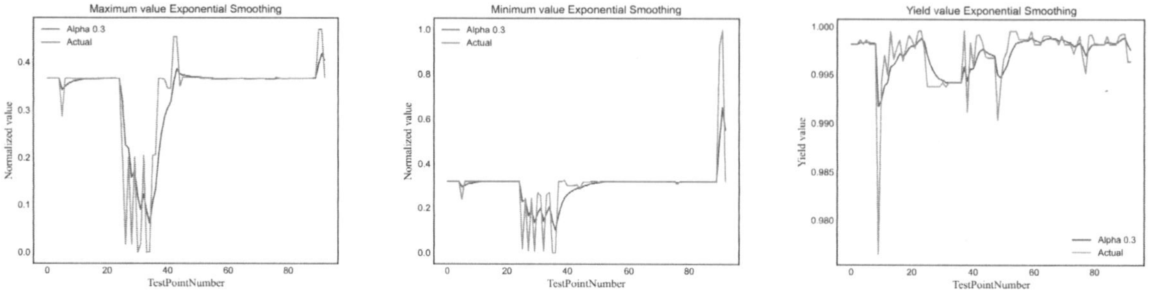

(a) Maximum test inputs. (b) Minimum test inputs. (c) Target test inputs.

Figure 5. The original and smoothed versions of maximum, minimum, and target test inputs for product A.

the final test yield as (2):

$$FY = \frac{Pass\ units}{Total\ processed\ units} \tag{2}$$

Moreover, *Total processed units* is the total number of times that a unit has been tested, then $0 < Yield \leqslant 1$. The yield values closer to 1 mean that the product is mature and around 100% of the products that have been tested have passed. While yield values lower than 0.94 are considered as low yield in our application.

- **Step 2. Pre-processing:** in order to eliminate undesirable characteristics in the data (e.g. anomalies) and use the results values from different test points, we need to normalize the data. Since the measurement results are largely divergent, such as *Temperature* equal to $+50C$ or the *Current* equal to $10mA$, normalization of all the studied test records needs to be done before training the data or feeding it to the machine learning models. For instance, the minimum and maximum measurement values of each test point can be normalized by all the test points in a form of a matrix [17]. Furthermore, to detect the test points' results that are considered abnormal or do not fit any particular pattern, noise removal needed to be applied. Noise in this context contains the values outside the yield range, i.e., 0 to 1 and also the outliers. In our current data set, most test points have extremely good yields because they belong to a mature product. In this study, we utilize smoothing methods to remove the noise in our data set. The smoothing process is based on (3),

$$y_i = \alpha \cdot y_i + (1-\alpha) \cdot y_{i-1} \tag{3}$$

where α is a smoothing factor that defines the forgetting rate of previous values. The lower α indicates the lower weights, which are applied to the true observed values. Moreover, y_{i-1} is the previous model value, and multiplying $(1-\alpha)$ is a solution for the recursive function to smooth the remaining data. We need to consider that α is between 0 and 1, which measures how much the true observation and previous model value influence the stability of data. Basically, the single exponential method here makes use of moving average in the exponential way to decrease the weights. The recursive behavior can be described as (4):

$$y_j = \sum_{i=1}^{j} \alpha(1-\alpha)^{j-i} y_i \tag{4}$$

where the hyper-parameter α is tuned by the grid search method to find the marginal point when the Root Mean Square Error (RMSE) starts to drop. Both, the input features and the target needed to be tuned individually. Therefore, the comparable best α for maximum value input, the one for minimum value input, and for the target all drop at $\alpha = 0.3$. Figure 5 shows the smoothing result for the test inputs (test points) and the target (final test yield) respectively.

- **Step 3. Regression Predicting Model:** as we can see in Figure 4, the output from Step 2 is a set of smoothed and normalized data. Moreover, the minimum and maximum measurement values from each test point execution are employed to build an FY model using regression methods. Our input data in Step 3 is represented as an array X. Each element of the array X has two columns: a minimum and a maximum of each test point. We need to consider that, the assumption here is that all row elements in X are independent:

$$X = \begin{bmatrix} x^{(1)} \\ x^{(2)} \\ \vdots \\ x^{(m)} \end{bmatrix} \tag{5}$$

and Y is the target value that represents the FY, where m is the number of test points.

$$Y = \begin{bmatrix} y^{(1)} \\ y^{(2)} \\ \vdots \\ y^{(m)} \end{bmatrix} \tag{6}$$

Since the relationship between features and target is

unknown, the following regression methods are applied in this paper in order to compare their performance. 1-Linear, 2-Polynomial, 3-Ridge, and 4-XGBoost regression. The mentioned regression methods are chosen due to their low complexity and computational efficiency, which easily can be adapted for solving industrial real cases. The linear regression models a linear relationship between two dependent and independent variables. It can also be modeled using simple linear approximation under the assumption if there is a linear relationship between variables. However, if this assumption is not entirely true and there is under-fitting, polynomial regression can be applied to model the non-linear relationship between inputs and target. In order to avoid the over-fitting problem proper of linear and polynomial regression, the Ridge regression utilizes regularization to punish the learning process to reduce the complexity. Extreme Grading boosting (XGBoost) is a type of Ensemble learning based on decision trees and can be used in regression prediction modeling by applying the advantages of regularization and weak learners. The XGBoost is known to be efficient and fast for prediction purposes. Later in this paper, the evaluation results of all the mentioned regression methods are compared using an industrial case study at Ericsson. The dynamic thresholds are found based on the regression models using three sigma and empirical approximations. This model provides feedback, which allows to update the constants of the formula, to avoid false anomaly detection.

- **Step 4. Classification of Imbalanced Data:** after performing the regression model for the prediction problem in step 3 for the FY measurement, the models are evaluated using RMSE, MAE, through comparing the prediction against the ground truth. In the utilized data set in this study, the best prediction is found for the XGboost model, which has a very low error rate and a much better prediction trend compare to other regression models. The results found using the XGboost model are then used to label the original data set, i.e., 0: Pass, 1: Warning, and 2: Stop. However, this auto-labeled data set is highly imbalanced. For instance, the imbalanced ratio (IR) between labels is 23.25. In order to balance the data set the SMOTE model is applied. The new balanced data set is used for the classification task. In a close consultancy with Subject Matter Expert (SME) at Ericsson, we classified all test points into three main classes: *Pass*, *Warning* and *Stop* using the SVM model. The number of classes is flexible and can be adapted based on the different optimization applications.
  Note that the model tends to find the best classification lines using the linear kernel function. The binary classification models can be seen as logistic regression but the SVM model does not support multi-class classification naturally and require meta-strategies.

Since the main goal of this study is to monitor the production of RBS and alarm the operator or the system manager for abnormal yield risks in advance, the outputs of the proposed solution in Figure 4 can be considered in form of different high-level applications. For instance, the proposed solution can be used as an alarm signal, a pop-up window, or a flag in a more advanced software of the testing process.

V. Industrial Case Study

In order to get a better understanding of the proposed solution in this study, an industrial case study is designed using an ongoing Telecom project at Ericsson AB, Sweden. The provided industrial case study in this work is following the proposed guidelines for conducting and reporting case study research in software engineering by Runeson and Höst [18] and specifically, the way guidelines are followed in [1] and [19].

The units of analysis in the case under study are test points, extracted from an internal database at Ericsson of a 4G RBS from now on called product A and a 5G RBS from now on called product B. The case study is performed in several steps.

TABLE II. Detailed information of product A and B, 4G and 5G RBS respectively, for the conducted case study at Ericsson.

Product A		Product B	
Description	**Quantity**	**Description**	**Quantity**
Test units	1581	Test units	8
Test Points (Pass) with limits	2737	Test Points (Pass) with limits	12643
Test Points (Fail) with limits	165	Test Points (Fail) with limits	408
Test Point classification	1103	Test Point Labeling/classification	286
Test Points yield (0-1)	93	-	-

1) A total number of $5,018,925$ test records are captured from Ericsson's database for product A and 836174 for product B.
2) The captured test records include the following information *Test units* and *test points results (pass or fail)* where the quantity of them are summarized in Table II for product A and B respectively.
3) The final yield, FY, for each test point is measured using (2). Its noise and outliers are smoothed as shown in Figure 5c.

VI. Result

The obtained prediction results in this study are presented in Figure 6 for the linear, polynomial, Ridge, and XGBoost regression models. The upper and lower dynamic thresholds illustrated in Figure 6 are based on our prediction models. The X-axis represents the different test points (sub-parts of test cases) and the Y-axis is FY. The predictions follow the ground truth in most cases, however, the best prediction is found using the XGBoost. For the linear regression, the prediction suffers from the under-fitting problem and finds one divergent point, while in the polynomial there is an over-fitting problem for some points. As can be seen in Figure 6, the yield prediction goes above 1 which is not acceptable, and therefore found three divergent points, which are false alarms. For the Ridge regression, the prediction seems highly optimistic and slightly under-fitting, where it does not consider the divergences proper of the test process and consider them as real divergent points.

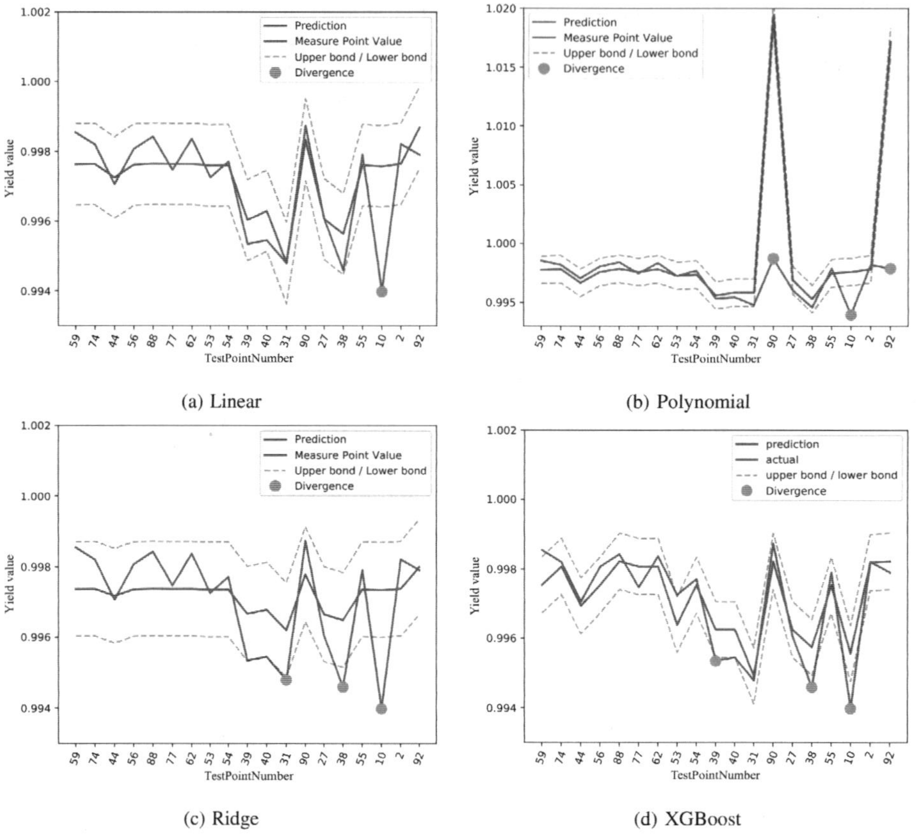

(a) Linear (b) Polynomial

(c) Ridge (d) XGBoost

Figure 6. The smoothed data utilized regression models on product A. The dashed lines are the predicted thresholds.

On the other hand, the XGBoost follows continuously the ground truth and finds also three divergent points which could mean anything according to the sensitivity of the application. In this case, all three divergent points can be classified as normal process behavior but their automatic discovery can save a lot of time for the engineers which otherwise will need to do this analysis manually. The classification model after auto labeling is evaluated by Receiver Operating Characteristic (ROC) curve from prediction scores. ROC curves represent the performance of the classification model. In order to get an optimum result, the iteration was done for a random state, which is a hyperparameter in the SMOTE method of K from 1 to 100 to get the best value to balance the data distribution and eliminate unnecessary noise then fix the random state value to get a consistent result. The best ROC score is 0.94 with K equal to 32. The optimized ROC curve is shown in Figure 7 for product A. The auto labeling process and the usage of the advantages of the SMOTE show an outstanding classification result.

A. Model Performance Evaluation

Besides the graphical results, the evaluation performance for regression predictive modeling is done using the RMSE and MAE, their results are displayed in Table III. The XGBoost model outperforms the other regression models as well, showing better results in both evaluation methods.

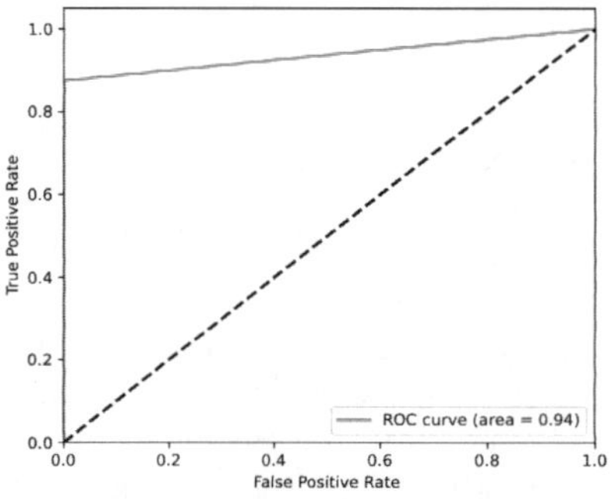

Figure 7. Classification evaluation using ROC for product A.

TABLE III. A SCORES SUMMARY OF THE SMOOTHED DATA VALIDATION.

Model Name	RMSE	MAE
Linear Regression	0.00099	0.067
Polynomial regression	0.0049	0.202
Ridge regression	0.0012	0.095
XGBoost	0.00073	0.00014

B. Model evaluation using unseen data

The problem of predictive modeling is to create models that have an acceptable performance making the predictions on new unseen data [20]. Therefore, the best model trained using product A data set is tested on product B to transfer the knowledge of the mature product and see if the model is still valid for another product with similar characteristics. The model prediction based on the XGBoost regression works for product B as well by detecting the yield divergences. Since product B is not as stable as product A and it is at the beginning of the production process, a minimum threshold of 0.94 of acceptance is necessary to be defined. Unlike product A, which does not have a definitive Fail, product B is labeled as follows: label *2* for yields lower than 0.94 - Fail, label *1* for divergence detected by the regression model- Warning, and label *0* as acceptable yield - Pass. After auto-labeling, this data set is a three-class classification task. The data set is obviously imbalanced. Referring to the solution of the imbalanced data set of product A, the SMOTE is implemented in the data set for product B by separating the data set into two classes at a time. The first one with labels *0* and *1*, the second with labels *0* and *2*, and then combining them. For the multi-label classification, the tool *OneVsRestClassifier* allows to build a classifier per class. For the unseen data set, we have three classes 0, 1 and 2. The evaluation is based on the ROC curve which is demonstrated in Figure 8 for each class. The Macro ROC score is based on the average of each label's individual Precision and Recall, unlike the Micro ROC score which combines all three labels' recall and precision to do the average. The Macro score emphasizes more the small class label and the Micro score is the opposite because considers more the label with the larger class. Here both scores are comparably demonstrating that our labeled data set is well balanced and classified.

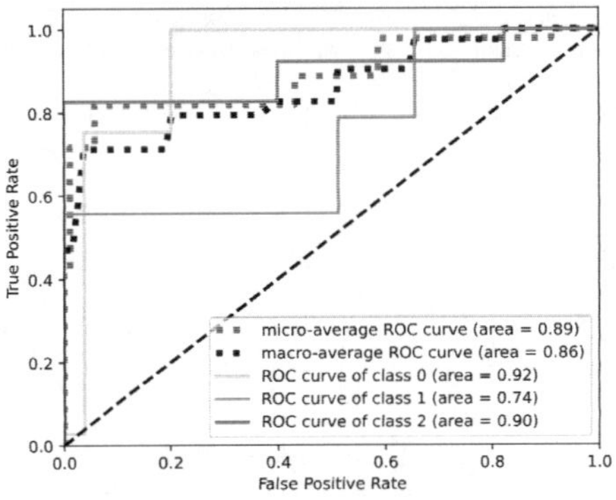

Figure 8. Classification evaluation ROC using unseen data captured from product B.

VII. Discussion

The main goal of this study is to design, implement and evaluate an ML-based solution that estimates the divergences points from dynamic thresholds based on yield predictions of two radio generations instead of using the traditional form to analyze the test process via fixed thresholds. To this end, we have made the following contributions:

- An ML-based approach is proposed for finding the dynamic thresholds for the final test yield (FY) with the purpose to develop a prognostic health management tool to work along the production process. The proposed approach has been implemented as a prototype in Python. It uses the XGBoost regression model to predict the test points' yield evolution and also the SVM model for classification of the predicted yield and automatic labeling of the input features.
- The evaluation of the proposed approach was performed using the test records of a 4G product at Ericsson. Furthermore, the risk of failure for the utilized product has been predicted by performing several regression models.
- The prediction error of the proposed regression models has been measured employing RMSE and MAE and for the classification, the ROC curve has been utilized.
- The proposed solution in this paper is applied to a set of unseen data, using test records of a 5G product. Moreover, the validation of the SVM model for the classification is showing good results. Considering the obtained result opens the possibility to transfer the knowledge learned in one product and use it in another product with similar properties. Furthermore, this approach can be used in an early stage of the testing process to find the largest sources of yield drop [3].

The yield prediction based on test points is modeled using normalized data inputs because the different kinds of testing processes, called test points in this paper, have different amplitude levels. For simplicity, all test points are assumed to have normal distributions and thereof are normalized. No further analysis is done in this paper on whether this normalization influences the final results. According to the reviewed stated of the art, this may differ depending on the application [21]. On the other hand, smoothing methods were implemented to remove the noise and the outliers in both inputs and targets before the prediction modeling was applied using several regression methods. Smoothing is a powerful technique uses in data analysis. Nevertheless applying smoothing in regression analysis to find divergences with respect to normal patterns can be very sensitive, especially when the smoothing process may remove important information one wishes to discover. Studies have been done regarding false positive reduction in networks using smoothing methods [22], the authors highlight the advantages of using smoothing as a method to averaging the unstructured false positives in anomaly detection, thus improve the accuracy. In this paper, we have also seen improvements in the prediction analysis after using smoothing instead of statistical approaches based on quartiles that are better applicable to variables with normal distributions. In this study, we assumed that test points are independent and the sequence of evaluation is not important, which is not always the case in different real-world applications. However, this assumption does not affect the prediction of the final yield because it is based on each test point and its respective evolution through time. The dependency between test points is outside of the scope of this paper but we consider it an important matter in the test optimization, therefore it is left as future work. An important variable in this study is the low computational complexity of the different machine learning methods because the monitor tool is planned to be used in an online mode. Although the whole modeling was done in offline mode due to the limitation of the data set, it is prepared to be implemented as part of a larger test program used at Ericsson production and can accept any kind of inputs, the normalization and removal of outliers are done automatically. The results of the execution of the monitoring tool in a production site are left as future work.

VIII. CONCLUSIONS

In this paper, we have introduced a novel framework to predict the final test yield, proposed new data-driven thresholds based on the predictions, found divergent points, and automatically labeled the results for two of the latest radio generations. This framework is generic and can be applied to any manufacturing process with continuous data sets. Besides, it is robust, scalable, and configurable to adapt to the sensitivity of the application. The pre-processing covers automatic noise and outliers removal by smoothing the inputs and target, inputs' normalization and solve the problem of imbalanced data sets for classification purposes. Four regression models were used successfully to model the historical trends of final test yield, whereof XGBoost showed better performance than linear, polynomial, and Ridge regressions. Firstly, divergent points were found using the prediction model and the dynamic thresholds. Secondly, automatic labeling of the prediction results was implemented using SVM. In our case labels: Pass, Warning, and Stop were relevant, however, the model can be scalable to many other cases where automatic labeling is needed. Hence, preventive actions can be executed before those divergences happen. These actions can be continuing execution with close monitoring or stop the production of one unit and continue with another one, instead of trying to pass the unit after many trials with a risk of suffering quality problems in the near future. Additionally, transfer learning has been briefly studied in this paper. The results show that it is possible to use the modeled trained in a 4G radio product and tested with excellent results in a 5G radio product, giving this approach some kind of generalization with a minimum amount of tuning. One pre-requisite is that the products have some kind of similarity to avoid a negative transfer. Future studies of this work can use the dynamic thresholds to update the test points' current thresholds to secure the values are in a safe region to guarantee acceptable final test yield. Besides, research the percentage of knowledge that is possible to transfer to future radio generations and still keep the quality of the product, thus reducing the amount of time consumed in the manual test optimization (which is still used in many manufacturing areas) will be in focus for future studies.

ACKNOWLEDGEMENT

This work has been supported by the Swedish Knowledge Foundation (KKS) and VINNOVA through CoAIRob industrial research school and INDTECH research school (20200132O1H) and also AIDOaRt project via the ECSEL Joint Undertaking (JU) under grant agreement No 101007350. The JU receives support from the European Union's Horizon 2020 research and innovation program and Sweden, Austria, Czech Republic, Finland, France, Italy, Spain.

REFERENCES

[1] S. Tahvili, L. Hatvani, E. Ramentol, R. Pimentel, W. Afzal, and F. Herrera, "A novel methodology to classify test cases using natural language processing and imbalanced learning," *Engineering Applications of Artificial Intelligence*, vol. 95, pp. 1–13, August 2020.

[2] H. . Chen, R. Hsu, P. Yang, and J. Shyr, "Predicting system-level test and in-field customer failures using data mining," in *IEEE International Test Conference*, 2013.

[3] D. Jiang, W. Lin, and N. Raghavan, "A novel framework for semiconductor manufacturing final test yield classification using machine learning techniques," *IEEE Access*, vol. 8, pp. 197885–197895, 2020.

[4] N. Chawla, K. Bowyer, L. . Hall, and W. Kegelmeyer, "Smote: Synthetic minority over-sampling technique," *J. Artif. Int. Res.*, vol. 16, p. 321–357, June 2002.

[5] L. Ma and S. Fan, "Cure-smote algorithm and hybrid algorithm for feature selection and parameter optimization based on random forests," *BMC Bioinformatics*, vol. 18, 03 2017.

[6] F. Pedregosa *et al.*, "Scikit-learn: Machine learning in Python," *Journal of Machine Learning Research*, vol. 12, pp. 2825–2830, 2011.

[7] S. Jin, K. Chakrabarty, and Z. Zhang, "Anomaly-detection-based failure prediction in a core router system," in *International Conference on Advances in System Testing and Validation Lifecycle*, 2016.

[8] A. Gainaru, F. Cappello, M. Snir, and W. Kramer, "Fault prediction under the microscope: A closer look into hpc systems," in *SC '12: Proceedings of the International Conference on High Performance Computing, Networking, Storage and Analysis*, pp. 1–11, 2012.

[9] J. Pan and Q. Yang, "A survey on transfer learning," *IEEE Transactions on Knowledge and Data Engineering*, no. 10, pp. 1345–1359, 2010.

[10] O. Khan, "A practical guide to utilizing cp and cpk," *Understanding Statistics for Quality by Design*, p. 1, 2015.

[11] V. Chandola, A. Banerjee, and V. Kumar, "Anomaly detection: A survey," *ACM Comput. Surv.*, vol. 41, pp. 1–58, July 2009.

[12] W. Cho, Y. Kim, and J. Park, "Hierarchical anomaly detection using a multioutput gaussian process," *IEEE Transactions on Automation Science and Engineering*, vol. 17, no. 1, pp. 261–272, 2020.

[13] L. Li and J. Chang, "Real-time detection for anomaly data in microseismic monitoring system," in *2009 International Conference on Computational Intelligence and Natural Computing*, pp. 307–310, 2009.

[14] J. Pang, D. Liu, Y. Peng, and X. Peng, "Multiple-output-gaussian-process regression-based anomaly detection for multivariate monitoring series," in *2018 Prognostics and System Health Management Conference (PHM-Chongqing)*, pp. 326–332, 2018.

[15] Y. Chae, N. Katenka, and L. DiPippo, "An adaptive threshold method for anomaly-based intrusion detection systems," in *2019 IEEE 18th International Symposium on Network Computing and Applications (NCA)*, pp. 1–4, 2019.

[16] Y. Chae, N. Katenka, and L. Dipippo, "Adaptive threshold selection for trust-based detection systems," in *IEEE 16th International Conference on Data Mining Workshops*, pp. 281–287, 2016.

[17] S. Tahvili, R. Pimentel, W. Afzal, M. Ahlberg, E. Fornander, and M. Bohlin, "sortes: A supportive tool for stochastic scheduling of manual integration test cases," *Journal of IEEE Access*, pp. 1–19, 2019.

[18] P. Runeson and M. Höst, "Guidelines for conducting and reporting case study research in software engineering," *Empirical Software Engineering*, vol. 14, no. 2, p. 131, 2008.

[19] S. Tahvili, *Multi-Criteria Optimization of System Integration Testing*. PhD thesis, Mälardalen University, December 2018.

[20] S. Tahvili, W. Afzal, M. Saadatmand, M. Bohlin, and S. Ameerjan, "Espret: A tool for execution time estimation of manual test cases," *Journal of Systems and Software*, vol. 161, pp. 1–43, September 2018.

[21] P. Sherman, "Tips for recognizing and transforming non-normal data." available at https://www.isixsigma.com/tools-templates/normality/tips-recognizing-and-transforming-non-normal-data/, Aug 2021.

[22] M. Grill, T. Pevný, and M. Rehak, "Reducing false positives of network anomaly detection by local adaptive multivariate smoothing," *Journal of Computer and System Sciences*, vol. 83, no. 1, pp. 43–57, 2017.

Developing for Testability: Best Practices and the Opinion and Practice of OutSystems Professionals

Fernando Reinaldo Ribeiro[1,2], José Carlos Metrôlho[1,2], Joana Salgueiro[2]
[1]R&D Unit in Digital Services, Applications and Content
[2]Polytechnic Institute of Castelo Branco
Castelo Branco, Portugal
e-mail: fribeiro@ipcb.pt, e-mail: metrolho@ipcb.pt, e-mail: joana.salgueiro@ipcbcampus.pt

Abstract— **Implementing best practices during the software development process can significantly influence the test automation process. This is true in all software applications, regardless of the platform or the programming language used, but it is even more important when the software is developed using low-code development platforms. These platforms are commonly used together with agile methodologies, and they are designed to accelerate software development with a minimum of hand-coding. Generally, when using these platforms and methodologies, the focus is on verbal and informal communication rather than documentation. The focus is on getting high-quality source code, adequate test sets, and greater interaction with the end customer. This highlights the need to use best practices in software development to achieve better quality software and facilitate the test automation process. In this work, we analyse the test automation on low-code development platforms and, more specifically, how the best practices for OutSystems development influence the test automation process. A survey on the opinion and practice of OutSystems platform professionals, 27 respondents, is also analysed and discussed. The goal is to understand how they recognise the influence that best development practices have on the testing automation process and how they apply these best practices in their daily activities.**

Keywords- low-code platforms; OutSystems; software quality, software testing; test automation.

I. INTRODUCTION

More than 3,300 IT professionals in all kinds of industries share their insights in a research report on the state of application development. Findings from this report [1] show that forty-one per cent of respondents said their organisation was already using a low-code platform, and a further 10% said they were about to start using one. They also report that the number of applications respondents had planned for delivery in 2019 was 60% higher than the assessment they had done in the previous year. This growing demand is one of the reasons why most organisations have invested in customer-centric practices in the past year (2018), including agile (60%), design thinking (30%), customer journey mapping (20%), and lean UX (11 %) [1]. These results show the growing interest in adopting agile methodologies and adopting Low-Code Development Platforms (LCDP). Similar conclusions are also presented by the Low-Code Development Platform Market [2], as it is notice that the global LCDP market size is projected to grow at a rate of 28.1% during the 2020-2026 period. These studies show the growing popularity of LCDP and its growing adoption by IT companies. They may help fill the gap between business and IT through abstraction and automation and accelerate the software release time.

Some of the reasons that have been used to justify this growth are the same ones that are often pointed out as advantages of these platforms: they allow to reduce the software delivery time and to update and deliver new features in shorter periods [3]; they allow applications to be built for multiple platforms simultaneously [3]; they integrate many of the same tools' functionalities that developers and teams use to design, code, deploy and manage their applications [4]; developers may still need to do some coding for a specific task, but a significant part of the job can be done through the drag-and-drop interface [5], and many of the data integration features have already been developed and can be easily customised. [3]. Also, LCDP are often associated with agile development (e.g., [6][7]), which have implications for the way tests are managed. This is because agile methodologies are based on reduced use of documentation and more frequent interactions with end-users. However, it is also because, in certain situations, the testing process may derail some of the benefits associated with the low-code development and agile methodologies. Bug fixing and application scalability are made easier in these platforms using high-level abstractions and models, but low-code development is not synonymous with error-free development. LCDP democratise application development to software practitioners with distinct backgrounds. This brings more professionals to IT areas, reskilling some of them from different areas of knowledge and greater employability difficulties, but the lack of specialised knowledge can lead to a higher number of bugs in the developed software. This further highlights the need to test the software developed on these platforms and the importance of studying various test strategies and tools that best suit these platforms. A study [8] of around 5K Stack Overflow forum posts that contain discussions of nine popular LCDP found that most of the questions are related to the development phase, and low-code developers also face challenges with automated testing. Low-code development introduces new concepts and characteristics that led to new challenges and opportunities in the software testing process.

Some of the best practices that should be used during software development are discussed, and a study to understand how OutSystems professionals know and apply these best practices and how they value testing activities in software developed at OutSystems LCDP is presented and discussed. We choose this platform because it is a platform widely used by software development companies in Portugal and because we have a collaboration with that company for several years, under which we have accessible software licenses. Another important fact in the choice is that this platform is one of the leaders in the low-code market [9]. The goal is to investigate the importance of the best practices in low-code development, their impact on the test automation process, and to understand how professionals know and apply these best practices. As a methodology to achieve this goal, the influence of best practices in low-code development in the software testing process was first analysed and then a survey was carried out to understand the professionals' opinion and practice. Section 1 presents a brief overview of the problem under study and presents its motivation and objectives. Section 2 describes some works that addressed test automation on low-code platforms. Section 3 presents background about test automation on LCDP and analyses the best practices for OutSystems development and its influence on test automation. Section 4 presents and discusses the results based on a survey about the opinion and practice of OutSystems platform practitioners about best practices in development in low-code software testing automation. Finally, Section 5 presents some conclusions that were obtained while conducting this study.

II. RELATED WORK

Software testing and test automation are essential topics that deserve the attention of everyone involved in the software development process, regardless of the technologies or the methodologies they used. However, in the specific case of software developed using LCDP, usually following agile methodologies, there is not much documentation and research on this topic.

Some well-known LCDP have made efforts to provide some documentation on this topic and provide tools to support testing activities. The Mendix Application Test Suite [10] is a suite of tools for embedding testing in the application lifecycle. These tools are built-in Mendix, on top of Selenium. In Power Apps, testing can be performed with test studio [11] that is developed specifically to support automated end-to-end UI testing of an application. OutSystems provide the BDD Framework [12] that is an open-source application that provides a set of tools for producing Behaviour Driven Development (BDD) Test Scenarios and can also be used for automated testing. Other studies have looked at various LCDPs to compare their approaches to testing. In [13] five commercial LCDP (Mendix, Power Apps, Lightning, Temenos Quantum, OutSystems) were analysed to identify low-code testing advancements from a business point of view. They analyse the testing facilities embedded in each platform and they identify some challenges when testing low-code software. When using LCDP, automation is possible on all test levels. Component testing is essential for developers to test the software they develop. Moreover, as low-code applications use many integrations to other services using APIs, besides system/ End-to-End tests, automated integration/API tests are also essential. A good testing strategy enables continuous quality assessment and is essential. It is well known that development practices influence the test automation process. It is therefore important that developers know and apply best practices in development to facilitate subsequent testing activities. In this context, some works have analysed the development/tests relationship when LCDP is used. A study of the test automation process on the OutSystems low-code development platform is described in [14]. Their focus is on Unit, Integration / API and System / End-to-End testing levels. Their examples illustrate that the implementation of best practices during the development process can have a significant influence on the test automation process.

Few research works address test automation on LCDP and how development practices influence testing activities. It is necessary to study this relationship and understand the awareness of LCDP professionals regarding the importance of testing the software developed using LCDP.

III. LOW-CODE SOFTWARE TESTING AUTOMATION

Automated testing is essential, and there are many situations where these approaches are more beneficial than manual testing approaches. These advantages are important, especially when it may be helpful to repeat tests already carried out, such as regression tests. Nevertheless, there are other advantages. Manual testing is often complex, or impractical, or can be time-consuming and vulnerable to inaccurate results. Test automation enables continuous quality assessment and may save significant time and effort. In LCDP, test automation is possible on different tests such as unit tests, Integration/API tests, System/E2E tests, etc. However, the specific features of those platforms raise a set of challenges in low-code testing. Some of these challenges are identified in [13], namely:

- The role of citizen developer and its low-level technical knowledge in the testing activities: Test cases are usually derived from the requirements, and it is common to involve partners with low-level technical knowledge in the testing activities, which poses some challenges.
- The importance, and the challenges, in offering high-level test automation: In software developed using LCDP, several situations should be continuously tested (e.g., many integrations to other services, and these integrations should be continuously tested). To facilitate test automation, these tools should allow high-level test automation,

be undemanding technical skills, and require little manual scripting for writing tests.

- Leveraging the cloud for executing tests and for supporting testing of cloud-based applications: LCDP are cloud-based and they support the development of cloud-based applications using cloud resources. Test automation must be adapted to this environment.

Despite the challenges it raises, test automation allows continuous quality assessment, and it is essential in agile and low-code development. To be efficient and beneficial, it is also vital that best practices are used during development. This can help to reduce the work required for test automation and significantly reduce the need to write manual scripting.

A. *Testing on the OutSystems Low-Code Development Platform*

Low-code development is often associated with error-free development. However, although these platforms provide several features that allow reducing the probability of errors occurring, they can always occur, introducing bugs that may later lead to failures in the software. In the OutSystems LCDP, several features are available that help developers to develop software with fewer bugs and consequently with better quality. The OutSystems platform performs continuous integrity validation that checks the impact of all changes in application layers (data model, business logic or presentation) to ensure that everything is integrated at the time of implementation. When changes are made in the applications data models, API, and architecture, the OutSystems platform automatically updated all existing dependencies. At a more general level, the OutSystems platform performs an impact analysis for multiple applications when creating deployment plans, evaluating the impact of moving new versions of selected applications to the target environment before the deployment is performed. As a result of this process, the number of bugs introduced is generally lower than traditional development technologies, leading to fewer test cycles and issue fixes, reducing the effort associated with development and delivery.

Despite this support provided by the OutSystems platform, there is no guarantee that errors will not occur, and the need for testing remains. Therefore, the life cycle of an OutSystems application includes several stages when testing activities must be performed. The four levels of testing, provided in the International Software Testing Qualifications Board (ISTQB) classification [15], are included:

- Component Tests are used to verify the behaviour of code units. In some cases, code units are not easily accessible to be tested. The developers deliver these tests as part of the activities developed in the sprint performed in the development environment (DEV) and the continuous integration environment (CI). Usually, they are automated tests performed using the BDD Framework [16].
- Integration Tests are tests to verify the integration with external systems. These tests are critical since it is widespread that LCDP make use of external API. These tests must be performed in the DEV environment by the developers or Quality Assurance (QA). These tests can be automated.
- System Tests are usually run through a web or mobile interface. They are performed considering the perspective of the end-user or the system (End-to-End tests). The quality team can automate this type of test if they are UI tests. Usually, they are performed in a quality QA environment.
- The clients perform Acceptance Tests. Usually, they are performed manually in the QA environment.

Also necessary, the Regression Tests. They must be used whenever new features are added. In addition to these tests, other tests are also planned, such as Security Tests and Performance Tests.

B. *Best Practices for OutSystems Development and its Influence on Test Automation*

Regardless of the development platform or programming language used, applications must be developed to facilitate testing activities to facilitate tests that validate its correctness. This is often called developing for testability. To make this possible, there is a set of good practices, architectural and design decisions, which must be followed. Some of these best practices are applicable when developing applications on the OutSystems platform, but they are also applicable when applications are developed on other LCDP or programming languages. Some of these practices can significantly facilitate test automation at various levels, and their influence on the testing process has already been studied (e.g., [14]). For example:

- Integration Tests (API tests): to facilitate the automation of these tests, it is important to isolate the API consumption in a specific module that exposes the API methods through public actions. Other modules, which need access to the API, will have to do it through this specific module, avoiding implement and run tests on every module that is consuming this specific API.
- System Tests: in this case, test automation usually involves simulating and recording a user's interactions in a browser to complete the functionality under test. To be less hard work, test automation tools, which are being used, should correctly identify the web elements found on the web page. To make it possible, it is necessary that the web elements identifiers (names and ID) are easily found and identified by the test tool. It often implies the use of personalised identifiers in place of the identifiers assigned by the development

platforms. In applications developed in OutSystems, those elements should be appropriately identified in Service Studio by the developer. The developer must customise the elements' identifiers to ensure that all elements have an identifier that would be uniquely identified during the test automation process. This will have a positive effect on the test automation process but, on the other hand, will require more time and more resources and can be a complex task for developers without specialised skills.

These practices, and their effect on the test automation process, are known. Nevertheless, it is important to know how they are applied and the opinion and practices of professionals regarding their use. This is particularly important when referring to LCDP professionals since the allocation of time to facilitate or develop the tests, and the adoption of certain development practices can undermine some of the benefits associated with the use of low-code platforms.

IV. Opinion and Practice of OutSystems Platform Practitioners

In this section, we present the survey addressed to IT professionals, with experience in OutSystems development. The goal is to analyse their perception of the importance of software testing in low-code development and the influence of the best development practices in test automation.

A. *Survey*

The survey was disseminated among professionals from 4 software companies that use the OutSystems LCDP to develop their products and was organised in two parts. The first part was aimed to characterise the respondents regarding their experience in the IT area and, in particular, their experience with LCDP and in the area of software testing and quality. This part had seven questions about: age; years of experience in IT; technologies/software development tools that they use, or have used, in their professional activity; LCDP that they use/have used in their professional activity; activities/roles to which they dedicate more time in their professional activity; if their professional activity involves development, for which platforms they develop; and most common development methodologies in the projects in which they have participated. With this first part of the survey, we were able to characterise the universe of respondents in terms of experience, roles, skills and dominant activity of their respective professional activities. We had the participation of 27 respondents.

The second part was intended only for participants who had some experience in testing activities. The objective was to allow a characterisation of the respondents to perceive testing activities and how functionality description and development practices influence test automation activities. Furthermore, it was also an objective to obtain a characterisation about the tools they use for testing. This part had nine questions, where information was collected about: the importance they give to testing; difficulty in deciding what should be tested; how the way of describing the functionalities (use cases, user stories, etc.) contribute to facilitating the test design; how the way the code is developed contributes to facilitating the test activity (write, implement, and execute the test cases); the way the test cases are written; types of functional tests that are performed more frequently; tools/platforms used to perform the tests; opinion about the BDD Framework (if used by the respondent); for those who use the BDD Framework, opinion on advantages and disadvantages of it. We had the participation of 25 respondents for this part.

From the analysis of the responses to the first part of the survey, we conclude that:

- Most of the participants in the survey (48.1%) are between 26 and 30 years old, and 25.9% are between 36 and 40 years old.
- In terms of years of experience in IT, 88.8% of the respondents have between 3 and 15 years of experience, 40.7% have between 3 and 5 years, 25.9% have between 6 and 10 years, and 22.2% have between 11 and 15 years.
- Regarding the technologies used, most of the respondents answered that they use, or have used, HTML/CSS, JavaScript, C#, Java, and PHP.
- Regarding the LCDP that they use/ have used in their professional activity, all the participants answered that they use, or have used, OutSystems. Two of them pointed out that they have also used two other LCDP.
- As for the feedback on the professional activity to which the participants currently devote more time, we found that almost 59.3% of respondents are developers and 22.2% of respondents are team leaders or managers.
- In terms of target platforms (web, Android, iOS or Multiplatform), we obtained 26 responses, of which 73.1 % of respondents indicated multi-platform and 26.9% for the web.
- Regarding the development methodology that is most common in the participants' projects, only 1 of the participants answered "Lean", while the remaining 26 participants answered Scrum.

In summary, the sample involved an experienced population, from 4 different companies, with development experience in OutSystems, experience in Agile Scrum methodology and in several development technologies, and mainly composed of staff dedicated to both web and multi-platform development tasks.

B. *Data analysis and discussion*

The second part of the survey was addressed only to professionals with experience in software testing.

- The question of this part was intended to find out how the participants see the testing activity. With a total of 25 answers, 100% of the participants considered that "Testing is important and should be performed regardless of the development methodology used".

- The second question, to evaluate the difficulty of the participants in evaluating what should be tested and how it should be tested, revealed that 52% of the respondents (13 of 25 feel these difficulties sometimes and still 16%, 4 participants, feel difficulties many times.
- From the 25 respondents, 13 answered that they strongly agree, and 9 that they agree that the way functionalities are described (use cases, user stories, etc.) contribute to facilitating the test design. The other 3 respondents had no opinion.
- To the question, "Does the way the code is developed contribute to facilitating the testing activity (write, implement, and execute the test cases)?", 11 out of 25 participants answered that they agree, eight answered that they strongly agree, five neither agree nor disagree, and only one answered that he disagrees. In other words, 76% (19 out of 25) of the respondents acknowledge that the way they develop their software has implications on the testing activities of that software.
- 33.3% of the participants (8 of 24) answered that they use common sense to write the test cases, and 45.8% (11 of 24) answered that they use recognised design techniques, such as BDD (Given - When - Then) and user stories acceptance criteria.
- To the question "In your testing activities, when you perform functional tests, at what level do you perform the most frequently?", 23 respondents answered, of which 73.9% of the participants (17 out of 23) answered that they perform unit/component tests, 17.4% (4 out of 23) answered that they perform system tests and, finally, 8.7% (2 out of 23) answered that they perform integration tests. These answers seem to be in line with the fact that a significant number of the respondents are currently developers, and therefore unit/component testing is more common.
- 14 respondents answered to the question "If your professional activity includes implementation and execution of tests, and if you use any testing tool, please indicate which you have used". All of them (14) pointed out that they have used BDD Framework, and 1 respondent has also used Tricentis Tosca and Katalon.
- Regarding the experience with the BDD Framework tool, it was asked that "If you use BDD Framework in your testing activity, how do you rate your experience with this tool?". In response, 53.3% of the participants (8 out of 15) answered that they have had or have a positive experience, 33.3% (5) answered that the experience was neither positive nor negative, and finally, 13.3% (2) of the participants answered that they have had or have a very positive experience with BDD Framework.
- Finally, the last question allowed respondents to write an open-ended answer to the following question "In relation to your answer to the previous question; please indicate the most positive aspect (strength) and the most negative aspect (weakness) of the tool you use". All respondents reported having used the BDD Framework tool. In their opinion the strengths of the BDD Framework, in the opinion of the participants are:
  - Ease of use and organisation of tests.
  - Tests are developed oriented to the user story, which enables task-test mapping.

  The weaknesses mentioned were the following:
  - Heavy reliance on the user story.
  - If the user story is not well written, the tests may not be implemented correctly.
  - Requires extra time to implement, which can have a significant impact on the project delivery time.
  - In agile, if the requirements change a lot, the tests developed may become useless, and therefore there is a waste of time.
  - It generates an extra effort in preparation.

  In other words, some limitations to the use of BDD Framework are pointed out by some of the survey respondents, but it is a user-friendly tool. The fact that tests are related to user stories is also a point of disagreement among the participants because some say that it enables task-test mapping while others say that they are dependent on user stories.

A cross-check was also done to analyse the impact of years of experience in the testing activities. That is, to analyse if there are some relationships between the number of years of experience and the knowledge or techniques applied at the testing process. First, the relationship between the number of years of experience and their perception of how the application code is developed to facilitate the testing activity was analysed. In this context, the inclusion of the best practices during the software development is of fundamental importance. As can be seen in Figure 1, only 25% of the participants who have between 11 and 15 years of experience disagree that the way code is developed can facilitate the implementation of tests. All professionals with more than 16 years of experience (despite the low number of respondents) strongly agree that the way code is developed to facilitate the implementation of tests. These results seem to suggest that professionals with more experience are more aware of this issue.

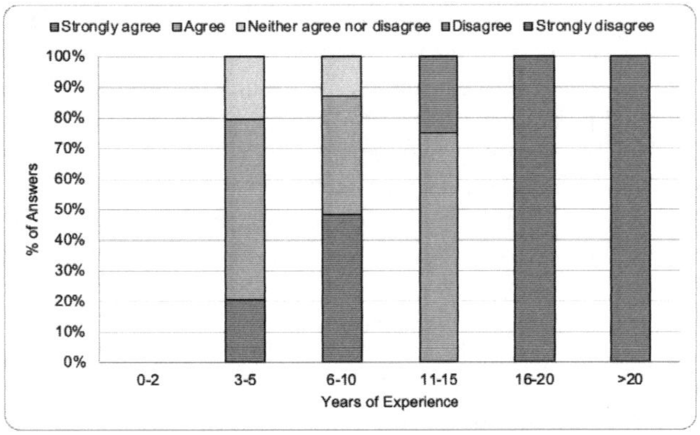

Figure 1. Years of experience vs how the code is developed.

The relationship between years of experience and difficulty in the testing activity was also analysed (see Figure 2). There are slots with more experience (6-10 and 11-15) that express difficulties more often than participants with between 3 and 5 years of experience. Overall, the results to this question seem to indicate that there is no cause-effect relationship between the years of experience and difficulty in the testing activity. The difficulties in testing, manifested by the respondents, were transversal to all professionals.

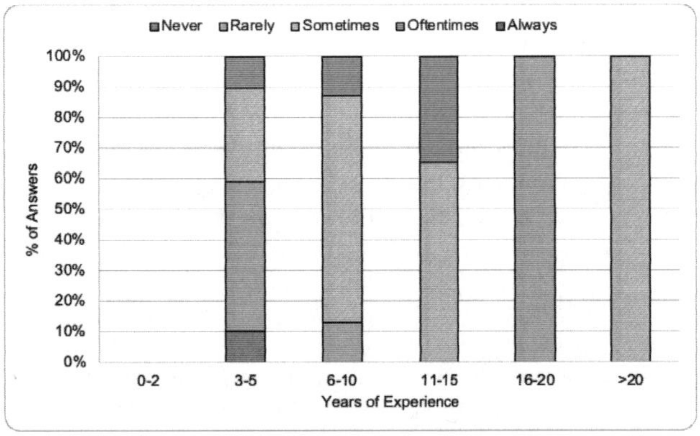

Figure 2. Years of experience vs difficulties in testing activities.

The relationship between years of experience and the way they plan and write test cases was also analysed and presented in Figure 3. In this case, the data is quite similar, and many participants still use only common sense as a way of writing tests regardless of their years of experience. These results reveal that participants do not have training in this area to know and use more test writing techniques to optimise this component of their work.

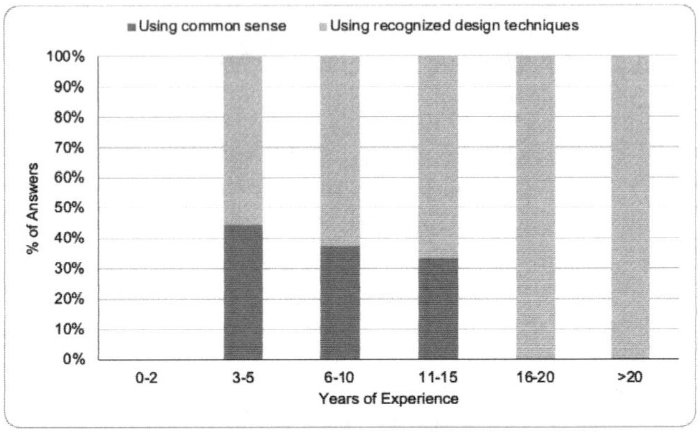

Figure 3. Years of experience vs the way they plan and write test cases.

V. Conclusion and Future Work

Regardless of the development platform or programming language used, applications must be developed to facilitate testing activities to facilitate tests that validate its correctness. To achieve this, a set of good practices, architectural and design decisions, must be followed. These practices, and their effect on the test automation process, are well known. This becomes particularly important when the software is developed using an LCDP since the allocation of time to facilitate or develop the tests, and the adoption of certain development practices can undermine some of the benefits associated with the use of LCDP.

To understand the opinion of IT professionals about the importance of software testing and their perception of the importance of best development practices and their influence on the process of test automation, a survey was conducted. The respondents that work with OutSystems, have some experience with testing activities and use the BDD Framework as a test implementation tool. Although it is the tool most used by the participants and is easy to use, it has some weaknesses in the participants' opinion. All of them recognise the importance of testing regardless of the type of application to be developed, and more than 50% recognise that they often have some difficulty assessing what should be tested and how. They also express the influence that the way functionality is described and how software is implemented have on the process of testing activity.

It results from the analysis made in the study presented in this paper that developing for software testability is recognized as very important also in the case of LCDP. The code abstraction allowed by these platforms does not exclude the need to follow best practices during the development cycle. It is also important that professionals have knowledge of adequate testing techniques and tools that allow more support for testing activities. This stage, due to the importance it assumes for the delivery of high-quality products, requires care so that (as with software development) it is carried out quickly and completely.

REFERENCES

[1] OutSystems, "State of Application Development Report 2019/2020," 2019.

[2] Marqual IT Solutions Pvt. Ltd (KBV Research), "Global Low-Code Development Platform Market By Component By Application By Deployment Type By End User By Region, Industry Analysis and Forecast, 2020 - 2026," Report, 2020. [Online]. Available: https://www.kbvresearch.com/low-code-development-platform-market/ (accessed Aug. 31, 2021).

[3] J. Idle, "Low-Code rapid application development - So, what's it all about?," *Platinum Business Magazine*, pp. 52–53, 2016.

[4] OutSystems, "The Low-Code Development Guide," 2019. https://www.outsystems.com/low-code-platforms/ (accessed Jul. 01, 2021).

[5] C. Boulton, "What is low-code development? A Lego-like approach to building software," *CIO (13284045)*, 2018. https://intellyx.com/2018/03/27/what-is-low-code-development-a-lego-like-approach-to-building-software/ (accessed Jul. 01, 2021).

[6] J. C. Metrôlho, F. R. Ribeiro, and P. Passão, "Teaching Agile Software Engineering Practices Using Scrum and a Low-Code Development Platform – A Case Study," in *The Fifteenth International Conference on Software Engineering Advances*, 2020, no. c, pp. 160–165.

[7] "Mendix Predicts Low-CodeOps Will Deliver Radical New Efficiencies for IT Operations," 2021. https://www.mendix.com/press/mendix-predicts-low-codeops-will-deliver-radical-new-efficiencies-for-it-operations/ (accessed Jul. 19, 2021).

[8] M. A. Al Alamin, S. Malakar, G. Uddin, S. Afroz, T. Bin Haider, and A. Iqbal, "An Empirical Study of Developer Discussions on Low-Code Software Development Challenges," in *Mining Software Repositories Conference*, 2021, p. 12.

[9] J. R. Rymer and R. Koplowitz, "The Forrester Wave^{TM}: Low-Code Development Platforms For AD&D Professionals, Q1 2019," 2019.

[10] Mendix, "Test Automation & Quality Assurance." https://www.mendix.com/evaluation-guide/app-lifecycle/test-automation-quality-assurance/ (accessed Aug. 31, 2021).

[11] "Test Studio," 2020. https://docs.microsoft.com/en-us/powerapps/maker/canvas-apps/test-studio (accessed Aug. 31, 2021).

[12] OutSystems R&D, "BDDFramework," 2016. https://www.outsystems.com/forge/component-overview/1201/bddframework (accessed Aug. 31, 2021).

[13] F. Khorram, J.-M. Mottu, and G. Sunyé, "Challenges & Opportunities in Low-Code Testing," in *Proceedings of the 23rd ACM/IEEE International Conference on Model Driven Engineering Languages and Systems*, 2020, pp. 1–10, doi: 10.1145/3417990.3420204.

[14] J. Salgueiro, F. Ribeiro, and J. Metrôlho, "Best Practices for OutSystems Development and its Influence on Test Automation," in *9th World Conference on Information Systems and Technologies*, 2021, pp. 85–95.

[15] International Software Testing Qualifications Board, "Certified Tester Foundation Level Syllabus (Version 2018 V3.1)." 2019.

[16] J. Proença, "BDDFramework: overview," 2016. https://www.outsystems.com/forge/component-overview/1201/bddframework (accessed Jul. 02, 2021).

A Test Concept for the Development of Microservice-based Applications

Michael Schneider, Stephanie Zieschinski,
Hristo Klechorov, Lukas Brosch,
Patrick Schorsten, Sebastian Abeck
Research Group Cooperation & Management
Karlsruhe Institute of Technology (KIT)
Zirkel 2, 76131 Karlsruhe, Germany
email: (michael.schneider | sebastian.abeck)@kit.edu
(stephanie.zieschinski | hristo.klechorov | lukas.brosch)@student.kit.edu

Christof Urbaczek
xdi360 GmbH
Leopoldstraße 252b, 80807 München
email: (christof.urbaczek@xdi360.com)

***Abstract*—A microservice-based application is composed of several distributed microservices. When developing the microservices of the application, it is important to test that the requirements are met and that the application works as intended. Especially end-to-end tests require all involved microservices to be available for testing. A common way is to execute the tests via a continuous integration / continuous delivery pipeline. In this paper, we present a test concept for developing microservice-based applications which covers the different test types according to the test pyramid, from end-to-end, integration tests, and consumer-driven contract to unit tests. The test concept considers the entire test pyramid as part of the microservice engineering process. Furthermore, we show how the test concept can be executed during the development process using a continuous integration / continuous delivery pipeline by the example of a PredictiveCarMaintenance application.**

Keywords*—*microservices; development process; behavior-driven development; test pyramid; test concept; code quality; CI/CD.

I. INTRODUCTION

A microservice-based application is composed of several independently developed and deployed small services. The microservices are loosely coupled into business-related cohesive functionalities that do one thing well [1]. Microservices communicate with each other via technology-independent interfaces to solve the more extensive business tasks. The architectural style Representational State Transfer (REST) by Roy Fielding [2] provides a lightweight way to define the microservices' web Application Programming Interfaces (APIs). As a result, each microservice can be developed separately by different development teams using different programming languages, and can be tested and deployed independently from each other. At the same time, testing the whole application becomes far more complex, since the microservices are distributed. Testing an application itself has to consider the whole test pyramid [3] and the different tests types. This includes unit, integration, Consumer-Driven Contract (CDC), and End-to-End (E2E) tests. However, especially E2E tests are important, since the interaction of microservices fulfill the business functionality of a microservice-based application which has to be tested [4]. In addition, all involved microservices need to be available for testing. To simplify the test process, a pipeline for Continuous Integration / Continuous Deployment (CI/CD) has to be set up to assist the development process and the use of the test concept. This enables the regression testing of the application on the level of the business requirements in form of user acceptance tests.

The development of microservice-based applications requires a systematic development approach so that developers know what to test. For the test concept, a systematic microservice engineering approach is followed. Therefore, the test concept is integrated into the microservice-based development process [5]. Testing is considered during the whole engineering process, including the requirements analysis, design and the implementation phase. Figure 1 displays an overview of the development process and the resulting test artifacts. In the requirements analysis, the required functionality is specified by several artifacts. For testing purposes, the acceptance criteria is specified as Gherkin features according to Behavior-Driven Development (BDD) practices, which are used for the development of end-to-end tests. Gherkin features embrace the natural language which simplifies the communication with the stakeholders requirements.

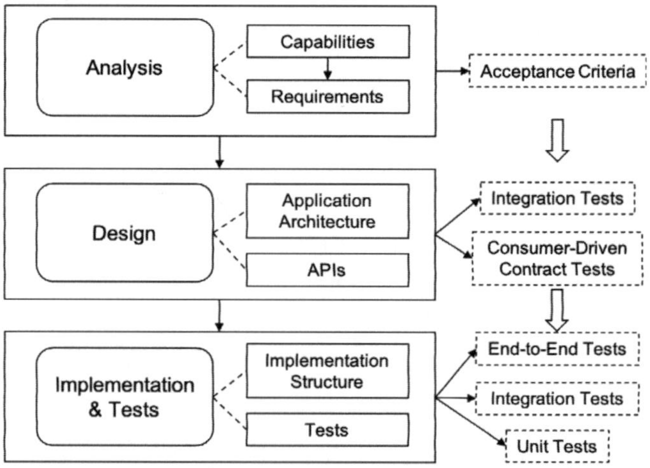

Figure 1. Development and Test Artifacts.

The design phase utilizes the artifacts from the analysis phase and forms the microservice architecture of the application by applying Domain-Driven Design (DDD) [6]. Important artifacts for the integration tests are the application architecture and the API specifications of the microservices. The design artifacts, especially the API specification, are important for the CDC tests. The implementation phase utilizes the artifacts created in the analysis and design phase for the test implementation. The applicability of the test concept and the different tests is shown in detail by the example of a concrete microservice application, PredictiveCarMaintainance (PCM).

The main contributions of the article are: (i) a systematic test concept considering the test types of the test pyramid, E2E, integration and unit tests, extended with CDC tests and considering all test types during development; (ii) the integration of the test concept into a CI/CD pipeline.

The article is structured as follows: Section 2 presents the state-of-the-art in the area of testing microservices. Section 3 introduces the system under test (i.e., PCM) and the required artifacts. In Section 4, the test concept is introduced and explained by the example application PCM. The problem of test automation through the use of a CI/CD pipeline is tackled in Section 5. Results of the test concept are presented in Section 6. Section 7 summarizes the main results of our test concept and the main research issues we currently work on.

II. Related Work

Software tests are well introduced by several sources and placed into software engineering processes. O'Regan [7] provides an introduction to the field of software testing which contains a broad spectrum of related aspects, and further topics including software processes, and requirements engineering.

A reusable testing architecture is introducing by Rahman et al. [8] and proposes a dedicated application for automated acceptance testing. The concept provides separation of concerns among developers, testers and business analysts and is part of the test concept that is presented in this paper.

Savchenko et al. [9] provide a general testing process which extends the microservice development by several test steps, e.g., (internal functional) component testing, integration testing, and continuous system testing.

The conclusion that a microservice-based architecture requires more high-level testing especially on the end-to-end-side is discussed by Faragó et al. [4]. The reasoning behind this is that the interaction of microservices is the key to a working application.

John F. Smart [10] provides a more technical coverage of BDD practices and showcases a number of tools for different languages and frameworks, which aid developers in creating robust and sustainable tests. BDD can be seen as further development of Test-Driven Development (TDD) [11].

A case study was conducted to examine how a microservice-based application can be tested effectively by Lehvä et al. [12]. They do so by extending the traditional test pyramid with Consumer-Driven Contract (CDC) tests between integration and component tests. The study suggests that CDC tests could even replace integration tests, as they provide similar feedback, but only have a fraction of the development effort and execution time.

Wang et al. [13] present an API testing process which automatically gathers the API specifications from cloud websites and transforms the interpreted syntax and semantics of service data and operations into internal semi-formal representations from which the test cases are derived. This may be considered in further versions of the test concept.

Microservice-based applications require additional considerations during development because the applications are distributed and the services may be developed independently by different teams. Related work has influenced the result of the systematic microservice engineering approach that considers the entire test pyramid.

III. Application under Test

The application under test is the microservice-based application PredictiveCarMaintenance (PCM) which provides insight about a vehicle health. The application is developed using a systematic microservice engineering approach conceptualized specifically for the test concept.

During the requirements analysis, the cohesive functionalities are grouped into capabilities. The requirements of such a capability are described by User/System Interactions (USI) which are further represented as graphical USI flows. For acceptance testing, the end-to-end tests are systematically derived using Behavior-Driven Development (BDD) and the specified user interactions. Each step within the scenarios has a corresponding step definition, implemented during the development of the end-to-end tests. Furthermore, the scenarios describe the USIs under test. Smart [10] illustrates how unit tests can be derived from step definitions. Utilizing the approach, the application logic contained within a scenario can be developed in an iterative way.

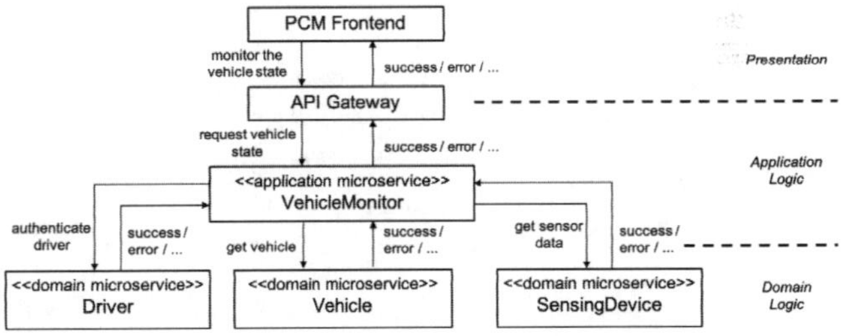

Figure 2. PCM Architecture Overview.

Figure 2 shows an overview of the derived architecture for the PCM application. The architecture was modeled during the design phase by applying Domain-Driven Design (DDD) concepts by Eric Evans [6]. The PCM application consists of the frontend, the API gateway, the application microservice VehicleMonitor, and the domain microservices Vehicle and Driver. Additionally, the application also communicates with the domain microservice SensingDevice. We differentiate between microservices which are only relevant for one application (the application microservices) and the application-agnostic microservices (domain microservices) which provide funcionality that can be reused by other applications. The frontend of PCM allows the user to interact with the system and presents the information provided by the VehicleMonitor by requesting all data via the API gateway. The application microservice VehicleMonitor needs to authenticate the user by sending the corresponding requests to the microservice Driver. If the authentication is successful, VehicleMonitor gathers the required information by the domain microservice Vehicle and executes the application logic needed to support the USIs. To retrieve the sensor data, the VehicleMonitor communicates with the microservice SensingDevice. The microservices need to be orchestrated to fulfill the desired functionality. Therefore, the orchestration of the services for an application microservice is specified by task processes which describe a chain of service calls. The task processes itself are based on the concepts of the Business Process Executing Language (BPEL) [14] and the Service-oriented architecture Modeling Language (SoaML) [15].

The test concept is exemplary applied on the USI "Monitor the Vehicle State". The frontend calls the API gateway, which in turn calls the application microservice VehicleMonitor to receive the state of a vehicle. The application microservice first calls the microservice Driver for authentication and then calls the microservice vehicle for the information about a vehicle and its components. The detailed sensor data for each component is requested from SensingDevice. This information is used to derive a vehicle component's health state and the result is returned to the frontend.

IV. Test Concept

The development of tests follows a logical order, bottom-up. An overview of different types of tests used and the related artifacts is shown in Figure 3. As the development

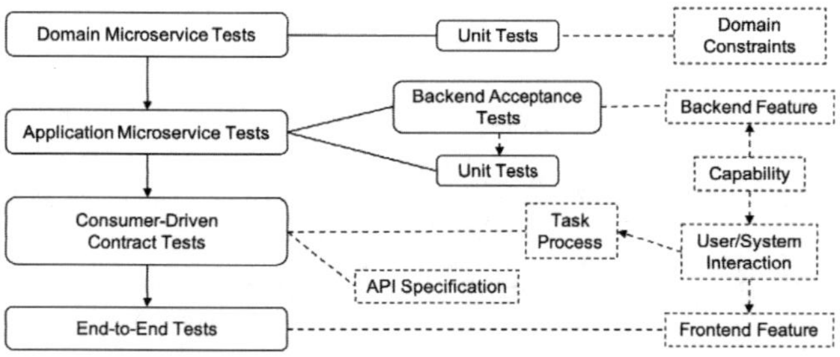

Figure 3. Overview of the Test Concept and Artifacts.

of microservice-based applications starts with the domain microservices, the tests for these microservices are created early. We differentiate between domain and application microservice unit testing, since domain microservices mostly contain simple functionality, i.e., CRUD operations. Therefore, corresponding tests are directly derived from the domain constraints. On the other hand, while implementing application microservices, two types of tests are developed: the backend acceptance and unit tests, which are derived from the former. After the implementation of, at least, one domain microservice, the development of one or more application microservices starts, including their tests, while deriving the functionality from the capabilities. When there are at least two microservices that communicate, Consumer-Driven Contract (CDC) tests can be applied, where the two most important artifacts are the task process and the API specification. The task process shows which microservices communicate and which data they access, whereas the API specification reveal how requests and responses are specified. The end-to-end tests form the highest layer of tests where great parts of the application under test are needed and are derived from the User/System Interactions (USI).

The BDD principle concentrates on the behavior and not on the concrete implementation of the software. The acceptance tests are written in the language Gherkin as features, that enable a common understanding of the software by using natural language. The Gherkin features formally specify the requirements of an application. The creation of those features involves a discussion between developers, testers and domain experts. The use of a ubiquitous language in those features helps additionally. For each capability, an application microservice is developed. The features are derived from the capabilities and contain scenarios comprised of steps. We derive the scenarios of a feature from the USIs which are further modeled as so-called USI flows. Figure 4 displays an example of the USI flow for monitoring a vehicle state.

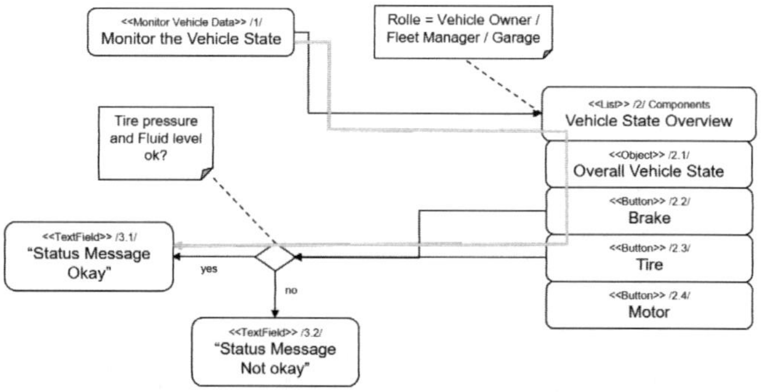

Figure 4. USI Flow for Monitor the Vehicle State.

Each path through a USI flow (one path is shown by the grey line) leads to a scenario. One of the resulting scenarios is shown in Figure 5.

```
Scenario: Monitor Component State (Success)
Given I am logged in as a vehicle owner,
    fleet manager or garage
  And the vehicle state overview is
      displayed
When I open the vehicle state overview for
    the motor
Then I see the detailed summary of the motor
  And a status message is displayed
```

Figure 5. Scenario for Monitor Component State.

A. Development of the Unit Tests for Domain Microservices

Due to the differences between domain and application logic, unit test development for domain microservices differs from the development of unit tests for an application microservice. Instead of application functionality, domain logic focuses on the application-agnostic domain logic which should be reusable by many applications from the same domain.

The domain knowledge of a bounded context can be expressed in an entity relation view which contains the domain objects and their relationships similar to a class diagram [16]. Figure 6 displays the entity relation view for the bounded context Vehicle. The entity relation view displays the entities Vehicle, VehicleComponent, Observation and Manufacturer. The vehicle is the most central domain entity. A vehicle consists of several vehicle components, such as brakes, tires and motor. These components are monitored by sensors. Sensors create observations that specify the time of the measurement and the observed measurement. Using the example of the method getObservationFromTimePeriod(), the constraints are defined and implemented in the following. This method makes it possible to display the observations of a sensor in a certain period of time.

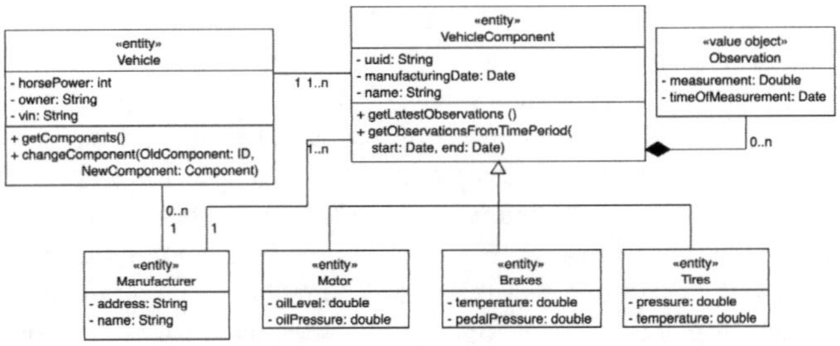

Figure 6. Entity Relation View of the Bounded Context Vehicle.

An observation is a measurement of a component value such as motor temperature at a specific time. The desired information may include only the latest observation or multiple observations for a specified time interval. The vehicle bounded context has no active influence on the observations itself. These observations are providedby a microservice SensingDevice.

The domain logic itself contains constraints which define the boundaries of the domain objects. The constraints of a domain are stated when the domain is modeled. This domain knowledge can be added formally to further specify the UML diagrams [17], e.g., the entity relation view of the bounded context vehicle, by the use of the Object Constraint Language (OCL). This leads to the advantage, that the model can be implemented and tested later. Constraints are derived from the domain knowledge (e.g., physical world constraints), gathered in the analysis phase and need to be enforced by implementation. Furthermore, the constraints need to be tested and therefore, are a valuable input for the unit tests of a domain microservice.

Figure 7 shows an excerpt of the constraints for the bounded context Vehicle. Using the method getObservationFromTimePeriod() and pre- and postconditions, the allowed transitions can be formally expressed with OCL. Lines 1-2 define the context and the considered method. In line 3, a precondition is specified. Here it is important that the end date of the observation is not before the start date. In lines 4-6, a postcondition is specified which ensures that the observations are not outside of the specified period.

```
1. context VehicleComponent::
       getObservationsFromTimePeriod(start:
       Date, end: Date):
2. pre: start.before(end)
3. post: forAll(o:Observation | (start.after(
       start)
4.     or start.equals(start))
5.     and (end.before(end) or end.equals(end)))
```

Figure 7. Excerpt of the Domain Constraints.

These constraints are implemented in the vehicle microservice's domain logic. Based on the underlying domain constraint the implementation of the method getObservationsForTimePeriod() is done, which is part of the VehicleComponent entity.

The pre- and post-conditions must be valid before and after the method is invoked, respectively. Therefore, each pre- and postcondition is checked through if statements. An example of a postcondition implementation is shown in Figure 8. If a condition is violated when a method executes, the method will throw an exception, which is an object that indicates that an error occurred.

Similarly, to guarantee that the requirements of the postconditions are met when the method has been called, the method uses an if statement in line 4. Only if all these conditions are met, the method returns a list with observations with regards to the specified time frame.

```
1. List<Observation> result = new ArrayList<>()
       ;
2. for (Observation o : this.observations) {
3.     ZonedDateTime t = o.getTimeOfMeasurement
           ();
4.     if((t.isAfter(start) || t.equals(start))
           &&
5.       (t.isBefore(end) || t.equals(end))) {
6.       result.add(o);
7.     }
8. }
```

Figure 8. Postcondition Implementation.

Test cases are derived from each constraint. There are two kinds of test cases and unit tests respectively: (i) the first kind asserts the method under test behaves as expected by feeding it with correct input and matching the output with expected output and (ii) the second kind asserts the input data is validated correctly by feeding the method under test with incorrect input and awaiting an exception to be thrown.

Test cases of type (i) use test data which conforms to all domain constraints. For the constraints presented in Figure 7, type (i) unit tests are going to test whether the correct set of observations is delivered as output by the method getObservationsFromTimePeriod(). Hence, two argument providers are presented in Figure 9 and 10. One serves as example for an arguments provider for unit tests of type (i) and the other - for unit tests of type (ii). It is good practice to develop one arguments provider class per unit test type.

ArgumentsProviderTypeI initializes the arguments for the test case (see lines 1-3) where the observations for the last month are requested. Those are a start date of one month ago, followed by an end date of today and the expected output which is provided by a separate class where expected result data is initialized or loaded from external files such as a test database or CSV table.

```
1. OutputProvider op = new OutputProvider();
2. ZonedDateTime start = ZonedDateTime.now().
       minusMonths(1);
3. ZonedDateTime end = ZonedDateTime.now();

4. return Stream.of(
5.   // Test Case 1: Last month
6.   Arguments.of(start, end, op.getOutput(1))
7. );
```

Figure 9. Class ArgumentsProviderTypeI.

The test data for type (ii) unit tests aims to violate the domain constraints. Each test case violates one specific constraint, thus accelerating the fault discovery process.

ArgumentsProviderTypeII initializes a test case that violates the time period constraint by having a start date after the end date (see lines 1-2). A minimal test suite must have at least one violating test case per domain constraint. Advanced test suites have multiple violating test cases.

```
1. ZonedDateTime start = ZonedDateTime.now();
2. ZonedDateTime end = ZonedDateTime.now().
       minusMonths(1);

3. return Stream.of(
4.     // Test Case 2: Time period violation
5.     Arguments.of(start, end)
6. );
```

Figure 10. Class ArgumentsProviderTypeII.

The resulting unit tests in Figures 11 and 12 receive the test data as a stream from the respective arguments provider class. The first unit test exemplifies unit tests of type (i). It receives input for the method under test and the expected output from the arguments provider. The expected output must abide by the constraints defined in the postcondition.

The second unit test is an example of type (ii) unit tests. Its arguments provider delivers the input and the unit test asserts

```
List<Observation> result =
    validTestComponent.
        getObservationsFromTimePeriod(start,
        end);
assertEquals(result, expectedResult);
```

Figure 11. Unit Test Type I.

```
assertThrows(IllegalArgumentException.class,
      () ->
    validTestComponent.
        getObservationsFromPeriod(start, end)
        );
```

Figure 12. Unit Test Type II.

that the proper exception is thrown. A method that throws multiple exceptions requires multiple type (ii) unit tests.

B. Backend Acceptance and Unit Tests of an Application Microservice

An application microservice is developed to support USIs for a specific capability. In order to ensure that the test suite exercises every bit of functionality developed for the capability, the BDD outside-in approach is adopted for the development of acceptance and unit tests for the application logic. First, the acceptance criteria is specified. Then, it is automated as backend acceptance tests. Unit tests are derived from the backend acceptance tests, whereby the behavior of the code is specified further. Finally, the application logic needs to satisfy the acceptance criteria and the tests are implemented.

The step definitions differ from those created for end-to-end tests in the way that UI step definitions manipulate frontend components (e.g., through page objects), whereas backend step definitions manipulate application code directly. Furthermore, these backend acceptance tests support the outside-in development approach, since unit tests can be derived from them. The implementation of a feature starts with the acceptance criteria and advances through the lower levels as illustrated by Figure 3. Backend Gherkin features are derived from the frontend step definitions. Figure 13 presents the backend scenario equivalent of the scenario in Figure 5.

There are multiple benefits from introducing backend acceptance tests. They provide assurance of the backend system functionality independent of the frontend. If an end-to-end test fails but its corresponding backend acceptance test is passed successfully, then the problem is located in the frontend. Backend acceptance tests execute faster than frontend acceptance tests, because UI slows down tests significantly [10]. Hence, testing the system without the UI layer allows for more tests in a shorter amount of time being both developed and executed.

The Gherkin features [11] are the central artifact for the testing of application microservices. For each of the (Given, When, Then) steps, the backend step definitions are specified by coding the function calls on the backend side. To fulfill the backend step definitions, the application logic is implemented

```
Scenario: Monitor Component State (Success)
Given the component with uuid "123..."
    exists
When the state of a component with uuid
    "123..." is requested
Then latest sensor information about the
    component is fetched
```

Figure 13. Scenario for Monitor Component State (Backend).

by writing the required unit tests in a first step and the application code to pass the unit tests in a second step. Smart [10] illustrates how unit tests can be derived from step definitions. Adopting this approach, in Figure 14, a step definition for the When step in Figure 13 is implemented. During the implementation of the step definitions, initial considerations for the application code are made. In the example, an operations class is modelled, which provides a method that fetches component information. The information itself is modelled as a list containing the various values provided by the domain microservice.

```
@When("When the state of a component with
    uuid <string> is requested")
public void request_component_info(String id
    ) throws Throwable {
  List componentInfo = operations.
      getComponentInfo(id);
}
```

Figure 14. Backend Acceptance Test Step Definition.

BDD treats unit tests as low-level executable specification, meaning the main focus is the behavior of the system, not the functionality of the separate methods. By following the method from Figure 3, this paradigm is enforced further. The unit tests are derived from the backend acceptance tests. Figure 15 illustrates the unit test derived from the When step in Figure 14. Infrastructural software units (e.g., database repositories, mappers, etc.) require unit tests as well.

```
public class StateOperationsTests {
    private StateOperations operations;
        ...
    @ParameterizedTest
    @ArgumentsSource(ArgumentsProvider.class)
    public void getComponentInfo_
    ShouldGatherComponentInfo(
        componentId, List expectedInfo) {
        assertThat(expectedInfo,
            samePropertyValuesAs(
          operations.getComponentInfo(
              componentId)));
    }
}
```

Figure 15. Unit Test Example.

C. Consumer-Driven Contract Tests

One of the main problems when dealing with a microservice-based application is the integration of microservices [18].

The main goal of integration tests is to find out whether changes break the application or not. For this, the affected services would need to be deployed which leads to slow tests. Testing the integration of microservices in an isolated way by using Consumer-Driven Contracts (CDC) can decrease the number of integrated tests and therefore decrease the duration of running all tests [18]. Those contracts document the communication between two services, where the caller of a service is called consumer and the callee is the provider. In this paper, the contract testing tool Pact is used for the CDC tests [19]. Pact offers implementations in many different programming languages, including Go and Java, meaning that Pact can directly be used for all of PCM's microservices. CDC tests in Pact consist of two steps: in the first step the contract is created by the consumer, by creating a Pact mock of the provider under test and specifying the expected response. In the second step, the previously defined request is sent to the provider and the real provider's response is compared to the expected response in the contract [20].

The needed contracts, where the microservice under test is the consumer, are derived from the task process of each of its microservice operation. An example for the microservice operation Monitor the Vehicle State is shown in Figure 16. Here, the microservice VehicleMonitor is the consumer and all the other microservices are providers.

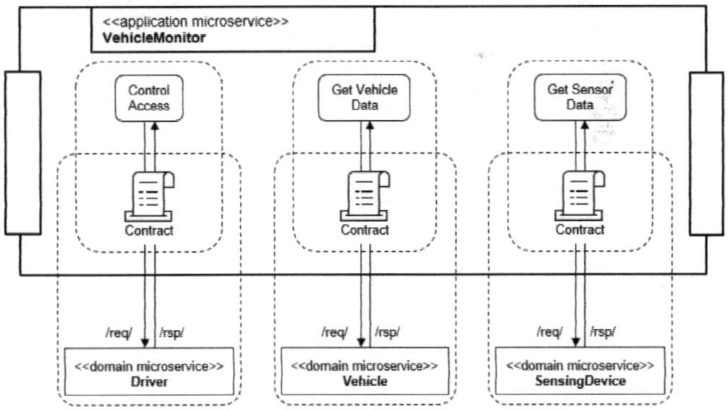

Figure 16. Contracts for the Microservice VehicleMonitor.

D. End-To-End Tests

The approach from [8] is adapted for the integrated tests, i.e., integration and end-to-end tests. As a result, a separate repository is used for those tests. Having those in each microservice repository would lead to high maintenance test suites, because step definitions cannot be reused across repositories. The test repository cannot access the internal code of the microservices, which means the whole application needs to be treated as a black box. Before the end-to-end tests can run, every required microservice needs to be deployed. The two main questions to answer when end-to-end testing are what and how is tested. The end-to-end tests should not be used to reach a high coverage for all paths in an application, instead they should describe examples for the software's behavior [10]. To find such examples, USI flows are used. From a USI flow every path through the application for the considered user interaction can be derived. For the user interaction in Figure 4 twelve different paths can be found: two different states for both, brakes and tires and there are three different roles involved. Taking into account more components or adding additional decisions would drastically increase the number of application paths. This means, not every path should be mapped to a test, as many slow end-to-end tests would also slow down development [21]. As the user interaction is exactly the same for every role, it is sufficient to run this test only for one of the roles. This decreases the number of tests to four. By choosing one component for the test, only two test cases are left: (1) the component is okay and (2) the component is not okay. The data for the other component(s) as well as the access for the other roles can be tested in the integration tests. The resulting Gherkin feature is depicted in Figure 17. To increase readability both tests are combined into one scenario outline.

```
Feature: Monitor the Vehicle State
  As a vehicle owner, fleet manager and garage
  I want to see the overall state of a vehicle
  So that I can continuously monitor its state

  Scenario Outline: Display correct tire state
    Given I have opened PCM
      And I am logged in as a vehicle owner
      And the tire pressure is <tire pressure state>
    When I open the overview for the tires
    Then I see the tire state is <tire state>

    Examples:
      | tire pressure state | tire state |
      | not okay | not okay |
      | okay | okay |
```

Figure 17. Feature derived from the USI Flow.

In the following, the question of how the application should be tested is answered by using guidelines for creating end-to-end tests to ensure a good quality of the tests. Quality of tests has to be considered on two aspects: the test specification, i.e., Gherkin features, and the test implementation, i.e., the step definitions. End-to-end tests often have a high maintenance effort when they are written in an imperative way, because the features contain UI-specific or other irrelevant information. When the UI changes, both the step and its step definition need to change. To improve this, declarative features should be written, so a UI change would lead to a change only in the step definition, in case of a declarative feature [21]. In the example above, one could instead specify which exact inputs the user makes in order to log in. In this case, every time this user needs to login the step would need to update if the credentials would change.

Tests should provide feedback for the developers whether a change broke the application or not. When they need to wait very long for the test execution to finish, it affects the productivity. Moreover, not every edge case needs to be verified by an end-to-end test, those should be tested with unit tests [21].

Another problem that could occur in the test above could be inaccuracy. This problem is often indicated by imprecise language (e.g., "a user") or the use of the word "or".

Figure 18 shows a scenario that violates these guidelines. This scenario is inaccurate as it does not specify which user is logged in to the application (line 2). To get this information one would need to look into the step definition, which defies the purpose of BDD. The same applies to lines 4 and 5, where the concrete component is not specified.

```
1. Scenario: Monitor the Vehicle State (Success)
2. Given I am logged in as a vehicle owner, fleet manager or garage
3.     And The vehicle state overview is displayed
4. When I open the vehicle state overview for a "component"
5. Then I see the detailed summary of the " component"
```

Figure 18. Example of a Flawed Scenario.

An improved version of this scenario is displayed in Figure 19. It is now clear which user is logged in for the test case and which component is viewed. If the scenario needs to be tested for the other roles as well, this can be easily accomplished by using a scenario outline.

```
Scenario: Monitor the Vehicle State (Success)
Given I am logged in as a vehicle owner
  And the vehicle state overview is displayed
When I open the vehicle state overview for the motor
Then I see the detailed summary of the motor
```

Figure 19. Example of an Improved Version of the Scenario.

Software should be easy to change, therefore especially the end-to-end tests should be robust against changes, as they take a lot of time to implement [10]. To realize this, the Gherkin features should not contain implementation details that are prone to changing and leave out irrelevant information. When an application's implementation changes, only the corresponding step definition needs to be updated, the step can remain the same.

For the automation of the Gherkin features, step definitions need to be written. For those there are also guidelines defined to support automated testing. To increase maintainability, useful selectors should be chosen. A poor selector is one that is likely to change and is difficult to understand, an example is XPath. It is recommended to use IDs or similar attributes. By using the page object model maintainability can be even further increased. The page object model implements all interaction with the applications into classes called page objects. The page objects hide UI details from the test code [22].

One common problem for automated end-to-end tests are tests that sometimes pass or fail without an apparent reason. The reason could be race conditions. In web applications many things happen asynchronously, so often the order in which calls return cannot be known beforehand. A quick fix could be using fixed-length waiting times. This is not a suitable solution, as this increases the test execution time and on the other side it does only decrease the possibility of a race condition. Conditional waiting times should be applied instead [21].

A similar problem could occur when tests change persistent state, but do not reset it. In this case the success of a test would depend on the execution order. These side effects can lead to false negative test results, i.e., the functionality works, but the test fails. To prevent this, such a state should always be reset.

V. Pipeline Integration

The pipeline considers all types of tests that are used. Each microservice's repository includes all of its isolated tests (i.e., unit and Consumer-Driven Contract (CDC) tests), the integrated tests (i.e., integration and end-to-end tests) are stored in a dedicated test repository, following the approach of the reusable automated acceptance test architecture from [8], where the end-to-end tests are extracted into their own repository. An example of executed pipeline jobs on a change in the microservice VehicleMonitor is shown in Figure 20. On a commit in a repository all of its pipeline stages are executed, starting with the unit tests. The next tests that are run are the CDC tests. These tests are split into separate pipeline jobs ConsumerContract and ProviderContract. In the job ConsumerContract new contracts are created or existing ones are updated by sending them to the Pact broker. If contracts are changed in this stage, the affected providers are tested by running their pipeline through Pact's webhooks, where only the provider tests are executed. Therefore, a pipeline trigger token is created in the corresponding providers' repositories to start their pipeline from Pact. This also enables differentiating how the pipeline was started. After the VehicleMonitor's consumer tests are finished, its provider contracts are retrieved from the Pact broker and the microservice is tested. If the jobs for unit and contract testing were successful, the new version of the changed microservice is deployed. This will trigger the test repository pipeline in the pipeline job Downstream with its two jobs that run integration and end-to-end tests.

One of the most important aspects of a continuous integration pipeline is to have a short build time [23]. This leads to

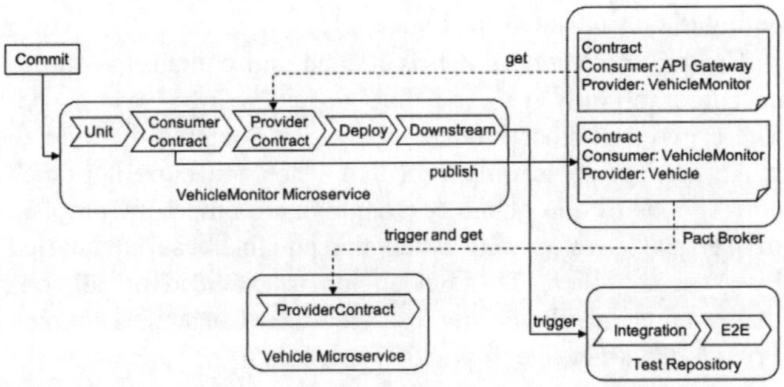

Figure 20. Pipeline for a Change in the VehicleMonitor Microservice.

quick feedback about breaking changes to the developers. One way to decrease the pipeline's build time is to test as much as possible on the lower levels of abstraction [24], without external dependencies that slow down testing. Typically, integration tests are used to test the communication between microservices, that often need to be deployed beforehand, and are therefore slow [9]. The communication between the microservices is tested with the much faster Consumer-Driven Contracts (CDC) that can greatly reduce the needed integration tests by replacing those [19]. The CDC tests are more stable than the integration tests as less moving parts are involved [12]. Error localization is simplified as in a CDC test only two services are considered at a time. By stopping pipeline execution on every failure and running the tests ordered by execution time, feedback times are additionally reduced: if there is an error in the unit tests this functionality will not work in the tests of higher level. Another important feature of a continuous integration pipeline is to run tests in a clone of the productive environment [23]. There are two deployment environments, called test and prod. Both deployment environments mirror the contents of one branch each. The test environment contains the state from the corresponding branch develop, and the contents of the branch master get deployed to the prod environment. As only those two branches get deployed, the integration and end-to-end tests are only applicable to those.

```
.no-trigger-token:
  rules:
    - if: '$CI_PIPELINE_SOURCE != "trigger"'

unit:
  extends: .no-trigger-token
  script: ...
```

Figure 21. Pipeline Configuration.

As GitLab is used, which only permits one pipeline per repository, a solution needed to be found that allows this structure with one single pipeline. Additionally, a goal was decreasing duplicates in this pipeline configuration as much as possible. This was achieved by the use of hidden pipeline jobs that contain the needed rules for all pipeline jobs and extend those as described in [25]. An excerpt for the pipeline configuration is shown in Figure 21.

The job .no-trigger-token is hidden and contains a rule to execute a job only if the pipeline was not started by a trigger. There exists another hidden job, which contains the rule to make sure a job is only executed when the current branch corresponds to one of the two deployment environments, i.e., master and develop, and when the pipeline was not started by a trigger token. This hidden job is extended by all jobs that require a deployed microservice, i.e., ConsumerContract, ProviderContract, Deploy and Downstream.

VI. Results of the Test Concept

In the context of unit testing, the domain constraints provide a structured approach. These constraints describe in a formal way, which values for attributes or parameters for method calls are permissible, before starting the implementation. Furthermore, the constraints are used as a reference during the implementation and writing of unit tests. This has the advantage that during the implementation the already defied edge cases (within the constraints) can be used. Because the constraints are created separately from the implementation, the unit tests are correspondingly less influenced by the implementation. The constraints provide a golden thread, which is helpful when writing the unit tests.

Constraints can be efficiently utilized to create test cases for edge cases. Edge cases are on one side of the constraint and thus cover the area of the constraint. As a result, test cases which do not increase the test coverage, are minimized.

During the implementation of the domain microservice Vehicle, we applied the test concept. The structured approach and the domain constraints were helpful for the developers. This is because the systematic procedure by the test concept subdivides the unit testing of the domain microservice in several tasks. Therefore, we were able to assign these tasks among us appropriately and thus work on some tasks in parallel. When writing the unit tests, it was still an open topic which test data should be used for the tests. Furthermore, these can be systematically derived from the other existing artefacts of the domain microservice.

The test concept distinguishes between domain and application microservices. Therefore, the test concept with its artifacts supports the scope of the respective microservices. For example, the focus of an application microservice is more on testing the behavior (e.g., through Gherkin features). This was an advantage during the development of the application PCM because a more targeted procedure to writing unit and integration tests is possible.

Moreover, by shifting the tested functionality to tests of lower layers whenever possible, the development time of the tests as well as their execution time is minimized. Especially CDC tests are important in a microservice-based application to verify that different parts of the tested application can communicate.

The guidelines for end-to-end tests (E2E) can help improving the maintainability of those tests, by enabling faster development and reducing test cases as much as possible. The application of the guidelines leads to more stable tests.

The introduction of the uniform pipeline structure presented in this paper will simplify the application of Continuous Integration / Continuous Deployment, especially when it is used as a template, where only the microservice-specific scripts need to be customized.

VII. Conclusion and Future Work

We have introduced a test concept for the development of microservice-based applications and showed its applicability by the example of an excerpt of the microservice-based application PredictiveCarMaintenance (PCM). One of the main goals was to systematically test the application by using the artifacts and different test types (end-to-end, integration, consumer-driven contract, unit tests) and assist the developers in this process. By starting with the domain and its constraints, we test the domain microservices with unit test by deriving the test from the constraints. Testing the application microservice and its operations is done by a systematic derivation of backend acceptance tests which are transferred to unit tests. Next, we test the integration of the microservices with consumer-driven contract tests to test the microservices in an isolated way. Finally, end-to-end tests are developed using the guidelines provided to test the whole application at once. BDD simplifies the communication with the stackholders. Overall, the test concept provides what should be tested with which tests.

In addition, we integrated the different tests into a CI/CD pipeline and described how the different pipelines need to be triggered. The pipeline approach can be reused for further projects with minor configuration adjustments. As a result, we are convinced that applying the test concept leads to well tested microservice-based applications with a small effort. At the same time, the development of the application is simplified.

A further point to look at is that the test issues a deterministic request to the system under test and expects a predefined output or response from the system. A request usually requires concrete values and parameters. Therefore, a suitable selection of the test data is necessary, for example, to cover edge cases.

In addition, a systematic representation of the test data needs to be researched. The goal here is to arrange the test data into an orderly format for the representation of the test data. One goal of further research is to assist the developer with even more support for writing tests by providing additional guidelines for applying the test concept. This includes optimizations and enhancements of the presented test concept. In the future, the test concept needs to be applied to more applications which may lead to further insights to adapt the approach.

Moreover, the versioning of the CDC tests needs to be revised in the future, as the tests are currently only executable in master and development branches. The developers can benefit from guidelines that will be created in the future and can simplify the development of CDC tests.

REFERENCES

[1] N. Alshuqayran, N. Ali, and R. Evans, "A Systematic Mapping Study in Microservice Architecture," in *9th International Conference on Service-Oriented Computing and Applications (SOCA)*. IEEE, 2016, pp. 44–51.

[2] R. T. Fielding, "Rest: Architectural styles and the design of network-based software architectures," Ph.D. dissertation, University of California, 2000.

[3] A. S. Bueno, A. Gumbrecht, and J. Porter, "Testing Java Microservices: Using Arquillian, Hoverfly, AssertJ, JUnit, Selenium, and Mockito," 2018.

[4] D. Faragó and D. Sokenou, "Keynote: Microservices Testen Erfahrungsbericht und Umfrage," *Test, Analyse und Verifikation von Software (TAV) der Gesellschaft für Informatik (GI), Stuttgart*, 2019.

[5] B. Hippchen, P. Giessler, R. Steinegger, M. Schneider, and S. Abeck, "Designing Microservice-Based Applications by Using a Domain-Driven Design Approach," in *International Journal on Advances in Software*. IARIA, 2017, pp. 432–445.

[6] E. Evans, *Domain-Driven Design: Tackling Complexity in the Heart of Software*. Addison-Wesley Professional, 2004.

[7] G. Regan, *Concise Guide to Software Testing*. Springer, 2019.

[8] M. Rahman and J. Gao, "A Reusable Automated Acceptance Testing Architecture for Microservices in Behavior-Driven Development," in *IEEE Symposium on Service-Oriented System Engineering*, 2015, pp. 321–325.

[9] D. Savchenko, G. Radchenko, T. Hynninen, and O. Taipale, "Microservice Test Process: Design and Implementation," in *International Journal on Information Technologies and Security*, 2018, pp. 13–24.

[10] J. F. Smart, *BDD in Action*. New York, NY, USA: Manning Publications, 2015.

[11] D. North, "Introducing BDD— Dan North & Associates," 2006.

[12] J. Lehvä, N. Mäkitalo, and T. Mikkonen, "Consumer-driven contract tests for microservices: A case study," in *International Conference on Product-Focused Software Process Improvement*, 2019, pp. 497–512.

[13] J. Wang, X. Bai, H. Ma, L. Li, and Z. Ji, "Cloud API Testing," in *10th IEEE International Conference on Software Testing, Verification and Validation Workshop (ICSTW)*, 2017.

[14] M. B. Juric, "A Hands-on Introduction to BPEL," *Oracle (white paper)*, p. 21, 2006, [retrieved 30/08/2021]. [Online]. Available: https://www.oracle.com/technical-resources/articles/matjaz-bpel.htm

[15] B. Elvesæter, A.-J. Berre, and A. Sadovykh, "Specifying Services using the Service Oriented Architecture Modeling Language (SoaML) - A Baseline for Specification of Cloud-based Services," in *CLOSER*, 2011, pp. 276–285.

[16] M. Schneider, B. Hippchen, P. Giessler, C. Irrgang, and S. Abeck, "Microservice Development Based on Tool-Supported Domain Modeling," in *Conference on Advances and Trends in Software Engineering (SOFTENG)*, 2019.

[17] Object Management Group, "Object Constraint Language," [retrieved 30/08/2021]. [Online]. Available: https://www.omg.org/spec/OCL/2.4

[18] S. Newman, *Building Microservices: Designing Fine-grained Systems*. O'Reilly Media, Inc., 2015.

[19] Pact, "Introduction," [retrieved 01/09/2021]. [Online]. Available: https://docs.pact.io/

[20] ——, "How Pact works," [retrieved 30/08/2021]. [Online]. Available: https://docs.pact.io/getting_started/how_pact_works

[21] M. Wynne and A. Hellesøy, *The Cucumber Book: Behaviour-Driven Development for Testers and Developers*. Pragmatic Bookshelf, 2012.

[22] M. Fowler, "PageObjects," https://martinfowler.com/bliki/PageObject.html, 2013.

[23] ——, "Continuous Integration," https://martinfowler.com/articles/continuousIntegration.html, 2006.

[24] H. Vocke, "The Practical Test Pyramid," https://martinfowler.com/articles/practical-test-pyramid.html, 2018.

[25] GitLab, "Keyword reference for the .gitlab-ci.yml file: Extends," [retrieved 30/08/2021]. [Online]. Available: https://docs.gitlab.com/ee/ci/yaml/#extends

Portable Fast Platform-Aware Neural Architecture Search for Edge/Mobile Computing AI Applications

Kuo-Teng Ding*, Hui-Shan Chen*, Yi-Lun Pan*, Hung-Hsin Chen†, Yuan-Ching Lin‡ and Shih-Hao Hung*
*High Performance Computing Division, National Center for High-performance Computing
*Hsinchu, Taiwan
*email: {tony.ding,chwhs,serenapan,2003002}@narlabs.org.tw
†Department of Computer Science and Information Engineering, National Taiwan University
†Taipei, Taiwan
†email: r09922038@csie.ntu.edu.tw
‡Department of Computer Science, National Tsing Hua University
‡Hsinchu, Taiwan
‡email: s105062329@m105.nthu.edu.tw

***Abstract*—The recent rise and progress of neural network-based artificial intelligence are obvious, and we have settled up many traditional machine learning problems by deep learning. However, problems were encountered when deploying neural networks on diverse hardware platforms, which needs lots of computational capability and time to "try out" the best architecture tipping the balance of model accuracy and execution latency. The proposed Portable Fast Platform-Aware Neural Architecture Search (PFP-NAS) system allows users to use the trained neural network model easily without considering the hardware architecture of the edge/mobile computing on the client-side. The portable neural architecture search device shrinks the data center and converts it to allow users to utilize it on-demand and dynamically. This just-in-time, secure, and portable neural architecture search method is mainly based on the platform-aware client-side and applying the neural network model trained on the data center. Another primary thing to remember is that users use the expandable modules of this device-Performance Prediction Module and Client Requirement-oriented Module, i.e., Accuracy, Latency, Throughput floating point operations per second (FLOPs), mean Average Precision (mAP), Cost, etc. and then the device can detect hardware architectures, such as Development Kit/Tensor Processing Unit (TPU)/Graphics processing unit (GPU)/Field-programmable gate array (FPGA) on edge/mobile computing. When detected, the device will send signals to connect the data center and drive the trained model in the data center for the corresponding hardware architecture. The proposed technique has the following characteristics: a. Only a boot medium is needed to detect and determine the hardware and then get the most suitable neural network from the server; b. Provide performance prediction module and client requirement-oriented module; c. Automatically match the model and the corresponding hardware architecture; d. Designed with modular scalability, and there is no need to configure any settings on the client-side. Consequently, the proposed framework achieves a portable data center.**

Keywords*—*Portable; Neural Architecture Search; Performance Prediction.

I. INTRODUCTION

Neural architecture search (NAS) issues are attracting more and more attention. Still, researchers try to cut into neural network search methods with its extreme computing cost and specific decentralized acceleration of neural network search.

Fig. 1. The demo of PFP-NAS

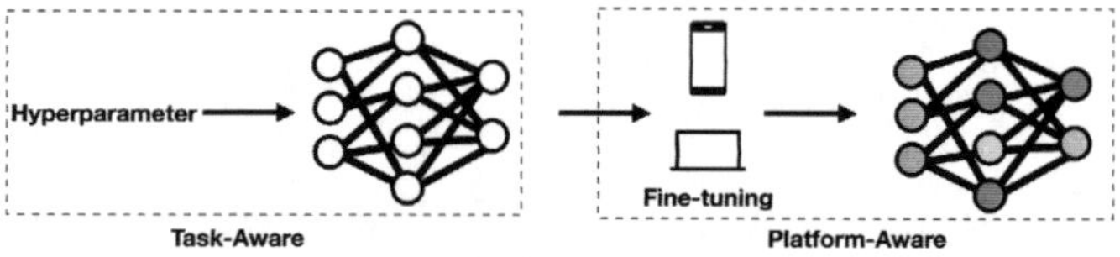

Fig. 2. Task-Aware Model Recommend and Platform-Aware Model Training

Acceleration methods from different aspects, such as Mathematical Model, Empirical Rule, and other methods have been proposed. However, these methods are often configured for special tasks and require fine-tuning and actual experiment feedback on the hardware platform. As we all know, it requires powerful computing capabilities and repeated training for the platform to get a good-quality model. This research places high hopes to solve the practical problems of insufficient computing power and data protection requirements.

Fig. 1 shows the simple demo of PFP-NAS. Users can install the NAS Agent program with a Universal Serial Bus (USB) device or download it from the internet and connect to its own target device. Users can also manipulate the PFP-NAS flow

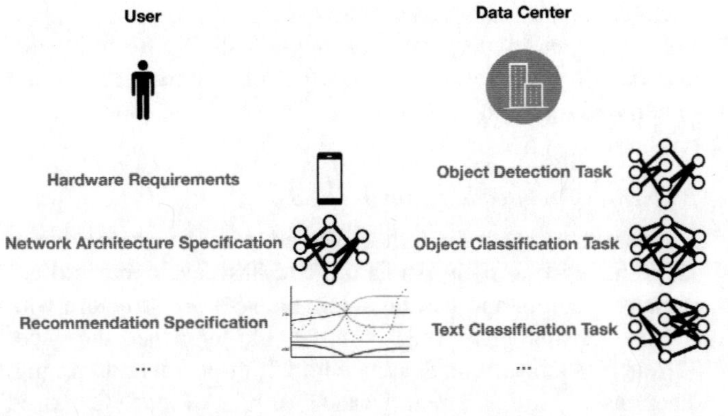

Fig. 3. Pre-trained Task-Aware Model Recommend for different tasks

with a modified Microsoft NNI user interface. The portable accelerated NAS service is proposed, which aims to split NAS into two important parts: the Task-Aware Model Recommend and the Platform-Aware Model Training, as shown in Fig. 2. The concept of pre-training is applied to model search in this architecture. The data center can learn in advance and discover the best structure of task-aware model. Moreover, the type of hardware architecture in the client-side can be paired with the recommended model in the data center to filter and select a suitable Platform-Aware model.

Fig. 3 shows that the data center will pre-train the model in advance and the pre-trained model will vary against different tasks. The pre-trained model can provide users with a hyperparameter recommendation set about a specific task. The user will need to provide platform-aware results (model accuracy and execution latency) to the data center, helping the whole hyperparameter search meet the requirements (shown in Fig. 4). In such a scenario, the client takes charge of network fine-tuning, and the data center recommends the hyperparameter. The communication process will take a few loops, and finally, the outcome is a slim and efficient model. Users can easily acquire the trained NAS model without considering their own hardware architecture on edge/mobile computing and without having to provide their own data sets. Through the designed portable accelerated neural network search device, the powerful computing power of the data center can be shrunk and converted into a dynamic and easy use for the end-users. Therefore, our design is the PFP-NAS framework to tackle the above problems.

To effectively select a suitable Platform-Aware model, the PFP-NAS can provide the Just-In-Time Performance module and the Platform-oriented module to the data center. These two modules can instantly evaluate the expected performance of the selected model and detect the user's hardware architecture. After detecting edge/mobile computing hardware architecture, such as TPU/GPU/FPGA, the user device will send relevant signals to contact the data center and drive the corresponding edge trained in the data center for mobile computing. Therefore, this research will design and provide the following three aspects of use scenarios and case solutions:

- Under the circumstance, when the client-side provides a personal dataset, the PFP-NAS only needs the module's description without the users' module. Then PFP-NAS can easily provide forecasting of the time-consuming and accuracy.
- When the client-side does not provide any personal dataset, PFP-NAS can provide a platform-aware recommendation service for protecting the client-side's privacy. The Just-In-Time Performance Predict Module and Platform-oriented module designed in this project can be used. The server side of the portable accelerated neural network search will be based on the existing information of the model and the user through the high-level description. The language interacts, and then the candidate models are screened out. The remaining part is to carry out portable training on the user device, allowing the user device to return the reward value or weight to adjust the recommendation logic.

The core concept of PFP-NAS is through portable accelerated NAS device services and NAS Agent to bring the powerful computing power of the data center to the user (Portable). Therefore, the following contributions are shown:

- Make computing resources portable: Through the designed PFP-NAS framework, the data center with powerful computing capability can be reduced and converted into a portable application service for users.
- Make dataset protective: It does not require users to upload datasets but allows users to interact and describe through high-level language to generate similar data sets, providing complete protection of user datasets.
- Make models speedup and optimized: The PFP-NAS framework proposed in this research will use powerful computing resources to automatically find and try every possible model in advance so that each model can be optimized to make full use of the back-end computing resources and provide them to the front-end good user experience.
- Make recommended models in real-time: With the benefit of the Just-In-Time Performance Predict Module, it can dynamically provide models that meet user needs.
- Make platform-as-a-service scalable: This research framework can bridge data centers (such as TWCC and AWS) to create tens of millions of portable computing power so that these data centers can provide accelerated NAS services.

The remaining of the paper is structured as follows: Section 2 presents backgrounds and related works. Section 3 presents the whole system design and system components. Section 4 indicates the experiement results around the system. Section 5 concludes the works and future works.

II. Related Works

This section will cover the related works ranging from automated machine learning and neural architecture search to hyperparameter tuning. The implementation of this work is based on Microsoft NNI opensource project which will be mentioned in the automated machine learning part. The proposed framework is mainly rose from the concept of Once-for-All network [1] and will be described in the neural architecture search part.

A. Automated Machine Learning (AutoML)

Automated machine learning [2] provides machine learning technology that non-experts in this domain can also get started quickly, such as data preprocessing, feature engineering, hyperparameter optimization and model post-processing, because the complexity of these tasks often exceeds the knowledge of non-experts in the domain of machine learning. The development and research of traditional machine learning models requires a lot of resources and cost. Therefore, AutoML can greatly improve the efficiency of machine learning and promote machine learning research. The following introduces and analyzes three AutoML technology:

a) MLflow (Machine Learning Workflow): MLflow [3] is an open-source project, which is created by the Apache Spark technical team. It is a platform to manage machine learning lifecycle. It can support a lot of existing machine learning applications and libraries. The main components of MLflow platform are MLflow Tracking-log and compare parameters, code, and experimental data, MLflow Projects-package training models for reproducible runs using Conda and Docker, MLflow Models-share and deploy the same training model on different platforms, and MLflow Model Registry-manage the full life cycle of MLflow models. MLflow UI adopts Flask's Web application framework to show visualization experimental results. In addition, in terms of model training alone, MLflow supports a wide variety of tools, including scikit-learn, PyTorch, Spark, TensorFlow, R, etc.; nevertheless, MLflow cannot perfectly solve model incompatibility problems caused by using different tools.

b) Microsoft NNI (Neural Network Intelligence): Microsoft NNI [4] is a lightweight toolkit for AutoML, which is released by Microsoft, but it has powerful functions and is easy to operate. It is one of the prevalent Automatic Machine Learning (AutoML) open-source tools, which can effectively help users to automatically tune and optimize the neural network architecture of the machine learning model. Its features include hyperparameter tuning, neural network architecture search, model compression, feature engineering, and provides many general-purpose NAS frameworks.

However, hyperparameter tuning and optimization is the core and basic function of Microsoft NNI. It provides a lot of popular auto-tuning algorithms (Tuner) to adapt to the hyperparameter tuning of different machine learning and deep learning applications; it also provides early stop algorithms (Accessor). It is used to predict and evaluate that if each trial's performance is not as good as the expected value, the trial will be terminated early. In this study, the research team integrated the proposed algorithms to efficiently and robustly search hyperparameters and NAS models in AutoML framework.

Based on the above discussion, only Microsoft NNI provides complete hyperparameter tuning and NAS technologies and functions, therefore, Microsoft NNI is introduced as the underlying infrastructure design for further development in this research.

B. Neural Architecture Search (NAS)

Neural network training has evolved from the original hand-made network to data extraction, and has developed into automated training and getting a suitable network structure with the least resources. Furthermore, Google published the paper - Neural Architecture Search with Reinforcement Learning. They used reinforcement learning for NAS and surpassed the previously hand-made network in image classification and language modeling tasks. At present, the effect of NAS has been comparable to the state-of-the-art model structure. Moreover, Nas-Bench-101 [5] emerged to evaluate the performance of NAS objectively in the fields of semantic segmentation, speech recognition, object detection, object classification, data enhancement, etc.

However, there are still some problems with NAS, such as the inability to find an objective method to compare NAS effects and reuse NAS results efficiently because various NAS methods have various different ways in search space and hyperparameter optimization. For example, for the hardware-aware NAS problem, the search space may be configured with different hardware specifications. Still, these found structures cannot be easily used for conversion learning on different tasks or on tasks with different datasets.

The traditional hand-crafted methods or NAS methods often require a lot of GPU resources. Han Cai1's lab published Once-for-All [1] and proposed the "Model Shrinking" method. It trains a large model while also training a small model, thereby reducing the cost of repeated training for the same type of neural network with similar architectures in order to select the best model. Model Shrinking will gradually reduce the scale of the trained neural network, and finally perform Fine-Tuning for each trained model. This paper proposes the neural network search strategy used in Model Shrinking, including Resolution, Kernel Size, Depth and Width in the convolutional neural network structure.

C. Hyperparameter Tuning

With the continuous expansion of the importance and application of machine learning tools, so does the demand for non-experts to use AutoML tools. Hyperparameter tuning is a common problem in many machine learning tasks, whether supervised or unsupervised. Some research has provided several different useful ways to solve these problems, such as cross-validation and excessive scoring functions. However, the scholars [6] discuss that some appropriate automated machine learning framework would include the automation of modeling and hyperparameters search which typically use black-box gradient-free optimization.

In addition, the other researchers [7], [8] focus on the information about the hyperparameter combination from the

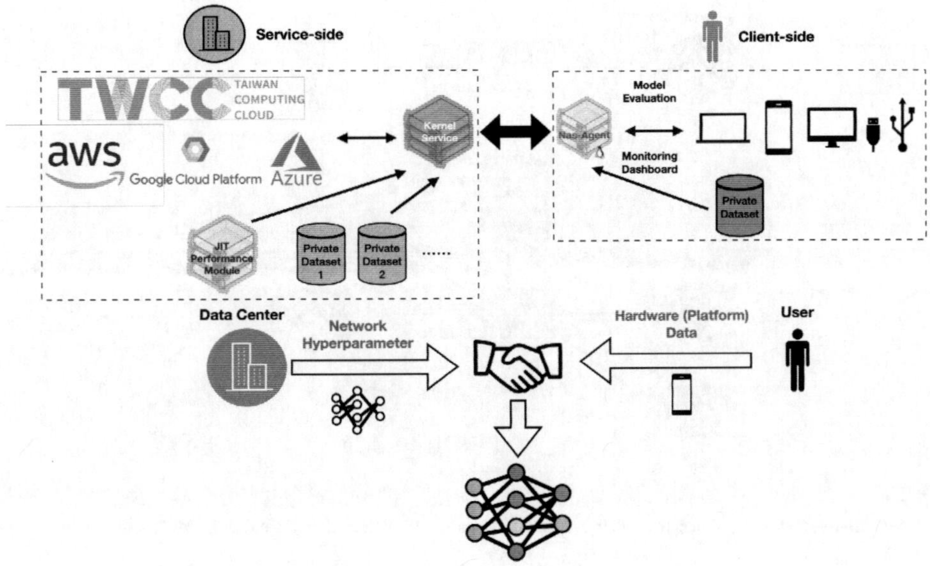

Fig. 4. Conceptual System Architecture Diagram

function f:X→R, and then output the data-generated model through the Bayesian optimization framework. The above method is also an effective method to search the hyperparameters. In AutoML setup, the f function may represent some hyperparameter definitions and the metric of the model that matches the given data, such as cross-validation residual, likelihood function, or risk function.

In addition, Bayesian optimization can be used to simultaneously tune multiple aspects of the machine learning model, such as data preprocessing and model hyperparameters [9]. Bayesian optimization can be utilized in various models, including Gaussian process (GP) [10], random forests (RF) [11], and tree-structured Parzen estimator (TPE); each of these models has its strengths. In this study, our team used two open-source hyperparameters tuning tools, Hyperopt [12] and Optunity [13], which are most widely used recently. The main purpose of applying the two above tools is to efficiently and robustly search hyperparameters in an AutoML framework.

III. System Architecture and Implementation

The architecture of PFP-NAS can be divided into several modules, which are the Just-in-Time Performance Prediction Module, Once-for-All Pre-training Module, Network Architecture Search Module, Network Architecture Searching Agent Module, and Kernel Service Module.

The Fig. 4 is the conceptual system architecture diagram. The main concept is to use the NAS Agent embedded on the client-side hardware platform. The NAS agent is a middleware between the datacenter and users, and is responsible for communicating with the kernel service module. The data center leverages its own powerful computing resources with the Once-for-All Pre-training Module; the Just-in-Time Performance Prediction Module will automatically suit the client-side hardware, enabling a customized NAS task host on the data center (server-side). A recommended model can be generated for the client-side hardware platform, such as USB/Tensor Processing Unit (TPU)/GPU/FPGA, but only needs a mere little amount of computing power. Users do not need to concern about dataset leaking.

When users actually use the PFP-NAS service, they only need to provide specific requirements and specifications. PFP-NAS will select the appropriate Just-in-Time performance prediction module and the appropriate pre-trained Once-for-All network to recommend the network structure.

Users use private data sets to test the recommended network on the hardware architecture of the client-side and then report the actual performance results to the server, as bottom left of Fig. 5 is shown. The server will revise the original network and further recommend the new network based on these results. Since there is already a pre-trained Once-for-All network, fine-tuning for different hardware is saved every time performing a platform-aware NAS for a specific large-scale network structure. It can save a lot of time because the user does not need to retrain the network on the client-side. The network scale of the Just-in-Time Performance Prediction Module is small, so the revision will be completed in a few seconds, and the calculation of the online model recommendation is fast and real-time. This research organizes the entire PFP-NAS training process and the interaction between the user and the server as shown in Fig. 9. Therefore, the procedures of the designed algorithm are shown as the following:

- Step 1. The user on the client-side submits the description file specifing the execution parameters and resouce requirements through web-based interface or Restful API. Kernel Service will perform data integration and create a new Python program execution task. During the execution

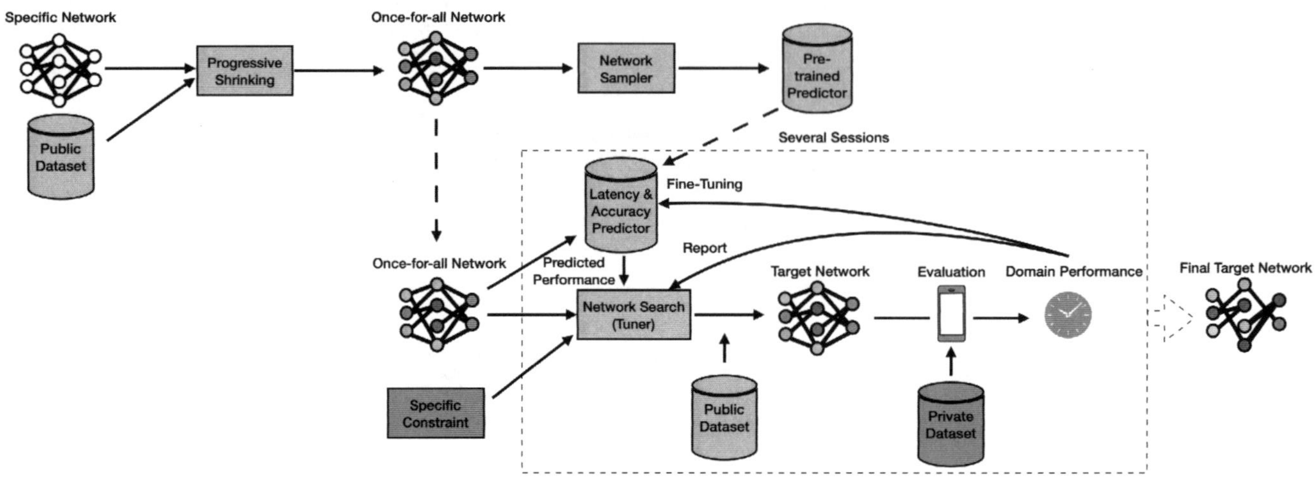

Fig. 5. The Interaction between the Once-for-All Pre-training Module, JIT Performance Predict Module and Client-side NAS Agent

of the Kernel Service, the related Input (Dataset, Criteria: Accuracy, Latency, Throughput, etc.) will be stored in MariaDB.

- Step 2. The python program and input parameters are sent to the NAS Module for execution, and the combinations of recommended hyperparameter of dedicated neural network are dynamically generated. The hyperparamether combinations will be stored in MariaDB performed by Kernel Service Module and visualized with a web-based interface which the client can browse on their device.
- Step 3. NAS Agent will gather performance metrics of hardware and the model inference result on the user platform, feedback to the server.
- Step 4. Kernel Service Module receives the user domain information sent by NAS Agent. The Just-in-Time Performance Prediction Module consists of the two three-layer multilayer perceptron neural networks and a joint score algorithm (shown in Alg. 1), and it will be automatically updated according to model inference latency and accuracy under user platform with private dataset. A new NAS task will be performed by Kernel Service following the prediction.
- Step 5: Repeat steps 2 to 4.
- Step 6. Generate an optimized candidate neural network model (NN) and send it back to the user.
- Step 7. (Optional) The client can effectively perform a fine-tuning with a recommended model with few epochs because the recommended model already has high-accuracy and low-latency.

We will dedicate each module of our PFP-NAS below.

A. Just-In-Time (JIT) Performance Prediction Module

JIT Performance Prediction Module comprises two 3-layer multilayer perceptron (MLP) prediction networks, divided into latency and accuracy prediction networks. PFP-NAS will train a set of specialized performances for each specific task's Once-for-All network and then predict the users' hardware status.

When each online mission of PFP-NAS is performed, the user will actually test the received recommended network structure on the user's hardware platform. Because there is no backward propagation process but only inference process, we can quickly get the actual performance results when the user tests the network with the private data set on the hardware platform. PFP-NAS will carry out the backward propagation of the prediction network based on the user domain results. Because of the networks in JIT Performance Prediction Module is relatively small, it only takes a few seconds to update the prediction network to obtain high accuracy during actual operation.

To acquire the base unit for latency and accuracy magnitude, we take both magnitudes into one base quantity - score (shown in Alg. 1; As we want to avoid a high latency model primarily, we will put a higher penalty coefficient to latency.

JIT Performance Predict Module will feed the score back to Kernel Service, and tune NAS modules.

B. Once-for-All Pre-training Module

The main purpose of the Once-for-All network is to deploy directly under different hardware restrictions without retraining and re-searching. Only the Lookup Table method is needed to determine the network architecture. It can flexibly deal with different depths, widths, kernel sizes, and resolutions, as shown in the Fig. 6 below (Once-for-All). In this way, continuous re-searching and continuous retraining can be successfully avoided. The problem that the NAS algorithm cannot handle the diverse hardware environment in the past can also be solved. Furthermore, the core service will interact with JIT Performance Prediction Module. When the Once-for-All module generates a new subnet architecture, it will be one-hot encoded and fed to the JIT Performance Prediction Module to obtain the delay and accuracy. Then NAS module uses this

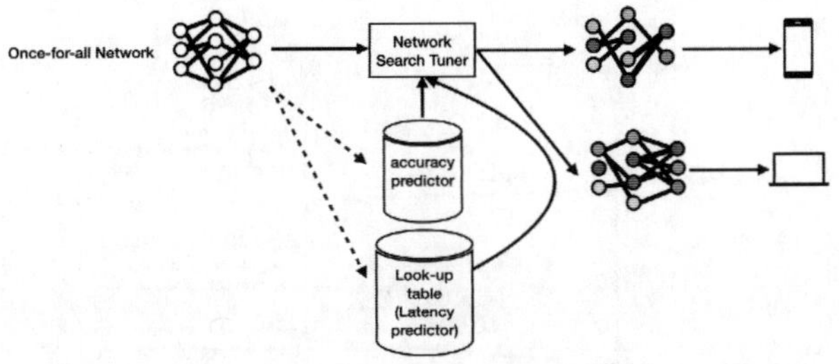

Fig. 6. The Original Once-for-All Training Flow

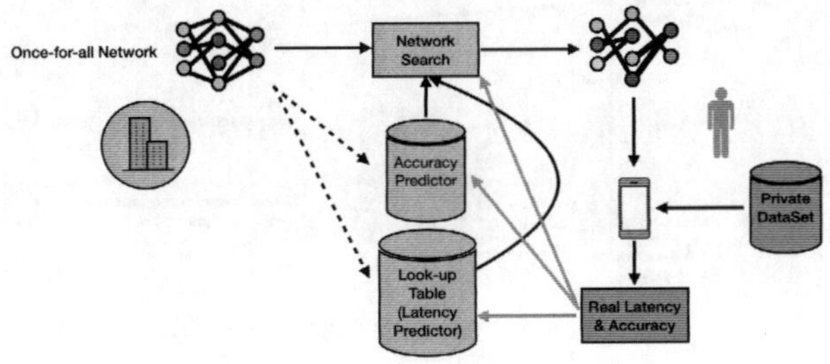

Fig. 7. The Proposed Once-for-All Module Flow

set of results to perform parameter recommendation and then hand it over to the Once-for-All module for model training and search of the next round. The implementation of the Once-for-All module is based on MobileNet V2, which mainly implements 5 large blocks and 1 small block, and the depth of each large block is 2-4 layers, as shown in the following Fig. 7. The user-side only needs to evaluate (not fine-tuning) the network and feedback the performance measure.

After integrating the Once-for-All Module into the system, the process architecture provided is shown in the right top of Fig. 5. Above all, we use many open data sets to train the Once-for-All network for a specific model architecture in the data center and pre-train a network of JIT Performance Prediction Module suitable for different hardware platforms. Considering the size of the open data set and the resources required to train a Once-for-All network, such a process requires a lot of time and computing resources. We will distribute these tasks to the computing center for preprocessing.

C. Neural Architecture Search (NAS) Module

This module can be easily replaced with any hardware-measurement-based NAS, such as ProxylessNAS, ENAS, and reinforce-learning-based NAS. The whole process of model searching will automatically adapt the target according to model performance (accuracy) and latency on hardware. In this article, we use ProxylessNAS for the default network searching algorithm, the ProxylessNAS adopts a method for making accuracy and latency magnitude differentiable, which is the loss function of a network model, and thereby use gradient descent to optimize the network searching model for finding a better network architecture.

D. Neural Architecture Search (NAS) Agent Module

NAS Agent Module is a client daemon for preliminary and simplified detection of hardware information on the client-side. At the same time, it collects the non-confidential performance metrics of testing results and feeds them back to the Server for prediction and optimization in the next cycle. The main purpose of NAS Agent is to allow users to communicate with the server easily. Users acquire the NAS model trained by the Server without considering their own hardware architecture on edge/mobile computing and without providing their own data sets. The entire data center is transformed to allow users to use it dynamically and easily through a portable fast NAS device. The device (NAS Agent) of the client-side receives the candidate models generated by the Kernel Service (Portable Fast Platform-Aware NAS) of the server-site, and these models can be tested on the client-side. Then, the following steps are performed on the client-side:

- Step1. Run the candidate model generated by the kernel service (Portable Fast Platform-Aware NAS) of the Server Site , and process the models of AI Framework in .prototext and .caffemodel formats;
- Step2. Execute Model Optimizer to output .xml and .bin formats;
- Step3. Inference Engine interacts with User Application and collects the information of hardware architecture;
- Step4. Automatically detect the hardware architecture running the inference job and send it back to the server-site.

E. Kernel Service Module

The Kernel Service Module provides the HTTP service with Restful API, the web-based interface, and task scheduling. The components of Kernel Service are introduced below.

1) Dispatcher: Dispatcher is responsible for the task scheduling of Tuner and Assessor, which are parts of NAS Module, and the generation of configuration files for each trial, including hyperparameter combinations and specific neural network architecture. During the training process, it analyzes the intermediate result value of each trial, and evaluate whether it should be terminated early.

2) NNI Manager: NNI Manager is responsible for each training experiment. With interaction with NAS Module, it can find the best hyperparameter combination and the best neural network architecture for the training model through experiments.

3) DBMS: The record of Once-for-All Pre-training Module and user domain information of each feedback with trail ID will be stored in MariaDB.

4) Training Service: The Training Service will gather and synchronize parameters along with related programs with the dispatcher, and perform the training task. The NAS Module mentioned above will automatically incorporate the Training Service as the computing resource for training.

Users can use built-in training services provided by Microsoft NNI to run trial jobs on the local machine, remote

Algorithm 1 The designed joint latency and accuracy score

Input: latency and accuracy
Output: score

```
if latency > LATENCY_THRES then
    score ← accuracy - (latency / LATENCY_THRES ) ∗ PENALTY_COEFF
else
    score ← accuracy
end if
```

Fig. 8. The designed joint latency and accuracy score

machines, and on clusters like PAI, Kubeflow, AdaptDL, FrameworkController, DLTS, and AML.

IV. EXPERIMENTS

Our experiments mainly focus on the effectiveness of AI training with PFP-NAS on multiple hardware requirements. In this section, we test the effectiveness of PFP-NAS on various hardware requirements with parallel multiple computing nodes. Our experiments apply PFP-NAS with Imagenet [14] as public dataset on five workstations with Intel(R) Xeon(R) Gold 5118 CPU @ 2.30GHz and test 6, 12, 24 NVidia GeForce GTX 1080 GPUs. The client task is Cifar-10 [15], and the pre-trained once-for-all network is based on mobilenet V2.

To prove the effectiveness of designed architecture, we test the PFP-NAS on the local workstation (the NAS agent and kernel service modules are hosted on the single workstation) and remote execution. We fix the hyperparameter search algorithm on annealing and set the same hardware requirements in this experiment. The results (Table I) show the top-1 and top-5 accuracy do not have much difference.

To verify the effectiveness of PFP-NAS under different hardware requirements, we set different latency, trial times, number of dispatched process in treatment of our experiments. We can see that the model performance will be better under the some treatment settings in Table II, and the same results (Table III) can be seen in treatment of hyperparameter search method.

We compared different hyperparameter tuning methodologies in PFP-NAS, such as Anneal, TPE, and Random search, and found that the result does not significantly differ; possible reasons might be the experiment network size are too small to have a large search space. Although the effectiveness of PFP-NAS is proven, the combination relationship with tuning methodologies still remains unclear, and the experiments of larger-scale neural network are needed.

V. CONCLUSIONS

In the era of artificial intelligence, while gaining convenience from advanced machine learning, deep learning, and

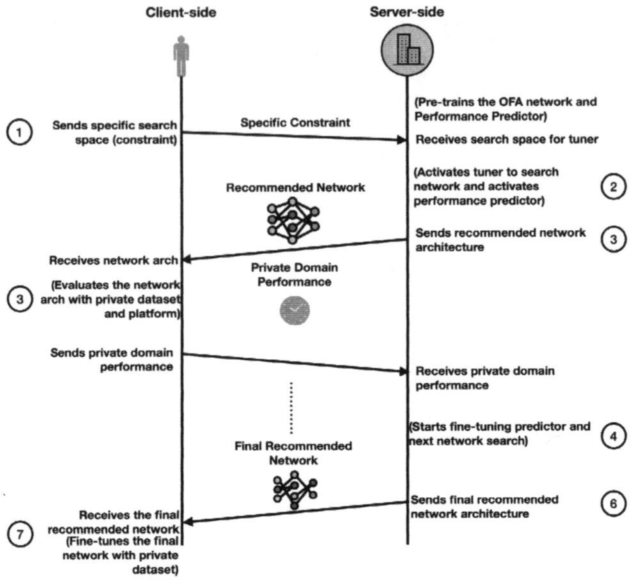

Fig. 9. The Model Recommendation Procedures

neural network search technology, it also faces data privacy issues and the risk of data leakage. When the user wants to keep its own private data set and does not provide it to the server, how the server can automatically determine the hardware architecture of the client-side and successfully recommend the NAS model becomes a tall order. The mechanism designed in this research solves this pain point. When the client-side data set and hardware architecture are confidential information and cannot be leaked, the kernel service of the server-side recommends a corresponding neural network model based on the preliminary information provided by the client-side. Then, the user actually runs the neural network model on its own hardware and feeds back the performance measurements to the server to update information and generate a new model.

The experiments around the different hardware settings show the effectiveness of our proposed PFP-NAS in the lightweight network, and further investigation about other network types and scales is ongoing. Also, through the designed PFP-NAS, the time-consuming training workout that originally required a lot of time is reduced to a few seconds for recommended models. For privacy, the PFP-NAS leverages the computing capability from the data center to help users create their own model but deals with the dataset privacy issue: users without powerful computing resources can utilize the cloud-based computing service and have no worries about the data leaking.

Next stage, we will leverage our proposed method into diversity experiments mainly to extend the Once-for-All module with other popular networks (not only the MobileNet V2), and apply the PFP-NAS to other application scenarios.

TABLE I
PFP-NAS PERFORMANCE IN SINGLE MACHINE AND MULTIPLE MACHINES

machine platform	dispatched process	tuner algorithm	psuedo trial	latency mape	avg_corr	max_latency	top-1 (%)	top-5(%)
local	2	anneal	0	0	1	85	94.22	94.16
local	4						94.39	94.18
controller	12						94.49	94.41

TABLE II
PFP-NAS PERFORMANCE IN DIFFERENT TUNER TRIAL REQUIREMENTS

dispatched process	tuner algorithm	psuedo trial	latency MAPE	avg_corr	max_latency	top-1(%)	top-5 (%)
12	anneal	0	0	1	85	94.49	94.41
		10	0.05	0.92		94.24	94.154
		150				94.47	94.418
		300				94.44	94.24
		1000				94.11	94.088
24		300				94.49	94.358
6					125	94.01	93.822
					165	93.96	93.886
					205	94.18	93.89
					245	94.08	94.036
					285	94.14	93.918

TABLE III
PFP-NAS PERFORMANCE IN DIFFERENCT HYPERPARAMETER SEARCHING METHODS.

dispatched process	tuner algorithm	psuedo trial	latency MAPE	avg_corr	max_latency	top-1 (%)	top-5 (%)
6	tpe	300	0.05	0.92	85	94.08	94.026
	random_search					93.99	93.762
	anneal					94.24	94.16

REFERENCES

[1] H. Cai, C. Gan, and S. Han, "Once for all: Train one network and specialize it for efficient deployment," *CoRR*, vol. abs/1908.09791, 2019. [Online]. Available: http://arxiv.org/abs/1908.09791

[2] M. Feurer, A. Klein, K. Eggensperger, J. Springenberg, M. Blum, and F. Hutter, "Efficient and robust automated machine learning," in *Advances in Neural Information Processing Systems*, C. Cortes, N. Lawrence, D. Lee, M. Sugiyama, and R. Garnett, Eds., vol. 28. Curran Associates, Inc., 2015.

[3] M. Zaharia, A. Chen, A. Davidson, A. Ghodsi, S. Hong, A. Konwinski, S. Murching, T. Nykodym, P. Ogilvie, M. Parkhe, F. Xie, and C. Zumar, "Accelerating the machine learning lifecycle with mlflow," *IEEE Data Eng. Bull.*, vol. 41, pp. 39–45, 2018.

[4] Microsoft Corporation, "Neural network intelligence," https://github.com/microsoft/nni , accessed: 2021-07-19.

[5] C. Ying, A. Klein, E. Christiansen, E. Real, K. Murphy, and F. Hutter, "NAS-bench-101: Towards reproducible neural architecture search," in *Proceedings of the 36th International Conference on Machine Learning*, ser. Proceedings of Machine Learning Research, K. Chaudhuri and R. Salakhutdinov, Eds., vol. 97. PMLR, 09–15 Jun 2019, pp. 7105–7114. [Online]. Available: http://proceedings.mlr.press/v97/ying19a.html

[6] C. Thornton, F. Hutter, H. H. Hoos, and K. Leyton-Brown, "Auto-weka: Automated selection and hyper-parameter optimization of classification algorithms," *CoRR*, vol. abs/1208.3719, 2012. [Online]. Available: http://arxiv.org/abs/1208.3719

[7] W. Burgard, O. Brock, and C. Stachniss, *Active Policy Learning for Robot Planning and Exploration under Uncertainty*, 2008, pp. 321–328.

[8] E. Brochu, T. Brochu, and N. de Freitas, "A bayesian interactive optimization approach to procedural animation design," in *Proceedings of the 2010 ACM SIGGRAPH/Eurographics Symposium on Computer Animation*, ser. SCA '10. Goslar, DEU: Eurographics Association, 2010, p. 103–112.

[9] A. Coates, A. Ng, and H. Lee, "An analysis of single-layer networks in unsupervised feature learning," in *Proceedings of the Fourteenth International Conference on Artificial Intelligence and Statistics*, ser. Proceedings of Machine Learning Research, G. Gordon, D. Dunson, and M. Dudík, Eds., vol. 15. Fort Lauderdale, FL, USA: PMLR, 11–13 Apr 2011, pp. 215–223. [Online]. Available: http://proceedings.mlr.press/v15/coates11a.html

[10] J. Snoek, H. Larochelle, and R. P. Adams, "Practical bayesian optimization of machine learning algorithms," in *Advances in Neural Information Processing Systems*, F. Pereira, C. J. C. Burges, L. Bottou, and K. Q. Weinberger, Eds., vol. 25. Curran Associates, Inc., 2012.

[11] F. Hutter, H. H. Hoos, and K. Leyton-Brown, "Sequential model-based optimization for general algorithm configuration," in *Learning and Intelligent Optimization*, C. A. C. Coello, Ed. Berlin, Heidelberg: Springer Berlin Heidelberg, 2011, pp. 507–523.

[12] J. Bergstra, D. Yamins, and D. Cox, "Making a science of model search: Hyperparameter optimization in hundreds of dimensions for vision architectures," in *Proceedings of the 30th International Conference on Machine Learning*, ser. Proceedings of Machine Learning Research, S. Dasgupta and D. McAllester, Eds., vol. 28, no. 1. Atlanta, Georgia, USA: PMLR, 17–19 Jun 2013, pp. 115–123. [Online]. Available: http://proceedings.mlr.press/v28/bergstra13.html

[13] M. Claesen, J. Simm, D. Popovic, Y. Moreau, and B. D. Moor, "Easy hyperparameter search using optunity," 2014.

[14] J. Deng, W. Dong, R. Socher, L.-J. Li, K. Li, and L. Fei-Fei, "Imagenet: A large-scale hierarchical image database," in *2009 IEEE conference on computer vision and pattern recognition*. Ieee, 2009, pp. 248–255.

[15] A. Krizhevsky, G. Hinton *et al.*, "Learning multiple layers of features from tiny images," 2009.

Dual-Track Agile in Early-Stage Startups

Elena Lape
School of Informatics
The University of Edinburgh
Edinburgh, United Kingdom
e-mail: elena@tardis.ed.ac.uk

Abstract—**Dual-Track Agile is a new type of Agile development where work is broken down into two parallel tracks: generating validated ideas for the development backlog (Discovery track) and turning those ideas into software (Delivery track). There exists a small body of research on Product teams within established companies using Dual-Track Agile. In contrast, this study focuses on how and for what reasons early-stage startups use this model in their product development processes. We interviewed five early-stage technology companies, and found that startups use Dual-Track Agile to ensure that their software meets customers' needs and to build lasting relationships with potential users who can be valuable in later development stages. Most researched startups who identify themselves as Dual-Track Agile adopters do not follow strict methodologies, but instead, their workflows are driven by Product management and software development tools they use. We also found that more defined product development processes are introduced as companies grow.**

Keywords—Agile software development; Software engineering; Engineering management; Product development.

I. Introduction

In an early 2021 publication, Porter and Heppelmann described how an increasingly interconnected world created a competitive landscape in digital product development [1]. Good quality software on its own is no longer enough to please people: consumers are looking for tools that solve their problems better than existing ones. Naturally, companies developing software products need to test, iterate, and experiment with the market constantly to keep up with the competition. Each time a new product enters the market, user expectations also rise — it gives them ideas about what other functionalities there could be.

In order to stand out from the competition and not waste time on features that bring little value to users, technology companies need to find ways to quickly validate product ideas and make sure that only validated ideas are implemented. The Dual-Track Agile, also known as the Continuous Discovery and Delivery model, offers Product development teams a solution to this challenge by combining the Discovery and Delivery activities in parallel. According to this model, teams need to align their software development processes with continuous market research and validation.

Startups' adoption of the Dual-Track Agile model is not widely researched in academia. This study focuses specifically on early-stage company product development practices.

The main goal of this study was to learn how startups adopt Dual-Track Agile in practice. We broke down this goal into three components, and so the following research questions were considered:

- What are startups' motivations for using Continuous Discovery and Delivery, provided they do use it?
- What Continuous Discovery and Delivery practices do startups adopt, and how are they built into their processes?
- How does the scale of the company affect its Continuous Discovery and Delivery practices?

The study was organised in two parts. First, we reviewed the existing work to understand Dual-Track Agile and the challenges that come with it. Then, we interviewed five different startups to learn about how they implement Discovery and Delivery in their teams.

Section 2 presents the related work relevant to this study, Section 3 describes the methodology used to sample and interview startups, Sections 4 and 5 present and analyze interview responses on the two topics of Discovery and Delivery respectively, Section 6 discusses the results of the interviews, Section 7 proposes some limitations to the study, and Section 8 concludes with a summary and future work.

II. Related work

Single- and Dual-Track Agile methodologies share a similar philosophy in that they both recognise the need for flexibility in software and product development.

A. Single-Track Agile

Many companies developing digital applications have adopted an Agile approach to software development. Traditional Agile methodology focuses on software functionality and is flexible to adapt to changing functional requirements [2]. However, there are at least two problems with Agile development, given today's competitive landscape.

First, Agile treats "working software" as the teams' primary measure of progress [3]. This measure emphasizes technical excellence and building out features but does not address the user perspective side of the development. Without a process to closely couple Delivery with market research, the products may end up being high quality

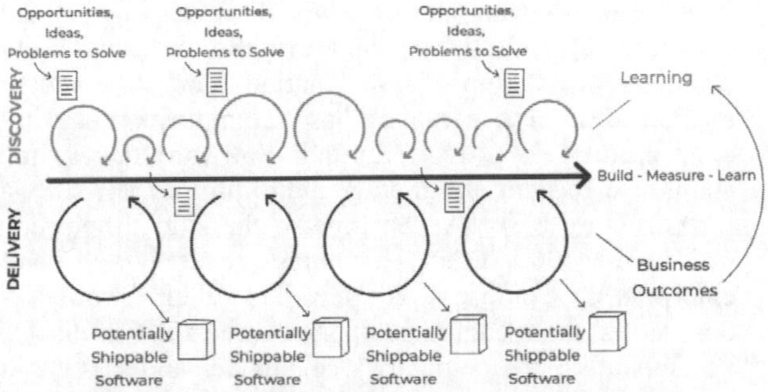

Figure 1: The Discovery-Delivery model (adapted from [9]).

engineering-wise, but something that the customers do not like or use. Without an approach that integrates more User Centered Design elements, Agile becomes not too dissimilar from Waterfall, where "testing and validating" is a discrete phase of software development that is usually final one [4].

Second, Agile assumes the presence of a "client" or a "customer", i.e., a stakeholder who creates and changes requirements and sets priorities for the Development team. Sedano et al. highlight that "Agile methods do not explain how to identify stakeholders, understand them, model them or turn this understanding into stories that developers can readily implement" [5]. Agile does not have inherent support for constantly evolving markets, frequent stakeholders changes, and an ecosystem where user requirements are yet to be uncovered.

Interestingly, the two issues highlighted above have been identified even before the Agile Manifesto was created in 2001. Gilb and Finzi's *Principles of Software Engineering Management* published in 1988, then introduced *Evolutionary Delivery* as a potential solution: delivering a system to users in "miniature incremental versions" to allow for changing markets dictating product pivots, and collecting plenty of feedback [6]. However, their Evolutionary Delivery model did not provide guidance on how exactly teams should prioritise ideas and requirements, or how and at what stage they should involve end-users in the feedback process.

B. Dual-Track Agile

Dual-Track Agile (or Continuous Discovery and Delivery) is a new type of Agile development. It offers to solve traditional Agile's shortcomings by combining Product Discovery (the ability of a company to validate products, services or features before implementation) and Delivery (the technical implementation and deployment of the identified outputs of Product Discovery) activities in parallel, as defined by Trieflinger et al. [7]. According to Cagan, Continuous Discovery and Delivery is a model as opposed to a methodology [8], as is illustrated in Figure 1.

Following the observation that companies see Product Discovery as a necessity but "struggle in finding an approach to conduct Product Discovery and Delivery activities", Trieflinger et al. found five different implementation approaches to Dual-Track Agile in grey literature:

- *Pay to Learn/Pay to Build Cycle.* Product Discovery is carried out in the "pay to learn" cycle, while Product Delivery is carried out in the "pay to build" cycle. In the "pay to learn" cycle, the process begins with the gathering of ideas, such as performing interviews with prospective clients and other related internal stakeholders. To test each idea, one or more hypotheses are established based on these ideas. Experiments are used to test theories, and good ideas may be added to the product backlog. A first iteration of a concept is introduced and shipped to consumers in the pay-to-build cycle, and then feedback is obtained — this serves as input for the next Discovery cycle.
- *Now-next-later Product Roadmap.* Product roadmaps that facilitate the Delivery of goods, features, or services focused on consumer and business value are known as now-next-later roadmaps. Theme-based roadmaps, in contrast to outcome-driven roadmaps, add an additional layer of aggregation (themes) from which the desired outcomes are derived. The three columns 'now', 'next', and 'later' in both roadmap formats indicate the time horizon (in contrast to time-based roadmaps)
- *Product Kata.* Product Kata is a four-step method for assisting Product teams in aligning around a common goal, learning about customer needs, and determining the best solution to build. It is a high-level model with three Discovery-related steps, after which the team must choose the Delivery implementation process ("solution optimization").
- *Lean Sprints.* This type of Dual-Track Agile implementation was introduced by Ash Maurya, author of "Scaling Lean". Sprints are typically two weeks long, and each phase of product development consists of one Discovery sprint and one or multiple Delivery sprints. To generate a variety of ideas and hypotheses, the author suggests forming a cross-functional Product development team that includes designers, software developers, and marketers [10].
- *Dual Track Scrum.* Each track has its own team in the 'Dual-Track Scrum' technique. Lead designers and developers usually make up the Discovery team, while developers and software testers make up the Delivery team. To improve communication and workflow between the two teams, it is recommended that a Product Owner be included on both teams. The Discovery team gathers data from users, creates prototypes, and tests ideas. Ideas are classed as "mature" (ready to be added to the scrum backlog and implemented), and

"immature" (not useful for users or not viable to be implemented by the Development team) [11].

Most Continuous Discovery and Delivery workflows from Trieflinger's literature review assume a cross-functional Product development team, which is largely a characteristic of larger established companies.

Finding suitable workflows is especially tough for smaller teams and startups who may have a limited budget and a small number of employees, but who need to move quickly to meet the market. It remains unclear how early-stage startups adopt this model in practice, how they structure it compared to larger teams, and what value Dual-Track Agile brings to their team or products.

III. Methodology

We interviewed five founders and early-stage employees at technology startups developing software-based products. The interviews took place between March and May 2021. In this initial study we had limited resources — therefore, we adopted a qualitative approach to interview a small number of startups showing signs of potential to be successful supported by a review of valuable literature. This means that our conclusions are tentative but they are indicative of the issues encountered by startups in developing new products in a Dual-Track Agile way.

A. Selection Criteria

The research target group were C-suite executives, Product Managers, and Engineers who were early employees — one of the first twenty — in companies that are younger than eight years old. The group self-identified as individuals who use Dual-Track Agile or Continuous Discovery and Delivery processes at work.

The target companies were for-profit businesses with a recent valuation (through equity investment received or EBITDA [12]) of at least 1 million US Dollars. Their core business must revolve around a software product(/-s) or a service(/-s) that at the time of the study had at least 50 individual users.

B. Research Participants

1) Participant A/Company A: Company A is a two-year-old SaaS company based in Canada valued at approximately 50 million USD. They develop virtual reality applications for showcasing 3D models of buildings' interiors and exteriors. The company employs 20 people full-time and outsources a remote Software development team overseas consisting of 30 software engineers-consultants. Company A's clients are typically property development firms. The company is a spin-off of another two-year-old company specialising in Virtual Machine (VM) provisioning for consumer applications. Participant A is the co-founder and Chief Technology Officer (CTO) of both companies. He has a professional background in full-stack software engineering and developing VM and Cloud Computing environments.

2) Participant B/Company B: Company B is a two-year-old United States-based software infrastructure cost analytics startup with a valuation of approximately 30 million USD. The company has 12 employees, and their core product is a platform that Software development teams use to plan and predict and optimise their software infrastructure costs. At the time of the study, the product had over 1000 users, including several well-known enterprises. Company B describes their product as open-core: their engine is open-sourced on GitHub [13]. Participant B, the company's co-founder and CTO, has a professional background in site reliability engineering at major technology companies and full-stack engineering at startups. They also have a Bachelor's degree in Computer Science from UC Berkeley.

3) Participant C/Company C: Company C is a two-year-old United Kingdom-based startup developing a digital application that allows users to manage the storage and insurance of their collectable assets. Their target market is primarily luxury car collectors with busy lifestyles who outsource the management of their car portfolio. The product is currently in its beta stage with over 100 user sign-ups, has a valuation of over 1.3 million USD, and five full-time employees. Participant C is a founding engineer of the company. Their professional background is in building full-stack web and mobile applications, and they have a Bachelor's degree in Political Science from The University of Edinburgh.

4) Participant D/Company D: Company D is a United Kingdom-based startup with a recent valuation of around 6 million USD, focusing on providing web scraping solutions for financial institutions and government organisations. Most of the company's work is project-based. Company D has been working on these types of projects since 2016 and currently has 20 full-time employees. Participant D is the Vice President of Technology in the company overseeing the Software development team's work. They have a professional background in low-level software infrastructure engineering and full-stack software development.

5) Participant E/Company E: Company E is a three-year-old company based in Romania, targeting the European higher education market. Their core product allows prospective students and university admissions consultants to manage multiple international university applications in one platform. Company E has recently been valued at 1.4 million Euros and has around 35 employees, half of which are full-time. Participant E is the company's Business Development Manager who joined the company within the first 20 employees. However, they were the first person to be hired to focus specifically on the Discovery Track. Their professional background is in data analytics and entrepreneurship-themed event organising, and they have a Bachelor's degree in IT and Business Management from Manchester University.

C. Interview Process

The nature of the study is exploratory, therefore the schedule was constructed in a semi-structured manner. To avoid researcher's bias and allow for rich qualitative data to be collected, we used open-ended questions. Interviews with each participant were conducted in a one-on-one over a video communications platform. Each interview took between one and two hours to complete.

At the start of the interview, each participant was asked a number of questions that called for discrete answers, such as company valuation, company size, their technology stack, or concrete product development methodologies. This data allowed us to compare and contrast the startups on the same terms, and draw more objective observations.

Later in the interview, each study participant was asked to first describe their Discovery processes: e.g., what Discovery means to them, who (if anyone) leads their Discovery efforts, what Discovery data (if any) they collect, and what they do with it. Then, they were asked to do the same with Delivery: e.g., how they define Delivery, who leads Delivery at their company, how they organize it and using which tools (if any). Towards the end of the interview, the participants were asked to talk about how they bridge Discovery and Delivery, naming any specific tools, people, or methodologies they rely on.

D. Data Processing

The audio extracted from the videos was processed using Amazon Transcribe to generate time stamped transcripts in JSON format [14]. To parse the JSON data into a human-readable format, we used the tscribe Python library to convert the transcripts into readable document format [15]. This way, we were able to find the participants' responses to specific questions and discussion themes based on the timestamps, summarize their responses, and compare with other startups' responses regarding that topic or theme.

IV. The Discovery Track

This section presents summarized and analyzed responses to Discovery-related interview questions and themes.

A. Interview Responses

1) Participant A/Company A: Company A business as project-based, where the deliverable is a 3D VR property visualisation. Each project starts with the client providing a property plan and is managed using a simple *to-do*, *in-progress*, *done* Trello board [16]. An initial prototype is then created and sent to the client for revisions.

To make revisions, in the earliest stages of the company Participant A would "initially meet the client every single week and walk with the client with a VR headset and listen to them what they wanted to fix in the VR deliverable". However, this proved to be inefficient and "such a hassle".

Participant A "ended up writing a very, very simple application". Clients were given access to a VR application where they could "draw a little red circle and write notes on what they want to change". This helped Company A speed up and scale their Discovery process. The red circle would automatically spawn up a "to-do card on Trello" in the product development Kanban board. This created "a closed feedback loop with the developers".

Automating their Discovery process helped Company A spot patterns across different clients and improve their initial prototypes and shorten the Delivery cycle from months to weeks.

2) Participant B/Company B: Company B operates in the software infrastructure space. In 2019, Participant B co-founded a two-person open source project on GitHub to test their idea. From early stages onward, open sourcing the core of their engine allowed them to verify that there is a market for the tool via growing GitHub popularity and incoming outside contributions. At the same time, they were collecting user feedback and feature requests through GitHub Issues.

As the tool's popularity grew, Company B created a community Slack workspace for the users, as a way to provide customer support and observe the pain points the company could address [17]. Slack also helped them build "close relationships with power-users who were willing to share more detailed feedback".

Feedback and feature requests are translated into "product themes, areas of improvement or new opportunities", which are then "added into quarterly roadmaps". Tasks are prioritized based on the "severity of the issue" (e.g., "a security bug will be very high priority"), implementation scope, and "how much revenue depends on getting this done" — for example, if a paying enterprise client is asking for a particular feature, and Company B identifies that there may be other potential customers facing similar problems, then the feature's priority will be high.

3) Participant C/Company C: Participant C describes the Discovery processes of their collectible asset management app as mostly ad-hoc and heavily based on "building personal relationships with potential customers" that emerged from the founders' personal network.

Participant C believes that that "clearly defined organised Discovery processes found in business manuals distract you from the goals when the company is small", and they remarked that "it would waste everyone's time and it would not fit in correctly; we are working very chaotically together, and that's how we get the best ideas, the best things ever". Participant C stresses that working with "experienced, intelligent teammates" is what allows them to communicate loose research and development plans and feature roadmaps verbally, and "keep them in their head".

In addition, Company C relies on readily available SaaS tools to conduct Discovery. For example, they use FullStory to collect usage statistics and user experience metrics from their private beta [18]. This data is verbally interpreted by the founding team as features and fixes that they then go on to implement.

4) Participant D/Company D: Company D develops web scraping and search products for clients on a project basis. Each project begins with the client providing a list of functional requirements. However, there is a "surprising amount of variance between clients", therefore Company D has to research government regulations and compliance documentation independently.

Given the nature of the contracts being confidential and subject to government regulations, Continuous Discovery happens in-house. Participant D said that after each iteration, they would have "demo days to pitch them to a range of cross-functional teams (sales, engineering) within the organisation". For Company D, the demo days "have become a very core way of being able to prove concepts quickly for things that might not necessarily be immediately visible even to clients". Demo day findings become input for the next Delivery cycle, organised as a 2-week sprint.

5) Participant E/Company E: Company E is developing an all-in-one platform for university application management. At the start of their business, they first quickly built a prototype based on their hypotheses, and then "participated in educational conferences in order to get access to a network of university admission consultant agencies". Then, they "started having phone calls with them presenting what they want to build in the future", showing them the value that the product brings and observing reactions.

Participant E highlights quality over quantity when gathering feedback for their releases. "Every two or three weeks", Participant E shows customers several versions of the product, observes them using it, going step by step, collecting answers to questions such as "What do you need here?", "What do you see there?", "Is this useful to you?", "We're working towards this feature, what do you think about it?".

Company E uses Productboard [19] "to organise answers and ideas into themes", which then go through a prioritisation process with Product Managers based on scope, urgency and "market opportunity" once a month. Once features are determined, they are added to the next Delivery cycle. For "small bug fixes, developers are contacted directly in a dedicated Slack channel".

B. Analysis

Discovery differs significantly in project-based companies versus companies who offer a single platform. Companies A and D typically have an initial list of requirements from clients to build a prototype they can iterate on, whereas Companies B, C and E have to validate the market and then navigate the problem ambiguity themselves.

Companies B, C and E value building personal relationships and directly talking with potential customers to understand their needs over having directed, streamlined Discovery processes. As such, the initial requirements that enter their Delivery Track are somewhat experimental in nature.

It is important to note that in the cases of Companies B, C and E, founders admitted that their personal experience and connections gave them a head start in understanding the market and customer' needs. It is unclear whether this a prerequisite for building a technology product, but it is likely that it helps them save time and resources that would have to be devoted to conduct initial market validation and research otherwise.

Another observation is that founders all emphasize specific tools (Trello, GitHub, Slack, FullStory, Productboard) that each carry a particular workflow. Similarly, automating user feedback collection is a common theme among A (with VR app), B (with GitHub Issues, Slack) and C (with FullStory). We may hypothesise that these tools themselves help startups define Discovery processes and link them with Delivery.

V. The Delivery Track

This section presents summarized and analyzed responses to Delivery-related interview questions and themes.

A. Interview Responses

1) Participant A/Company A: Company A bridges Discovery and Delivery via a Trello Kanban board that is set up for each project. All development is outsourced to a remote Software development team overseas, and the "developers are managed by in-house Project Managers". The Project Managers are responsible for review and verification, as well as task distribution amongst developers.

Each project is set up using a CI/CD (Continuous Integration/Continuous Deployment) framework that the sister company previously built. At the start of each project, the project manager extracts feature requirements from the client's specification and puts them in the *to-do* list. Once a card is moved to *done* by a developer (whether it's for the initial version, or part of a client's revision), this triggers the CI/CD pipeline and generates a build.
Project and revision scope varies from client to client and revision to revision, therefore, time-constrained sprints are not used.

2) Participant B/Company B: Company B's Engineering team works in one-week sprints, which begin with a sprint planning meeting. When Participant B was asked why just one, they said that "the priorities change too much from week to week" at a startup, and contrasted this experience with Google, where sprints were two weeks long.

Company B has a CI/CD pipeline which generates local builds nightly, and a new software version (a production build) is released to customers every two weeks. Participant B notes that "if something is missed in a sprint, it should get picked up and done for the next release". However, security fixes "jump all the possible queues".

3) Participant C/Company C: Company C prioritised building their first version to be "robust, modular and scalable", which took them over a year to implement, and then released a private beta to a select number of customers that they had already built close relationships with for testing and qualitative feedback.

Participant C noted they built the software in a way that would account for pivots and make adding and subtracting new features easy and intuitive. Currently, Company C adds new improvements to their production environment daily.

4) Participant D/Company D: Participant D sees Delivery as "parallel to Discovery, but something that needs to be done in a different part of the brain".

Their engineering division consists of two teams: DevOps engineers, and software developers. For projects that are just starting out, DevOps engineers are responsible for scaffolding out the architecture and implementing a CI pipeline, and the Software team builds out the applications, and then does feature iterations. The engineers work in two week sprints, in line with the internal bi-weekly demos.

However, Participant D notes that this is a new process to them and at the beginning it was not standardised. Company D introduced sprints and teams' division as they scaled.

5) Participant E/Company E: Participant E is not directly involved in the Delivery process, therefore, it is unclear how those are managed in Company E's Engineering team.

B. Analysis

Project-based companies A and D work off an initial set of requirements, therefore, the process is more or less the same for each product they build. They both use CI/CD pipelines to generate incremental and production builds.

Company B delivers their product continuously by definition, starting with incremental commits to their public GitHub repository. Once the paid product was released and the team grew, more streamlined CI/CD processes were implemented to allow for scheduled releases. Bi-weekly releases help them set customer expectations, and help organise Delivery efforts internally for their grown team.

Company C described a different approach to building their software. It is somewhat similar to the Waterfall software development process because only a sophisticated version of the application was released as beta. However, it is different from Waterfall in that Company C conducts research alongside building their product, rather than following an initial set of requirements they set out. Moreover, the software is built in a scalable, modular way to allow for future changes. The reason behind releasing a polished beta and not a makeshift prototype could be the nature of C's target market: their users are busy, high net-worth individuals. These people may have limited time to provide feedback for several prototyped versions, and if the initial version does not appear to bring them value, they may lose interest in the product. In a market that is exclusive and limited in size, this could be detrimental.

All of the research participants but E indicated a strong software engineering background.

VI. Results

To address the three research questions proposed in Section 1, we formulated the results of the study based on summarized and analyzed interview responses.

A. Startups' motivations to use Dual-Track Agile

Provided that the research participants were recruited based on self-identification as "applying Dual-Track Agile (or Continuous Discovery and Delivery) in their product development processes", we can conclude that this Product Management model is indeed used by early-stage companies. In their own words, participants use the model to "verify the market", "verify need", "build incrementally and test user behaviour", "not make too many irreversible assumptions", "test hypotheses".

In addition, the model brings another important benefit for single-product startups: it helps them build relationships with potential customers. Large companies already have existing users, but new entrants face the problem in that they do not have a user base to test with. Therefore, continuously engaging with the market and talking to their users on a one-to-one basis helps create buy-in from customers and use that buy-in to gather feedback and ideas.

B. Continuous Discovery and Delivery practices

Some similarities do exist between startups and literature findings: Companies B, C, E highlighted some form of a roadmap as a way to bridge Discovery and Delivery. However, none of the study participants follow as streamlined of a Dual-Track Agile process as was found by Trieflinger et al., and instead adopt a similar mentality to Evolutionary Delivery [5].

We observed that each company's implementation of the Dual-Track model differed to an extent, which suggests that there is no universal tool or process that startups all adopt. Single product-based startups' (B, C, E) processes are overall quite simple and are largely influenced by specific tools.

Where possible, some of our study participants aim to automate their CI/CD processes and some user feedback collection (e.g. through FullStory for C, GitHub Issues and Slack for B, Trello for A) early on to save time and resources.

The implementation of the model varies also by type of startup's business model. Project-based companies (A and D), or companies that have already grown (B) aim to invest in implementing robust Discovery and Delivery processes, because they are not building for a market whose problems' solutions need to be researched, but instead — for clients who know what they want, or a user base that they already know well.

Early stage single product-based companies Discovery and Delivery processes appear to be characterised by the tools they use (Trello, FullStory, GitHub, etc.). Not over-focusing on the workflows allows them to prove concepts quicker.

Continuous Delivery practices across startups are more uniform and more streamlined than Discovery practices. They all appear to be building software in a modular, scalable way, and most use CI/CD pipelines. Their Discovery practices differ because markets, users and customers they are developing for are not uniform and each require a different approach. For example, a product aimed at asset collectors (C) requires forming personal relationships and trust via meetings and phone calls, whereas a developer tools company (B) can collect feedback via platforms that developers, conveniently, are already using every day, such as GitHub Issues.

Another reason why Continuous Delivery across most startups appears more streamlined than Discovery could be that most participants indicated a background in software engineering. It is likely that they already have experience in developing scalable, modular software for other startups or large modern companies, and so they know how to do it quickly and effectively. In addition, Continuous Delivery as a whole is a well-documented domain and so it is easier to find appropriate practices from the onset.

C. Dual-Track Agile as startups scale

We observed that in small-scale and very early-stage startups, defined Dual-Track Agile methodologies are not used, presumably because the companies are optimising for reducing time spent on tasks that are seen as counterproductive and administrative, and because small team size allows for coordinating efforts ad-hoc.

Companies do introduce some elements of organisation (e.g., sprints, quarterly roadmaps) at early-stage, though, as they scale (A, B, D) and hire more people, and employees take sole ownership of certain parts of the product.

VII. Limitations

First, the sample size of research participants is small as only five startups were interviewed. However, there are thousands of technology product startups incorporated each year. It is unclear whether it is common for early-stage companies in the world to adopt the Dual-Track Agile model in their work. Another important note is that participants were selected from an open call for participation, which means that not all founders and industries are represented. Therefore, the study results may not be generalized to the whole software startup ecosystem.

Second, the interviews are retrospective. It is possible that the participants forgot how their processes evolved over time and did not mention or purposely excluded some details they felt were unimportant, but could have been valuable for the study.

Third, the *Hawthorne Effect* may have played a part — this occurs when participants in a study are aware that they are being observed by scientists and, either consciously or unconsciously, alter the way they act or the answers they give [20]. Even though the participating companies were anonymised in the final study, some participants may have concealed important information about their processes to avoid risking the company's reputation. For example, if a company revealed that their processes change often and are chaotic, and a potential/existing investor recognises the company based on its description, the investor may choose not to invest in the following round.

VIII. Conclusion

In this study, we set out a goal to investigate how startups use Dual-Track Agile in practice, and considered three research questions:

- What are startups' motivations for using Continuous Discovery and Delivery, provided they do use it?
- What Continuous Discovery and Delivery practices do startups adopt, and how are they built into their processes?
- How does the scale of the company affect Continuous Discovery and Delivery practices?

A. Summary

We found that Dual-Track Agile is used by some startup technology companies and not just Product teams within established enterprises. The startups' motivation for using this approach is to not only verify the demand for their products or product features, but also to build close relationships with their users who can be useful in further development stages.

Most interview participants do not use the workflows found in Trieflinger et al.'s review and often rely on a set of particular tools to aid them in their broad Delivery and Discovery efforts. Where possible, early stage companies aim to automate their feedback collection and deployment processes to reduce the length of the feedback loop and speed up development time.

We found that instead of investing in processes, very early-stage products rely on verbal communication and direct prototyping to plan, validate and test their ideas. But as organisations grow in size, more concrete workflows and prioritisation processes, such as quarterly roadmaps or sprints, are introduced for visibility and organisation purposes.

As the research was carried out with five startup case studies, we recognise that our observations and results may not be representative of the whole early-stage software company ecosystem.

B. Future work

A more systematic study of startups' product development practices should be done. Longitudinal case studies and overt observations of startups would allow us to see how and why exactly their processes evolve over time, as well as validate that the startups' own descriptions of their processes align with their actions.

As this study only involved five early-stage companies, the results may not be representative of startups as a whole. In the future, a larger sample size should be examined to draw more meaningful observations.

The five case studies indicated a relationship between specific SaaS platforms and their product development workflows. However, more research needs to be conducted to assess whether chosen tools are dictating the processes, or processes dictating tools.

This paper does not examine how the early stage companies' chosen practices affect their products' usability and success. A controlled real-time study examining startups who use Continuous Discovery and Delivery versus those who do not, could provide some insight into whether chosen processes contribute to some companies' success and/or failure.

REFERENCES

1. G. M. Porter and J. Heppelmann, "How smart, connected products are transforming competition," Harvard Business Review, no. 92, pp. 64-88, 2021.
2. D. Salah, R. F. Paige, and P. Cairns, "A systematic literature review for agile development processes and user centred design integration,", 18th International Conference on Evaluation and Assessment in Software Engineering (EASE '14), no 5, pp. 1-10, 2014.
3. O. Hazzan and Y. Dubinsky, "The Agile Manifesto," in Agile Anywhere," Springer International Publishing, pp. 9–14, 2014
4. M. Light, "How the Waterfall Methodology Adapted and Whistled Past the Graveyard," Gartner Research, 2009.
5. T. Sedano, P. Ralph, and C. Peraire, "Dual-Track Development," IEEESoftw., vol. 37, no. 6, pp. 58–64, 2020.
6. T. Gilb and S. Finzi, Principles Of Software Engineering Management.Boston, MA: Addison Wesley, 1988.
7. S. Trieflinger, J. Münch, B. Heisler, and D. Lang, "Essential approaches to dual-track agile: results from a grey literature review" in International Conference on Software Business, pp. 55-69, 2020.
8. M. Cagan, Inspired: How to create tech products customers love, 2nd ed. Nashville, TN: John Wiley & Sons, 2017.
9. "Product Discovery," Aktiasolutions.com, 2020. Available: https://aktiasolutions.com/product-discovery/. [Accessed: 28 June 2021]
10. A. Maurya, "Scaling Lean: Mastering the key metrics for startup growth", Penguin, 2016.
11. J. Ciecholewski, "How to set up Dual-Track Scrum in Jira", Devbridge. Available: https://www.devbridge.com/articles/how-to-set-up-dual-track-scrum-in-jira [Accessed: 1 September 2020]
12. D. T. Emott, "EBITDA Valuation Engine" in Practitioner's Complete Guide to M&As, Hoboken, NJ, USA: John Wiley & Sons, Inc., pp. 264–275, 2015.
13. GitHub. Available: https://github.com [Accessed: 10 September 2021].
14. Amazon Transcribe. Available: https://github.com [Accessed: 10 September 2021].
15. Tscribe. Available: https://aws.amazon.com/transcribe/ [Accessed: 10 September 2021].
16. Trello. Available: https://trello.com [Accessed: 10 September 2021].
17. Slack. Available: https://slack.com/ [Accessed: 10 September 2021].
18. FullStory. Available: https://www.fullstory.com/ [Accessed: 10 September 2021].
19. Productboard. Available: https://www.productboard.com/ [Accessed: 10 September 2021].
20. S. R. G. Jones, "Was there a Hawthorne effect?," American Journal of Sociology, vol.98, no. 3, pp. 451–468, 1992.

On the Model Continuity in Control Systems Design Using DEVS, UML, and IEC 61499

Radek Kočí and Vladimír Janoušek

Brno University of Technology, Faculty of Information Technology,
Bozetechova 2, 612 66 Brno, Czech Republic
email: {koci,janousek}@fit.vut.cz

***Abstract*—This paper deals with various ways of design and implementing Distributed Control Systems (DCS). The authors are familiar with the Unified Modeling Language (UML), the Discrete Event System Specification (DEVS) formalism, the IEC 61499 standard, and different tools, such as 4diac, Node-RED, or PowerDEVS. The paper presents the basics of methodology for the design and implementation of control software, which will allow the use of any of these approaches following a conceptual model based on UML. The main reason is to describe the whole development process, from the standard UML models to their implementation, and enable the developers to use modeling or design techniques they are familiar with. The promising way is to apply the model-continuity principle in conjunction with the DEVS formalism, which can be used as a unifying platform for design, and in some cases, as the most appropriate path to implementation. Using DEVS, we get the possibility of directly applying the simulation during the design, thus a more straightforward validation of the proposed system. The DEVS model can also be transformed into alternative implementation models. The considered principles is demonstrated on a case study of a simple system, Central heating with zone valves.**

Keywords*—*Control systems; IoT; UML; DEVS; IEC 61499; simulation; model continuity.

I. INTRODUCTION

The paper presents the basics of methodology for the design and implementation of control systems. We consider the tree-level structure of such a system: sensors/actuators, distributed controllers, and a Supervisory Control And Data Acquisition (SCADA) system. The standard IEC 61499 addressing function blocks for industrial processes and control systems was established in 2005. It defines a generic model for distributed control systems. Various environments and tools follow IEC 61499 principles, e.g., 4diac with the corresponding runtime environment FORTE [1]. Different approach to the implementation of control systems or their parts is represented by, e.g., Node-RED [2]. Nevertheless, a uniform procedure including a problem analysis or requirements specification is not defined. The motivation for this work is to describe the whole development process, from the conceptual models to their implementation following the Model-Driven Development (MDD) and model-continuity principles, and allow any of the commonly available approaches. Our goal is to define and use a unified approach independently of the target implementation environment.

MDD is a development methodology that supports the use of models as significant artifacts [3]. The development process is a series of constant refinement and transformation of models. Ideally, more specific models are generated and, in the last step, the code for a particular platform. Unified Modeling Language (UML) is a standard language for modeling various aspects of software systems, both in academia and in industrial development, thanks to a sophisticated graphical representation. However, the ability to simulate and investigate models in real conditions limits the use of UML [4]. It is, therefore, appropriate to look for proper formalisms or approaches that can build on UML models and simplify the simulation and transition from models to implementation.

A typical example of a combination of formal modeling and simulation is the Discrete Event System Specification (DEVS) [5]. DEVS is a modular and hierarchical formalism for modeling and simulation of discrete event systems, systems of differential equations (continuous systems), and hybrid systems. DEVS models can be interconnected through input/output ports to create modular and hierarchical topologies of blocks. In the context of modeling and development of control systems, the Model Continuity for DEVS has been introduced [6][7]. The main idea of model continuity is that a DEVS simulation model for a controller can evolve during the development process from a pure simulation (in a simulated environment) until its final deployment in the target environment without re-implementation. The DEVS simulation engine becomes a run-time execution environment for the target system. This approach leads to the fact that no errors are introduced into the target implementation during the development.

For our work, we chose DEVS because it is well-defined, intuitive, understandable, and universal. DEVS-based real-time simulation engine (in our case PowerDEVS [8]) can be used in the role of runtime execution environment. In addition, we also consider the possibility of using other environments for implementation. These environments interpret DEVS similar models such as Node-RED flows or IEC 61499 applications (in our case, we use the open-source development environment 4diac with the runtime environment FORTE).

The paper is structured as follows. We discuss related work in Section II. Section III addresses the conceptual modeling of control systems, introducing a case study. In Section IV, we describe the possibilities of creating the Platform Independent Model (PIM) using UML and DEVS. Subsequently, in Section V, we will show the ways of creating the Platform Specific

Model (PSM) from DEVS PIM. Finally, in Section VI, we will show the possibility of extending to a distributed environment.

II. Related Work

Similar works are dealing with control system design using UML and the IEC 61499 standard. Many of them, e.g., [9]–[11], propose generating IEC 61499 from UML, or System Modeling Language (SysML), typically from a class diagram. Other works, such as [12], deal with the behavior of atomic components and propose a transformation of activity diagrams to the IEC 61499 execution control charts (ECC). Unlike these works, which interconnect UML and IEC 61499, we propose a step from UML to DEVS during the development process.

Other approaches, e.g. [13], [14] deal with the behavioral model of atomic components. In contrast, we focus only on the structure of components and sub-components in this paper. We assume the availability of a library of well-defined atomic components in the target environment.

There are also approaches that attempt to transform conceptual models, such as those described by SysML, into simulation models [15]. In contrast, we do not consider the simulation model a goal but a potential option in the development. Our main goal is a unified methodology leading to the implementation of a control system in different environments. The novelty of our approach is that we use DEVS as a basis for various ways of implementation. DEVS, IEC 61499, and Node-RED execution environments are presented as examples.

III. Conceptual Model of Control System

In this part, we will present the basic approach to creating conceptual models using the UML language and then a simple example (case study), on which we will demonstrate our approach to the design of control systems.

A. UML in Control Systems Design

UML is an acknowledged and used language for conceptual design of software systems, including control systems. Their advantage is that they can offer different views of the same system to get a complete overview of the complex system. Now, we briefly recall the basic way of designing software systems using the UML language. Although UML itself does not define the methodology and assumes that different approaches will use it, it is possible to identify basic processes, activities, and models applied to most design methodologies.

- *Requirements specification.* In the context of software design, we could also use the term system usage model, as a use case diagram is often used.
- *Structure specification.* To capture the structural elements of the system, which then contribute to the solution of individual use cases. Class, component and package diagrams are commonly used.
- *Behavior specification.* Diagrams capturing the behavior of classes (objects), use cases, or components. The most commonly used ones are activity diagrams (for use cases), state-charts, and interaction diagrams.

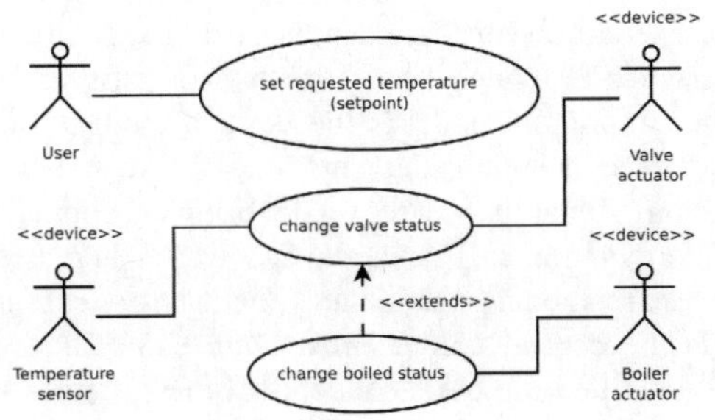

Figure 1. Use case model of the Case study.

The models designed in this way can be subjected to a more thorough analysis. Nevertheless, UML, including the object-oriented approach, retains features that are advantageous in the design of control systems — complexity, the ability to capture and formalize control system requirements, or the availability of tools. So, the full use of the object-oriented approach in the practical design and implementation of control systems was too demanding and expensive. From these reasons, standards for implementing control systems in the automation domain, e.g., IEC 61499, have gradually emerged. However, even in these approaches, UML models can be used to specify requirements and domain concepts (*conceptual modeling*), which can either be further developed by other paradigms, used as part of a simulation, or transformed into a language or environment that better suits the needs of the control system [16].

B. Case Study

We will use a simple example (case study) of Central heating with zone valves to demonstrate our approach. Each zone contains a temperature sensor, valve actuator allowing On/Off control, and Human-Machine Interface (HMI) capable of displaying all relevant data points and setpoint adjusting. The zone controller compares sensor data and setpoint and decides whether to open or close the radiator valve. In our example, we consider two zones. Zone controllers are connected to the central controller. The central controller sets the boiler On/Off according to the state of zone valves; if and only if at least one of the valves is open, the boiler is instructed to heat. It also contains interface to central HMI/SCADA.

C. UML Conceptual Model of the Case Study

The first step in creating conceptual models is defining the system's requirements. As already mentioned, a use case diagram from UML is usually used. The initial overview is in Figure 1. We have identified four actors who interact with the system and are always involved in specific use cases. The actor can be a person (*User*), but also other systems or hardware components. We have identified three types of these components in our example—*temperature sensor*, *valve actuator*, and *boiler actuator*. The primary use cases are then the temperature setting by the user and the change of the valve setting (open/closed) based on the change of the sensor temperature. This case can cause a change in the boiler settings, which is modeled by the extension case.

Another important model is the domain model. It captures the system's conceptual elements (classes) that are needed to solve individual use cases. The primary domain model is shown in Figure 2. The model is divided into two parts. The first part models the zone (*ZoneController*), and the second is the central unit (*CentralController*). In each part, we have identified the basic concepts of the system – sensors, actuators, the user interface (HMI) representation, and the basic controller. These parts communicate with each other, as indicated by the association between the *CentralCore* and *ZoneCore* classes.

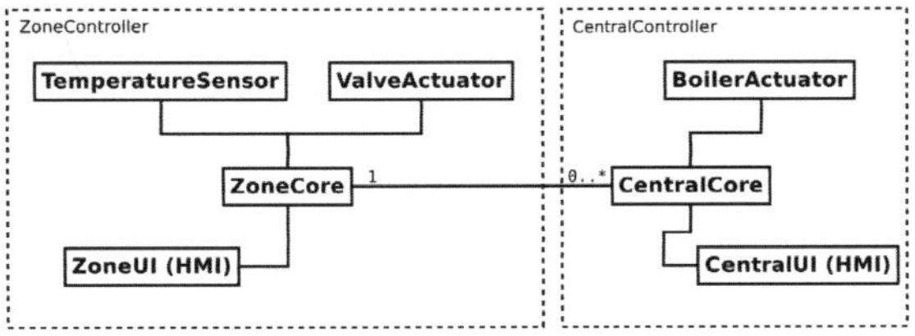

Figure 2. Basic domain model of the Case study.

Of course, conceptual classes are not sufficient for a more detailed description of the structure and behavior of the system; they serve primarily for the initial identification of concepts in the system design. In a further development, more detailed design models are created based on these concepts and use cases. It will be taken into account in Section IV.

IV. Platform Independent Model

The Platform Independent Model (PIM) is used to design a detailed system structure and behavior regardless of the specific platform on which the system will run. For the creation of PIM, modelling techniques should be used that allow simple automated transformation into PSM. We will continue with UML models. To use them as a starting point for further generation, we will mainly use the component diagram, because components are close to the concept of control software design. We will show that a similar effect can be achieved with the DEVS formalism, which can be directly simulated with a suitable tool and considered an actual control system model and its implementation.

A. UML Component Model of the Case Study

The UML component is a specialization of a structured class and as such forms a hierarchical model. It can be understood as an entity encapsulating a more complex structure of classes (and thus other components) and interchangeable with another component that meets the required interface.

Figure 3 shows the component corresponding to the *ZoneController* sets of conceptual classes. The component works with representations (classes or interfaces) for the temperature sensor, valve actuator and user interface (HMI), and contains the *ZoneCore* class implementing the decision algorithm. The component has one input and one output port, each associated with an interface. The component offers the interface (provided interface, in the UML terminology) *ZoneInterface*, through which it receives external events, and requests the interface (required interface, in the UML terminology) *CentralInterface* from the connected components.

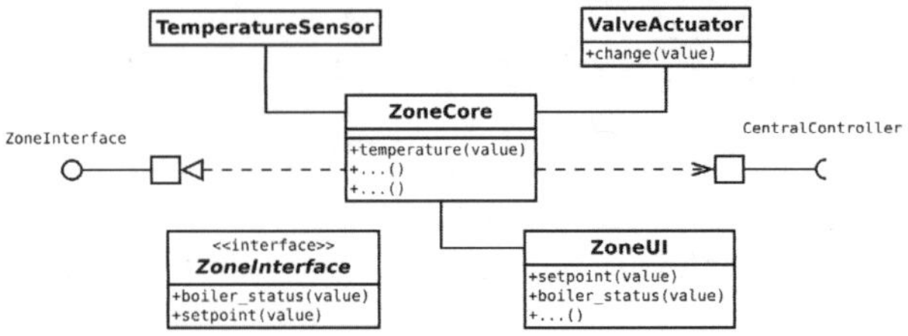

Figure 3. Component model of the ZoneController conceptual class.

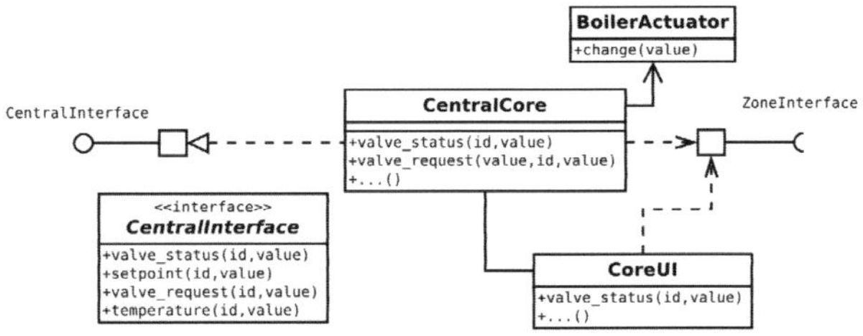

Figure 4. Component model of the CentralController conceptual class.

Figure 4 shows the component corresponding to the *CentralController* sets of conceptual classes. The component is structured similarly to the *ZoneController*. The component has the provided interface *CentralInterface* and the required interface *ZoneInterface*. Each event corresponds to the method of the respective interface. We assume that only simple data (temperature, on/off, etc.) is passed between the system elements, which can be annotated—the method attributes model annotations. In the example, only the identification of individual zones is used.

B. From UML Component Model to the DEVS

From the control systems design point of view, it is better, especially for clarity, that each event is associated with an individual port of the component. This is achieved by deriving specific interfaces from the original interface in the component diagram, following the principle of interface separation, where each such interface contains only one method corresponding to the event. The modified component model is shown in Figure 5.

It is possible to create a composite component that consists of other interconnected components. Figure 6 shows such the composite component for a simple system consisting of one zone controller. Simple, so-called atomic components, which are no longer further divided into internal parts, can be described by some of the behavior models, or another suitable formalism can be attached to them.

Finally, we can create the same component diagram using the DEVS formalism. Compared to the UML component

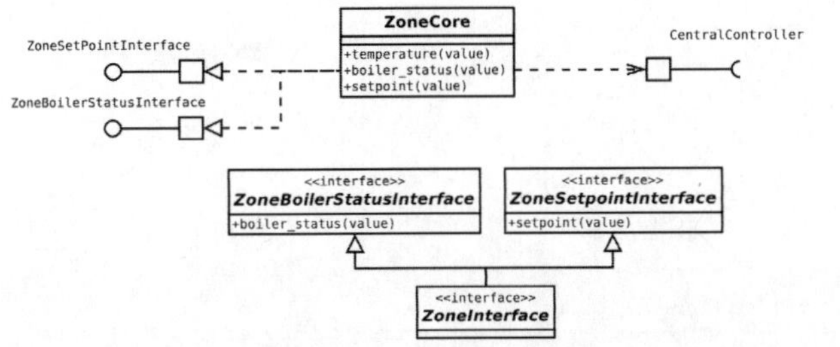

Figure 5. Part of the ZoneController component model having individual ports for each event.

model, which captures the system's static structure, the DEVS (component) model represents specific elements (objects) of the system. Thus, it represents both the model and the implementation of a specific system. In Figure 7, we see a DEVS model for a system with one central control and two zones. These components can be imagined as instances of the corresponding components in Figure 6, but they also define the structure.

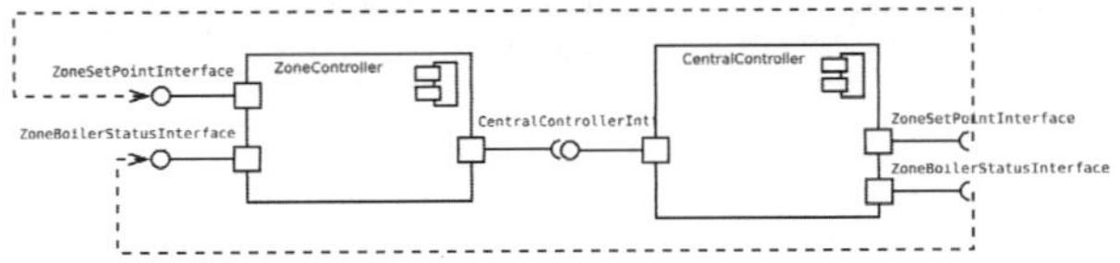

Figure 6. System component model.

It is then possible to derive systematically implementation for a specific platform, like PowerDEVS Node-RED, and 4diac/FORTE. In our approach, we understand this as a straightforward implementation of the Model-continuity principle [6]. It follows that in the case of DEVS, the PIM and PSM models merge–they differ mainly in the implementation of atomic components. Therefore, the DEVS models of the case study will be further discussed in Section V.

V. Platform Specific Model

In this section, we will present various ways of control system implementation, which are based on DEVS PIM models.

A. *PowerDEVS implementation*

The transformation of the DEVS model for a specific version of the DEVS platform is straightforward (various implementations differ only in detail). We use PowerDEVS [8] because it enables real-time simulation and can serve as runtime environment for DEVS models deployment.

The control model is in Figure 7. It contains two components, modeling zone controllers and one component, modeling the central controller. The interconnected component models the transfer of data between components (in DEVS terminology, these are events).

The model of the central controller is in Figure 8. The *or* component is responsible of deciding to keep the boiler on if and only if at least one of the zone controllers requires to

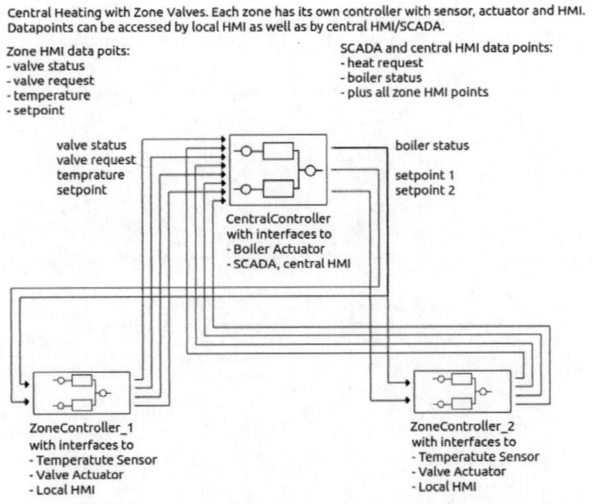

Figure 7. PowerDEVS model of the system.

heat. In addition to the basic functionality it also includes an interface on central HMI/SCADA.

By comparing with the domain model (see Figure 2) and the component model (see Figure 4), we find that the *Boiler_Actuator* component models the *BoilerActuator* concept, the *HDMI_SCADA_Pub_Sub* component represents the *CentralUI* user interface, and other components and their interconnections model the decision-making algorithm (*CentralCore*). The interface is then made up of ports and data transfer instead of interfaces and method calls.

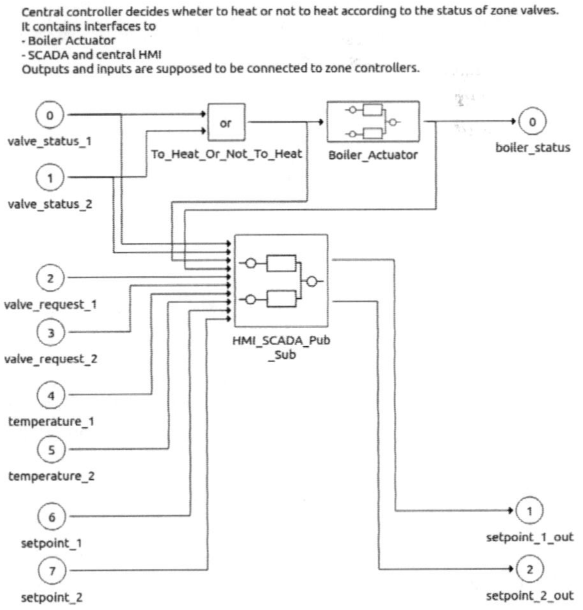

Figure 8. PowerDEVS model of central controller.

The zone controller model is shown in Figure 9. It contains an interface to a temperature sensor (in our case, it is a client of MQTT broker, which subscribed messages from the

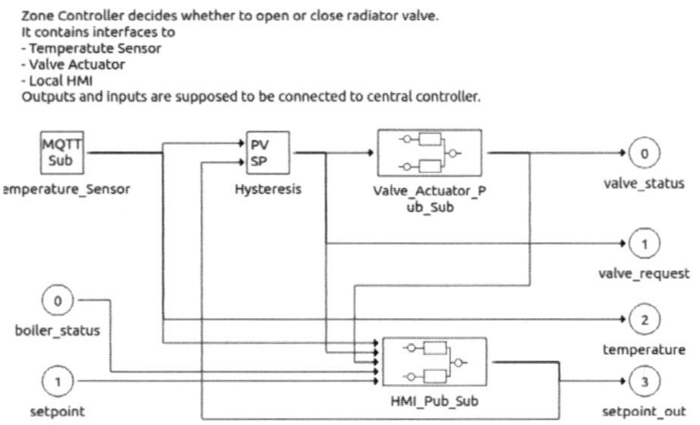

Figure 9. PowerDEVS model of zone controller.

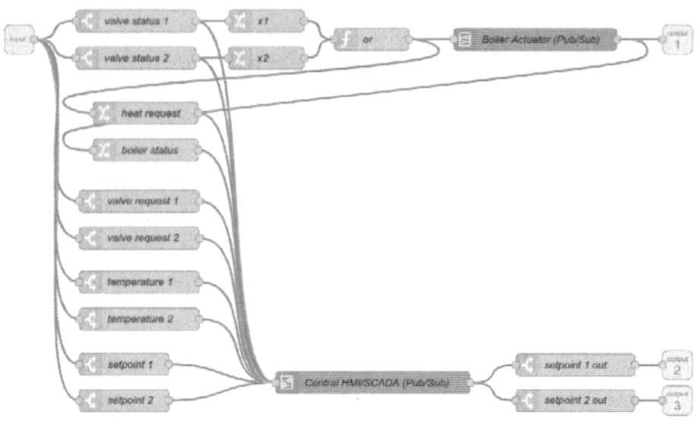

Figure 11. Node-RED model of central controller.

required temperature sensor), comparison with the setpoint available from the HMI (connected via MQTT pub-sub client too) is performed by the hysteresis component. The output is connected to the actuator interface (again via MQTT pub-sub component). The inputs and outputs of the zone controller enable the connection and transfer of data from/to the central controller. These data are used to operate the potentially distributed control and for presentation to the user via the HMI. Setpoints, i.e., required temperature values in zones, can also be set via local HMIs or the central HMI.

B. Node-RED implementation

Node-RED [2] is a popular tool for coordinating and automating the IoT systems. It is a platform for modeling and interpreting so-called flows, which is a concept similar to DEVS. DEVS is thus easily transformable into Node-RED.

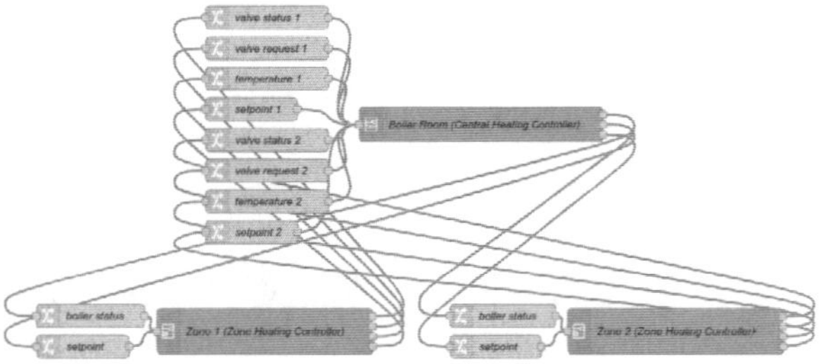

Figure 10. Node-RED model of the system.

The difference between Node-RED and DEVS is that it is not intended for simulations nor hard real-time applications. However, for implementation of soft real-time applications (typically IoT or home automation), it can be successfully used. It provides the concept of interconnecting function blocks (in Node-RED terminology, these are nodes) into flows, which corresponds to composites in DEVS. These can be organized hierarchically. When transforming DEVS into Node-RED, it is practically only necessary to overcome a small problem. The Node-RED node has only 0 or 1 input. Nevertheless, the specific meaning of the input data can be distinguished by the topic specification in the incoming message structure (the message object always contains the topic and payload slots). For the systematic transformation of DEVS into Node-RED, it is necessary to express the existence of input ports of the component by a corresponding modification of the message topic. In our case we solve this by nodes of type change (in Figures 10, 11, and 12 they are colored yellow). Such a node sets msg.topic to the corresponding DEVS port name. In a case when DEVS does not define port names explicitly (in our case, the *or* component in Figure 8), generic names like x1, x2 are used (see Figure 11).

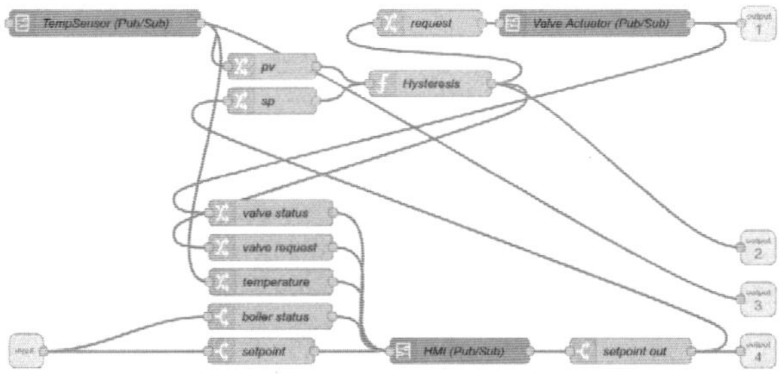

Figure 12. Node-RED model of zone controller.

According to this information, the next node then knows the port name and can handle the message adequately. Node-RED flows in Figures 10, 11, 12 correspond to DEVS models in Figures 7, 8, 9.

C. IEC 61499 implementation

Transformation into IEC 61499 also requires overcoming a slight difference compared to DEVS. IEC 61499 distinguishes between data and events due to the optimal implementation of complex real-time control applications. If data appears on the input port, it does not mean that it should be processed immediately. For the input data to be processed, the corresponding input event has first to be accepted. Which data is processed in which input event is specified by the interface. Figure 13 shows the interface of the Central Heating block type. The jumpers between event and data inputs specify which data is processed at which events. For the purpose of systematic transition from DEVS to IEC 61499, it makes sense for each data input or output to specify its own event.

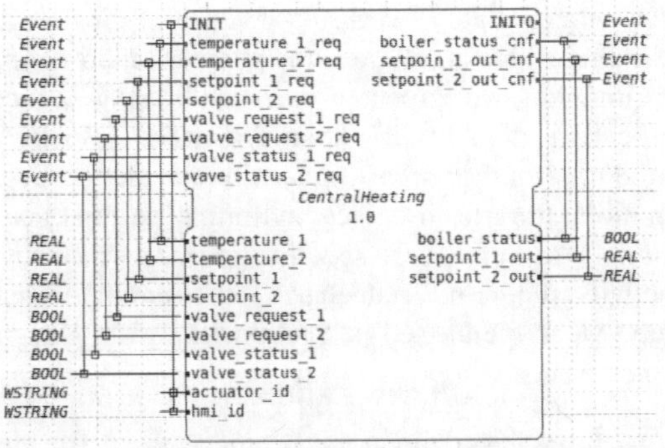

Figure 13. Interface of Central controller. To be DEVS-compatible, each data input and output has its associated event.

Another difference of IEC 61499 from DEVS is that data from multiple sources cannot be sent to single data input. However, this can be solved by including a special component that forwards any of its inputs to a single output. In our example, we do not have such a situation, but in general, it is necessary to count with it.

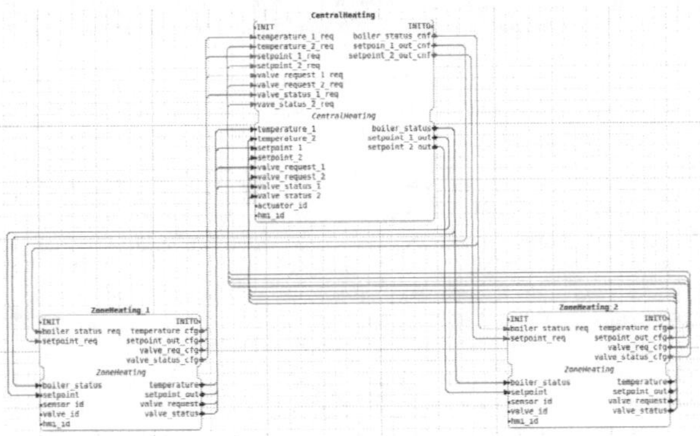

Figure 14. IEC 61499 model of the system.

Figure 14 shows the system model according to IEC 61499 (modeled in 4diac development environment), corresponding to the DEVS model in Figure 7. The other models would be derived from DEVS analogously.

VI. Platform Specific Model – distributed version

The entire control application, comprising two zone controllers and one central, can be easily deployed to a single computer or Programmable Logical Controller (PLC), equipped with a runtime environment for PowerDEVS, Node-RED, or IEC 61499. Now let's look at the distributed implementation of the control application. IEC 61499 supports distributed deployment natively. In DEVS and Node-RED, we can do it analogously. We will demonstrate the principle using the IEC 61499 approach.

The first step is a model of a distributed computing environment, see Figure 15. In our case, there are two networked Raspberry Pi computers. The second step is to map the components of the control application to the compute nodes. In Figure 16, it is visualized by different colors of the components

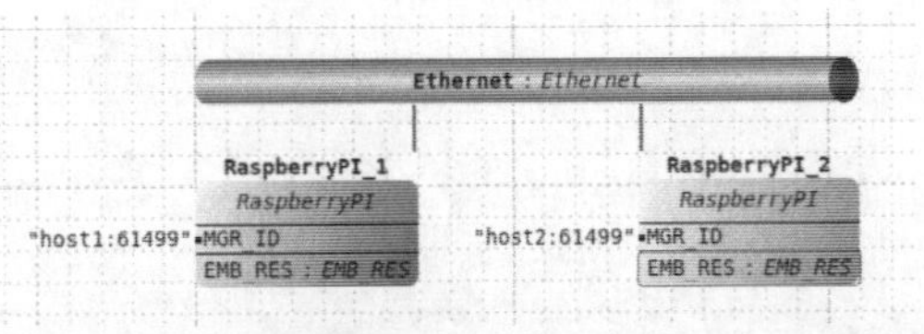

Figure 15. IEC 61499 distributed system model. One RPi hosts Central controller and Zone 1 controller, The second one hosts Zone 2 controller.

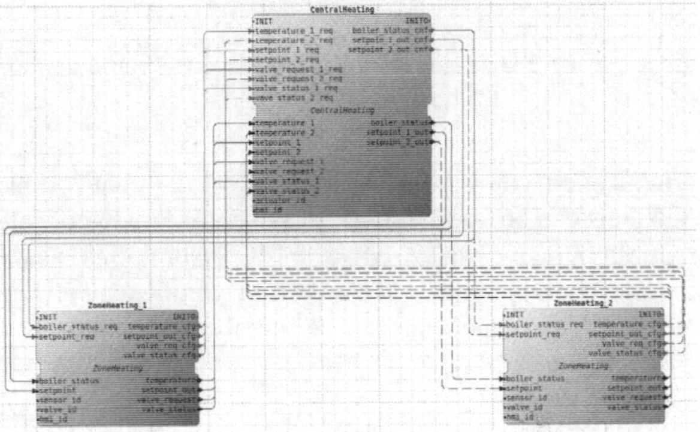

Figure 16. IEC 61499 model of the system - distributed version. Different component colors mean that they are mapped to different nodes of the distributed system. Dotted lines model network connections between parts of the system.

(the colors correspond to the colors of the computational nodes in Figure 15). The third step is to ensure communication between the distributed components using a suitable network protocol. These are the dashed links between the components in Figure 16. The application running on the first or second node must be equipped with communication components for each link that leads out of the node, respectively inside the node, see Figures 17 and 18. In addition, it is also necessary to ensure the initialization of components at the start of the platform (see the component E_START). The selection of

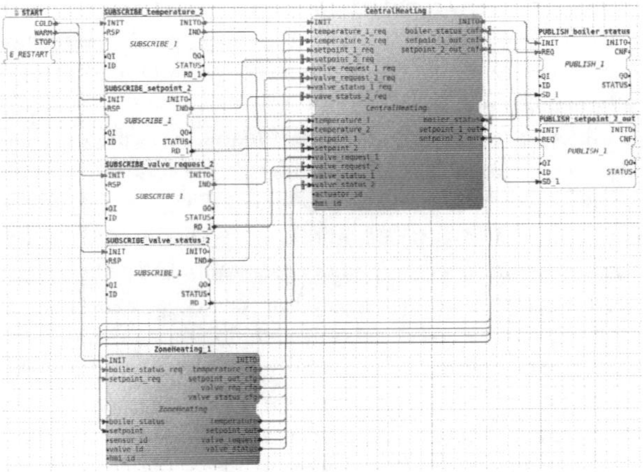

Figure 17. Central controller and Zone 1 controller with an interface to the Zone 2 controller is deployed on Rasberry Pi 1

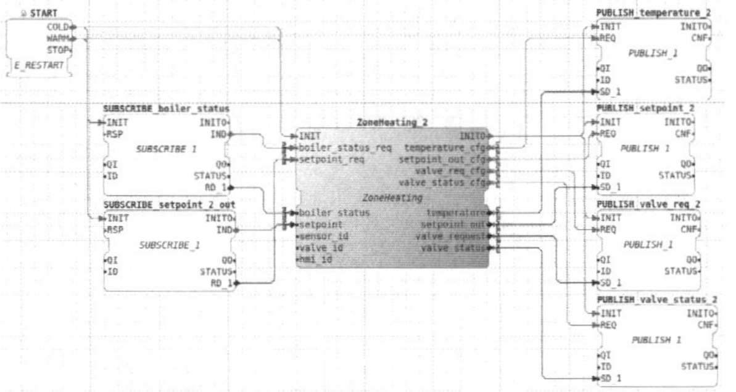

Figure 18. Zone 2 controller with and interface to central controller is deployed on Raspberry Pi 2.

communication components and the way of initialization of components can be standardized for the considered application domain. In our case, we use only the MQTT protocol, message topics are unambiguously derived from component and port names, and all components can be initialized concurrently.

VII. Conclusion

This paper has shown by example the transition from a conceptual model through a platform-independent model to platform-specific models in several environments usable for control applications. The initial modeling tool was the UML language, which is followed by the DEVS formalism. We understand DEVS as an essential tool and concept for modeling and implementing control systems in our approach. We demonstrated the transition from DEVS to three implementation environments. Each of them has specifics regarding distribution, real-time responses of runtime availability for given hardware (e.g., PLC, soft PLC, or PC), and semantics of block diagrams, flows, etc. Specifically, PowerDEVS is suited for time critical regulatory control, but it is also applicable in another way (like in our example). On the other hand, Node-RED is designed to typically run on an IoT gateway or in the cloud, not on a PLC. Finally, IEC 61499 is applicable for PLC as well as for higher levels of control. In addition, it has the means for distributed application deployment. Besides the implementation environments we dealt with, there is possible to consider any other modeling and programming means based on hierarchically organized and interconnected function blocks with semantics similar to DEVS.

An interesting feature of our methodology is the continuity of the DEVS model in all considered implementation environments. The transformation of the DEVS model into the target environment is based on relatively simple rules, and the original structured DEVS model is retained. Because DEVS is at a higher level of abstraction than, for example, IEC 61499, where data and event ports are distinguished, modeling is easier. This more direct modeling is then at the cost of slightly less efficient implementation (the component in DEVS always reacts to any change in any input port). However, it is still usable for hard real-time in the same way as, e.g., PowerDEVS. At the same time, it allows transformation to Node-RED (unless hard real-time behavior is required).

Unlike other related works, we do not deal with the level of atomic blocks. We do not generate them from their specification, but we expect a standard library (concerning the application domain) of atomic function blocks in all considered environments. However, to provide the necessary function block libraries in target environments, their automatic generation from behavioral specifications can be considered using activity diagrams, statecharts, etc., similar to some of the related work mentioned in Section II.

Acknowledgment

This work has been supported by the internal BUT project FIT-S-20-6427.

References

[1] Eclipse. (2021) 4diac documentation. online. [Online]. Available: https://www.eclipse.org/4diac/. [Retrieved: 08, 2021]

[2] OpenJS Foundation, "Node-red," online, 2021. [Online]. Available: https://nodered.org. [Retrieved: 08, 2021]

[3] R. Manione, "A full model-based design environment for the development of cyber physical systems," *Design*, vol. 3, no. 1, pp. 1–30, 2019.

[4] F. Ciccozzi, I. Malavolta, and B. Selic, "Execution of uml models: a systematic review of research and practice," *Software & Systems Modeling*, vol. 18, no. 3, pp. 2313–2360, 2018.

[5] B. Zeigler, T. Kim, and H. Praehofer, *Theory of Modeling and Simulation: Integrating Discrete Event and Continuous Complex Dynamic Systems*. Academic Press, Inc., London, 2000.

[6] X. Hu and B. Zeigler, "Model continuity in the design of dynamic distributed real-time systems," *IEEE Transactions on Systems, Man, and Cybernetics - Part A: Systems and Humans*, vol. 35, no. 6, pp. 867–878, 2005.

[7] E. P. Marcosig, J. I. Giribet, and R. Castro, "Devs-over-ros (dover): A framework for simulation-driven embedded control of robotic systems based on model continuity," in *2018 Winter Simulation Conference (WSC)*. IEEE, 2018.

[8] F. Bergero and E. Kofman, "Powerdevs: A tool for hybrid system modeling and real-time simulation," *Simulation*, vol. 87, pp. 113–132, 01 2011.

[9] T. Hussain and G. Frey, "UML-based Development Process for IEC 61499 with Automatic Test-case Generation," in *IEEE Conference on Emerging Technologies and Factory Automation*. IEEE, 2010.

[10] C. A. Garcia, E. X. Castellanos, C. Rosero, and Carlos, "Designing Automation Distributed Systems Based on IEC-61499 and UML," in *5th International Conference in Software Engineering Research and Innovation (CONISOFT)*. [Online]. Available: https://ieeexplore.ieee.org/abstract/document/8337936

[11] I. A. Batchkova, Y. A. Belev, and D. L. Tzakova, "IEC 61499 Based Control of Cyber-Physical Systems," *Industry 4.0*, vol. 5, no. 1, pp. 10–13, November 2020.

[12] S. Panjaitan and G. Frey, "Functional Design for IEC 61499 Distributed Control Systems using UML Activity Diagrams," in *Proceedings of the 2005 International Conference on Instrumentation, Communications and Information Technology ICICI 2005*, 2005, pp. 64–70.

[13] H. T. Park, K. Y. Seong, S. Dangol, G. N. Wang, and S. C. Park, "An Approach to Obtain a PLC Program from a DEVS Model," in *In Proceedings of the Fifth International Conference on Informatics in Control, Automation and Robotics - RA*. [Online]. Available: https://www.scitepress.org/papers/2008/14924/14924.pdf

[14] A. Gonzalez, C. Luna, M. Daniele, R. Cuello, and M. Perez, "Towards an automatic model transformation mechanism from UML state machines to DEVS models," *CLEI Electron. J.*, vol. 18, no. 2, 2015. [Online]. Available: https://doi.org/10.19153/cleiej.18.2.3

[15] G. D. Kapos, V. Dalakas, A. Tsadimas, M. Nikolaidou, and D. Anagnostopoulos, "Model-based system engineering using SysML: Deriving executable simulation models with QVT," in *IEEE International Systems Conference Proceedings*, 2014.

[16] M. Moallemi and G. A. Wainer, "Modeling and simulation-driven development of embedded real-time systems," *Simulation Modeling, Practice and Theory. Elsevier*, vol. 38, pp. 115–131, November 2013.

A Developer Portal for DevOps Environment

Niklas Sänger, Stefan Throner,
Simon Hanselmann, Michael Schneider, Sebastian Abeck
Research Group Cooperation & Management
Karlsruhe Institute of Technology (KIT)
Zirkel 2, 76131 Karlsruhe, Germany
email: (niklas.saenger | stefan.throner | michael.schneider | sebastian.abeck)@kit.edu

***Abstract*—A good microservice architecture divides a complex system into separate microservices, which can then be reused in several applications. To achieve efficient reuse of components, it is necessary to provide the developers with the required information on how they can use the running microservices and their application programming interfaces (APIs). A tool for this kind of information is the developer portal, which enables the administration of the interfaces and documentation of individual microservices and makes them available to all developers on a central platform. The diversity that arises from multiple teams and different environments makes it difficult to manage the information in the developer portal manually and in a central location. In this paper, we describe the development of a developer portal and focus on the following aspects: (i) designing a domain that represents a service environment, (ii) requirements for the developer portal to support the developer workflow, (iii) environment-agnostic approach for automated data gathering for the developer portal, (iv) microservice monitoring during runtime.**

***Keywords*—DevOps; microservices; api; development; developer portal.**

I. INTRODUCTION

Agile methods and microservices are the main concepts to deal with today's complexity of modern software systems [1]. This is achieved by splitting a monolithic system into microservices [2], allowing to reduce the overall complexity of single components. Additionally, a good microservice architecture, designed according to the principles of Domain-Driven Design (DDD), results in reusable microservices which can be consumed by other microservices and applications [3]. Due to the use of APIs and the separation of functionality, microservices can be developed and maintained by small individual development teams as it is common in agile development. To enable efficient reuse of microservices and their APIs, the microservice information and API specifications have to be accessible to all developers. One solution for APIs is a developer portal [4].

A developer portal allows the provisioning of API specifications and documentation of the corresponding services and provides access to the data in a central spot. However, this requires that developers provide the data and publish them to the developer portal manually. While this approach is suitable for the classical use of the developer portal, the offering and marketing of APIs, it can lead to problems when the data (e.g., API specification) should be provided continuously in larger projects, with multiple distributed teams during the development process. Since agile methods aim to deliver new features and bug fixes on a daily basis, manually updating data can lead to an overhead for the developer, potential data inconsistencies (e.g., different API specifications), and distributed knowledge (i.e., teams have a different understanding of an API specification).

To overcome these problems, we propose an automated solution for a developer portal, which uses a development and operations (DevOps) approach to automate the process of service registration and lifecycle management of API specifications and service documentation, thus providing a continuous source of truth. The automated provision of data is supported by a template-based pipeline approach [5], which allows central adaptation and extension of the Continuous Integration / Continuous Deployment (CI/CD) pipelines.

The requirements on the developer portal are formally specified and implemented by applying a microservice engineering process. This results in a microservice-based application, called MicroserviceDeveloperPortal (MDP) and a business domain called ServiceEnvironment. In the context of this application, microservices play two different roles, which must be distinguished: on the one hand, the MDP application provides support to develop microservices, and on the other hand, the MDP itself is built as a microservice-based application.

This present article is structured as follows: Section II presents the state-of-the-art in microservices and DevOps. Section III provides our approach to the domain and application engineering. Section IV describes the microservice registration process. Section V introduces our health monitoring approach for microservices. Section VI describes the use of the MDP in our environment. Lastly, Section VII summarizes the main results of our approach and future work.

II. RELATED WORK

The term microservice goes back to the year 2011. A group of software architects chose it as an appropriate name in 2012. Among them, Lewis was the first researcher using the term in a presentation [6]. Three years later, Lewis and Fowler published the first description of microservices and the microservice architecture style [1]. Based on this work, Newman published a well accepted and often cited book on microservices [7].

A strong motivation for the microservice architecture style is provided by the disadvantages of a monolithic software architecture in regard of change cycles and complex deployments [2]. This is because even small changes require a complete rebuild and redeploy of the monolith. This aspect is especially important for companies wanting to reduce the time-to-market or improve robustness of the provided services [2].

A microservice architecture reduces the complexity for each service but increases the overall amount of microservices [8]. When compared to a monolithic application, the urgent need for a service orchestration arises. A common solution for this problem is to use Kubernetes which is a widely used container orchestration system developed by Google [9] [10]. While Kubernetes can solve the orchestration of microservices, Kubernetes is inherently complex and introduces its own tools and paradigms [11].

The complexity of microservice architectures requires additional communication and contracts among development and operations teams. To overcome these obstacles, DevOps principles can be used. While there is no general definition of DevOps, various authors tried to define the term. Lwakatare et al. [12] perform a study to define the term DevOps and come up with five dimensions: collaboration, automation, culture, monitoring, and measurement. Erich et al. [13] find that companies have different definitions on DevOps but share a common understanding that team, culture, and automation are key aspects.

Moreover, Wilsenach [14] stated that the DevOps culture should have no silos between Dev and Ops. This is where agile methods, such as a CI/CD pipeline can be efficiently used [8]. It allows for cross-functional teams which are responsible for the development, deployment, and operation of their microservice. One aspect of this work is to use DevOps for the automation of data provisioning which in turn ensures up to date data for a developer.

In general, a developer portal must provide the developer with all necessary information required for the development of an application. De [4] refers to a developer portal in the context of API management which is a common use-case for a developer portal. It supports a developer by providing API documentation, API access, or API analytics information. The counterpart of a developer portal is the provider portal in which a service developer provides information (e.g., API specifications, API version) of a service. Generally, the API specifications Examples can be found in the developer portals by Amazon Web Services (AWS) [15] or Mercedes-Benz [16]. Existing solutions, such as the developer portal offered by AWS, work best with products of the same vendor, creating a vendor lock-in effect. They also neglect information about the backing services (i.e., microservices) and require manual data upload. We propose a microservice-based solution, which can be deployed in an arbitrary Kubernetes environment able of running Docker containers. Moreover, a CI/CD pipeline is used to automate the provisioning of data including the state of microservices running in a cluster.

The microservice engineering process we have applied to systematically implement the requirements on a developer portal into a microservice-based application is based on the Domain-Driven Design (DDD) from Eric Evans [3] and has been described by us in several publications. In [17], the process is introduced and applied to the domain of connected cars to provide a solution for the charging of electric cars (i); [18] describes the microservice architecture based on the domain-driven design concept of a context map in detail (ii); and [19] shows how we use the profiles of the Unified Modeling Language (UML) to formally specify the domain model by different types of UML diagrams (iii).

III. Domain and Application Engineering

The development of the MDP follows a previously mentioned microservice engineering process. Therefore, the first step is to develop a suitable domain in which the application is located. The difficulty lies in placing the components needed for a microservice environment in the domain.

A. *ServiceEnvironment Domain*

Since the MDP touches a variety of aspects related to microservices, DevOps, and container orchestration, we decided to name the domain ServiceEnvironment. The ServiceEnvironment domain should further include everything that is required for the deployment and operation (e.g., orchestration and monitoring) of microservices.

After setting the scope of the domain ServiceEnvironment, the engineering process requires a definition of a ubiquitous language and a context map. The ubiquitous language defines terms that are relevant (i.e., because they are frequently used) for the domain and its applications. This ensures that developers have a common understanding of the terms throughout the engineering process. Hence, the ubiquitous language must follow a previously fixed set of guidelines in order to be consistent. In case of the ServiceEnvironment domain, an extract of the ubiquitous languages defining terms such as Service, HealthState or Observation can be found in Table I.

TABLE I
Excerpt of the Ubiquitous Language of the Domain ServiceEnvironment.

Term	Definition
HealthState	Data which describes the availability state of a service (e.g., latency, liveness).
Observation	Part of the domain that observes services after the deployment
Service	Part of the domain that represents a deployed application that can be accessed by the user

The next artifact for the ServiceEnvironment domain is a context map that defines the domain, its subdomains, and bounded contexts. The development of the artifact is motivated by DDD. Figure 1 illustrates the context map of the ServiceEnvironment domain, which includes the subdomains Observation, MicroserviceManagement, and Deployment. Each subdomain provides a bounded context that the MDP can interact with. To reduce the overall complexity of the ServiceEnvironment, the domain currently only includes subdomains that the MDP requires. If the functionalities of the MDP would be extended or another application would require additional data from the domain, the ServiceEnviornment should be extended accordingly.

Typically, bounded contexts are implemented as domain microservices. This means that they must have no dependencies on other services. We decided that a domain microservice should only provide Create, Read, Update, and Delete (CRUD) operations to handle data requests (e.g., monitoring data) and not contain any application logic. This makes the microservices, and thus the data, reusable for multiple applications. Moreover, it allows the application microservices to be stateless since the data is stored within the domain microservices following the 12 Factors App paradigm [20].

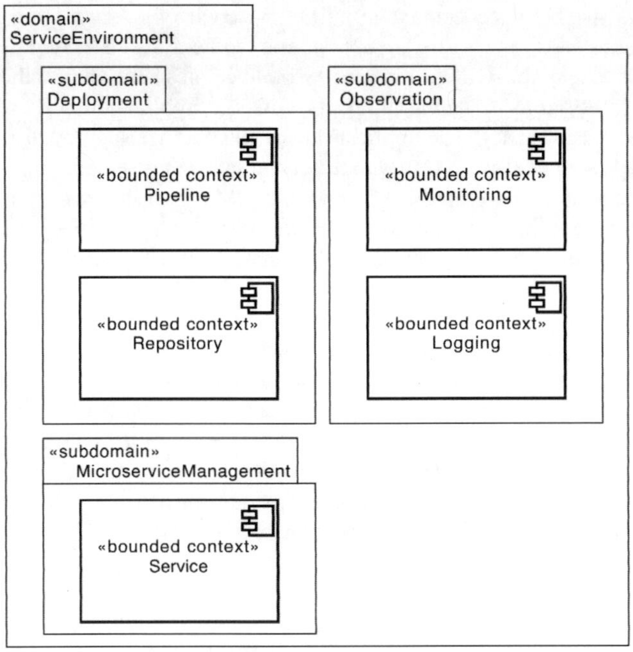

Figure 1. ServiceEnvironment Context Map.

The subdomain Observation includes everything regarding the observation of a microservice. The bounded context Monitoring is implemented as a domain microservice that stores monitoring events (e.g., if a container has been created). Logging data can be stored within the bounded context Logging. If tools such as Prometheus were to be used, they would be located in the subdomain Observation and replace or complement the domain microservice Monitoring.

The subdomain Deployment includes a bounded context Pipeline, which represents a CI/CD pipeline including its steps that are used across the ServiceEnvironment domain (e.g., build or test). Furthermore, the bounded context Repository stores the microservice source code, documentation, API specification dependencies, or design artifacts. Such bounded contexts are later not implemented as domain microservices. Instead, the functionalities are provided by GitLab.

Finally, the subdomain MicroserviceManagement includes a bounded context called Service which should store information about a deployed microservice (e.g., API, deployment name, version, or dependencies). This bounded context is also implemented as a domain microservice.

The context map and the ubiquitous language are not final. Another application, requiring additional subdomains, bounded contexts or terms can add them to the domain and reuse existing subdomains.

B. *MicroserviceDeveloperPortal*

The MDP is the first application in the ServiceEnvironment domain. The basic idea of the MDP is to have a single source of truth for developers and operators alike. For example, whenever a developer wants to find out which microservices are currently running in a Kubernetes cluster or find the API specification of a specific microservice, the portal should be the first place to look for this information. Figure 2 presents the application sketch, which defines how a developer interacts with the ServiceEnvironment to get the information they are looking for. These interactions lead to two distinct capabilities which must be provided by the MDP.

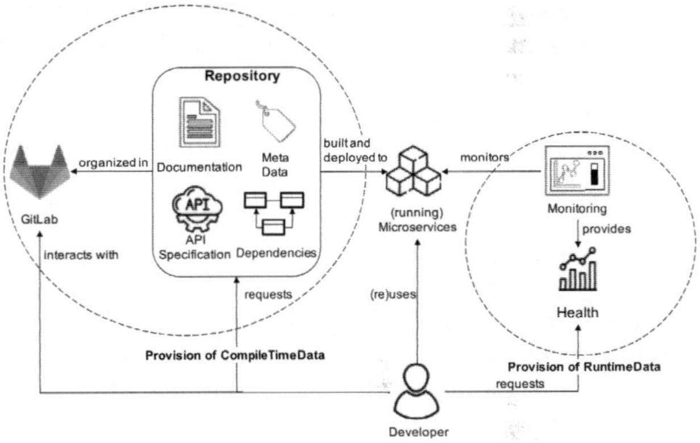

Figure 2. Application Sketch of the MDP.

1) **Provision of CompileTimeData:** Data already present during the compilation of a microservice should be collected and provided to the user. This data includes information of the repository provided by Git (e.g., commit reference or name of the branch), API data in form of OpenAPI specifications or dependencies on other microservices (e.g., databases). This information is of particular interest to developers who plan on reusing existing microservices and therefore are looking for their documentation.
2) **Provision of RuntimeData:** This data can only be collected while the microservice is running. For now, the MDP is only capable of monitoring a simple health state of microservices. This information of the health state is interesting to developers who are troubleshooting problems that occur during runtime.

While the introduced application sketch captures interactions between various actors and objects, a relation view captures the data entities, called shared entities, that are used for these interactions. Figure 3 shows the entity relation view of the MDP, which contains the entities shared by the bounded contexts of the domain ServiceEnvironment (i.e., shared entities) relevant for the MDP. Furthermore, the shared entities are set into a relationship with one another.

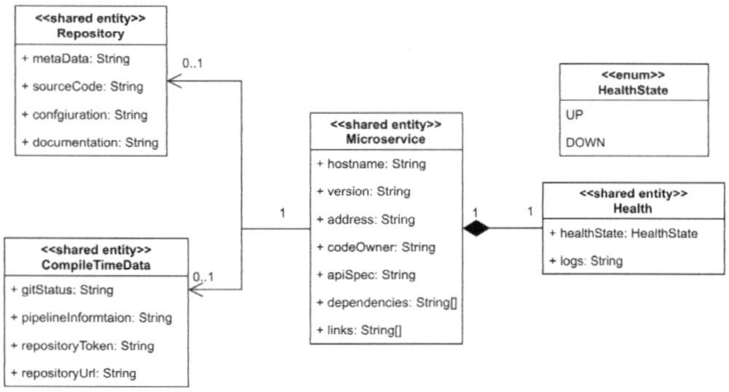

Figure 3. The Entity Relation View of the MDP.

The shared entity Repository represents a Git repository provided by GitLab. Thus, it contains source code, configuration artifacts, and documentation. The CompileTimeData entity represents all data that is available during the compilation of the microservice source code. Furthermore, the CompileTimeData contains a reference to a Repository and data about the event (e.g., Git commit) that triggered the pipeline that executed the compilation. This data is then combined into the shared entity Microservice. Each shared entity Microservice has an associated shared entity Health. This entity contains the most recent HealthState of a microservice, which can be *UP* or *DOWN*, together with logs that were written when the health state was observed.

Different services are responsible for creating and storing these data entities. The application sharing view in Figure 4 visualizes relations between shared entities and bounded or application contexts. Bounded contexts represent reusable services that are part of the ServiceEnvironment domain. Applications contexts provide the application specific logic for the MDP and are not reusable by other applications in the ServiceEnvironment.

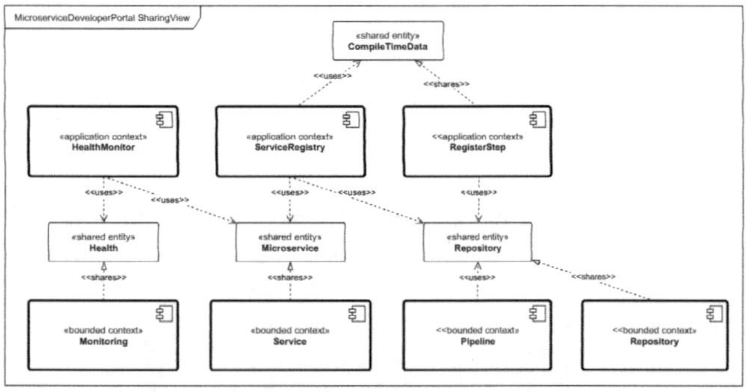

Figure 4. The Application Sharing View of the MDP.

While the bounded contexts Pipeline and Repository are already present in the system, the bounded contexts Service and Monitoring are implemented as domain microservices. The domain microservice Service stores the currently registered microservices and provides the data through CRUD operations. The domain microservice Monitoring stores the monitoring events for the currently registered microservice and provides the data through CRUD operations. The application contexts HealthMonitor, ServiceRegistry and RegisterStep perform specific tasks for the MDP. Hence, they are placed in the application layer instead of the domain layer.

The general flow of data starts with the bounded context Repository, which triggers the Pipeline. The bounded context Repository shares the shared entity Repository, which is used by the bounded context Pipeline and each of its steps (e.g., build, test, deploy). An application context RegisterStep is added to the CI/CD pipeline, which creates and shares the shared entity CompileTimeData with the application context ServiceRegistry. The application context ServiceRegistry uses the shared entity CompileTimeData and the shared entity Repository to create a shared entity Microservice which is persisted by the bounded context Service. The application context HealthMonitor uses the shared entity Microservice to determine which microservices in the cluster have to be monitored. The shared entity Health is created from the results of the application context HealthMonitor and persisted and shared in the domain by the bounded context Monitoring.

The application contexts Pipeline, RegisterStep, ServiceRegistry and bounded context Service fulfill the capability to provision CompileTimeData, while the remaining two contexts HealthMonitor and Monitoring are needed to fulfill the capability provision of RuntimeData.

IV. Microservice Registration

Each deployed microservice in a Kubernetes cluster should be represented by a shared entity Microservice. To create these entities, either the current state of the ServiceEnvironment has to be observed at all time or the deployments and undeployments have to be monitored. Because the pipeline can be used to perform a job after each successful deployment, the latter approach was chosen. Thus, an extension for the pipeline was developed with the goal of automatically registering a microservice after a successful deployment. The pipeline extension represents the application context RegisterStep.

To use the RegisterStep, the pipeline receives two new stages. First, the register stage is triggered after a successful deployment of a microservice. Second, the unregister stage is executed parallel to the undeployment of a microservice. The RegisterStep is a Docker image that contains Python scripts for each stage. Depending on the stage, either the register or the unregister script is executed. The scripts send a HTTP request to the representational state transfer (REST) endpoint of the ServiceRegistry to either register or unregister the microservice.

Figure 5 shows the process for registering a new microservice. The Repository triggers the execution of the Pipeline (1)

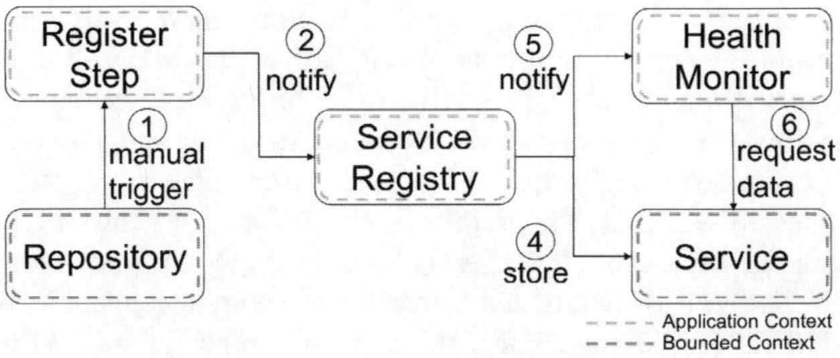

Figure 5. The Service Registration Process.

which notifies the ServiceRegistry that a new microservice has been successfully deployed (2). This notification includes data about the name of the deployment and the URL to the Git repository. The ServiceRegistry then requests relevant information from the repository such as the API specification and the dependencies to other microservices (3). After gathering all relevant information, the data is passed to the domain microservice Service which persists it in a database (4). In the last step, the HealthMonitor is notified about the new deployment (5). This will cause the HealhMonitor to request an updated list of the currently running microservices from the domain microservice Service (6).

The process to unregister a microservice is similar to the registration process with three essential differences. First, the pipeline is not necessarily triggered by the repository but can also be triggered manually by a developer. Second, after the ServiceRegistry is notified, it will not request data from the repository. Finally, the ServiceRegistry will delete the microservice entity from the domain microservice Service instead of saving it.

Figure 6 presents an excerpt of the GitLab pipeline. The columns specify the different stages of the pipeline and the boxes specify the tasks which should be executed in each stage. The lines between the boxes visualize a dependency relationship between the tasks. A microservice is only registered after a successful deployment. A microservice is unregistered when the undeploy stage is executed. In this step, the connected entry will be deleted from the domain microservice Service and the HealthMonitor is notified about the update. The undeploy stage should be executed whenever the base branch for the deployment is deleted or the microservice is not needed anymore.

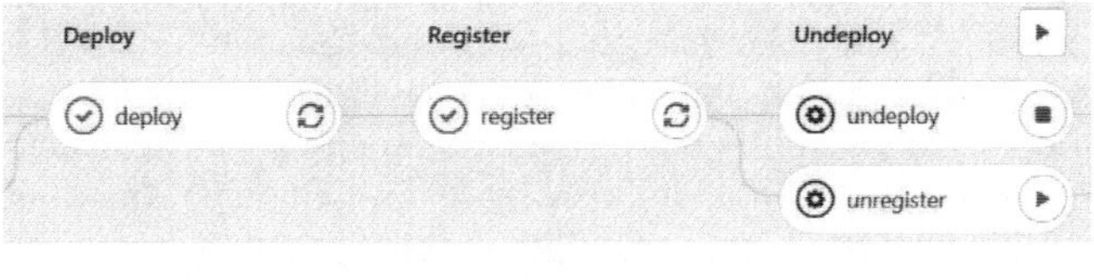

Figure 6. Extract of the GitLab Pipeline.

This workflow ensures that the domain microservice Service always holds an up-to-date list of the shared entities Microservice which represent the microservices that are running in the cluster. The name of the deployment in the Kubernetes cluster is used as a unique identifier for the running instances of the microservice and its dependencies (e.g., database container). Other services can now request a list of deployments and collect further information with a reference to the deployment. The dashboard can request the list of all registered deployments and get more detailed information by querying data from other data sources using a specific deployment name. This process is described in the following section with the example of a service that monitors the health states of deployed and registered microservices.

V. HEALTH MONITORING

One of the MDP's capabilities is the provisioning of runtime data. In the initial version of the MPD, the focus is set on the health data of running microservices that are registered with the MDP. In the ServiceEnvironment, microservices are running in a Kubernetes cluster which offers a pod lifecycle that is used to determine the health state of containers running inside a pod. The health state is stored in a health data entity, which includes the current state of the pod (e.g., running or terminated) and a log message.

Two microservices are responsible to track the current state of a deployed microservice and storing the health data. Those are the application microservice HealthMonitor and the domain microservice Monitoring, which can also be found in Figure 4. Since the microservice Monitoring is part of the ServiceEnvironment domain, it offers CRUD functionalities and is responsible for storing health data. The stored health data can later be displayed in a dashboard. HealthMonitor is responsible for extracting the health data from the microservices and is implemented as a Kubernetes operator in Go. An operator is a software extension for Kubernetes and has access to Kubernetes cluster resources such as pods and events. If the status of a pod changes (e.g., container running or container stopped), an event is created. The operator works in a control loop and will receive the new event. Afterward, the operator can process the event accordingly.

An overview of the operator process can be found in Figure 7. HealthMonitor fetches a list of registered services from the domain microservice Service. This list determines which deployed microservices must be monitored. The list is fetched whenever the ServiceRegistry registers a new microservice and notifies HealthMonitor through an API endpoint (see Figure 5). If the state of a microservice in the cluster changes, HealthMonitor is notified and will check if the microservice is registered with ServiceRegistry (i.e., the microservice is in the fetched list of registered microservices). If this is the case, HealthMonitor will process the event and store the data in the domain microservice Monitoring. The dashboard can then access the health state for a microservice through REST calls to the domain microservice Monitoring.

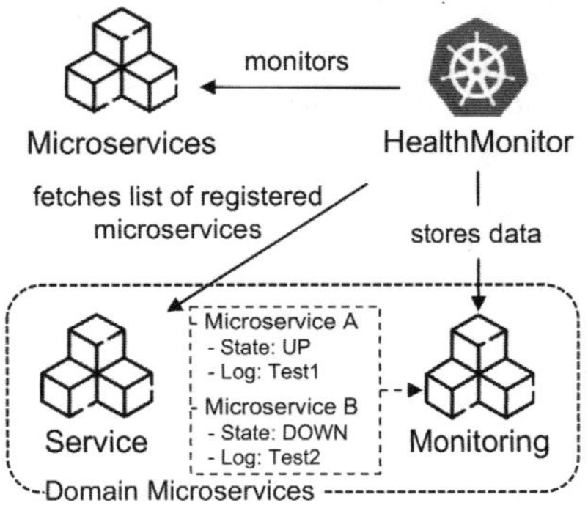

Figure 7. Overview of HealthMonitor.

VI. USE OF THE MDP APPLICATION IN A REAL SERVICE ENVIRONMENT

Currently, the MDP is deployed in a Kubernetes cluster and is used by up to 20 users including academic staff and students. The cluster runs five containers for the MDP including the domain microservices Service and Monitoring, as well as the application microservices ServiceRegistry, HealthMonitor, and a container for the front-end. The Git repositories as well as the pipeline and the pipeline runner are provided by GitLab. Each academic semester, students develop microservice-based applications using DevOps templates which configure and set up the CI/CD pipeline [5]. The DevOps templates automatically include the additional register and unregister step. Hence, the microservices are all automatically deployed to the Kubernetes cluster and registered to the MDP.

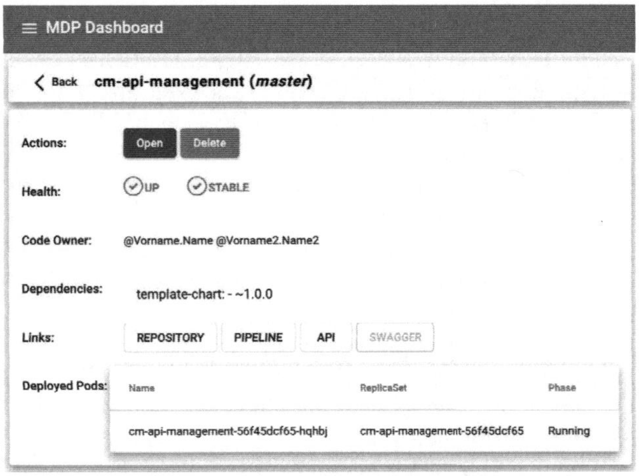

Figure 8. Excerpt of the MDP Dashboard.

In the context of a practical lecture, students (i.e., developers) fluctuate throughout the semesters. This makes the continuous development of microservice-based applications difficult. The MDP provides an entry-point for new students to see which microservices are currently running in the cluster, who developed them, how they can be accessed (i.e., API specification), and other microservices they depend on. Therefore, they can get into the actual microservice development work faster. In Figure 8, an extract of the dashboard of the MDP shows a selected registered microservice (i.e., cm-api-management). The user can see which version of the microservice is deployed and can automatically open it if a Kubernetes Ingress resource is created (i.e., HTTP traffic from outside the cluster is allowed). Moreover, the user is presented with information about the code owner, dependencies (e.g., Helm dependencies) and links to the repository, the executed pipeline, the API specification, and a Swagger UI (if available). Finally, the user can see the health status of the deployed instances of the microservices.

While the MDP currently works in a real microservice environment, further validation of the results has to be done. Especially regarding the correctness of the stored data including the API specifications and information of a deployed microservices (i.e., CompileTimeData and RuntimeData). Moreover, analyzing if the MDP does support developers and improve their workflow should be performed through a questionnaire or case study.

VII. CONCLUSION AND FUTURE WORK

Reusing existing software components should be a high priority in a sustainable software development environment. Microservice-architectures offer a good opportunity to reuse or exchange individual components in the form of microservices.

Before an existing microservice can be reused, a developer has to know where a microservice is located and how it can be accessed. Keeping track of the currently deployed microservices in a cluster can be difficult once the amount of microservices increases. Therefore, we developed an application called MicroserviceDeveloperPortal (MDP) to provide users with all necessary information.

A key contribution of our approach is a first solution for the architecture of an environment which contains everything that is necessary to build, deploy, run, and operate microservices and its dependencies. We call this environment ServiceEnvironment. The ServiceEnvironment provides domain microservices which offer operations to store and retrieve relevant data. The domain microservices are used by the MDP but can also be reused by other applications.

The data is differentiated in CompileTimeData and RuntimeData. CompileTimeData contains data generated during the build process and is sent by the pipeline step to the MDP. The RuntimeData contains health information and is collected by the MDP through a Kubernetes operator. Finally, the user can retrieve the data through a front-end. Since the MDP is a microservice-based application running in Docker containers, it can be deployed in any Kubernetes environment. Although the paper used GitLab as a solution for a Git repository and CI/CD solution, exchanging GitLab for another solution such as AzureDevops or Jenkins should be easily possible.

The future development of the MDP includes an improvement of the architecture and the additions of new capabilities. Currently, the RegisterStep is modeled as an application context. Logically, the RegisterStep is closer to the bounded context Pipeline and thus should be part of the ServiceEnvironment domain. Moreover, the monitoring aspects of the MDP uses a custom solution to monitor the Pods running in the cluster. The monitoring aspects of the MDP should rather be replaceable by an arbitrary existing monitoring solution (e.g., Prometheus) which has to be modeled accordingly. Then, the application microservice HealthMonitor has to perform a mapping to the existing monitoring solution rather than performing the monitoring itself.

Future research will focus on the management of APIs, which includes researching what is required for the management of APIs and how it can be done by creating a reusable microservice architecture. The management of APIs is mostly neglected in the current version of the MDP and should be added in a future version. Since APIs and microservices depend on each other, the information about APIs could also be stored within the ServiceEnvironment domain. Ideally, the RegisterStep is extended to store the API specification of a registered microservice. This would also allow further API management capabilities such as the versioning of APIs as well as the configuration of API gateways to directly allow developers to access a microservice.

REFERENCES

[1] M. Fowler and J. Lewis, "Microservices," Thouhtworks, Tech. Rep., 2014, [retrieved 21/08/2021]. [Online]. Available: http://martinfowler.com/articles/microservices.html

[2] S. Newman, *Monolith to Microservices: Evolutionary Patterns to Transform Your Monolith*. O'Reilly Media, Inc., 2019.

[3] E. Evans, *Domain-Driven Design: Tackling Complexity in the Heart of Software*. Addison-Wesley Professional, 2004.

[4] B. De, *API Management: An Architect's Guide to Developing and Managing APIs for Your Organization*. Apress, 2017. [Online]. Available: http://link.springer.com/10.1007/978-1-4842-1305-6

[5] S. Throner *et al.*, "An advanced devops environment for microservice-based applications," in *2021 IEEE 16th International Conference of System of Systems Engineering (SoSE)*, 2021, in press.

[6] J. Lewis, "Micro services - the java way," Thouhtworks, Tech. Rep., 2012, [retrieved 21/08/2021]. [Online]. Available: http://2012.33degree.org/talk/show/67

[7] S. Newman, *Building Microservices: Designing Fine-grained Systems*. O'Reilly Media, Inc., 2015.

[8] L. Chen, "Microservices: Architecting for continuous delivery and devops," in *Proceedings - 2018 IEEE 15th International Conference on Software Architecture, ICSA 2018*, 2018, pp. 39–46.

[9] Sysdig, "2019 container usage report," Sysdig, Tech. Rep., 2019, [retrieved 21/08/2021]. [Online]. Available: https://dig.sysdig.com/c/pf-2019-container-usage-report

[10] Portworx and Aqua Security, "2019 container adoption survey," Porworx and Aqua Security, Tech. Rep., 2019, [retrieved 21/08/2021]. [Online]. Available: https://portworx.com/wp-content/uploads/2019/05/2019-container-adoption-survey.pdf

[11] Cloud Native Foundation, "CNCF survey 2020," Cloud Native Foundation, Tech. Rep., 2020, [retrieved 21/08/2021]. [Online]. Available: https://www.cncf.io/wp-content/uploads/2020/11/CNCF_Survey_Report_2020.pdf?utm_source=thenewstack&utm_medium=website&utm_campaign=KCCNC-NA-2020-Referral

[12] L. E. Lwakatare, P. Kuvaja, and M. Oivo, "An exploratory study of devops extending the dimensions of devops with practices," *ICSEA 2016*, vol. 104, pp. 91–99, 2016.

[13] F. Erich, C. Amrit, and M. Daneva, "A qualitative study of devops usage in practice," *Journal of Software: Evolution and Process*, vol. 29, no. 6, p. e1885, 2017. [Online]. Available: https://onlinelibrary.wiley.com/doi/abs/10.1002/smr.1885

[14] R. Wilsenach, "Devops culture," Tech. Rep., 2015, [retrieved 21/08/2021]. [Online]. Available: https://martinfowler.com/bliki/DevOpsCulture.html

[15] Amazon Web Services, "Aws for developers — programming languages, tools, community — aws developer center," AWSb, Tech. Rep., 2021, [retrieved 21/08/2021]. [Online]. Available: https://aws.amazon.com/de/developer/

[16] Mercedes-Benz, "Mercedes–benz /developers – the api platform by daimler," Mercedes-Benz, Tech. Rep., 2021, [retrieved 21/08/2021]. [Online]. Available: https://developer.mercedes-benz.com

[17] S. Abeck *et al.*, "A context map as the basis for a microservice architecture for the connected car domain," in *INFORMATIK 2019*, 2019, pp. 125–138.

[18] B. Hippchen, M. Schneider, I. Landerer, P. Giessler, and S. Abeck, "Methodology for splitting business capabilities into a microservice architecture: Design and maintenance using a domain-driven approach," in *Conference on Advances and Trends in Software Engineering (SOFTENG)*, 2019, pp. 51–61.

[19] M. Schneider, B. Hippchen, P. Giessler, C. Irrgang, and S. Abeck, "Microservice development based on tool-supported domain modeling," in *Conference on Advances and Trends in Software Engineering (SOFTENG)*, 2019, pp. 11–16.

[20] A. Wiggins, "The twelve-factor app," 12factor, Tech. Rep., 2012, [retrieved 21/08/2021]. [Online]. Available: https://12factor.net/

Relational Databases Ingestion into a NoSQL Data Warehouse

Fatma Abdelhedi
CBI² research laboratory, Trimane,
Paris, France.
E-mail : fatma.abdelhedi@trimane.fr

Rym Jemmali
Toulouse Institute of Computer Science
Research (IRIT), CBI²- Trimane,
Paris, France
E-mail : rym.jemmali@trimane.fr

Gilles Zurfluh
IRIT, Capitole University,
Toulouse,France
E-mail : gilles.zurfluh@ut-capitole.fr

Abstract— **The digital transformation of companies has led to the evolution of databases towards Big Data. Our work is part of this context and concerns more particularly the mechanisms to extract datasets stored in a Data Lake and to store the data in a Data Warehouse. The latter will allow, in a second time, decisional analysis. In this paper, we present the extraction mechanism limited to relational databases. To automate this process, we used the Model Driven Architecture (MDA), which offers a formalized environment for schema transformation. From the physical schemas describing a Data Lake, we propose transformation rules that allow the creation of a Data Warehouse stored on a document-oriented NoSQL system. An experimentation of the transformation process has been performed on a medical application.**

Keyword-Data Lake; Data Warehouse; NoSQL; Big Data; Relational Database; MDA; QVT.

I. INTRODUCTION

Due to the considerable increase of data amount generated by human activities, Data Lakes have been created within organizations, often spontaneously, by the physical grouping of datasets related to the same activity. A Data Lake [1] is a massive grouping of data consisting of structured or unstructured datasets. These datasets generally have the following characteristics: (1) they can be stored on heterogeneous systems, (2) each of them is exploited independently of the others, (3) some of them can contain raw data, i.e., data stored in their original form and without being organized according to the use that will be made of them, (4) the types and formats of the data can vary. In practice, a Data Lake can group together different datasets [2] such as relational databases, object databases, Comma Separated Values (CSV) files, texts, spreadsheet folders, etc. The massive data contained in a Data Lake represents an essential reservoir of knowledge for business decision makers. This data can be organized according to a multidimensional data model in order to support certain types of decision processing [3]. For example, in the French health sector, a Data Lake has been created by the French public health insurance company under the name of "Espace Numérique de Santé" (ENS); it includes the electronic health records of insured persons, health questionnaires, and care planners. However, the heterogeneity of storage systems
combined with the diversity of content in the Data Lake is a major obstacle to the use of data for decision-making. To manipulate a Data Lake, a solution consists in ingesting the data into a Data Warehouse and then transforming it (grouping, calculations, etc.). Ingestion is a process that consists in extracting data from various sources and then transferring them to a repository where they can be transformed and analyzed. For example, in [4] massive data from various sources are ingested into a Data Warehouse and exploited in the context of information retrieval on the Web. Other works have introduced the concept of polystore, which preserves the initial data sources (no ingestion) and allows querying them by creating "data islands", each of which contains several systems sharing a common query language. For example, all relational databases are connected to the "relational island", which is queried using standard SQL. This solution, developed in particular in the BiGDAWG [5] and ESTOCADA [6] projects, keeps the data in their native formats.

Our work aims at performing decisional processing on a Data Lake. This problem is part of a medical application in which, massive data are stored in a Data Lake that will be used by medical decision makers. We have chosen to ingest the data from the Data Lake into a Data Warehouse that will later be reorganized for Big Data Analytics. This paper is limited to the ingestion of relational databases and excludes for the moment other forms of datasets present in the Data Lake.
Our paper is organized as follows: in the following Section 2, we present the medical application that justifies our work's purpose. Section 3 describes the context of our study as well as our research problem which aims at facilitating the querying of data contained in a Data Lake by decision makers. Section 4 describes the databases metamodels used in our application. Section 5 presents our contribution which consists in formalizing with the Model Driven Architecture (MDA), the process of transforming the Data Lake databases into a unique NoSQL Data Warehouse. Section 6 describes an experimentation of the proposed process based on our medical application. Section 7 contrasts our proposal with related works. Finally, Section 8 concludes this paper and highlights possible directions for exploring the continuity of the work.

II. CONTEXT OF WORK

In this section, we present the case study that motivated our work, as well as the problem addressed in this paper.

A. Case Study

Our work is motivated by a project developed in the health field for a group of private health insurance companies. These insurance companies, stemming from the social and solidarity economy, propose to their customers a coverage of the medical expenses, which comes in complement of those refunded by a public institution: the public health insurance fund.

To ensure the management of their clients, these private health insurance companies are facing a significant increase in the volume of data processed. Indeed, some of these companies carry out all the computer processing related to a record. A digital health platform (ENS) has been developed by the the public authority to store the medical data of each insured person. Private health insurance companies can extract data from the ENS to process the files of their clients and, more broadly, carry out analyses of any kind (in compliance with confidentiality rules). For each insured person, the ENS contains administrative data, medical files (civil status, medical imaging archives, reports, therapeutic follow-ups, etc.), the history of refunds and questionnaires. When the ENS is fully deployed at the national level, its volume will be considerable since it concerns 67 million insured persons.

In the context of this project, the ENS constitutes a real Data Lake because of (1) the diversity of data types and formats (2) the volumes stored which can reach several terabytes and (3) the raw nature of the data. The objective of the project is to study the mechanisms for extracting data from the ENS and organizing it to facilitate analysis (Big Data Analytics).

B. Problematic

Our work aims to develop a system allowing private health insurance companies to create a Data Warehouse from a Data Lake. This paper deals more specifically with the mechanisms of extraction and unification from commonly used databases, we limit the framework of our study as follows:

-The ENS Data Lake is the source of the data; in this paper, we voluntarily reduce its content to relational databases. Indeed, this category of datasets represents an important part of the ENS data:

- The generated Data Warehouse is managed by a document-oriented NoSQL system. This type of system offers (1) a great flexibility to reorganize objects for analysis and (2) good access performances to large volumes of data (use of MapReduce).

To achieve our goal, each database in the Data Lake is extracted and converted into another model to allow its storage in the Data Warehouse. We do not address here the problems related to the selective extraction of data and their aggregative transformation.

To test our proposals, we have developed a Data Lake with several relational databases managed by MySQL[7] and PostgreSQL[8] systems. These databases contain respectively data describing the follow-up of the insured and the processing of the files in a medical center. The available metadata are limited to those accessible on the storage systems (absence of ontologies for example). The Data Warehouse, which is supported by an OrientDB [9] platform, must allow the analysis of the care pathways of insured persons with chronic pathologies. We chose the OrientDB system to store the Data Warehouse. Indeed, this document-oriented NoSQL system allows to consider several types of semantic links such as association, composition and inheritance links; it is thus well adapted to our case study where the richness of the links between objects constitutes an essential element for decisional processes.

III. OVERVIEW OF OUR SOLUTION

Although a Data Lake can contain files of any format, we focus in this paper on the extraction of relational databases and the feeding of a NoSQL Data Warehouse. Several works have dealt with the transfer of a relational database to a NoSQL database. Thus, some works have proposed algorithms for converting relational data to document-oriented systems, such as MongoDB [10]; however, these works transform relational links into embedded documents or DBRef links. However, these NoSQL linkage solutions are not satisfactory with respect to object systems[11]. Moreover, to our knowledge, no study has been conducted to convert several relational databases contained in a Data Lake into a NoSQL Data Warehouse.

In our ingestion process, we have defined three modules: the first module named CreateDW, the second ConvertLinks and the last one MergeClasses.We used a Data Lake as a source database for our process, which we limited in this paper to Relational databases and as a target database,we used a NoSQL Data Warehouse that will contain the final processed data. We named our process RDBToNoSDW. Our proposal is based on Model Driven Architecture (MDA) which allows to describe separately the functional specifications and the implementation of an application on a platform. Among the three models present in MDA (CIM, PIM and PSM), we are located at the PSM level where the logical schemas are described. We also use the declarative language Query View Transformation (QVT) [12] specified by the Object Management Group (OMG) [13], which allows us to describe the ingestion of data by model transformations.

To use the MDA transformation mechanism, we proposed two metamodels describing respectively the source and target databases. From these metamodels, we specified the transformation rules in QVT language to ensure data ingestion.

IV. METAMODELING

We present successively our metamodels proposal of a source Relational database and a target document-oriented NoSQL database.

A. Relational Metamodel

The Data Lake, source of our process, can contain several relational databases. A relational database contains a set of tables made of a schema and an extension. The schema of a table contains a sequence of attributes. The extension is composed of a set of rows grouping attribute values. Among the attributes of a table, we distinguish the primary key whose values identify the rows and the foreign keys, which materialize the links. Figure 1 represents the Ecore[14] metamodel of a relational database.

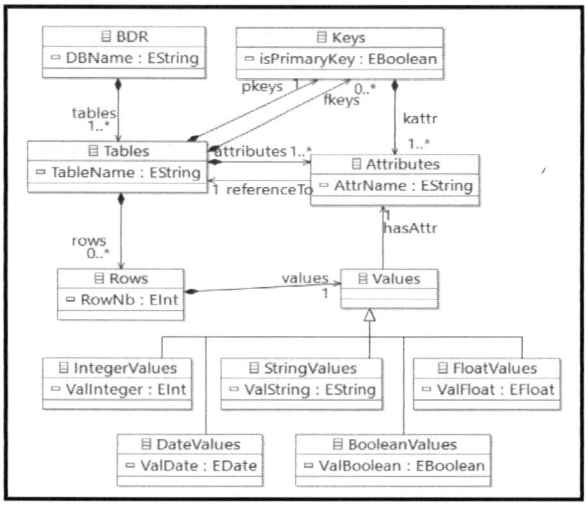

Figure 1. Metamodel of a relational database

B. *Document-Oriented NoSQL Metamodel*

The target of our process corresponds to the Data Warehouse represented by a NoSQL database. A document-oriented NoSQL database contains a set of classes. Each class gathers objects that are identified (by a reference) and composed of couples (attribute, value); a value is defined by a type, it can be either multivalued or structured. We distinguish a particular type, the reference, whose values make it possible to link the objects. These concepts are represented in Figure 2 according to the Ecore formalism.

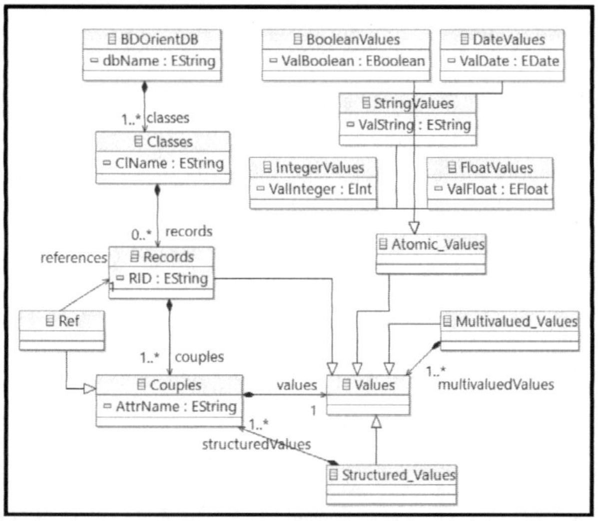

Figure 2. Metamodel of a document-oriented NoSQL database

V. DATA MANAGEMENT

This involves transferring relational databases from the Data Lake to a NoSQL database corresponding to the Data Warehouse. To carry out this ingestion process, we have defined three modules that will successively ensure (1) the transformation of relational data into NoSQL data (CreateDW module), (2) the conversion of relational links (foreign keys) into references (ConvertLinks module) and (3) the merging of tables containing objects of the same semantics (MergeClasses module).

A. *CreateDW Module*

This module transforms each relational database of the Data Lake into a unique NoSQL database according to the MDA approach. The NoSQL warehouse being unique, it will contain the data coming from the different relational databases of the Data Lake. The application of a set of transformation rules defined on the metamodels of Section 4, generates a set of classes in a NoSQL database. We informally present the rules that have been expressed in the QVT language.

Rule 1: Each table in a relational database is transformed into a class in the NoSQL database. To avoid synonymy, the name of the class will be prefixed by the name of the original database.

Rule 2: Each row of a table, associated with its schema, is transformed into a record in the corresponding target class; the record then contains a set of couples (attribute, value). The primary key is stored as any attribute. At this stage, the foreign keys are also stored with their relational values; they will be converted into references by the ConvertLinks module. These two rules, that we formalized in QVT language, are applied for each relational database of the Data Lake and feed the NoSQL DB; we will present their syntax in Figure 4 of the experimentation section. In parallel with the application of these transformation rules, an algorithmic processing allows to record metadata; these metadata match each relational primary key with the Record Identifier (RID) of the corresponding record in the NoSQL database.

B. *ConvertLinks Module*

In the standard object-oriented systems[15], links are materialized by references. Since this principle is used in NoSQL systems, it is necessary to convert relational foreign keys that have been transferred to the Data Warehouse into references.

The mechanism we have developed in ConvertLinks is not based on the expression of MDA rules but corresponds to an algorithmic process. In the NoSQL database, all records of a class are systematically marked with identifiers (RID for Record ID). During the transfer of data into the records, the relational primary and foreign keys were transferred in the form of pairs (attribute, value). Thus, thanks to the metadata recorded by the previous CreateDW module, the values of the foreign keys are converted into RID.

C. MergeClasses Module

The ingestion of data from the Data Lake has been done by transferring the data from the different relational databases into the NoSQL database. However, it is common for tables with the same semantics to be transferred from different relational databases; these tables are said to be "equivalent", for example the DB1-Insured table and the DB2-Patients table containing data on the insured. It is therefore useful to group the data contained in "equivalent" tables within a single class of the NoSQL database. To achieve this grouping, we relied on an ontology establishing the correspondences between the terms of the relational databases contained in the Data Lake. This ontology is provided by relational data administrators bringing their business expertise. These administrators, after consultation, have associated the tables considered as semantically equivalent.

Using this ontology, the MergeClasses module creates new classes in the NoSQL database; each of these classes groups the data from the various equivalent tables. This process is not limited to a union operation between records.

In fact, distinct records concerning the same entity can have complementary attributes that will be combined in a single record.

VI. IMPLEMENTATION AND TECHNICAL ENVIRONMENT

In this section, we describe the techniques used to implement the RDBToNoSDW process. We used the Eclipse Modeling Framework (EMF) technical environment that is suitable for modeling, metamodeling, and transforming models. EMF has the Ecore metamodeling language to create and manipulate metamodels. Ecore is based on XMI to instantiate models and QVT to transform metamodels. Algorithmic processing was coded in Java because of its compatibility with Eclipe which is the development environment used.

The CreateDW module of our process generates a unique NoSQL database from the Data Lake databses. It uses a relational metamodel and a NoSQL metamodel as represented with Ecore in Figures 2 and 3. The instantiation of the two relational databases is done with the XMI language. Figure 3 shows the XMI instantiation of a source relational database. The transformation rules have been translated with the QVT language (Figure 4) and apply to all relational databases, independently of the RDBMS used.

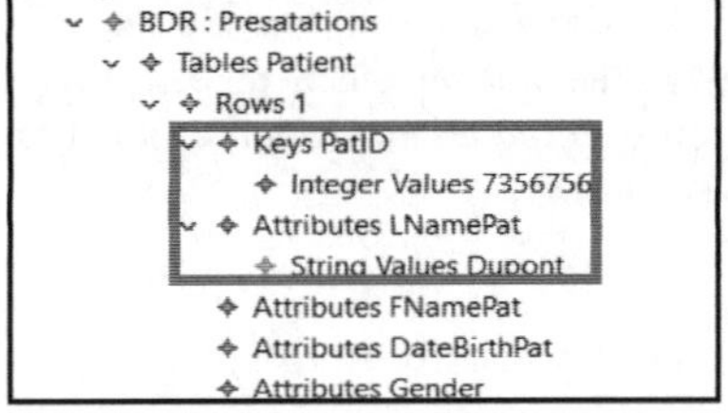

Figure 3. XMI instantiation of a source relational database

```
//Transform a relational database into an OrientDB database
mapping BDR::RDBtoODB(): BDOrientDB{
dbName:=self.DBName;
classes:= self.tables.map toTable();
}

//Transform a relational table into an OrientDB class
mapping RDB::Tables:: toTable():ODB::Classes{
ClName := self.TableName;
records:= self.rows.map toDoc();
}

//Transform a row into an OrientDB Record
mapping RDB::Rows:: toDoc():ODB::Records{
couples:=self.hasAttributes.map toCouple();
```

Figure 4. QVT transformation rules from relational to NoSQL databases

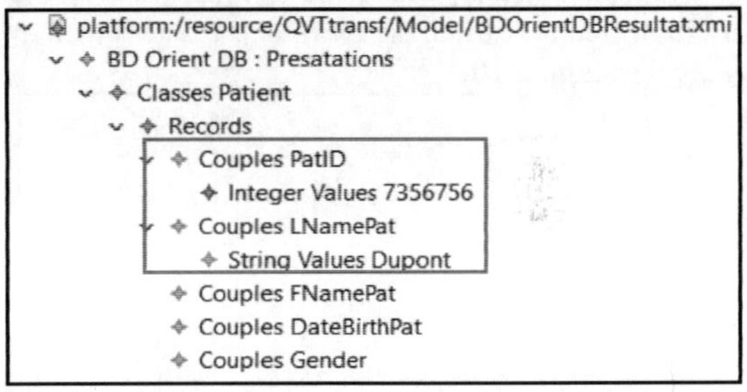

Figure 5. Result XMI file of a target NoSQL database (after QVT rules execution)

The result of applying the QVT transformation rules (Figure 4) is shown in Figure 5.

At the end of the execution of the CreateDW module, we obtain a NoSQL Data Warehouse containing a set of classes as shown in Figure 6. Each of them corresponds to a relational table without any filtering having been carried out (possible presence of "equivalent" tables stored in different databases from the source).

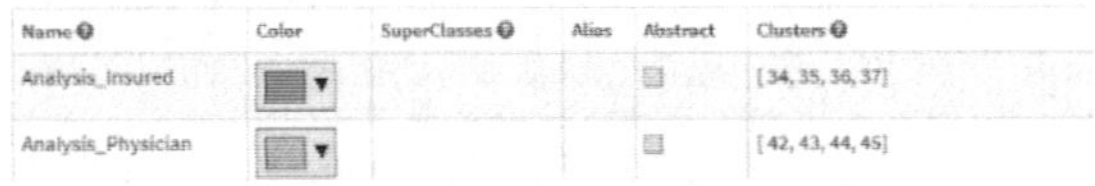

Figure 6. Extract from the list of the Data Warehouse classes stored in OrientDB

The ConvertLinks module converts relational foreign keys into RID. For example, we consider a table "Patient" containing a patient information's with a field "Doctor" representing a foreign key. This field will, therefore, be converted to a reference (RID). Figure 7 shows a record of the "Patient" class after running the ConvertLinks module.

```
{
  "@type": "d",
  "@rid": "#26:0",
  "@version": 1,
  "@class": "Analysis_Patients",
  "Email": "ramon.saadi@gmail.com",
  "FNamePat": "Ramon",
  "LNamePat": "Saadi"
  "NoPat": "45657709",
  "Doctor": "#22:0"
}
```

Figure 7. Extract from the "Patient" class after limks convertion

Finally, the MergeClasses module groups the records of the classes considered as "equivalent" based on the ontology provided by the experts. Figures 8 and 9 represent respectively two records from two classes "ServiceProvision_Insured" and "Analysis_Patients". The two records, having in common several semantically equivalent attributes, will be merged into a single record stored in the same class "Insured_DW" as shown in Figure 10.

```
{
  "@type": "d",
  "@rid": "#34:0",
  "@version": 1,
  "@class": "ServiceProvision_Insured",
  "Gender": "M",
  "FNameIns": "Ramon",
  "LNameIns": "Saadi",
  "NoInsured": "45657709",
  "Spouse": "#36:0"
}
```

Figure 8. Record from the « ServiceProvision_Insured » class

```
{
  "@type": "d",
  "@rid": "#26:0",
  "@version": 1,
  "@class": "Analysis_Patients",
  "Email": "ramon.saadi@gmail.com",
  "FNamePat": "Ramon",
  "LNamePat": "Saadi"
  "NoPat": "45657709",
  "Doctor": "#22:0"
}
```

Figure 9. Record from the « Analysis_Patients » class

```
{
  "@type": "d",
  "@rid": "#62:0",
  "@version": 1,
  "@class": "Insured_DW",
  "Email": "ramon.saadi@gmail.com",
  "FNameIns": "Ramon",
  "LNameIns": "Saadi",
  "NoInsured": "45657709",
  "Doctor": "#22:0",
  "Gender": "M",
  "Spouse": "#36:0"
}
```

Figure 10. Record fron the new created « Insured_DW » class

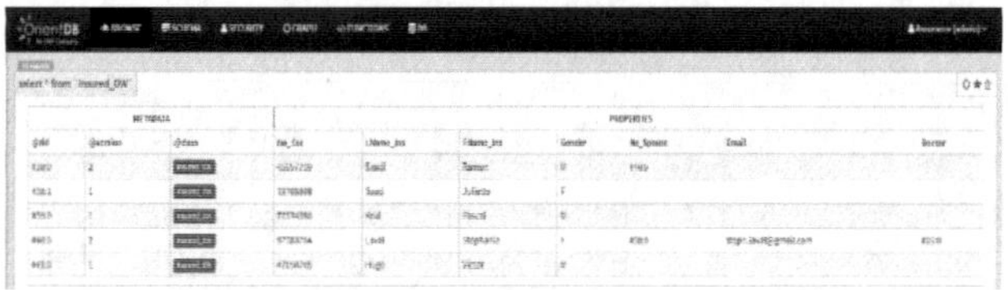

Figure 11. Extract from the "Insured_DW" class

Figure 11 represents an extract of the new class "Insured_DW" containing a record resulting from merging records belonging to the two classes "ServiceProvision_Insured" and "Analysis_Patients".

VII. RELATED WORKS

In this section, we present research work on extracting data from a Data Lake and more specifically data from several relational databases and creating a NoSQL Data Warehouse. The advent of Big Data has created several challenges for the management of massive data; among these we find the creation of architectures to ingest massive data sources as well as the integration and transformation of these massive data (Big Data) allowing their subsequent query. In this sense, some works have focused on the proposal of architectures (physical and logical) allowing the use and the management of Data Lakes. The work in [16] proposes an approach to structure the data of a Data Lake by linking the data sources in the form of a graph composed of keywords. Other works propose to extract the data of a Data Lake from the metamodels of the sources. The authors in [17] have proposed a metamodel unifying NoSQL and relational databases. There are several formalisms [18] to express model transformations such as the QVT standard, the ATL language [19], which is a non-standardized model transformation language more or less inspired by the QVT standard of the Object Management Group, etc.

Other works have studied only the transformation of a relational database into a NoSQL database. Thus in [20, 21] the authors developed a method to transfer data from relational databases to MongoDB. This approach translates the links between tables only by nesting documents. In [22], the authors present MigDB, an application that converts a relational database (MySQL) to a NoSQL one (MongoDB. This conversion is done over several steps: transforming tables into JSON files, then transmitting each JSON file to a neural network. This network allows to process the links at the JSON file level, either by nesting or by referencing. This work considers association links only. The same is true in [23], where the authors propose a method for transferring relational databases to MongoDB by converting the tables into CSV files that are then imported into MongoDB. However, the proposed method simply converts tables into MongoDB collections without supporting the various links between tables.

Our solution is based on the metamodeling of the sources of a Data Lake, the transformation of these metamodels thanks to the QVT standard and then the creation of a NoSQL Data Warehouse stored under OrientDB allowing to query the data of the Data Lake.

VIII. CONCLUSION

We have proposed a process to ingest data from a Data Lake into a Data Warehouse. The Data Lake contains several databases. This paper focuses on a specific problem, we have limited the content of the Data Lake to relational databases.

Three modules ensure the ingestion of the data. The CreateDW module transforms each relational database into a unique NoSQL database by applying MDA rules. This mechanism will be extended to transform other types of databases stored in the Data Lake. The ConvertLinks module translates relational links (keys) into references in accordance with the principles of object databases supported by the OrientDB system. Finally, the MergeClasses module merges semantically equivalent classes from different Data Lake databases; this merge is based on an ontology provided by business experts.

Currently, we are continuing our work on the ingestion of data from a Data Lake by extending it to other types of data sources, ingesting and processing data coming from CSV files, NoSQL databases (document and column-oriented databases) and text files. Indeed, these types of files are present in the Data Lake of our medical case study.

REFERENCES

[1] F. Nargesian, E. Zhu, R. J. Miller, K. Q. Pu, and P. C. Arocena, « Data lake management: challenges and opportunities », Proc. VLDB Endow., vol. 12, no 12, p. 1986-1989, August 2019.

[2] P. P. Khine and Z. S. Wang, « Data lake: a new ideology in big data era », ITM Web Conf., vol. 17, 2018.

[3] M. El Malki, A. Kopliku, E. Sabir, and O. Teste, « Benchmarking Big Data OLAP NoSQL Databases », in Ubiquitous Networking, vol. 11277, Ed. Cham: Springer International Publishing, 2018, p. 82-94.

[4] Meehan, J., Aslantas, C., Zdonik, S., Tatbul, N., & Du, J. (2017). Data Ingestion for the Connected World. CIDR.

[5] J. Duggan, J. Kepner, A. J. Elmore, and S. Madden, « The BigDAWG Polystore System », SIGMOD Rec., vol. 44, no 2, p. 6, 2015.

[6] R. Alotaibi, B. Cautis, A. Deutsch, M. Latrache, I. Manolescu, and Y. Yang, « ESTOCADA: towards scalable polystore systems », Proc. VLDB Endow., vol. 13, no 12, p. 2949-2952, August 2020.

[7] https://www.mysql.com (Accessed: 19 March 2021)

[8] https://www.postgresql.org (Accessed: 19 March 2021)

[9] https://orientdb.com/docs/3.0.x/ (Accessed: 01 March 2021)

[10] A. A. Mahmood, « Automated Algorithm for Data Migration from Relational to NoSQL Databases », Al-Nahrain J. Eng. Sci., vol. 21, no 1, p. 60, feb. 2018.

[11] http://www.odbms.org/odmg-standard/reading-room/odmg-2-0-a-standard-for-object-storage/ (Accessed: 30 June 2021)

[12] https://www.omg.org/spec/QVT/1.2/PDF (Accessed: 12 May 2021)

[13] https://www.omg.org (Accessed: 12 May 2021)

[14] https://download.eclipse.org/modeling/emf/emf/javadoc/2.9.0/org/eclipse/emf/ecore/package-summary.html (Accessed: 22 June 2021)

[15] http://www.odbms.org/wp-content/uploads/2013/11/001.04-Ullman-CS145-ODL-OQL-Fall-2004.pdf (Accessed: 30 June 2021)

[16] C. Diamantini, P. Lo Giudice, L. Musarella, D. Potena, E. Storti, and D. Ursino, « A New Metadata Model to Uniformly Handle Heterogeneous Data Lake Sources: ADBIS 2018 Budapest, Hungary, September 2-5, 2018, Proceedings », 2018, p. 165-177.

[17] C. J. F. Candel, D. S. Ruiz, and J. J. García-Molina, « A Unified Metamodel for NoSQL and Relational Databases », ArXiv210506494 Cs, May 2021.

[18] J. Bruel and al., « Comparing and classifying model transformation reuse approaches across metamodels », Softw. Syst. Model., 2019.

[19] A. Erraissi and M. Banane, « Managing Big Data using Model Driven Engineering: From Big Data Meta-model to Cloudera PSM meta-model », International Conference on Decision Aid Sciences and Application (DASA), Nov. 2020, p. 1235-1239.

[20] Hanine, M., Bendarag, A., Boutkhoum, O. (2015) « Data Migration Methodology from Relational to NoSQL Databases ». International Journal of Computer and Information Engineering, 9(12), 2559 - 2563.

[21] L. Stanescu, M. Brezovan, and D. D. Burdescu, « Automatic Mapping of MySQL Databases to NoSQL MongoDB », Proceedings of the Federated Conference on Computer Science and Information Systems, Oct. 2016, p. 837-840.

[22] G. Liyanaarachchi, L. Kasun, M. Nimesha, K. Lahiru, and A. Karunasena, « MigDB - relational to NoSQL mapper », in 2016 IEEE International Conference on Information and Automation for Sustainability (ICIAfS), Dec. 2016, p. 1-6.

[23] S. Chickerur, A. Goudar, and A. Kinnerkar, « Comparison of Relational Database with Document-Oriented Database (MongoDB) for Big Data Applications », in 2015 8th International Conference on Advanced Software Engineering Its Applications (ASEA), Nov. 2015, p. 41-47.

A Communities Engagement Tool for Assessing the Resilience and Deterioration of Cultural Heritage Sites

Nikolaos Tousert, Antonis Kalis, Maria Krommyda, Nikos Frangakis, Spyridon Nektarios Bolierakis, Angelos Amditis
Institute of Communication and Computer Systems
Athens, Greece
e-mails: {nikos.tousert, antonis.kalis, maria.krommyda, nikos.frangakis, spyros.bolierakis, a.amditis}@iccs.gr

Abstract—**Climate change and geo-hazards (such as landslides and earthquakes) may have a negative impact on historic areas hosting Cultural Heritage (CH) sites and monuments, which in turn yields significant adverse impacts on economies, politics and societies. The deterioration of CH sites is one of the biggest challenges that needs to be addressed through structural responses, preventive measures, restoration strategies, resilience and adaptation methodologies. In order to assess the resilience and deterioration of the historic areas and also the potential impacts due to various hazards through a community-based participatory environment, a web tool has been developed, entitled "Communities' Engagement Information and Communication Technology (ICT) Tool". This paper presents the aforementioned tool which aims at engaging cultural heritage aware communities through a web platform. This specialized software is an advanced application that will encourage citizens to give direct feedback to the relevant cultural authorities in order to assist them in assessing the deterioration of the cultural heritage sites and determining the needed reconstruction needs and expectations.**

Keywords-deterioration; hazards; cultural heritage sites; communities engagement tool; monuments.

I. INTRODUCTION

The Communities Engagement ICT Tool (hereafter referred to as "Engagement Tool") is a web based software that specializes in preservation and damage assessment of cultural heritage. It serves as a collaborative environment that can be used directly by the citizens so as to submit stories (or else reports) concerning cultural heritage sites deterioration. Rather than being a standalone tool, it aims at incorporating active communities' participation through the secure integration with the Pluggable Social Platform for Heritage Awareness and Participation (PLUGGY) [1]. PLUGGY, which is a social network platform for heritage gives voice to citizens across Europe and enables them to safeguard and enrich the European cultural heritage landscape. It is also an open source platform specializing on the preservation and promotion of everyday all-around heritage, using crowd-sourced techniques. The developed tool presented in this paper has taken advantage of the pluggable nature of PLUGGY in terms of integration potential and focuses on the engagement of local communities and business owners in reporting significant problems posed in CH sites or businesses that are caused by extreme events associated with the impacts of climate change and natural hazards.

Concerning the technical integration aspects, the Engagement Tool, which is a pluggable application makes use of already developed PLUGGY's Application Programming Interfaces (APIs) and database. The tool has been developed by taking advantage of the already registered PLUGGY community and its flexible data model. A user-friendly interface has been developed for the innovative presentation of stories to users in order for them to experience the content and better understand the changes imposed by climate change and extreme events concerning the monuments and the operation or disruption of businesses.

Section III reports the functional requirements which define the specifications and behaviours of the Tool. Section IV addresses the integration aspects between the Engagement Tool and PLUGGY. More specifically, Subsection A presents the PLUGGY flexible data model and the way it is used by the Engagement Tool. Concerning the security and user account management issues, they are analysed in Subsection B. The user interface and the available functionalities of the Engagement Tool are documented in Section V.

II. RELATED WORK

Plenty of research has been conducted on damage assessment of cultural heritage sites. According to [2], assessing damage to cultural heritage is complex and has to be broken down into two phases: an on-site assessment is needed first to estimate costs for salvaging, stabilizing and mitigating risks to cultural heritage and then, a detailed condition assessment of the damaged objects and structural elements is needed to estimate the costs. In [3], through the case study of Syria, it is highlighted the need for adopting well defined methodologies, methods and tools for recording both the inventory of sites and monuments and also the damage, threats and causes. Moreover, as stated in [4], remote sensing techniques (e.g., Unmanned Aerial Vehicle (UAV) photogrammetry) can also be used for the damage assessment of monuments based on the successful post-earthquake damage assessment carried out for "Sulamani" temple in Myanmar. Research has also been made on damage assessment through crowdsourcing involvement, however most of the published work has mainly focused either on improving the effectiveness of crowdsourcing results (e.g., mitigating bias due to unreliable participants) [5] or on improving the motivation of people to contribute (e.g., through media, influencers, memory of the city, etc.) [6]. On the contrary, the aim of this research was through integration efforts to get damage assessment content not from the wider public (which could lead to poor crowdsourcing results), but from the users of a cultural heritage aware community and more specifically from PLUGGY platform through the proposed developed plugin (i.e., the Engagement Tool).

III. FUNCTIONAL REQUIREMENTS

Table I lists the most important functional requirements (FR) of the Engagement Tool which drove its design, development and integration with PLUGGY platform. FR are program features or functions that software systems must implement so as to enable users to accomplish their tasks. It is therefore important to make them clear both for the development team and the stakeholders. FR describe system behaviour under specific conditions, so they consist the descriptions of the services that the software must offer. As shown in Table I, considering the Engagement Tool, FR are mostly relevant to integration aspects, user interaction, and type of content stored.

TABLE I. FUNCTIONAL REQUIREMENTS OF THE ENGAGEMENT TOOL

Functional Requirement No.	Functional Requirement Description
FR 1	The Engagement Tool must provide a user friendly interface so as for a citizen to be able to store or update info relevant to monument deterioration or business damages (i.e., Engagement Tool stories)
FR 2	The Engagement Tool must provide a user friendly interface so as for logged in users to be able to view citizen and business owners stories
FR 3	The Engagement Tool must be integrated with the identity manager and authorization services of a platform specialized in cultural heritage so to be able to attract its users with their same credentials
FR 4	The Engagement Tool must store the content generated by the users (i.e., business and citizen stories) in the database of the aforementioned platform. This would enhance the integration.
FR 5	The information relevant to the monument deterioration should include at least the following: description of the damage, location of the monument, photos and tags
FR 6	The content relevant to the business damages should include information useful to local authorities (e.g., business damage description, relevant tags, location, business risk, etc.)

IV. INTEGRATION OF THE COMMUNITIES ENGAGEMENT ICT TOOL WITH PLUGGY PLATFORM

The Engagement Tool has been integrated into PLUGGY which is a Pluggable Social Platform for Heritage Awareness and Participation. This social platform enables citizens to share their local knowledge and everyday experience with others. The reasons for integrating with PLUGGY, rather than creating a standalone tool, are the following:

- To take advantage of the visitors already engaged in PLUGGY platform [1]. This means that a user already logged in to PLUGGY platform will be able to interact with the Engagement Tool without leaving PLUGGY. This can be achieved through the plug-in mechanism of PLUGGY.
- To be able to retrieve content from PLUGGY platform (monuments information, used tags, photos, etc.) by making use of its APIs.
- To take advantage of the number of PLUGGY's users. This is achieved with the integration between the Engagement Tool and PLUGGY's authorization component. To this end, users that have already created an account in PLUGGY, they are not obliged to create another account in a separate authorization component.
- All the content of the Engagement Tool (monuments deterioration, business losses, etc.) can be viewed both through the current tool and the PLUGGY platform.

However, the integration of the Engagement Tool with PLUGGY is not only seen as a technical integration that will just exploit already developed technical units of PLUGGY, but the objective is the semantic integration in a way that content related to cultural heritage (CH) stored in PLUGGY database and especially monuments geo-localised information, will be exploited by the Engagement Tool. Figure 1 depicts the integration of the Engagement Tool with PLUGGY platform and its interaction with the user. The stories related to the deterioration of CH sites or business damages can be retrieved by any other web client through PLUGGY's Representational State Transfer (REST) services.

A. *Usage of the flexible PLUGGY database*

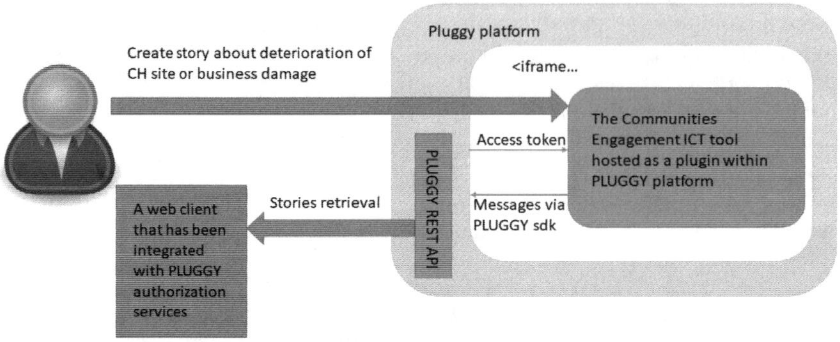

Figure 1. Integration of the Engagement Tool within PLUGGY platform.

PLUGGY, being a new paradigm in cultural heritage [7], provides the necessary tools to allow users to share their local knowledge and everyday experience with others. More specifically, it aimed at creating communities of people interested in cultural heritage, from simple citizens to cultural institutions that would have the opportunity to share their own personalized stories of local cultural knowledge and experiences. It is a social platform that aims at building extensive networks around a common interest in connecting the past, the present and the future. However, apart from being a heritage-centric social platform that will bring citizens together for creating stories with meaningful narratives resulting in Virtual Exhibitions, the architecture of the social platform [8] has been designed in a way that it allows the easy integration of external applications (or else plugins). External applications can make use of PLUGGY REST services so as to either retrieve content from social platform's database or curate cultural heritage content.

To this end, the Engagement Tool makes use of PLUGGY's flexible data model [8] which is depicted in Figure 2. As shown in Figure 2, the PLUGGY data model is generic enough to be used by other apps and more specifically by PLUGGY's plugins. This is why the Engagement Tool, which is a PLUGGY plugin makes use both of PLUGGY's APIs and database. The main entities used in PLUGGY data model along with their interpretation are the following:

- **Asset**: It is the elementary unit of content in PLUGGY. An asset is a media file with an identified owner, a title, a description, a set of tags and a license, which specifies how this file can be reused. The Asset can be used as a digital representation of cultural heritage artifact, tangible or intangible. The media file can be text, image, audio, 3d model or any type of binary data.
- **Exhibition**: Cultural heritage stories curated by users of PLUGGY using one or more assets. An exhibition can be of several types: media stories, timelines, geolocated tours, augmented reality exhibitions and games.

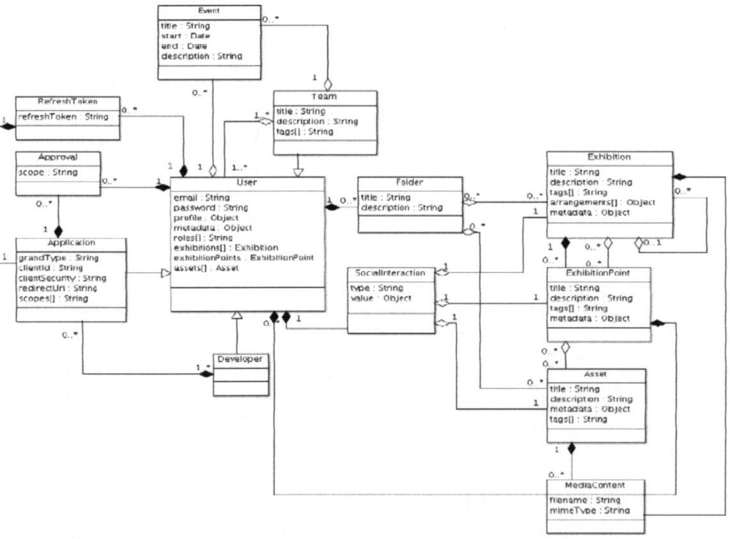

Figure 2. PLUGGY flexible data model.

- **Exhibition Point**: Exhibition points link exhibitions and assets. An exhibition point is the usage of an asset in an exhibition and an exhibition is composed of one or several exhibition points. For example, events are the exhibition points of timelines and chapters are the exhibition points of media stories.

As reported in [8], the PLUGGY provides the four basic operations for persistent storage (i.e., create, read, update and delete (CRUD)) for manipulation purposes of all aforementioned entities. The entities of PLUGGY entitled exhibition, exhibition point and asset are being used by the Engagement Tool but in a different manner as described below:

- **Exhibition in the Engagement Tool:** Each citizen story and each business owner story concerning the Engagement Tool corresponds to an exhibition. In the Engagement Tool, the exhibition has the meaning of a story (either citizen or business owner story). This exhibition may contain many exhibition points. Apart from the linking to exhibition points, the exhibition may contain among others: link to other exhibitions, the date when the exhibition was updated or created, the owner and the creator of the exhibition, and finally the title and description of the exhibition. For instance, the title of an exhibition concerning a citizen story could be the following: "Notable landmark in Wiltshire has deteriorated" and a title for an exhibition concerning a business owner story could be the following: "Restaurant in Athens has damage due to hurricane". The description of an exhibition relevant to a business owner story could be: "Restaurant Kitro in Athens has suffered damages. A hurricane has caused damage in restaurant 'Kitro' and is now out of service".
- **Exhibition Point in the context of Engagement Tool:** The exhibition point is linked to a specific exhibition (see Figure 2) and contains more detailed information regarding the story. Especially for the case of business stories for the Engagement Tool, a separate JavaScript Object Notation (json) file is linked to the exhibition point that when downloaded and parsed by the client, it contains the following attributes: (this json file is only applicable to business owner stories and not to citizen stories):
    - **Business Damage Description** (e.g., extensive damage to the building. The building has completely flooded over the weekend. As such, the restaurant has been closed).
    - **Business Risk Description** (e.g., since the restaurant is closed for the past week, there is the risk to loose high percentage of customers).
    - **Local Authorities info** (e.g., there is absolute devastation in the surrounding area. A fundraiser needs to be set up to help families who lost everything. Police has informed us that all businesses are under water).
    - **Customers Lost Percentage** (e.g., -80%. Loses related to last year's value).
    - **Priority of the issue** (possible values: Urgent, High, Medium, Low, Very Low)
    - **Criticality of the Issue** (possible values: Very High, High, Medium, Low, Very Low)
    - **Relevant Tags** (e.g., restaurant, flooded, damage)
- **Asset in the context of Engagement Tool:** Similarly to PLUGGY assets, an asset in the context of the Engagement Tool plays the role of a media file with an identified owner, a title, a description, a set of tags and a license, which specifies how this file can be reused. Currently, the kind of assets that the Engagement Tool can support are images. It has to be noted that the asset contains file metadata (tags, file length, name of file, chunk size, date of creation/update, file title, file description, etc.) and also the identification (ID) of the actual file which is required in order to later call the relevant API so as to retrieve the binary data.

This chapter addressed the main data entities of the Engagement Tool (i.e., exhibition, exhibition point, asset) and their relation to PLUGGY's data model. The Engagement Tool takes advantage of the flexibility concerning PLUGGY data model and stores all the relevant information into PLUGGY's database by making use of its APIs. To this end, as stated previously the citizen stories and the business owner stories curated by the Engagement Tool are stored in the PLUGGY's back-end in the form of exhibitions.

B. Integration with PLUGGY Authorization Server

PLUGGY is a pluggable platform and multiple applications can access users' content through Open Authorization (OAuth 2.0) security protocol. OAuth 2.0 is an open standard for access delegation, commonly used as a way for Internet users to grant websites or applications access to their information on other websites but without giving them the passwords [9]. Generally, OAuth 2.0 provides clients a "secure delegated access" to server resources on behalf of a resource owner. It specifies a process for resource owners to authorize third-party access to their server resources without providing credentials. Designed specifically to work with Hypertext Transfer Protocol (HTTP), OAuth 2.0 essentially allows access tokens to be issued to third-party clients by an authorization server, with the approval of the resource owner. The third-party then uses the access token to access the protected resources hosted by the resource server.

In this paper, we consider the third-party client to be the Engagement Tool. However, any other tool that can be integrated into PLUGGY through the OAuth 2.0 protocol, will be able to be a third-party client, and as such, it could retrieve the relevant content (i.e., citizen stories concerning a monument deterioration or business owner story concerning business interruption) through PLUGGY's APIs. Moreover, the resource server is considered to be the back-end of the PLUGGY platform that holds all the information that has been populated through the Engagement Tool. The resource owners are the users that created the stories through the Engagement Tool.

Figure 3 depicts the interaction between the aforementioned components so as for both the Engagement Tool and any other willing third-party module to be able to access PLUGGY protected resources (i.e., citizen and business stories). Before this interaction, and as depicted in Figure 4, the client (e.g., the Engagement Tool) has to register itself to PLUGGY authorization services by providing a client ID and a redirect Uniform Resource Identifier (URI). Then, the client is able to participate to PLUGGY OAuth 2.0 workflow which is the following:

a) The user wants to login to the client (i.e., the Engagement Tool) and therefore is redirected to PLUGGY login page.
b) The user inserts in the form their PLUGGY credentials.
c) After successful login, the access token is provided to the client from PLUGGY authorization services.
d) The user through the Engagement Tool asks for a resource (e.g., for the content of a citizen story) and therefore the access token is passed to PLUGGY resource server (i.e., the PLUGGY back-end).
e) The PLUGGY resource server validates the token and then it passes to the client the resource.
f) The user is able through the client to view or edit the citizen or business owner stories.

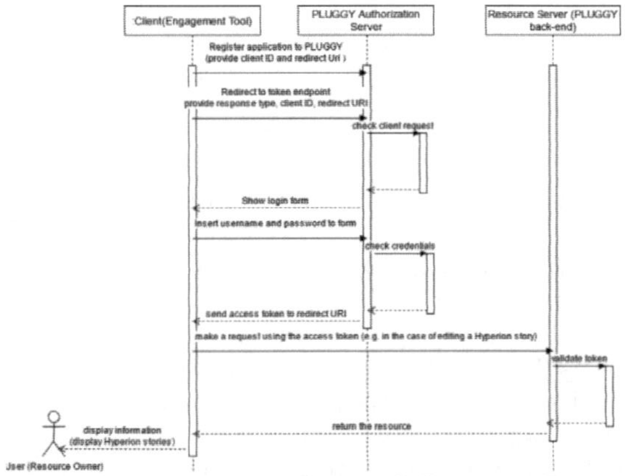

Figure 3. OAuth 2.0 workflow between the Engagement Tool, the PLUGGY authorization services and the PLUGGY back-end.

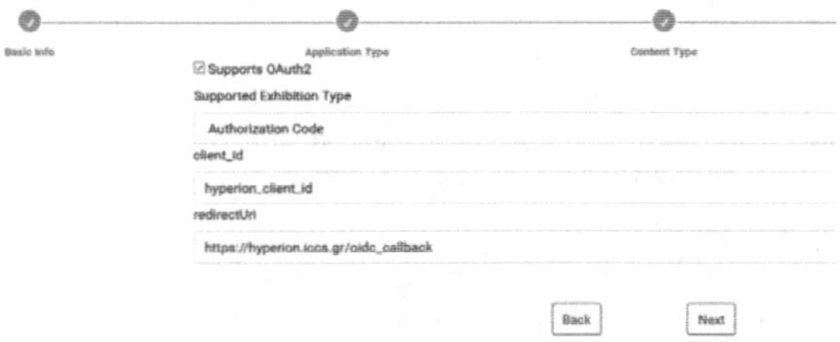

Figure 4. The Engagement Tool is registered into PLUGGY authorization services.

After successful authentication, the access token is granted to the client and the user is able through the client app to view or edit the stories. It has to be noted that through the PLUGGY login page, users are also able to reset password or create new accounts.

The registration of the application client to PLUGGY authorization services is a prerequisite for integrating into PLUGGY security mechanism (i.e., OAuth 2.0 protocol), however, this step is automatic for any developer and it is provided through PLUGGY platform [10]. According to Figure 4, the developer of the app has to provide a client ID and a redirection URI to PLUGGY platform so as to initialize the integration of the app with PLUGGY OAuth 2.0 mechanism. Every application can be integrated into PLUGGY platform and the security workflow and procedure is straightforward [10]. The Engagement Tool has already completed this procedure.

V. USER INTERFACE OF ENGAGEMENT TOOL

The user interface (UI) is the space where interactions between the users and the Engagement Tool occur. The goal of these interactions is to allow effective operation and control of the Engagement Tool by citizens and business owners. The following Subsections document the user interface which aims at making easy and efficient the creation and managing of citizen and business owner stories.

A. *Wizards for creating stories*

There are two kinds of stories that a user can store within the Engagement Tool through wizards:

- Citizen Stories: Citizens are able to create stories about the deterioration of cultural heritage sites. In this case the user is able through a wizard to store the following info: title of the story, monument damage description, and relevant photo and tags.
- Business Owner Stories: Local business owners are also able to report about their damages, so as to promise the business continuity. More specifically, business owners are able to report through the Engagement Tool the following: business damage, business risk assessment, information useful to local authorities, customers lost percentage, priority and criticality of the issue, and relevant tags.

The two aforementioned kinds of stories can both contain relevant images, location details and general information. Figure 5 depicts the first step of the wizard of the Engagement Tool for creating a citizen story concerning a monument damage. In this step the user has to enter information concerning story title and monument deterioration description along with location. Concerning the creation of a business story, the wizard is pretty much the same. The only difference lies in the fact that there is one more (second step) of the wizard, where the user has to insert

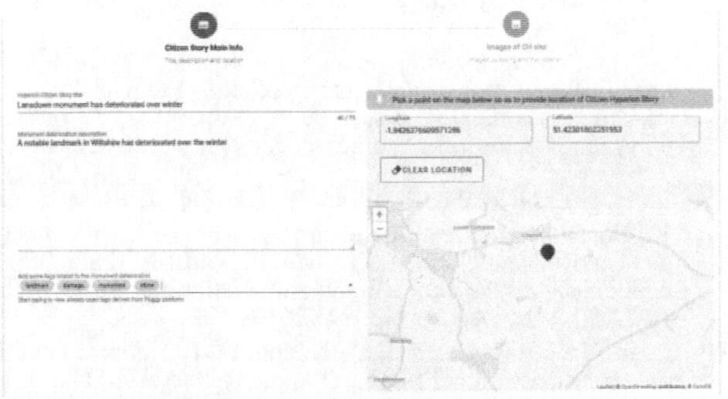

Figure 5. First step of the citizen story wizard.

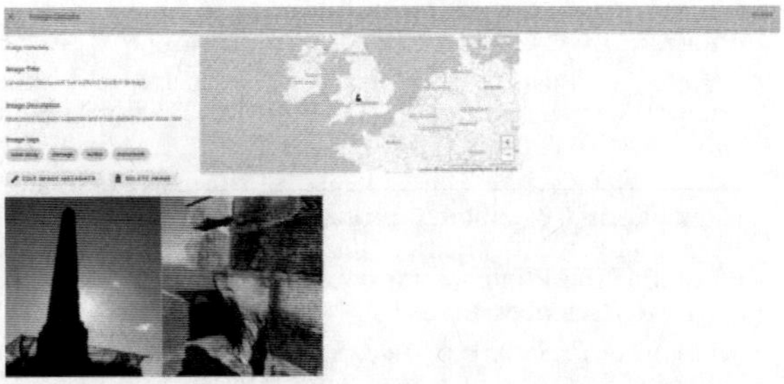

Figure 6. Photo along with its metadata is displayed.

information relevant to business damages (i.e., business damage, risk assessment for the business, information useful to local authorities, customers lost percentage, priority and criticality of the issue and relevant tags). After the completion of each wizard, all relevant information concerning the stories is stored in the PLUGGY back-end and can be retrieved through its APIs. Thereafter, the content could be retrieved by any third party app that has been integrated into PLUGGY authorization server.

B. *Presentation of created stories to users*

In addition to uploading these two kinds of stories, the users of the Engagement Tool are also able to view already stored stories. The page of the app that renders a photo along with its metadata concerning the monument damage is shown in Figure 6. In addition to the presentation of both citizen and business owner stories, the owners of the stories are also able to edit or delete them, and therefore dedicated pages exist for these functionalities.

C. *Responsive Design of the Engagement Tool*

Responsive web design (RWD) is an approach to web design that makes web pages render well on a variety of devices and window or screen sizes [11]. Responsive web design has become more important as the amount of mobile traffic has come to account for more than half of total internet traffic. Taking into consideration this, the Engagement Tool has been driven by RWD best practices and Figure 7 demonstrates a page of the Tool if it was to be viewed in a small screen. The Engagement Tool adapts the layout to the viewing environment by using fluid, proportion-based grids, flexible images, and Cascading Style Sheets (CSS3) media queries so as for the user to be able to use the tool and view the content of citizen and business stories from any device independent on its screen size.

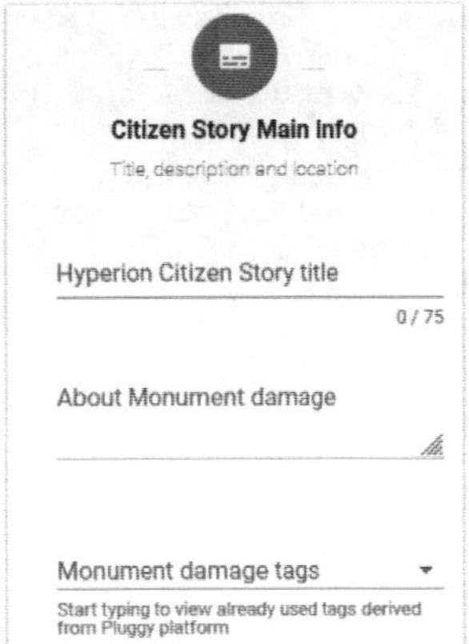

Figure 7. First step of the citizen story wizard if it was to be viewed in a screen 320 * 510.

VI. CONCLUSION

This paper presented the Communities Engagement ICT Tool which is a software component designed and developed in the context of the European project entitled "Hyperion". This tool aims at supporting communities' participation in the process of evaluating monument damages through the uploading of stories (i.e, reports). The textual and graphical content of the stories could be inspected and evaluated by the authorities so as to enhance the overall resilience and reconstruction planning of cultural heritage sites. The content of both citizen stories (relevant to monument damages) and business owner stories (relevant to business disruptions due to climate change and extreme events) could be combined, as proposed by Hyperion project, with atmospheric modeling, geotechnical analysis of CH sites and vulnerability maps so as to assess the threats of CH sites and support sustainable reconstruction plans. Last but not least, rather than developing an isolated and standalone tool, an integration with a pluggable social platform was performed and most specifically with PLUGGY. This integration benefits the Engagement Tool in terms of the free availability of PLUGGY data both in terms of existing users (aware of cultural heritage), and cultural heritage relevant data (e.g., monuments).

ACKNOWLEDGMENT

This work is a part of the Hyperion project. Hyperion has received funding from the European Union's Horizon 2020 research and innovation programme under grant agreement no 821054. Content reflects only the authors' view and European Commission is not responsible for any use that may be made of the information it contains.

REFERENCES

[1] V. Lim, N. Frangakis, L. M. Tanco, and L. Picinali, "PLUGGY: A pluggable social platform for cultural heritage

awareness and participation. InAdvances in Digital Cultural Heritage" 2018 (pp. 117-129). Springer, Cham.

[2] A. Tandon, "Post-disaster damage assessment of cultural heritage: Are we prepared." In: ICOM-CC 18th Triennial Conference 2017. 2017. (pp. 2017-12).

[3] A. Vafadari, G. Philip, and R. Jennings, "Damage assessment and monitoring of cultural heritage places in a disaster and post-disaster event--a case study of syria." International Archives of the Photogrammetry, Remote Sensing & Spatial Information Sciences 42 (2017).

[4] E. Baranwal, P. Seth, H. Pande, S. Raghavendra, and S. K. P. Kushwaha, "Application of unmanned aerial vehicle (UAV) for damage assessment of a cultural heritage monument." In International Conference on Unmanned Aerial System in Geomatics, pp. 123-131. Springer, Cham, 2019.

[5] A. B. Khajwal and A. Noshadravan, "An uncertainty-aware framework for reliable disaster damage assessment via crowdsourcing." International Journal of Disaster Risk Reduction. 2021 Mar 1;55:102110.

[6] P. Kumar, "Crowdsourcing to rescue cultural heritage during disasters: A case study of the 1966 Florence Flood." International Journal of Disaster Risk Reduction. 2020 Feb 1;43:101371.

[7] N. Frangakis et al., "PLUGGY: A pluggable Social Platform for Cultural Heritage Awareness and Participation." InCIRA@ EuroMed 2018 (pp. 21-30).

[8] J. Hreno, D. Toledo, and S. Bolierakis, "Architecture specification. Deliverable D3.1 of the PLUGGY project funded under the European Union's Horizon 2020 research and innovation programme under grant agreement No 726765." Available at https://www.pluggy-project.eu/deliverables/, [retrieved: 9, 2021].

[9] K. Dodanduwa and I. Kaluthanthri, "Role of trust in OAuth 2.0 and OpenID connect." In2018 IEEE International Conference on Information and Automation for Sustainability (ICIAfS) 2018 Dec 21 (pp. 1-4). IEEE.

[10] L. M. Tanco, P. Smatana, D. Toledo, L. Torrico, "Guidelines and Instructions for PLUGGY Apps. Deliverable D4.5 of the PLUGGY project funded under the European Union's Horizon 2020 research and innovation programme under grant agreement No 726765." Available at https://www.pluggy-project.eu/deliverables/, [retrieved: 9, 2021].

[11] A. Hussain and E. O. Mkpojiogu, "The effect of responsive web design on the user experience with laptop and smartphone devices." Jurnal Teknologi. 2015;77(4):41-7

An Ontology-based Approach For Conformance Checking of Decision Mining Rules

Sahar Toumia
RIADI Laboratory, Manouba University, Tunisia
High Institute on Management of Sousse, Sousse University, Tunisia
sahartoumia@gmail.com

Asma Mejri
RIADI Laboratory, Manouba University, Tunisia
High Institute of Computer Science of Kef, Jendouba University, Tunisia
mejri.assma@gmail.com

Sonia Ayachi-Ghannouchi
RIADI Laboratory, Manouba University, Tunisia
High Institute on Management of Sousse, Sousse University,Tunisia
sonia.ayachi.ghannouchi@gmail.com

***Abstract*—The decision mining field allows identifying decision points and analyzing rules for each choice depending on the available attributes in the business process. While significant advances have been made in this regard, little attention has been given to the manner of exploring the discovered rules, analyzing them and addressing the issue about their meaning and appropriateness. In order to alleviate this issue, in this work, we explore the possibility of investigating the conformance checking between the discovered rules that are generated by decision mining techniques and the knowledge rules of the corresponding ontology. We propose an Ontology-based approach for Conformance Checking of Decision mining rules (O2CD) in order to discover from event logs the decision models for a given process model and check the conformity between the corresponding discovered decision rules and the rules of an existing ontology. Our approach was evaluated using the COVID-19 case study in the COVID-19 crisis unit of the Farhat Hached University Hospital Center.**

Keywords-Decision mining; DMN; decision rules; ontology rules; conformance.

I. INTRODUCTION

Information systems are becoming more and more intertwined with the operational processes they support. As a result, multitudes of events are recorded by information systems. Nonetheless, organizations have problems when extracting value from these data. In this context, the goal of process mining is to use event data to extract process-related information. It aims to discover, to monitor, and to improve real processes by extracting knowledge from event logs readily available in today's systems [1]. However, the majority of algorithms, which are used for this purpose, produce models that describe the flow of activities, but do not detail how decisions are made along it. In this regard, Decision Mining (DM) is a method of deriving and analyzing event logs with the aim of extracting information from such event logs in order to extract rules, to check compliance to business rules, and to show performance information [2]. In this respect, decision making is one of the most important aspects of Business Processes (BPs) in organizations and making the right decisions during the BP execution is crucial for accomplishing the business goals of an enterprise [3]. Furthermore, due to importance of decision making, many organizations started to address a need for a standardized notation to represent decisions in BP models. Recently, in 2015, the Decision Model and Notation (DMN) [4] standard was published by the Object Management Group (OMG). In addition to that, an ontology is a way of representing a common understanding of a domain [5]. Lately, the scientific communities attempt to explore the decision support in organizations by emerging approaches on different decision ontologies [6]. In this context, the main objective of this paper is to check the conformance checking between decision rule models, elicited using process mining techniques, against the rules of a given ontology. The evaluation of our approach has been done on the basis of a real-life case study, which concerns COVID-19 patients care in the Farhat Hached University Hospital Center (UHC) in Tunisia.

This paper is organized as follows: Section 1 introduces basic background knowledge relative to the different concepts used in our approach. A detailed description of the proposed approach is presented in Section 2, and in Section 3 we illustrate our O2CD approach application and the main results of our case study. In Section 4, we describe briefly the different related works that we consider relevant to our research. Finally, section 5 concludes the paper.

II. BASIC CONCEPTS

In this section, we start by providing short and simple definitions of some important concepts which are decision mining, DMN standard and ontology.

A. Decision Mining

The term of DM was first introduced in process literature in the work of [8]. It was defined as the field that aims at the identification of data dependencies that affect the routing of a case. Moreover, it is based on the idea that a control flow decision can be transformed into a classification problem. Hence, machine learning techniques can be used to discover structural patterns in data based on a set of training instances. In order to solve such a classification problem, there are several algorithms, such as C4.5 and support vector machines.

B. DMN

Due to the appearance of decision making and decision mining, several organizations and companies started to address a need for a standardized notation to represent decisions in BP models. In 2015, the Object Management Group (OMG) published the first version of DMN. According to [5], the DMN standard includes two levels; the Decision Requirements level (DRD) and the Decision Logic level (DL). The DRD level shows the structure of decision. It consists of few elements that are used to capture essential information with regards to decisions. The DL defines how decisions are made.

One of the most largely used representations for decision logic is a decision table, which is used in the rest of this paper.

C. Ontology

The term ontology is taken from philosophy, where ontology describes the science of being and, with this, of descriptions for the organization, designation and categorization of existence [9]. Gruber was the first to formulate the term ontology in the field of Computer Science [10] and defined it as "a set of representational primitives with which to model a domain of knowledge or discourse".

In addition to that, ontology is composed of a set of elements: (1) Concepts also named terms or classes, which represent the class of entities or things within a domain, (2) Relations between concepts, which describe the interactions between concepts or concept's properties, (3) Properties, which are the set of attributes of the concepts that capture further knowledge about the relationships between concepts, (4) Rules also named predicates are used to constrain values for classes or instances.

III. O2CD APPROACH

One of the main objectives of this paper is to discover from event logs the decision models for a given process model and check the conformity between the corresponding discovered decision rules and the rules of an existing ontology. Therefore, we propose a six-step approach to verify this conformity, as depicted in Figure 1.

- Phase 1: Data extraction

Generally, organizations have the opportunity to store information about their activities that are conducted through information systems. In addition to that, since most BPs are supported by at least one information system, the amount of data being stored about process executions is rapidly growing. As well, the execution of a case results in a sequence of events being recorded. The goal of the data extraction phase is to obtain event log from data that is extracted from the original data source.

However, event data exist but some efforts are needed to extract them. Often, data preprocessing is an important step in process mining. As a result, in this phase, we try to build an event log from the data available within the organization. This step is part of the most crucial steps in the field of process mining. In fact, the different steps that are followed in our proposed approach are based on the event log that is constructed in this step. Thus, this event log will be used to discover a suitable process model. This process model discovery step will be discussed in the next section.

- Phase 2: Process Model Discovery

Based on the results of the previous phase, which is event log the next step is the creation of a process model by means of process mining. Therefore, the field of process mining can be categorized in three categories [1]: discovery, conformance, and enhancement. In the scope of this phase, we only consider the first category, which is process discovery. Its aim is to use the data stored in event logs in order to generate automatically a process model that describes the execution of a process. Moreover, the first step in process discovery is the selection of the algorithm responsible for mining the event log from which process discovery can be done. Over time, many process mining algorithms have been proposed to generate a process [11]. In this paper, we select the inductive Miner [12] algorithm to discover our process model. The main advantage of this algorithm is that it allows to discover models corresponding to hidden transitions and invisible tasks as well as the model always fits, i.e., the model can generate the traces in the log [13].

- Phase 3: Decision Mining Rules Discovery

The input of this phase is event log generated from Phase 1 and process model generated from Phase 2. In this sense, DM is the study of the decision-related characteristics of a process based on a process model of the process and log of previous process executions. It enhances process models with additional data on why specific decisions are made. Therefore, in accordance with [14], in this step, we use the Multi-perspective Process Explorer (MPE) plugin, which is available in ProM tool. In this phase, we are interested in the data discovery mode to express the set of rules. So, in the MPE mode 'Discover Data-Perspective' it is possible to enrich the process model with decision rules discovery based on the event log. Therefore, the output of this phase is a process model enriched with appropriates guards and conditions.

- Phase 4: Ontology selection

Nowadays, there exists a significant and explosion of the number of ontologies, which are available in the semantic web. Therefore, ontology selection is one of the most important steps in order to determine which of the several ontologies would be one of the best ontologies for a specific context or goal. Thus, in this phase, we aim at identifying and selecting the existence of one or more ontologies that are the most appropriate and adequate for a given domain. In this context, several methods have been proposed to select ontologies according to a variety of criteria. For example, more specifically, in this step we have based on the work presented in [15]. The authors proposed a set of elements and criteria that allows selecting the adequate and appropriate ontology. The output of this phase is the selected ontology.

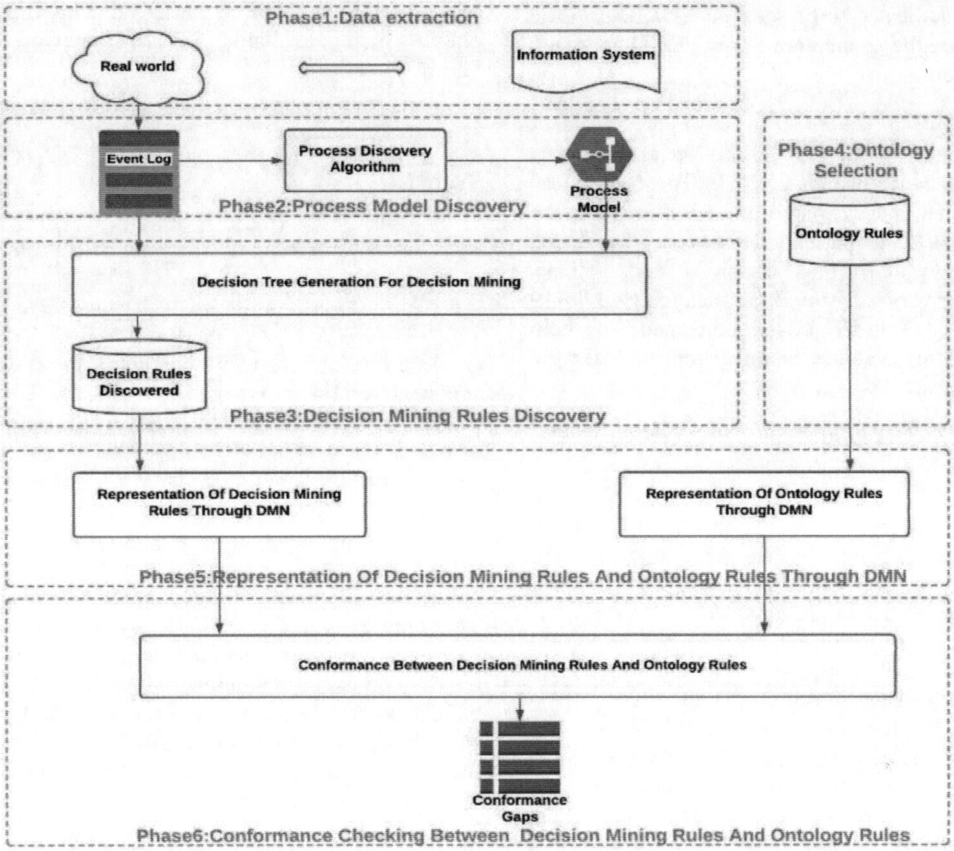

Figure 1. An Ontology-based approach for Conformance Checking of Decision mining rules: O2CD.

- Phase 5: Representation of Decision Mining Rules and ontology Rules through DMN

In this phase, we present how the decisions, which were discovered in process models, can be represented into the corresponding elements of the DMN based on the extraction of both decisions and process model from event log. These important steps were described in the previous phases. Our main idea is that process decision making can be captured and analyzed based on an event log. Further, the development of the proposed approach to transform DM rules into DMN models is inspired by results published by [4]. Secondly, we present the ontology rules through DMN. In this step, we start by extracting from the selected ontology the set of rules corresponding to the represented knowledge. Then, in the same way as we did for DM rules, we expressed them through DMN elements.

- Phase 6: Conformance checking between decision mining rules and ontology rules

In this phase, we try to check the conformity between the rules of ontology which define the acknowledged structured knowledge and those obtained by decision mining. In fact, rules incorporated in ontologies reflect ideal knowledge of a domain, while those from the event log reflect real actual execution. In order to do this, we compare the decision logic presented as tables with each other. The first table references to the corresponding decision tables containing the extracted DM rules and the second one references to the corresponding decision tables containing the extracted ontology rules. Then, we compare them according to a set of output, which are obtained according to a set of input data. In such tasks, the decision maker observes the cases of similarity and differences based on the analysis of the current situation. He/she is able of forming a comprehensive overview of the result and makes decisions using his/her professional experience and intuition, as well as, he /she can review the taken decisions.

IV. O2CD APPROACH APPLICATION AND PROOF OF CONCEPT

This section is dedicated to present the COVID-19 case study and to describe the application of our O2CD approach in a real-life situation.

A. Context of our exprimentation

In Tunisia, the coronavirus disease pandemic has officially developed since March 2, 2020. The COVID-19 crisis unit of the UHC has prepared an action plan for the management of COVID-19 patients. However, it has faced many difficulties in federating decisions and actions. Thereby, our aim is to consider the BP of managing covid-19 patients in the COVID-19 crisis unit and to help physicians/stakeholders evaluate their decisions and take the most appropriate ones.

B. Case study: COVID-19 patients care in the departement of infectious diseases

To evaluate our approach entitled O2CD, we have applied it on a real-life case study, which concerns COVID-19 patients care in the infectious diseases department. For the experimental study, we considered the covid-19 event log, which was extracted from the Electronic Health Record EHR information system. Therefore, we have prepared the log for the application of our proposed approach. Then, we conducted the different steps of our O2CD approach.

- Application of phase 1

First, we need to acquire an event log of the process in this stage. In the context of our case study, the information system records data about its operations in SPSS (Statistical Package for the Social Sciences). Then, we obtained a snapshot of the database that was taken between March 1, 2020 and May 31, 2020. It was converted into CSV extension. In our case, the purpose was to select patients who were suspected to have COVID-19, as shown in the examples in Figure 2.

patient_ID	task	start_date	end_date	entry_modes	fever	engelure	headache	muscle_or	congestion_	skin_rash	ageusia
50n	receive patier	21/04/2020 08:00	21/04/2020 08:10	emergency	1	0	0	0	0	0	0
50n	examine patie	21/04/2020 08:30	21/04/2020 08:40	emergency							
50n	start of isolati	21/04/2020 09:10	21/04/2020 09:30	emergency							
50n	assessment o	21/04/2020 09:40	21/04/2020 09:45	emergency							
50n	doing PCR tes	21/04/2020 10:45	21/04/2020 10:55	emergency							
50n	preparing for	21/04/2020 12:19	21/04/2020 12:40	emergency							
50n	decide diagnc	21/04/2020 13:40	21/04/2020 14:00	emergency							

Figure 2. Screenshot from the Excel sheet.

Then we convert the CSV file into an event log in the form of XES file. This dataset concerns 100 patients in the infectious diseases department which was the unique dataset considered in this phase of our research: 1024 events were recorded involving 18 distinct activities, and 24 data attributes. These attributes encompass the different symptoms of covid-19 such as fever, headache cough,etc and the outcome of test results of coronavirus.

- Application of phase 2

After extracting and preparing the event log, the BP which is mined from the event log, was discovered as a Petri net BP using the "Mine Petri Net with Inductive Miner" plugin which is available in ProM framework as depicted in Figure3.

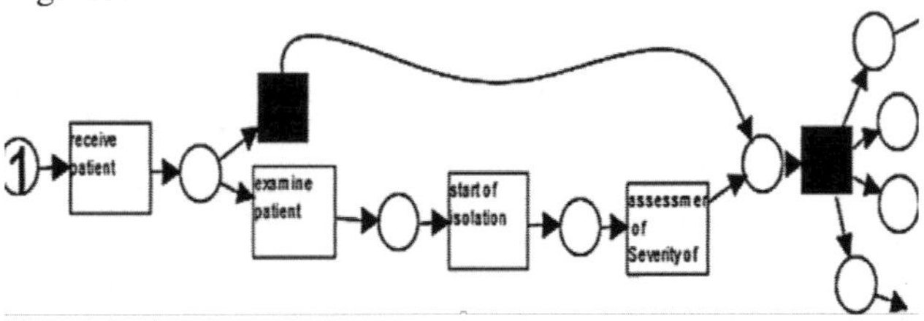

Figure 3. An excerpt of the discovered BP model.

As a result, as shown in Figure 3, the discovered model can be interpreted. We can see that the BP of managing COVID-19 patients starts by receiving the patient. The doctor examines the patient and evaluates the degree of emergency, and then the isolation is started according to clinical documents. Then, a set of activities is activated simultaneously which are: doing Polymerase Chain Reaction (PCR), preparing for hospital stay as well as deciding the appropriate diagnostic protocol and the clinical examination. Then, the PCR test is retrieved by the head of department. However, the patients can have negative or positive PCR test. On the one hand, the patient, with negative PCR result, can be discharged (ending of isolation). On the other hand, concerning patients with positive PCR result, the staff member has to evaluate whether the patient's status is mild, moderate, or severe. As well, the physician proceeds with the "keep isolated" activity and he/she can choose the Covid-19 procedure.

- Application of phase 3

In this phase, the Petri net model and the event log, which were obtained in previous steps, served as inputs for a "Multi-Perspective Process Explorer" plug-in (MPE plug-in). This step was carried out to discover the rules on the Petri net model. Firstly, the value of the "min instances" parameter was modified to the lowest possible value (0.001), which allowed the discovery of very large and complex rules related to some activities. In our case, the process model involved 10 rules base. But in this work, we mainly focused on 3 principal rules. In Figure 4, it is possible to visualize the large and complex discovery rules in the "Discover Data Perspective" mode of MPE found in the position called "p 19" in the Petri net model. These rules, shown in Table I, refer to the arc that takes the transition (activity) " consider case as mild ", " consider case as moderate", and " consider case as severe" transition. The rules, which were discovered in this step, were evaluated and then validated by the hospital staff. The goal was to verify if the discovered rules could be considered as correct and as well, if they are really applied within this process. The hospital staff agreed on the rules. We concluded that the applied method may possibly discover correct rules. However, this is not enough in this case to provide insights to the hospital staff. Therefore, we proceeded to explore the discovered rules and check if this information is conformed to acknowledged structured knowledge available in a selected ontology.

TABLE I. THE DISCOVERED RULES RELATED TO THE " CONSIDER CASE AS MODERATE", " CONSIDER CASE AS MILD", " CONSIDER CASE AS SEVERE" ACTIVITIES

Activity Name	Min instances	Guard
Consider case as moderate	0.001	(((respiratory_rate>22.0&& respiratory_rate<=28.0)&&testresult== "positive")&&entry_mode=="urgent medical aid service")
Consider case as mild	0.001	((presence_of_fever>0&& respiratory_rate<=22.0)&&testresult== "positive")
Consider case as severe	0.001	(((respiratory_rate>28.0&& respiratory_rate<=30.0)&&testresult== "positive")&&entry_mode== "urgent medical aid service")

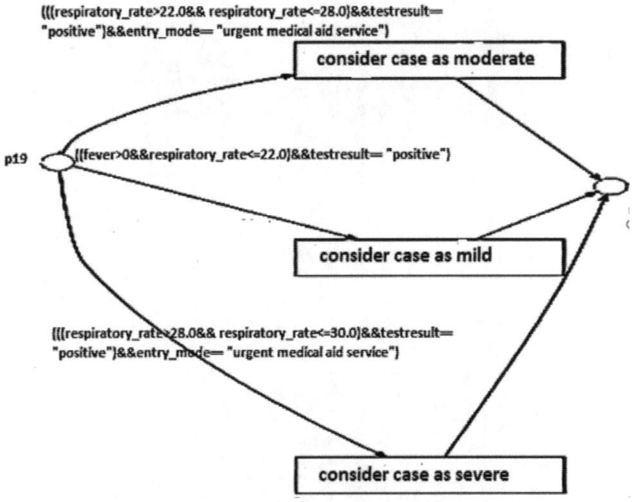

Figure 4. Process fragment representing a set of rules discovered by decision tree algorithm.

- Application of phase 4

In this stage, we try to identify and to select the most appropriate ontology in the context of COVID-19 pandemic. Therefore, we choose COVID-19 ontology for cases and patient information (CODO) [16], in accordance with a set of criteria, which provides a model for the collection and analysis of data about the COVID-19. The ontology already has incorporated real world and has uploaded thousands of cases from data collected by the government of India. As well, the inference rules were written in the Semantic Web Rule Language (SWRL), which is the rule representation language recommended by the Semantic Web community.

- Application of phase 5

After identifying and discovering the decision logic from the process models and the selected ontology, we try to derive a corresponding DMN model according to the proposed approach discussed in previous section. In the fragment process model shown in Figure 4 when place p19 is marked with a token, then, an exclusive choice between the execution of transitions needs to be made: “consider case as mild”, “consider case as moderate” and “consider case as severe”. The doctor evaluates whether the patient's status is mild, moderate or severe. As discussed before, DMN defines two levels: the decision requirements diagram level and the decision logic level. Figure 5 shows the DRD which is based on the fragment in Figure 4 from the health care domain.

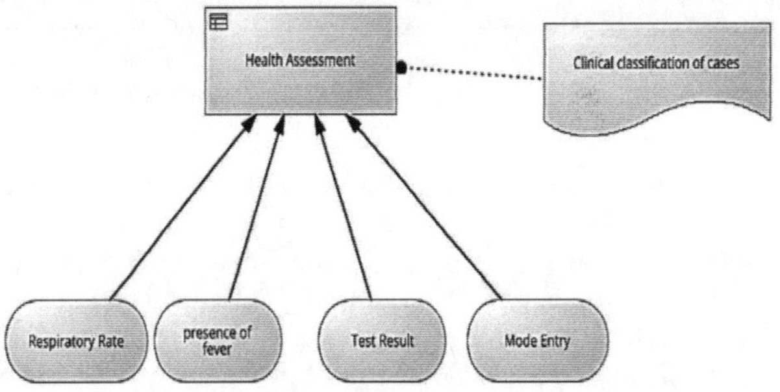

Figure 5. Decision Requirement Diagram of the decision point p19.

The decision to be taken refers to the health assessment and can directly be derived from the input data respiratory rate, presence of fever, test result, and mode entry. We noticed that the decision about how to assess a patient's health depends on the clinical classification of cases, which is a document performed by the staff of Farhat Hached UHC. Moreover, Figure 6 presents the DRD of CODO ontology. Therefore, the decision to be taken refers to the health assessment; can directly be derived from the input data respiratory rate, presence of fever, test result, cough, SpO2, and measured fever.

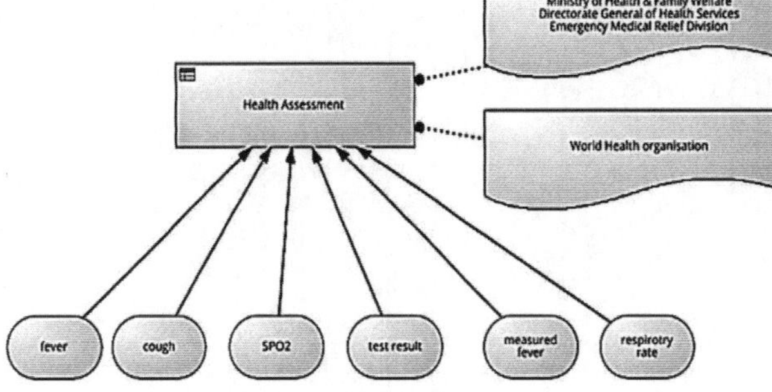

Figure 6. Decision Requirement Diagram of CODO ontology.

We noticed that the decision about how to control a patient's health depends on the clinical documentation of WHO (World Health Organisation) and a guidance document on appropriate management of confirmed cases of COVID-19 from the ministry of health and family welfare directorate general of health Services EMR (Emergency Medical Relief) Division of India. In addition to that, according to [17], decision logic can be represented in many ways, e.g., by an analytic model or a decision table. In this paper, we used decision tables.

F	Inputs								Outputs
	Respiratory Rate		Fever		Test Result		Mode Entry		case type
	Number		(has symptom fever)		(positive)		(SAMU)		Text
1	≤	22	=	has symptom...	=	positive		-	"mild"
2	∈	[22..28]		-	=	positive	=	SAMU	"moderate"
3	>	28		-	=	positive	=	SAMU	"severe"

Figure 7. Decision table for the rules at place p19 as specified by the DMN standard.

Figure 7 shows the decision rules regarding transitions consider case as mild, consider case as moderate, and consider case as severe, as a decision table. Figure 8 presents the decision rules of CODO ontology as a decision table. It can be seen for example from this figure that if the respiratory rate is between 15 and 30 and the SpO2 between 90 and 94 and the patient has a positive test result then the patient status is considered moderate.

F	Inputs												Outputs
	fever		cough		SpO2		measured fever		respiratory rate		test result		case type
	(has symptom fever)		(has symptom cough)		Number		Number		Number		(positive)		Text
1		-		-	∈	[90..94]		-	∈	[15..30]	=	positive	"moderate"
2		-		-		-		-	≥	30	=	positive	"severe"
3		-		-	<	90		-	≥	30	=	positive	"severe"
4	=	has symptom...		-		-		-		-	=	positive	"mild"
5	=	has symptom...	=	has symptom...		-	≥	38		-	=	positive	"mild"

Figure 8. Decision table for the rules of ontology as specified by the DMN standard.

- Application of phase 6

In this phase, we try to check the conformity and similarity between the discovered rules that were generated by DM technique with the ontology rules, which correspond to acknowledged structured knowledge. For this purpose, we attempt to compare these rules for a specific set of cases. More precisely, for each case, we compared the results respectively obtained by the discovered rules on one hand and the rules from the ontology on the other hand. As a result, in our case study, we used the two decision tables: the first one for DM rules (blue) and the second one for ontology rules (green). In this step, we want also to find out why a test case is producing a certain output and we want to see exactly which rules fire for the input data set. Thus, the formula returns true if the results are exactly the same. If there are any differences, the result returned is false and the decision maker should check his/her result. Thus, the decision maker can observe the cases of similarity and differences and form a comprehensive overview of the result.

CaseId	Respiratory Ra	Measured F	Test Resu	Fever	Cough	SPO2	Result	Name	CaseId	Respirat	Test Resu	Fever	Mode Ent	result		
1	19	38,2	positive	has symptor	has sympt	100	mild	testCases	1	19	positive	has symptom fever		mild	True	Conformance
2	30	37	positive	has symptor	has sympt	100	severe	testCases	2	30	positive	has symp	SAMU	severe	True	Conformance
3	20	38	positive	has symptor	has sympt	96	mild	testCases	3	20	positive	has symp	SAMU	mild	True	Conformance
4	16	39,6	positive	has symptor	has sympt	98	mild	testCases	4	16	positive	has symp	SAMU	mild	True	Conformance
5	16	39,2	positive	has symptor	has sympt	98	mild	testCases	5	16	positive	has symp	SAMU	mild	True	Conformance
6	19	38,2	positive	has symptor	has sympt	93	moderate	testCases	6	19	positive	has symp	SAMU	mild	False	Please check the patient status
7	18	38,1	positive	has symptor	has sympt	98	mild	testCases	7	18	positive	has symp	SAMU	mild	True	Conformance
8	24	37,1	positive	has symptor	has sympt	92	moderate	testCases	8	24	positive	has symp	SAMU	moderate	True	Conformance
9	28	37	positive			92	moderate	testCases	9	28	positive			moderate	True	Conformance
10	24	37,3	positive	has symptor	has sympt	98	mild	testCases	10	24	positive	has symp	SAMU	moderate	False	Please check the patient status
11	24	37	positive	has symptor	has sympt	99	mild	testCases	11	24	positive	has symp	SAMU	moderate	False	Please check the patient status
12	30	36,5	positive			100	severe	testCases	12	30	positive		SAMU	severe	True	Conformance
13	24	37	positive			94	moderate	testCases	13	24	positive		SAMU	moderate	True	Conformance

Figure 9. The result of conformance between decision rules and ontology rules.

As can be seen in the Figure 9, the formula compares the two tables, identifies cells with differences or finds similar values and displays the differences and similarities in corresponding cells. In our cases, we have around 75% cases of conformance and 25% cases of *divergence,* which are highlighted with the red color.

V. RELATED WORKS ON DECISION MINING AND ONTOLGY

In this section, we present the reviewed literature that we considered relevant to our research. The related works can be divided into two groups. The first group refers to the works dealing with the using of decision mining technique in processes. The second group is related to approaches that incorporate ontology in the field of decision-making. In fact, in recent Business Process Management (BPM) literature, DM appears as a frequent term [18]. In literature of DM, we identify three approaches: The first category focuses on improving decisions without considering DMN. The term of DM was first introduced in process literature in the work of [8]. The work identifies and describes the routing and choices in Petri nets by using a decision tree algorithm. However, De Leoni et al. [2] stated that the technique proposed in the work of [8] has several limitations, such as the technique cannot discover conditions associated with XOR-splits and many loop. To address these problems, the authors proposed a new approach, which was implemented by De Leoni et al. [2]. Later on, this plug-in was reused and integrated into the Multi-perspective Process Explorer plug-in for ProM introduced by [14]. The second category is dedicated to different approaches to derivate DM within DMN standard. In fact, in [19], the authors proposed an approach, which is based on using information about decisions incorporated implicitly in the process execution data. Furthermore, they proposed a technique to rebuild decision trees and to identify the dependencies between the discovered decisions. Recently, in [20], the authors proposed a new approach to produce DMN models from BPMN process models while focusing on the data perspective of process models. The third category is dedicated to Decision-aware control-flow discovery approaches. In [18], the proposed approach revised the way in which the decision and the process model can be retrieved in holistic manner. This work considered process activities as the drivers of decisions, whereas in our work we assumed that the decision drivers were control flow decision points and data attributes. In the second group of the related work have been proposed works dedicated to conceptual decision ontologies complementary to BPM techniques. The literature shows that few works addressed the relationship between discovering decision models from process and ontology. For example, in [7], the authors presented a decision ontology for supporting decision-making in information systems. This work derived components to decision processes and created independent decision-making ontologies. In [21], the investigated problem is whether a DM technique allows to identify business rules in Knowledge-Intensive Processes points. More specifically, in this work, the authors were interested in exploring the decision making associated to business rules of KIPO (Knowledge-Intensive Process Ontology), which is an ontology proposed in [22].The literature shows that the most studied works relies on the presentation and the discovery of decisions in process models on the one hand. On the others hand, a few academic works proposing their own decision-making ontology exist. However, those works are more conceptual and do not provide means for operationalizing of the decision-making ontologies. Moreover, we concluded that there is no existing works that try to check the conformity and similarity between the discovered rules that are generated by decision mining techniques with the ontology rules. So, what distinguishes our work from the existing works, is that we aim to check this conformity.

VI. CONCLUSION AND FUTURE WORK

In this paper, we presented our ontology-based approach for conformance checking of DM rules using ontologies. Our approach deals with discovering from event logs the decision models for a given process model and checking the conformity between these discovered rules with ontology rules, which are already existing. The proposed approach was evaluated using a real-life case study. We concluded that the proposed approach provided valid and accurate conformance gaps that can serve for improving the organization's decision making and hence its overall performance. In the future, we plan to extend our approach. We can improve our approach by considering more data from the various information systems to ensure the diversity of data. We can also collect data during a long period in order to examine more cases and check the correctness of the results. With more data and for a long period, more specific scenarios can be encountered which favors obtained better conclusion. Moreover, we aim to create an automatic tool for extracting the divergent cases when comparing DM rules and ontology rules. Recent technologies, such as reinforcement learning [23] and deep learning [24] algorithms, could be helpful for achieving this purpose. In addition to that, in future work, we will rely on similarity metrics specifically dedicated to semantic similarity such as semantic cosine similarity [25] and we will use different data sets for training and testing. Besides, in this work, the assessment stage and the accuracy evaluation are still based on a limited test case selection. In future work, we will plan for more test cases.

ACKNOWLEDGMENT

The experimental part of the work was carried out in the framework of the SMART2C RRV project in Tunisia (Research Results' Valorization project) which deals with developing a smart system for a COVID-19 Crisis Committee. The authors would like to thank the COVID-19 Crisis Committee in Farhat Hached hospital for providing the datasets and for validating the results.

REFERENCES

[1] W. Van Der Aalst, "Data science in action," in *Process mining*, Springer, 2016, pp. 3–23.

[2] M. De Leoni and W. M. P. Van Der Aalst, "Data-aware process mining: Discovering decisions in processes using alignments,"

Proc. ACM Symp. Appl. Comput., no. January, pp. 1454–1461, 2013, doi: 10.1145/2480362.2480633.

[3] S. Leewis, K. Smit, and M. Zoet, "Putting Decision Mining into Context: A Literature Study," *Lect. Notes Inf. Syst. Organ.*, vol. 38, no. September, pp. 31–46, 2020, doi: 10.1007/978-3-030-47355-6_3.

[4] E. Bazhenova, "Discovery of Decision Models Complementary to Process Models." University Potsdam, 2018.

[5] D. Model, "Notation (DMN). Version 1.1," *Object Manag. Group, Inc*, 2016. Available at: http://www.omg.org/spec/DMN/1.1/, 2016.

[6] R. Kishore and R. Ramesh, *Ontologies: a handbook of principles, concepts and applications in information systems*, vol. 14. Springer Science & Business Media, 2007.

[7] E. Kornyshova and R. Deneckère, "Decision-making ontology for information system engineering," *Lect. Notes Comput. Sci. (including Subser. Lect. Notes Artif. Intell. Lect. Notes Bioinformatics)*, vol. 6412 LNCS, pp. 104–117, 2010, doi: 10.1007/978-3-642-16373-9_8.

[8] A. Rozinat and W. M. P. Van Der Aalst, "Decision mining in ProM," in *Lecture Notes in Computer Science (including subseries Lecture Notes in Artificial Intelligence and Lecture Notes in Bioinformatics)*, 2006, vol. 4102 LNCS, pp. 420–425, doi: 10.1007/11841760_33.

[9] M. Rebstock, F. Janina, and H. Paulheim, *Ontologies-based business integration*. Springer Science & Business Media, 2008.

[10] T. R. Gruber, "Toward principles for the design of ontologies used for knowledge sharing?," *Int. J. Hum. Comput. Stud.*, vol. 43, no. 5–6, pp. 907–928, 1995.

[11] E. Gupta, "Process mining algorithms," *Int. J. Adv. Res. Sci. Eng.*, vol. 3, no. 11, pp. 401–412, 2014.

[12] S. J. J. Leemans, D. Fahland, and W. M. P. van der Aalst, "Discovering block-structured process models from event logs-a constructive approach," in *International conference on applications and theory of Petri nets and concurrency*, 2013, pp. 311–329.

[13] R. Ghawi, "Process Discovery using Inductive Miner and Decomposition," *arXiv Prepr. arXiv1610.07989*, 2016.

[14] F. Mannhardt, M. De Leoni, and H. A. Reijers, "The Multi-perspective Process Explorer.," *BPM*, vol. 1418, pp. 130–134, 2015.

[15] M. Sabou, V. Lopez, and E. Motta, "Open Research Online," *Choice Rev. Online*, vol. 51, no. 06, pp. 51-2973-51–2973, 2014, doi: 10.5860/choice.51-2973.

[16] B. Dutta and M. DeBellis, "CODO: An Ontology for Collection and Analysis of Covid-19 Data," no. November, pp. 76–85, 2020, doi: 10.5220/0010112500760085.

[17] K. Batoulis, A. Meyer, E. Bazhenova, G. Decker, and M. Weske, "Extracting decision logic from process models," in *International conference on advanced information systems engineering*, 2015, pp. 349–366.

[18] J. De Smedt, F. Hasić, S. K. L. M. Vanden Broucke, and J. Vanthienen, "Towards a holistic discovery of decisions in process-aware information systems," *Lect. Notes Comput. Sci. (including Subser. Lect. Notes Artif. Intell. Lect. Notes Bioinformatics)*, vol. 10445 LNCS, pp. 183–199, 2017, doi: 10.1007/978-3-319-65000-511.

[19] E. Bazhenova, S. Bülow, and M. Weske, "Discovering decision models from event logs," in *International Conference on Business Information Systems*, 2016, pp. 237–251.

[20] E. Bazhenova, F. Zerbato, B. Oliboni, and M. Weske, "From BPMN process models to DMN decision models," *Inf. Syst.*, vol. 83, pp. 69–88, 2019, doi: 10.1016/j.is.2019.02.001.

[21] J. Campos, P. Richetti, F. A. Baião, and F. M. Santoro, "Discovering Business Rules in Knowledge-Intensive Processes Through Decision Mining: An Experimental Study," 2018.

[22] J. B. S. França, F. A. Baião, and F. M. Santoro, "Towards characterizing knowledge intensive processes," in *Proceedings of the 2012 IEEE 16th International Conference on Computer Supported Cooperative Work in Design (CSCWD)*, 2012, pp. 497–504.

[23] R. S. Sutton and A. G. Barto, *Reinforcement learning: An introduction*. MIT press, 2018.

[24] Y. LeCun, Y. Bengio, and G. Hinton, "Deep learning," *Nature*, vol. 521, no. 7553, pp. 436–444, 2015.

[25] F. Rahutomo, T. Kitasuka, and M. Aritsugi, "Semantic cosine similarity," in The 7th International Student Conference on Advanced Science and Technology ICAST, 2012, vol. 4, no. 1, p. 1.

Towards a Smart Feature Model Evolution

Olfa Ferchichi[1]
[1] Laboratoire de Recherche en GénieLogiciel, Applications distribuées, Systèmes décisionnels et Imagerie intelligentes (RIADI), Université de Manouba
Tunisie
Email:olfaferchi@yahoo.fr

Raoudha Beltaifa[2]
[1] Laboratoire de Recherche en Génie Logiciel,Applications distribuées, Systèmes décisionnels et Imagerie intelligentes (RIADI), Université de Manouba
Tunisie
Email :raoudha.beltaifa@ensi.rnu.tn

Lamia Labed Jilani[3]
[1] Laboratoire de Recherche en Génie Logiciel, Applications distribuées, Systèmes décisionnels et Imagerie intelligentes (RIADI), Université de Manouba
Tunisie
Email : lamia.labed@isg.rnu.tn

Raúl Mazo[4]
Lab-STICC,
ENSTA Bretagne,
Brest, France.
GIDITIC, Universidad Eafit, Medellin - Colombia.
Email: raul.mazo@ensta-bretagne.fr

***Abstract*— With the proliferation of new technology platforms, new operational requirements, different contexts and so on, agility remains more and more solicitated for software evolution. For software evolution of Software Product Line Engineering (SPLE), the Feature Model (FM) is the basic instrument that supports the evolution of SPL at the variability level. We would like to improve FM diagrams to make them understandable during the evolution of the corresponding product lines. More precisely, FM evolution can become more systematic and more intelligent. In our work, we aim to evolve FMs by means of smart techniques. Hence, we represent feature models by an ontology. This latter will permit, among others, the inference of knowledge about the evolution of the FMs. By obtaining different versions of the FMs, these can be used as a learning base of a learning algorithm. So, for a given FM, a new version can be predicted as being an evolution version of the FM. In this paper, we present the FM metamodel extension necessary to represent the semantics of the evolution rules. Thus, with a model driven approach, FMs are transformed into FM ontologies. A running example about an Electric Brake Parking System extracted from the SPLOT repository is presented.**

Keywords- Software Product Line Engineering; Variability Modeling; Feature Models (FM); Feature Oriented Domain Analysis (FODA); non-functional features.

I. INTRODUCTION

"A software product line is a set of software-intensive systems sharing a common, managed set of features that satisfy the specific needs of a particular market segment or mission and that are developed from a common set of core assets in a prescribed way" [19]. In the SPLE approach, variability is seen as a key concept in its processes and artifacts, and it is usually defined in terms of features, variants, variation points (Variation Point (VP) and the relationships among them. According to Bosh, *"a feature is a logical unit of a behavior defined by a set of functional and non-functional requirements"* [17] while variants (VA) represent the different possibilities that exist to satisfy a PV [5] and [23]. Kang et al. [2] define a (VP) "*as being identification at one or more locations at which variation may occur".* A FM is a tree with the root representing a concept, and its descendent nodes are features, see Figure 1 as an example. A FM is a compact representation of all possible products of an SPL. In the Feature Oriented Domain Analysis (FODA) [2], features can be mandatory or optional, and be related through choice (alternative or multiple), requires and excludes relationships. Feature models are feature diagrams plus additional information such as feature descriptions, binding times, priorities, stakeholders, and so forth. The purpose of using FM is to express the existing relationships between the different features of the product line. A FM is a tree– like structure and consists of: i) relations between a parent feature and its child features. ii) cross–tree constraints that are typically inclusion or exclusion statements of the form "if feature F is included, then feature X must also be included (or excluded)" [12].

Software product lines are long-lived systems that undergo significant evolution throughout their lifespan. This latter concerns domain engineering (development for reuse) and application engineering (development with reuse) processes. This evolution allows companies to align their products with new technological platforms, the evolution of commercial strategies, the emergence of new customers operational needs and new technological challenges in general. Therefore, a product line development process must make evolve the whole product line taking into account the changes at the Domain Engineering level. The evolution of domain assets, as for example the feature models, has received a great attention from researchers as it represents a key success aspect of SPLs. It does not only consist in adding, modifying or deleting features in the FM, but also adding semantics about the features' characteristics. Given a feature, it can represent a quality feature, a software feature, a structural feature, a hardware feature, etc. and can be in constantly evolution. Some studies propose to improve FM models [11] [20] [22] and [27] but despite these various attempts, the semantics extension of FMs remains limited and no promising approach has been proposed to develop FMs as part of a common evolution approach.

In our work, we aim to evolve FMs by means of smart techniques. In this paper, we present the FM metamodel extension necessary for representing semantics important for the evolution rules. Thus, with a model driven approach, FMs are transformed into FM ontologies. This is a first attempt to define a smart FM evolution approach in a knowledge-based framework. Thus, ontology of a FM will permit among others, the inferring of knowledge about FM evolution. Our running example of feature model is about an Electric Braking Parking system shown in Figure 1.

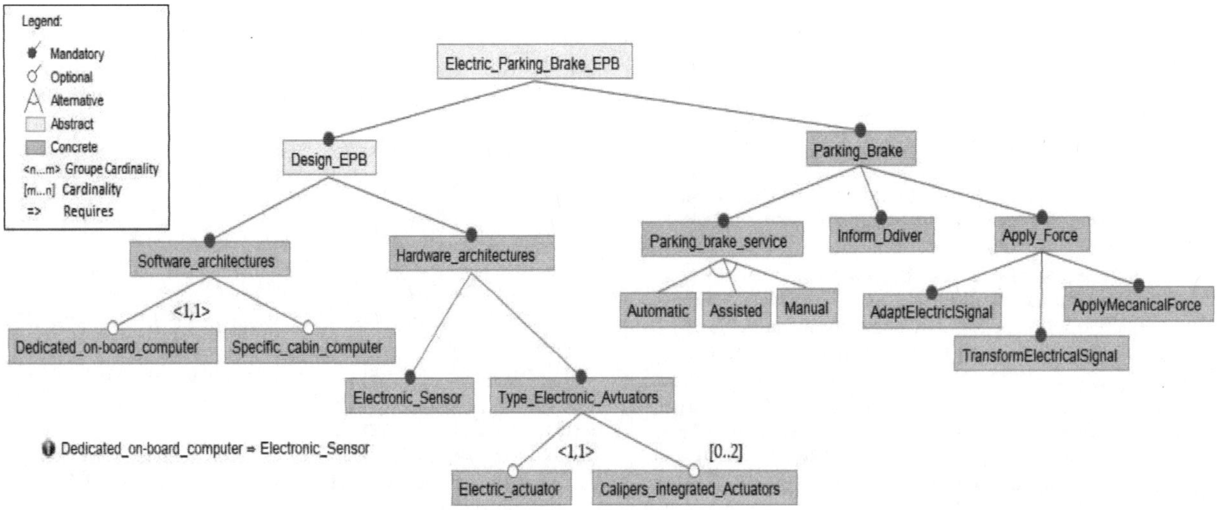

Figure 1: Electric Brake System FM [16]

The remainder of this paper is structured as follows: section 2 presents the related work of modeling variability with FM. Section highlights the issues treated in this paper. In section 4, the metamodel of an extended feature model (EVO-FM metamodel) is presented in the context of a model driven approach. It enriches the FM semantics in order to better handle evolution concerns. In the same section we present the transformation rules between the EVO-FM metamodel and the ontology metamodel to enable reasoning on the enriched models. Section 5 is devoted to present the implementation of the proposed approach under the Eclipse Framework. This operational aspect serves as a proof of concept. A conclusion summarizes the work and presents future workas perspectives in section 6.

II. RELATED WORKS AND ISSUES

Concerning the literature review on modeling feature models, several works have been done for making improvements and extensions to FM. The variability in the product family is represented by feature cardinality [1][2][5][14][16] and [25], a cardinality group of features [7][14][16][17][23] and [25], cardinality-Based feature models with constraints and feature attributes [17]. In our case, we also make extensions to FM for enriching its semantic. This latter is essential for evolution rules. Bhushan and al. [27] present the managing of Software Product Line using an Ontological Rule-Based Framework. Nieke and al [28] provide an ontology to check FM evolution. This latter is defined by feature models supporting temporal concepts. Rincón, Giraldo et al [29] propose an ontological rule-based approach to analyze dead and false optional features in FM as well as identifying certain causes of these defects, and explaining these causes in natural language. Our approach is also based on an ontology but it provides more semantic to FM features and relationships. In our work, we have temporal evolution rules. Feature modeling is the most popular technique to represent domain requirements variability in SPLs.

However, FMs have several limitations related to the lack of means to represent explicitly the semantics of features and their relationships. In fact, it needs improvements to provide semantics to its components for dealing with agility.

In order to better understand the problem, we present in the sequel, some limitations of feature models [14] and [21].

– Lack of distinction between behavioral and structural features. In the running example presented in Figure 1, we need to precise that "electronic_Sensor" and "Type_Electronic_Actuators" are structural features, but "adaptElectricSignal", "TransforElectricSignal" and "ApplyMecanicalForce" are behavioral features. Evolution rules can need the feature semantics in order to decide how to make changes in the FM.

– Evolutions of features in time and in space are not expressed. Variants of a feature may represent its evolution in time or space. For instance, in Figure 1, "Manual", "Assisted" and "Automatic" features represent the evolution of the "Parking_Brake_Service" feature.

- Features such as quality attributes are rarely specified in feature models and their variability is neglected. QoS feature can have different attributes such as response time, availability, reliability, throughput, etc. For a given product line, quality attributes can change during time so evolving from one kind to another.

– Distinguishing the nature of each feature; for specifying software concerns. This kind of information can be helpful for expressing evolution rules and/or inferring knowledge about evolution.

– Dependencies between a parent feature (variation point) and its children features (variants) should be more precise. For instance, a (VP) can represent an aggregate feature or a super-feature. To select features correctly, the semantics of these relationships have to be defined explicitly. In the running example, the "adaptElectricSignal", "TransforElectricSignal" and "ApplyMecanicalForce" features are mandatory regarding their corresponding father (i.e., "apply_force"). It is clear that "apply_force" aggregates these three variants; however, this information is not explicitly represented in the feature model and we consider that this information is useful to represent evolution rules.

III. MODEL DRIVEN APPROACH FOR EVO-FM CONSTRUCTION

EVO-FM is a feature model that represents knowledge and information for its evolution. Thus, EVO-FM is a feature model enriched with some concepts to support its evolution. In order to construct the EVO-FM, we adopt a model driven approach as shown in Figure 3. Hence, EVO-FM metamodel be transformed into an ontology metamodel supporting semantics information and allowing intelligent reasoning. In the sequel, we first recall some aspects of the model driven approach. Then, we present the EVO-FM metamodel conforms to ecore meta metamodel. This is done in the syntactic domain level and then as we will see in the next section, the Eclipse environment offers an ATL transformation facility to defined the transformation rules between EVO-FM metamodel and the ontology metamodel (semantic domain) [15].

A. *Modeling and metamodeling*

A well-defined language is a language with well-defined form (syntax), and meaning (semantics), which is suitable for automated interpretation by a computer. For a model to be useful, OMG [9] and [13], recommends that: "*A model needs to be expressed in a way that communicates information about a system among involved stakeholders that can be correctly interpreted by the stakeholders and supporting technologies. This requires the model to be expressed in a language understood by these stakeholders and their supporting technologies.*"[8].

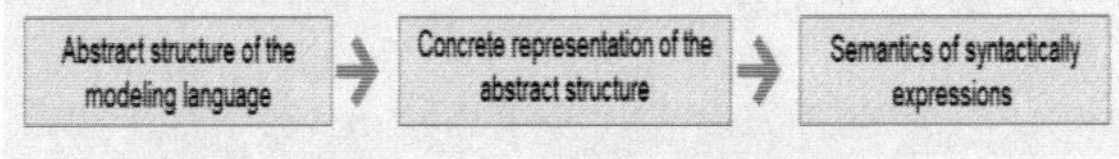

Figure 2: Meta model, model and concrete model

As illustrated in Figure 2, a modeling language is defined by an abstract structure, a concrete model and a model representing a real case enriched with additional semantics, which is in fact an instance of the concrete model [16].

B. Model transformation

Another key activity of model driven engineering [10] is the concept of model transformation, which is the automatic process to transform a source model into a target model. According to Bézivin et al [9] transformation is done by a collection of transformation rules that are "a description of how one or more constructs in the source language can be transformed into one or more constructs in the target language". More precisely, there are different levels of transformations as illustrated in Figure 3. Once the FM metamodel is created, a transformation to the FM ontology metamodel [15] is done. The extended metamodel (level 2) is consistent to the corresponding meta metamodel (level 3) and the FM model (level 1) is consistent to its corresponding metamodel (level 2). The transformations can be done horizontally in each level. The final real case ontology (level 0) can be obtained by instantiation of the meta ontology in OWL language and SWLR for the reasoning rules to be added manually [15]. The meta-model specification uses the TOPCASED ECORE editor. We checked the correctness of that transformation by verifying that each item in the source model has its corresponding item(s) in the target model. These are some transformation rules :

```
-- @path MM=/ATL_FM/Papier.ecore
--@path MM1=file:/C:/Users/HP/Desktop/OCTA_2019
/onto_FM/Ontology_FM.owl
module FM;
create OUT : MM1 from IN : MM;
rule Concept_Feature { from f : Feature!Feature
to out : Feature!Feature (
name <- f.name,
FeatureID <- f.FeatureID()
)}
rule Concept_Hardware_Feature{ from b : Feature!Feature
to out : Hardware_Feature!Hardware_Feature ()}
```

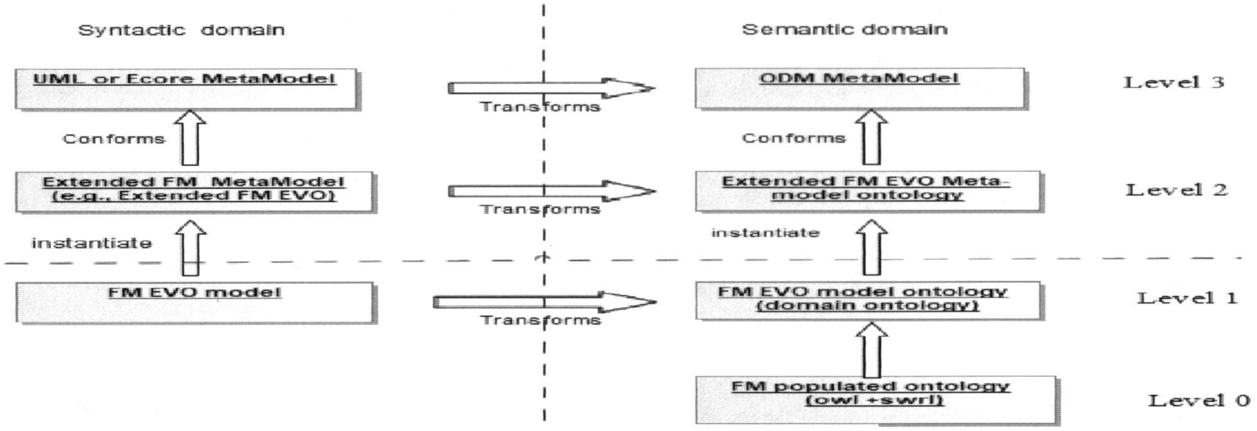

Figure 3 : Model-driven approach for EVO-FM construction

C. EVO-FM: Extended Feature Model Meta-Model

To help evolving feature models, we extend the FM metamodel using the UML notation [10] and [13]. In particular, we improved FM with three aspects: 1) the semantics of the features so that each feature of a FM can be characterized in one of the following four categories: software, hardware, structure and behavior, 2) the possibility to represent non-functional requirements (i.e., security, performance and accuracy) in the features of each FM and 3) the semantics of three new relationships: “compose”, “aggregate” and “is_a”. The concepts we integrate into the FM language are represented by the colored boxes in Figure 5. A non-functional feature represents the quality that the product family must have in order to meet the requested needs. We use the notion of stereotype [1] to specify the new concepts to the extended FODA language. Creating a non- functional feature should add the «stereotype_name» to the feature. For example, a feature that represents security will be stereotyped «Security» and similarly for the «Structural», «Behavioral», «Hardware» and «Software» features. The sample model shown in Figure 4 shows how to use the new relationships and quality requirements in our Electric Brake Parking System example.

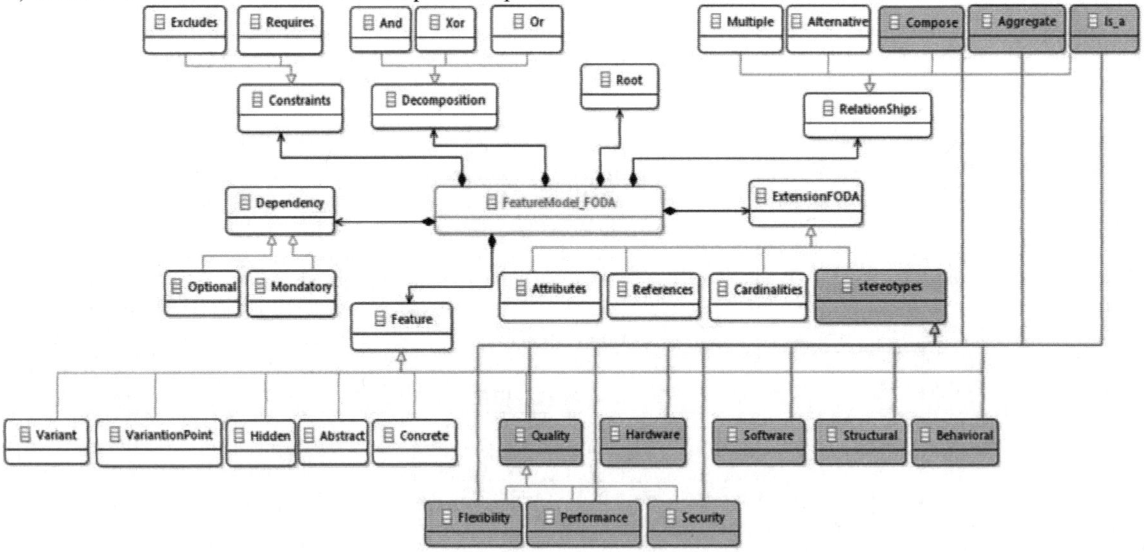

Figure 4: EVO-FM extended Feature model

IV. IMPLEMENTATION FRAMEWORK

In order to be able to construct EVO-FM, we implement ourmodel driven approach with the Eclipse family of integrated development environments, FeatureIDE and Xtext that we present in the sequel..The Eclipse community, withsupport from the Eclipse Foundation, provides integrated development environments (IDEs) targeting different developer profiles. It is a framework and code generation facility for building Java applications based on simple model definitions. Among the development tools provided by the IDE we used three complementary Eclipse frameworks: EMF, Xtext and FeatureIDE..

The Eclipse Modeling Framework (EMF) [6] provides a modeling and code generation framework for Eclipse applications based on structured data models. Although EMF supports the key MDA concept of using models as input to development and integration tools, it does not use however any one of the MOF compliance points previously described. Instead, EMF uses ECore, a not fully alignedvariant of OMG's EMOF. Essentially, among other elements, an ecore meta-model allows to define an EClass, an EAttribute, an EReference. To overcome this issue, EMF supplies model transformation and grammar capabilities. Model transformation can be model-to text (M2T) by the Textual Modeling Framework (TMF) [26]. It is an EMP's project aiming to support the development of textual concrete syntax. TMF is based on a meta-model and syntax specification, offering several functionalities that include a parser that reads the textual representation of the model and instantiates the corresponding EMF model, an eclipse text editor that supports syntax highlighting, code completion, navigation, and other features.

Xtext is a framework for development of programming languages and domain- specific languages. With Xtext you define your language using a powerful grammar language. With Xtext, we define grammars that implement stereotyped non-functional features.

FeatureIDE [24] and [25] is an Eclipse-based IDE that supports all phases of feature-oriented software development for the development of SPLs: domain analysis, domain design, domain implementation, requirements analysis, softwaregeneration, and quality assurance. Different SPL *implementation* techniques are integrated such as feature- oriented programming (FOP), aspect-oriented programming (AOP), preprocessors, and plug-ins. Full infrastructure, including parser, linker, type checker, compiler as ell as editing support for Eclipse, any editor that supports in [15] shows the ontology that we obtained for our running example.

V. CONCLUSION

In this paper, we have proposed EVO-FM, an extension to the FODA metamodel, which enriches it with knowledge and information to support the evolution phase of the models created with this engineering language. In particular, we enrich the feature models with quality and semantic features. Hence, we also add support for new types of feature relationships and extensions with stereotypes. We have adopted a model driven approach for constructing EVO-FM with also the possibility to transform them to ontologies that enforce the feature model semantics and intelligence by inferring new information. The obtained ontologies are not just enriched with SWRL rules for checking the EVO-FM consistency but also with the mechanisms to run the evolution rules [15]. To implement our approach, we advocate the adoption of metamodeling tools such as Eclipse modeling Framework and Xtext. Thus, the main contributions of our approach are:

- Add semantic features in the form of stereotypes such as «software», «hardware», «structural» and «Quality»
- Add quality features in the form of stereotypes such as «security», «Performance», «Flexibility».
- Import a textual specification into grammars using the Xtext framework to process it and transform it into XML;
- Import the EVO-FM in XMI, XML and Java format and soenhance reuse of it.

The main perspectives of our work are: 1) apply our model driven approach to different system families and validate the evolution rules that are behind the EVO-FM ontology 2) enable a smarter evolution of feature models by using different versions of EVO-FM feature model, these can be used as a learning base of a learning algorithm. So, for a given EVO-FM, a new version can be predicted as being a new FM evolution version. More specifically, suppose that we have the trace (history) of

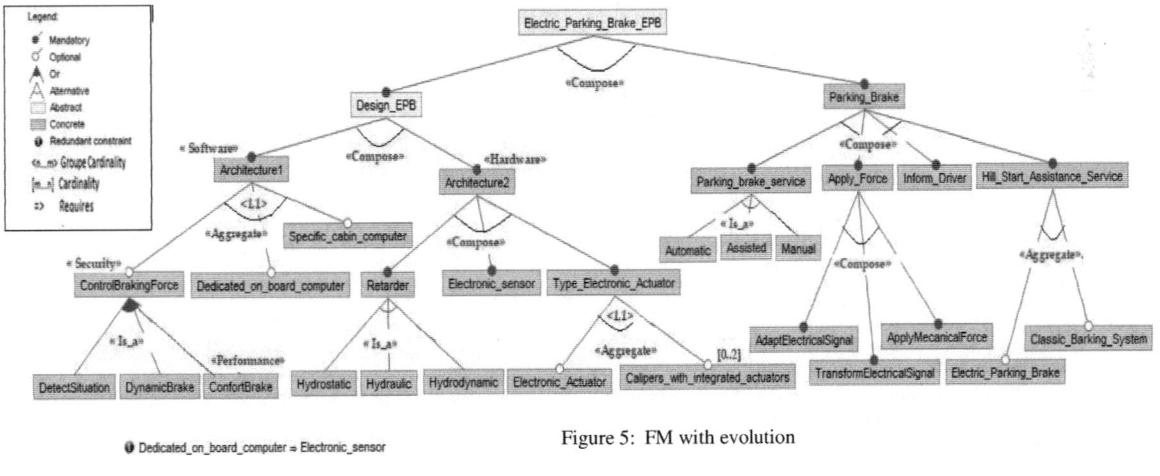

Figure 5: FM with evolution

the 50th previous versions of the EBP where the feature "Type-electronic-actuator" feature was "electric-actuator" in 10th first versions and after the 11th version becomes always "calipers_integrated_actuator" so the Type-electronic-actuator feature will evolve to become mandatory "calipers_integrated_actuator" instead of having two optional features. Also, we can have an aggregation of features that evolve to a composition of features because the learning algorithm find that after a certain number of FM versions, this happens. A quality feature can also evolve from performance to agility because this was learned from previous versions. We would like to investigate these concerns in the near future.

REFERENCES

[1] H. Papajewskiand D. Beuche and W. Schroder-Preikschat. Variability management with feature models. Science of Computer Programming, December 2004, vol. 53, no 3, pages333{352, 2004..

[2] K-C. Kang, S-G. Cohen, J-A. Hess, W-E. Novak, and A-S. Peterson,"Feature Oriented Domain Analysis FODA Feasibility Study", Technical Report CMU/SEI-90-TR-21, Software Engineering Institute, Carnegie Mellon University, Pittsburgh,PA, USA, November 1990.

[3] J. Christophe, " The Reuse and Variability software product lines ", Periodic publication smals,Junary 2009

[4] N. Noda, and T. Kishi,"Aspect oriented Modeling for Variability Management", 12th International Software Product Line Conference, September 2008.

[5] B. Frank, E.Raymond, S.David G.Timothy M.Ed .Eclipse modeling framework: a developer's guide. Addison-Wesley Professional. December 2004

[6] A. Classen, P. Heymans, and P. Schobbens,"What's in a Feature: A Requirements Engineering Perspective", In J. Fiadeiro and P. Inverardi (Eds.): FASE 2008, LNCS 4961 .Proceedings of the 11th International Conference on Fundamental Approaches to Software Engineering, held as part of ETAPS, Budapest, Hungary, pp.4-- 30,April, 2008.

[7] L. Moigne, Jean-Louis. Modeling of complex systems. Paris: Bordas,1990

[8] J Bézivin, O Gerbé. Towards a precise definition of the OMG/MDA framework. Proceedings 16th Annual International Conference on Automated Software Engineering,pp 273—280, IEEE , November 2001.

[9] OMG, "Unified Modeling Language TM (OMG UML)",Superstructure ,2011.

[10] M-A. Laguna, B. González-Baixauli, J-M. Marqués, and R. Fernándezet,"Feature Patterns and Multi Paradigm Variability Models",GIRO Technical Report 2008/01, v0.91, 2008.

[11] E-A.Oliveira, I-M. Gimenes, E. Hatsue, and M. Huzita, "A Variability Management Process for Software Product Lines",In Proceedings conference of the Centre for Advanced Studies on Collaborative research , IBM Press, pp.225-241,October 2005

[12] OMG Unified Modeling Language (OMG UML, OMG Document Number:formal/2007-11-04Standard document:URL:http://www.omg.org/spec/UML/2.1.2/Infra structure V2.1.2/PDF, Associated Schema Files.

[13] R. Mazo, Advantages and limitations of feature models in modeling variability requirements., Software engineering NO 11, Paris France, January 2015

[14] O. Ferchichi. R.beltaifa , L.Elabed. , *An ontological Rule-Based Approach for Software Product Lines Evolution.* International Multi-Conference on: "Organization of Knowledge anddvanced Technologies" (OCTA), IEEE, Tunisie. September 2020

[15] http://www.splot-research.org/Decenber 2010,

[16] J. Bosch, G. Florijn, D. Greefhorst, and J. Kuusela, "Variability issues in software product lines", In Software Product-Family Engineering (pp. 13-21). Springer Berlin Heidelberg,pp. 13-21, April 2001.

[17] D. Beuche, H. Papajewskiand, and W. Schroder-Preikschat, "Variability management with feature models", Science of Computer Programming, vol. 53, no 3, pp.333—352, 2004.

[18] P. Clements and L. Northrop. Software Product Lines: Practices and Patterns. SEI series in software engineering. Addison- esley,2002.

[19] D. Benavides, P.Trinidad, and A. Ruiz-Cortes, "Using Constraint Programming to Reason on Feature Models", In The Seventeenth International Conference on Software Engineering and Knowledge Engineering (SEKE05), Juillet, 2005.

[20] J. Christophe, " Reuse and variability software product lines ", Publication périodique smals , March 2009.

[21] D. Benavides, S. Segura, P. Trinidad, and A. Ruiz-Cortes," Using Java CSP Solvers in the Automated Analyses of Feature Models", LNCS, to be asigned, TIC2003-02737-C02-01 (AgilWeb), January 2006.

[22] D.Benavides, "Automated Reasoning on Feature Models",In The 5th Conference on Advanced Information Systems Engineering (CAiSE05), LNCS, 3520:491503,Juin, 2005.

[23] T. Kastner, C.Benduhn, *et al.* FeatureIDE: An extensible framework for feature-oriented software development. *Science of Computer Programming*, vol. 79, p. 70-85. January 2014.

[24] K. Christian, T. Thomas, S.Gunter, *et al.* FeatureIDE: A tool framework for feature-oriented software development .

[25] W.Edward Daniel. "Re-engineering eclipse MDT/OCL for xtext." *Electronic Communications of the EASST* 36 . March 2011.

[26] K. Czarnecki,"Generative Programming",Principals and Techniques of Software Engineering Based on Automated Configuration and Fragment Based Component Models, Tools, and Applications, Addison Wesley,ISBN 0201309777, Mai, 2000.

[27] M. Bhushan, S. Goel, A. Kumar and A. Negi. Managing Software Product Line using an Ontological Rule-Based Framework. International Conference on Infocom Technologies and Unmanned Systems (2017).

[28] M. Nieke, C. Seidl, T. Thum. ,Back to the future: avoiding paradoxes in feature-model evolution, SPLC (2), 2018.

[29] L. Rincón., G. Giraldo, R .Mazo and C. Salinesi. An ontological rule-based approach for analyzing dead and false optional features in feature models. Electronic notes in theoretical computer science, 302(0): 111 – 132. 2013.

Continuous Information Processing Enabling Real-Time Capabilities: An Energy Efficient Big Data Approach

Martin Zinner*, Kim Feldhoff*, Wolfgang E. Nagel*
* Center for Information Services and High Performance Computing (ZIH)
Technische Universität Dresden
Dresden, Germany
E-mail: {martin.zinner1, kim.feldhoff, wolfgang.nagel}@tu-dresden.de

***Abstract*—A considerable part of data aggregation during information processing in industry is still carried out in nightly batch mode. In contrast, using our method termed Continuous Information Processing Methodology (CIPM), the aggregation can be started as soon as the data collection is initiated. Our method was motivated by a real-world application scenario at a semiconductor company. During the data collection process, partial aggregated values are determined, such that, after the data collection phase has been completed, the final aggregated values are available for evaluation. In order to benefit from the rigour of a formal approach, a mathematical model is introduced and the conversion from batch mode to CIPM is exemplified. The most common aggregation functions used in various field of industry and business can be easily adapted and used within CIPM. The major additional benefits of the CIPM are reduced and spread aggregational effort over the whole collection period as well as tightened and straightforward computational design strategies. To conclude, the CIPM supports a paradigm shift from more or less subjectively designed individualistic conceptions in software design and development towards objectively established optimal solutions.**

***Index Terms*—Continuous information processing; Continuous aggregation; Energy efficient computation; Real-time capabilities; Data Analytics; Data processing; Stream processing; Batch processing; Business Intelligence; Big Data.**

I. Introduction

At first, the core of our aggregation theory in a nutshell is succinctly addressed, some definitions such as Big Data are tightened up and the principal motivation of our paper, i.e., increased real-time requirements in the industry, is presented. Cisco, in a white paper, identified the deficiencies of the classical nightly batch jobs aggregation strategy and summarised them in five Pain Points. All except for Pain Point 3 regarding ad-hoc reporting, will be addressed within this paper. The statistical function *standard deviation* is used to illustrate our methodology. The usual representation of the standard deviation is adapted to fit our needs. ,

Aggregation is an operation to obtain summarised information by using aggregate functions. A new methodology for information aggregation based on a very simple and straightforward starting point is formulated in this paper – namely, that within the information flow, *the process of information aggregation should be started as early as possible*, best as soon as the collection phase is initiated. This strategy assumes a strict and clearly defined architectural design strategy of the computational framework and enables real-time capabilities of the system, therefore, the new methodology is termed *Continuous Information Processing Methodology* (CIPM). In order to be able to in-depth analyse the CIPM, a formal, mathematical model is set up, the conversion of the underlying structure is defined and the pros and cons of CIPM, as opposed to the classical batch jobs strategy, are discussed.

According to [1] "Big Data is the information asset characterised by such a *high volume*, *velocity* and *variety* to require *specific technology* and *analytical methods* for its transformation into value". According to the definition above, Big Data is much more that high volume of data and needs unconventional methods to be processed.

At the same time, a cultural change should accompany the process of investing in interdisciplinary *Business Intelligence* and *Data Analytics* education [1], involving the company's entire population, its members to "efficiently manage data properly and incorporate them into decision making processes" [2].

A. Motivation

1) Rapidly increasing data amount: The total amount of data created, captured, and consumed globally is forecast to increase rapidly, reaching more than 180 Zettabytes in 2025, as opposed to 64.2 Zettabytes in 2020 and 15.5 Zettabytes in 2015 [3]. Real-time information processing has become a significant requirement for the optimal functioning of the manufacturing plants [4]. Worldwide by 2022, over 50 billion *Internet of Things* (IoT) devices including sensors and actuators are predicted to be installed in machines, humans, vehicles, buildings, and environments.

2) Real-time requirements: Demand is also huge for the real-time utilisation of data streams instead of the current batch analysis of stored Big Data [5]. The operations of a real-time system are subject to *time constraints* (deadlines), i.e., if specified timing requirements are not met, the corresponding operation is degraded and/or the quality of service may suffer and it can lead even to system failure [6]. In a real-time system deadlines must always be met, regardless of the system load. A system not specified as real-time cannot usually guarantee a response within any time frame. There are no general restrictions regarding the magnitude of the values of the time constraints. The time constraints do not need to be within seconds or milliseconds, as often they are understood. There is a general tendency that real-time requirements are becoming crucial requisites.

Travellers require current flight schedules on their portable devices to be able to select and book flights; in order to avoid overbooking, the flight plans and the filled seats must be kept reasonably current. Similarly, people expect instant access to their business-critical data in order to make informed decisions. Moreover, they may require up-to-date aggregated data or even ad-hoc requests. This instant access to critical information may be crucial for the competitiveness of the company [7].

B. Aim

Cisco [8] identified a couple of *Pain Points* in the Business Intelligence (BI) area, but these Pain Points carry a more general validity:

1) *the race against time*; managing batch window time constraints,
2) *cascading errors and painful recovery*; eliminating errors caused by improper job sequencing,
3) *ad hoc reporting*; managing unplanned reports in a plan-based environment,
4) *service-level consistency*; managing service-level agreements,
5) *resources*; ETL resource conflict management.

Our approach will address all points except Pain Point 3), which is subject for future research.

In conclusion, continuous information processing enables a new perspective on aggregation strategies, such that aggregation is performed in parallel to the data collection phase. Preliminary aggregated values corresponding to the current state of the retrieved data are available for evaluation. Nightly batch aggregation becomes obsolete.

C. Outline

The remainder of the paper is structured as follows: Section II gives an overview regarding existing work related to the described problem. An informal presentation of the continuous aggregation strategy is presented in Section III, whereby Section IV introduces the mathematical model and describes how the batch aggregation can be transformed into continuous aggregation. The presentation of the main results and discussions based upon these results constitute the content of Section V, whereas Section VI concludes this paper and sketches the future work.

II. Related work

The focus of this Section is primarily on algorithmic approaches regarding the previous art. The analysis of different one-pass algorithms [9] and their efficient implementation is beyond the scope of this paper as well as pure technical solutions based on database technologies.

A. SB-trees

A B-tree is a balanced tree data structure, that keeps data sorted and allows searches, sequential access, and deletions in logarithmic time; the tree depth is equal at every position, whereas the SB-tree is a variant of a B-tree such that it offers high-performance sequential disk access [10], [11]. Zhang [11] outlines the key challenges of spatio-temporal aggregate computation on geo-spatial image data, focusing primarily on data having the form of raster images. She gives a very detailed overview of the state of the art regarding efficient aggregate computation. Her approach is based on *aggregate queries* common in the database community, including data cubes, whereas our approach (CIPM) does not focus on database technology when calculating the aggregation functions. For example, the improved multi-version SB-tree consumes more space than the size of raw data. Other approaches use only a small index, reducing the space needed, but supporting only count and sum aggregate functions. The main idea behind the SB-trees is to provide through a depth-first search, – by accumulating partial aggregate values – a fast look-up of computed values [11], [12].

B. Scotty

Scotty [13] is an efficient and general open-source operator for sliding-window aggregation for stream processing systems, such as Apache Flink, Apache Beam, Apache Samza, Apache Kafka, Apache Spark, and Apache Storm. It enables stream slicing, pre-aggregation, and aggregate sharing including out-of-order data streams and session windows [14]. The aggregate window functions are: avg(), count(), max(), min(), sum(). Being a toolkit, the out-of-the-box aggregate functions are restricted to the above. Implementation details are disclosed in a preprint paper [15]. Scotty can be extended with user-defined aggregation functions, however, these functions must be associative and invertible. Since Scotty is open source, additional user extensions are always possible.

Sliding window aggregation is also a main topic regarding this paper, even if sliding windows are not used for reporting/evaluation. There is always the possibility that erroneous data is captured. This cannot be avoided, since a data set may look formally correct, but may be wrong with regard to its content. Such anomalies can be detected hours after the data has been processed and should be corrected.

According to [16] research on sliding-window aggregation has focused mainly on aggregation functions that are associative and on FIFO windows. Much less is known for other nontrivial scenarios. Is it possible to efficiently support associative aggregation functions on windows that are non-FIFO? Besides associativity and invertibility, what other properties can be exploited to develop general purpose algorithms for fast sliding-window aggregation? Tangwongsan et al. [17] present the Finger B-tree Aggregator (FiBA), a novel real-time sliding window aggregation algorithm that optimally handles streams of varying degrees of out-of-orderness. The basic algorithms can be implemented on any balanced tree, for example on B-trees.

C. Holistic functions

The median is the middle number in an ordered list of items. The median is a holistic function, i.e., its result has to rely on the entire input set, so that there is no constant bound on the size of the storage needed for the computation. An algorithm suitable for continuous aggregation based on heap technology can be found in [7]. For the sake of completeness, the main idea is presented below. Two heaps are used, one for the higher part and one for the lower part of the data. The newly collected dataset is inserted into the corresponding heap; if the total number of items is even and if the case arises, the heaps are balanced against each other, such that the two heaps contain the same number of items, etc. Hence, holistic aggregation functions can be used with continuous aggregation techniques, they should however satisfy the foreseen time constraints.

D. Quantile

A survey of approximate quantile computation on large-scale data is given by Chen [18]. In streaming models, where data elements arrive one by one in a streaming way, algorithms are required to answer quantile queries with only one-pass scan. Formulas for the computation of higher-order central moments or for robust, parallel computation of arbitrary order of statistical moments can be found here [19], [20], some of them are one-pass incremental approaches.

In conclusion, the main focus of the existing research has been to develop aggregate queries for efficient retrieval and visualisation of persisted data. However, with Scotty a general open-source operator for sliding-window aggregation in stream processing systems, such as, for example, the Apache family, has been developed. Scotty incorporates the usual aggregate functions like avg(), sum(), etc., and it has the possibility to include special user defined functions. Tangwongsan [16] points out that much less is known for nontrivial scenarios, i.e., functions that are not associative and do not support FIFO windows. Our approach, however develops the strategy and technology for continuous information processing, abbreviated CIPM and shows that functions, which allow efficient one-pass implementations are suitable for CIPM. Moreover, holistic functions allowing appropriate implementation, for example median [7] can be used with CIPM.

III. Problem Description

The term information function and aggregation function [21] are used synonymously within this paper. Corporate reporting aims to provide all of the counterparties with the information they need in order to transact with a company. This can be termed the *information function* of corporate reporting [22]. Within this paper, we assume that the data collection and the subsequent data transformation are continuous processes, aggregation being the process that succeeds transformation. The terms continuous information processing and continuous aggregation are used alternatively, emphasising that within the continuous information processing, the continuous aggregation is the challenging part.

1) Overview of the CIPM : Following, the fundamental issues of the continuous aggregation strategy are outlined by using two simple flow diagrams, Figure (1) presenting the classical nightly jobs aggregation strategy, whereas Figure (2) describing very succinctly the continuous aggregation strategy. It is assumed, that reporting is based on daily aggregated data. Data collection starts at 00:00:00 for the current day and it ends, retrieving data generated till 23:59:59 of the same day. Whenever applying the classical batch jobs strategy, the transformation/aggregation is started only after the data is fully retrieved/collected for the current day, which we are referring to. In this case, the transformation/aggregation can be started only after midnight.

On the other hand, the CIPM is carried out on small chunks of data, usually such that the transformation/aggregation is performed on data loaded into memory during the collection phase. This way, reloading data into memory for aggregation purposes is obsolete.

The continuous aggregation strategy is quite straightforward: after midnight, the collection phase for the current day is started, i.e., the chunks $C_1, C_2, ..., C_n$ are retrieved one after another. While the second chunk C_2 is retrieved, the first chunk C_1 is transformed/aggregated, and so on and so forth. At the end of the current day, most of the collected data is aggregated. The subsequent day, the remaining chunk(s) are transformed/aggregated and a post-aggregation phase is started, during which the final calculations are performed. In the end, the aggregated values are ready for reporting soon after midnight.

In order to keep the presentation simple and accessible and to avoid technical complications, it is required that the time to perform the transformation/aggregation of a chunk is slightly lower than the corresponding time of the collection phase. In real-world systems, under some circumstances, this is obviously not necessary. Let us suppose that the time to retrieve a chunk is t, but the time to transform/aggregate the values of a chunk is slightly lower than $3t$ and let A_i be the phase of aggregation of chunk C_i. Then, the start of A_i is phase-shifted by t with regard to C_i, i.e., A_1 is started simultaneously with C_2, etc. As a consequence, A_i completes before $C_{(i+4)}$ is started. Hence, in this example there are three instances of the aggregation algorithm running in parallel. Possibly, information between the aggregation instances running in parallel need to be exchanged.

In order to keep the presentation simple, it is assumed within this paper, that the chunks are of the same size and the time to retrieve them does not change. Of course, this assumption in not necessary in real-world systems.

2) Exemplification using Standard Deviation (SD): Next, the complexity of our approach is illustrated by exemplifying the technology on the *standard deviation of the sample*. The standard deviation shows how much variation (dispersion, spread) from the mean exists. It is easy to present without being trivial.

Let $\{x_1, x_2, \ldots, x_N\}$ be the observed values of the sample items, let $\bar{x} := 1/N \sum_{i=1}^{N} x_i$ be the mean value of these observations. The common representation of the (uncorrected

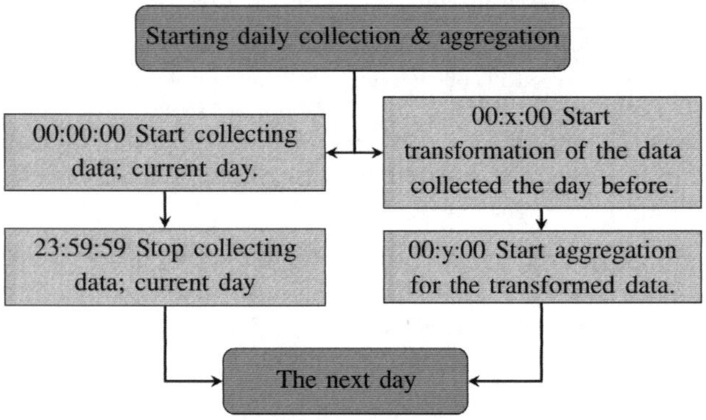

Figure 1: Simplified flow diagram exemplifying the batch job strategy(x is the time gap due to collection delay; y is the time gap due merely to transformation).

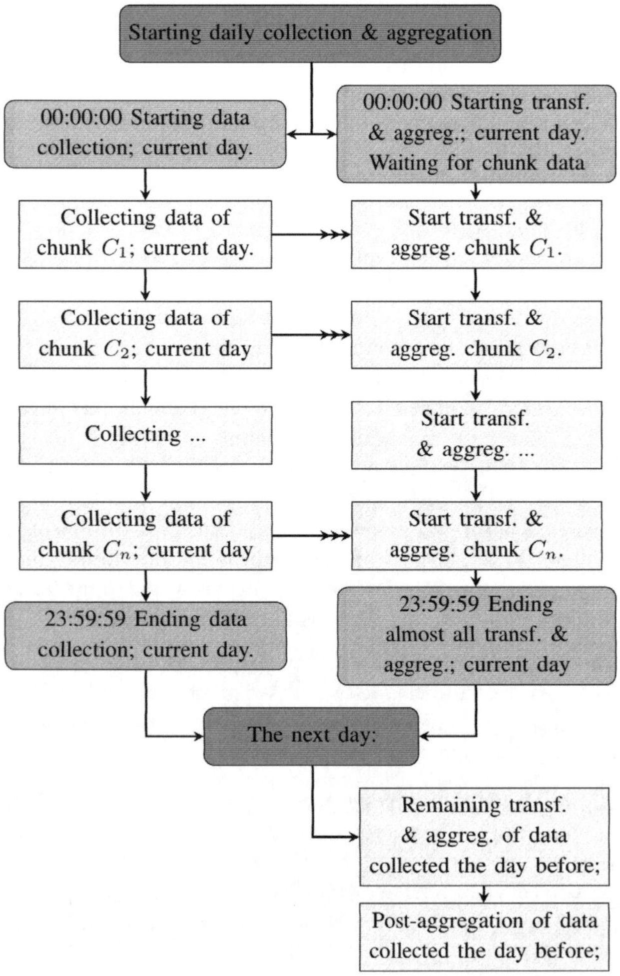

Figure 2: Simplified flow diagram exemplifying the continuous aggregation strategy. The arrow with three heads signifies that the aggregation phase waits till the respective chunk data has been collected.

sample) standard deviation is:

$$SD_N := \sqrt{\frac{1}{N}\sum_{i=1}^{N}(x_i - \bar{x})^2}. \tag{1}$$

At first glimpse, the above representation of the standard deviation cannot be applied to continuous computing techniques. The impediment is the term $\bar{x}$. In order to be able to apply the formula (1), all the data involved has to be first collected. Chan et al. [23], [24] call the above representation *two-pass algorithm*, since it requires passing through the data twice; once to compute $\bar{x}$ and again to compute SD_N. This may be unwanted if the sample is too large to be stored in memory, or when the standard deviation should be computed dynamically as the data is collected.

Regrouping the terms in the formula above, the well known representation is obtained:

$$SD_N = \frac{1}{N}\sqrt{\left|N\sum_{i=1}^{N}x_i^2 - \Big(\sum_{i=1}^{N}x_i\Big)^2\right|}. \tag{2}$$

Let $1 \leq n \leq N$. Let $S_n = n\sum_{i=1}^{n}x_i^2 - \Big(\sum_{i=1}^{n}x_i\Big)^2$, let $A_n := \sum_{i=1}^{n}x_i^2$, let $B_n := \sum_{i=1}^{n}x_i$. The alternative representation (2) of the standard deviation is suitable to be used within the continuous computation approach.

During the data collection phase, the functions A_n and B_n are updated, either after each item x_n, as soon as it in known to the system, or considering small batches. Thus, at each point in time, during the data collection phase, the values of $A_{(n+1)}$ and $B_{(n+1)}$ can be easily calculated by adding up the corresponding value of the new item. Hence $A_{(n+1)} = A_n + x^2_{(n+1)}$. Similar results hold for $B_{(n+1)}$. Accordingly, at each point in time, the standard deviation can be easily calculated, if needed, as a function of S_n, A_n, B_n. It follows:

$$S_{(n+1)} = S_n + A_n + n \cdot x^2_{(n+1)} - 2x_{(n+1)} \cdot B_n.$$

Hence, intermediary results and trend analysis are possible during data collection.

For example, almost all *Key Performance Indicators* (KPIs) used in the semiconductor industry can be adapted to be applied within CIPM [25]–[28]. The same is true in other areas of the industry or business.

3) Reason for choosing SD: The considerations above were drafted merely to illustrate the continuous computation technology, in real-world systems the representation (2) without using absolute values in the square root function can lead to negative values. When A_N and B_N are calculated in the straightforward way, especially when N is large and all of x-values are roughly of the same order of magnitude, rounding or truncation errors may occur [29]. Please note that the representation (2) using absolute values, has been adapted in order to avoid negative values under the square root. Using double precision arithmetic can possibly avoid the occurrence of anomalies as above.

4) Counterexample: Unfortunately, there are also some simple and well known functions, such as the *Average Absolute Deviation (AAD)*, which generally speaking cannot be used with continuous computing techniques; AAD is calculated as the mean of the sum of the absolute differences between a value and the central point of the group:

$$AAD_N = \frac{1}{N}\sum_{i=1}^{N} |x_i - M|.$$

The central point M can be a mean, median, mode, etc. For some distributions, including the normal distribution, AAD can be related to or approximated with the corresponding standard deviation [30]–[32].

IV. The Formal Model

The description of our methodology is formalised, we introduce a mathematical model in order to use the advantages of the rigour of a formal approach over the inaccuracies and the incompleteness of natural languages. It is assumed that the streams are *finite*, i.e., there are two points in time, t_s, the initiating and t_e, the termination point, such that within this time interval, the data is collected and aggregated.

If the aggregation occurs after the entire raw data have been previously collected, involving technologies that process all of the collected data at once, then the process is termed *batch aggregation mode* or *large scale aggregation*. On the contrary, if the collected data $[t_s, t_e]$ can be split into $k \geq 2$ smaller (equal) units of length l, such that

$$U_1 := [t_s, t_{s+l}],\ U_2 := [t_{s+l+1}, t_{s+2l}], \ldots,$$
$$U_k := [t_{s+(k-1)\cdot l+1}, t_e]$$

also termed chunks and *partial aggregation* is performed on these units, such that the final aggregation values are calculated out of the corresponding partial values of the chunks, then the process is termed *small scale aggregation*.

Some authors specify the terms large scale or small scale aggregation regarding their ability to perform the computation in memory. Within this paper, a more algorithmical than a technical approach is followed.

A. Notation

1) General notations: Let $l_X \in \mathbb{N}$ be the number of streams and let

$$X := \{X^{(1)}, X^{(2)}, \ldots, X^{(l_X)}\}$$

be the set of streams. In order to keep our model simple, it is supposed that each stream delivers data at the same point in time, let $\{1, 2, \ldots, T\}$ be the points in time when the data is collected and known by the system.

Let $1 \leq t \leq T$. The value of the stream $X^{(l)}$ collected at time t is denoted by $x_t^{(l)}$. The streamed values can be represented as a matrix

$$(x_{tl})_{1\leq t\leq T; 1\leq l\leq l_X}.$$

2) Grouping: Let l_F be the number of the aggregation functions. In order to perform the computation of the streams – the aggregation functions are in general functions of several variables – a grouping

$$G := \{G^{(1)}, G^{(2)}, \ldots, G^{(l_G)}\}$$

is defined on the space of the streams, such that

$$G^{(l)} := \{X^{(l_1)}, X^{(l_2)}, \ldots, X^{(l_l)}\}.$$

and $l_F = l_G$. Accordingly:

$$g_t^{(l)} := x_t^{(l_1)} \times x_t^{(l_2)} \times \cdots \times x_t^{(l_l)}$$

is the value of the grouping $G^{(l)}$ at time t. This way, new compound streams are created. In order to keep our model as simple as possible, it is supposed – without limiting the generality – that the number of groupings is equal to the number of aggregation functions.

3) Aggregation functions: Let

$$F := \{F^{(1)}, F^{(2)}, \ldots, F^{(l_F)}\}$$

be the set of the aggregation functions, such that

$$F^{(l)} : G^{(l)} \to \mathbb{R}$$

for $1 \leq l \leq l_F$.

In order to keep the model as general as possible, small scale aggregation is considered as the overall approach. This means especially, that data is collected and computed/aggregated in small batches. In order to be able to continuously compute – i.e., retrieve/collect, transform, aggregate – the time to aggregate the small batch should not exceed the collection time of the same batch. Obviously, if this is not the case, the aggregation cannot be performed during the data collection phase. During the transformation phase, the data is verified for accuracy, consolidated/aligned (i.e., data from multiple sources is harmonised), grouped and adapted such that it is best finalised for aggregation. During the transformation phase data is not altered and has the level of granularity of the original raw data.

4) Standard deviation as exemplification: Let $1 \leq l \leq l_F$. Let us suppose that $F^{(l)} : G^{(l)} \to \mathbb{R}$ is the standard deviation, see representation (2) and let $x \in G^{(l)}$ a particular stream. Let $1 \leq t \leq T$ and let:

$$f_t^{(l,1)}(x) := \sum_{i=1}^{t} x_i^2,$$
$$f_t^{(l,2)}(x) := \sum_{i=1}^{t} x_i,$$
$$f_t^{(l,3)}(x) := t\sum_{i=1}^{t} x_i^2 - \Big(\sum_{i=1}^{t} x_i\Big)^2$$
$$= t \cdot f_t^{(l,1)}(x) - (f_t^{(l,2)}(x))^2. \quad (3)$$

Let $F_t^{(l)}(x)$ be the value of the function $F^{(l)}$ applied on the values subscripted by $\{1, 2, \ldots, t\}$.

Then $F_t^{(l)}(x)$ can be calculated out of the values of $f_t^{(l,1)}(x)$, $f_t^{(l,2)}(x)$, i.e., by considering $f_t^{(l,3)}(x)$, namely:

$$F_t^{(l)}(x) = \frac{1}{t}\sqrt{\left|f_t^{(l,3)}(x)\right|}. \quad (4)$$

B. Information processing

1) Chunk-wise processing: Let $j, q \geq 1$ and let us suppose that the streams are retrieved in small chunks:

$$C_j := \{C_j^{(1)}, C_j^{(2)}, \ldots, C_j^{(l_X)}\}$$

of q items, i.e., the chunk $C_j^{(l)}$ consists of partial streams

$$C_j^{(l)} := \{x_{((j-1)q+1)}^{(l)}, x_{((j-1)q+2)}^{(l)}, \ldots, x_{(jq)}^{(l)}\}.$$

The information is processed chunk-wise, first C_1 is retrieved. As long as the next chunk C_2 is retrieved, aggregations is performed on C_1 simultaneously, then chunk C_3 is retrieved by simultaneously aggregating chunk C_2, and so on and so forth. As already mentioned, in order to assure continuous computation, the time to perform the aggregation on the chunks should not exceed the retrieval time of a chunk, else the aggregation cannot be performed during the retrieval period. The values of $f_{(j+1)q}^{(l,1)}$ and $f_{(j+1)q}^{(l,2)}$ can be easily calculated out of $f_{jq}^{(l,1)}$ and $f_{jq}^{(l,2)}$, for example:

$$f_{(j+1)q}^{(l,1)}(x) = f_{jq}^{(l,1)}(x) + \sum_{i=1}^{q} x_{jq+i}^2.$$

The value $F_{jq}^{(l)}$ can be calculated at each step, or alternatively, after having reached the end of the collection phase. This phase is termed *post aggregation phase,* since calculations are not done during the small scale aggregation phase (i.e., chunk aggregation), but after all chunks have been retrieved and aggregated. Since the small scale aggregation should be as fast and effective as possible, the functions $f_{jq}^{(l,3)}, F_{jq}^{(l)}$ must not be necessary calculated for each chunk, – if there is no requirement in this direction – they can also be calculated on a case by case basis by the tool that visualises intermediary results.

2) Truncation errors: A discussion regarding the truncation errors is beyond the scope of this paper. As already mentioned, when N is large and all of x-values are roughly of the same order of magnitude, rounding or truncation errors may occur when $f_t^{(l,1)}$ and/or $f_t^{(l,2)}$ for $1 \leq t \leq T$ are evaluated in the straightforward way [29]. A greater accuracy can be achieved by simply shifting some of the calculation to double precision, see [23], [24] for a discussion on rounding errors and the stability of presented algorithms. Barlow presents an *one-pass-through* algorithm [33], which is numerically stable and which is also suitable for parallel computing.

The scope of the presentation above is merely to illustrate the technology. Of course, if a function does not allow an one-pass algorithm, it cannot be used directly for continuous computation. A classical example in this direction is the average absolute deviation, as mentioned before, in some cases there are approximative one-pass implementation of the algorithms.

3) General case: Now, let us consider the general case. Let $1 \leq l \leq l_F$, let $j, q \geq 1$, such that j is the index and q is the length of the chunks. Let

$$F^{(l)} : G^{(l)} \to \mathbb{R} \text{ such that:}$$

a) there exists l_f real valued functions

$$f^{(l,1)}, f^{(l,2)}, \ldots, f^{(l,l_f)} \text{ defined on } G^{(l)}$$

such that for each chunk $C_j^{(l)}$, the values of

$$f_{(j+1)q}^{(l,i)} \quad (1 \leq i \leq l_f)$$

can be calculated out of the values of $f_{jq}^{(l,i)}$,

b) $F^{(l)}$ is a function of $f^{(l,i)}$ for all $1 \leq i \leq l_f$.

Then, intermediary results, such as the value of $F_{(j+1)q}^{(l)}$ can be calculated out of $f_{(j+1)q}^{(l,i)}$.

Let j_f be the index of the final chunk to be processed. Obviously, the algorithms should ensure that the value $F_{j_f \cdot q}^{(l)}$ does not depend on the size of the chunks.

4) Reprocessing: In practical systems, in general, there should be a technology in place that allows recalculation. This is necessary, if for what reason whatsoever, some stream values are erroneous. Sometimes, it takes time to correct them, since not all wrong values can be detected and corrected automatically. Regarding the standard deviation, two new functions $df_t^{(l,1)}, df_t^{(l,2)}$ can be introduced, such that

$$df_{jq}^{(l,1)}(x) := \sum_{i=j\cdot q}^{(j+1)\cdot q} x_i^2$$

and

$$df_{jq}^{(l,2)}(x) := \sum_{i=j\cdot q}^{(j+1)\cdot q} x_i.$$

Then, correct and updated computed values can be achieved, for example by adding to $f_T^{(l,3)}$ the new value of $df_{jq}^{(l,1)}$ and subtracting the corresponding old value $df_{jq}^{(l,1)}$, similar considerations for $df_{jq}^{(l,2)}$. This means especially, that the corresponding values for the initial chunk and the corrected chunk have to be (re)calculated. In the end, the value $F_{j_f \cdot q}^{(l)}$ has to be recalculated. As already mentioned, the above considerations are included in order to illustrate the methodology. In practice, better suited algorithms can or should be used instead.

C. Pseudo-code algorithm exemplification

A simplified algorithm to exemplify our continuous aggregation strategy is sketched. It is based on disassembling the standard deviation $F_t^{(l)}$ using $f_t^{(l,1)}, f_t^{(l,2)}, f_t^{(l,3)}$, see equation (3) and (4). In order to keep the representation of the algorithm simple, it is supposed that the chunks have the same length equal to l_{chunk}. The corresponding algorithm is presented in Figure (3). In real-world systems, the data collection may involve also time limits t_{Max}, such that the combination of both t_{Max} and l_{chunk}, restrict the length of the chunks.

```
/*
* Sample code to exemplify the continuous aggregation
    strategy
*/
double precision f^(l,1) = 0; //component function
double precision f^(l,2) = 0; //component function
double precision F^(l)  = 0; //intermediary value of the
    standard deviation corresponding to the state of
    collection
int l_chunk = 10,000; //number of the items of a chunk
float[l_chunk] c; //contains the retrieved values of the chunk
float[l_chunk] c_prev; //contains the data of previous chunk
int L_col = 0; //length of the collection
//-----------------------------------------------------------
/*
* data corresponding to the length of a chunk is collected
*/
procedure data_collection(){
   int l_cur = 0; //number of the collected items
   repeat
      collect data into c;
      l_cur ++;
   until (l_cur = l_chunk)
   for (int i; i < l_chunk; i++){
      c_prev[i] = c[i]; //copy the values of c into c_prev
   }
};
//-----------------------------------------------------------
/*
* data of the previous chunk is aggregated
*/
procedure data aggregation(){
   float[l_chunk] x; // contains data of the previous chunk
   for (int i; i < l_chunk; i++){
      x[i] = c_prev[i]; //copy the values of c_prev into x
   }
   // calculation of the functions composing the standard
       deviation
   f^(l,1) := f^(l,1) + \sum_{i=1}^{l_chunk} (x[i])^2;
   f^(l,2) := f^(l,2) + \sum_{i=1}^{l_chunk} x[i];
   L_col := L_col + l_chunk; //number of items already collected
   //
   F^(l) := (1 / L_col) \sqrt{ |L_col · f^(l,1) − (f^(l,2))^2| }; // only if required
};
//-----------------------------------------------------------
/*
* final calculation of the standard deviation
*/
procedure data_post_aggregation(){

   F^(l) := (1 / L_col) \sqrt{ |L_col · f^(l,1) − (f^(l,2))^2| };

};
//-----------------------------------------------------------
/*
* start aggregation in parallel to data collection
*/
void main(){
   data_collection();
   repeat
      start: in parallel
         thread: data_collection();
         thread: data aggregation();
      wait until both threads finished;
   until collection_phase_has_ended;
   data aggregation();
   data_post_aggregation();
}
```

Figure 3: Pseudo-code based algorithm using standard deviation exemplifying the continuous aggregation strategy.

D. Benefits in the software development process

1) Transparent software development: One of the outstanding advantages of the continuous aggregation strategy is the possibility to simplify and align/harmonise the set-up process of aggregation, thus leading to faster, modularised and more effective and transparent software development. This involves improved maintenance possibilities due to its conceptual unity. Moreover, people can be trained much easier on maintenance, since the software developed is not the outcome of individual abilities and unique skills, but of very well specified methodologies.

2) Paradigm shift: Lewis [34], [35] stated that *software construction is an intrinsically creative and subjective activity and as such has inherent risks.* Lewis added: *the software industry should value human experience, intuition, and wisdom rather than claiming false objectivity and promoting entirely impersonal "processes".*

Our contribution is a step in setting up objective criteria regarding software developing processes, such that it *can be a science, not just an art,* paraphrasing Roetzheim's statement [36] regarding software estimate. This way, our approach facilitates the *paradigm shift* from a subjective software construction activity, towards objectively verifiable straightforward strategies. Our approach does not claim that the overall effort of the transition from large scale aggregation to small scale aggregation is diminishing, the complexity of converting multi-pass algorithms to one-pass algorithms should not be underestimated. It does require *intrinsically creative* and *subjective activity* as formulated by J.P. Lewis, but merely on the algorithmic side.

E. Real-time capabilities

1) Real-time systems: The term *continuous information processing* involves incessant data collection and steady aggregation, such that preliminary aggregated results corresponding to the current status of the collected data are available for evaluation purposes. Continuous processing of large amounts of data is primarily an algorithmics problem [37].

Real-time systems are subject to time constrains, i.e., their actions must be fulfilled within fixed bounds. The perception of the industry of real-time is first of all fast computation [38]. Moreover, TimeSys [39] requires the following features for a real-time system:

a) *predictably fast response to urgent events,*
b) *high degree of schedulability*: the timing requirements of the system must be satisfied at high degrees of resource usage,
c) *stability under transient overload*: when the system is over-loaded by events and it is impossible to meet all the deadlines, the deadlines of selected critical tasks must still be guaranteed.

The characterisation above exemplifies the different requirements in some fields of the industry. A real-time system requires real-time capability of the underlying components, including the operating system, etc. These considerations show the immanent difficulties of the industry to cope with the complexity of real-time requirements of opaque and incomprehensible systems.

2) Real-time capability of CIPM: In order to point out the real-time capabilities of a continuous information processing system, its behaviour is analysed and it is shown that it satisfies the given time limits. In real-world systems, it is supposed that the maximum extent of the streams, i.e., the *maximum size of the streaming data* and the *streaming speed* are known and these thresholds are not exceeded.

With the aim to keep the argumentation simple and straightforward, it is assumed that the streaming speed is constant, i.e., the same amount and type of data is collected within equal time intervals. Hence, it is appropriate to setup chunks of data of the same size collected within equal time spans, such that the aggregation time of different chunks is equal. The aggregation time t_{agg} of a particular chunk should not exceed its retrieval time t_{ret}, i.e., $t_{agg} \leq t_{ret}$, else data to be aggregated will accumulate.

The strategy to achieve real-time behaviour based on continuous stream computing is straightforward. Let t_C be the time constraint such that within the time interval specified accordingly, aggregated data should be available. In order to have real-time capabilities, the condition $t_{ret} + t_{agg} \leq t_C$ should be satisfied. Obviously, to achieve this goal, some fine tuning should be performed by choosing the appropriate size for the chunks. Hence, continuous computation including small scale aggregation, pave the way for real-time capabilities.

In conclusion, within this Section a formal model has been introduced in order to best describe the concepts of the continuous information processing strategy. The focus is on the terms of one-pass algorithm, small scale aggregation, continuous computing, and real-time capability. One-pass algorithms enable small scale aggregation, which can pave the way for real-time capabilities, on the condition that the timely constrains can be satisfied by the underlying computing environment. Actually, the one-pass requirement of the algorithms is not necessary, it suffices that the partial results of the computation of the chunks can be merged such that the expected aggregated values can be calculated.

V. Outline of the Results; Discussions

Our objective has been to work towards developing practical solution to overcome the difficulties related to batch jobs, identified by Cisco in a white paper [8] as Pain Points. The pros and cons of the newly developed continuous information processing strategy versus the traditional batch jobs approach are outlined in this Section and additional weak points of each technique are identified.

A. Cisco's Pain Points

1) Toughest challenge: The main challenge – which led to the outcome of this paper – was to investigate whether it is possible to give satisfactory answers to the Pain Points raised by Cisco [8] concerning batch aggregation on data streams. Except Pain Point No. 3 regarding ad hoc reporting, to all other Pain Points, such as batch window time constraints, painful recovery, service-level agreements, etc., methods of resolution have been established. In order to be able to properly present our methodology, a formal model is set up and it is shown that under some circumstances (for example if the aggregation functions can be processed efficiently in one-step) the data collection and data aggregation can be performed continuously and thus comprise real-time capabilities.

2) Sticking point – additional implementation effort: The one-pass implementation (alternatively using small scale technology) of aggregation functions can be meticulous and may require additional effort. Most of the aggregation functions also termed *measures* used in the industry permit such implementations; one of the well-known counterexample is the average absolute deviation. Since the computation is continuous and final results are available soon after the data collection has been completed, the Pain Point No. 1 regarding the question of batch window time constraints is obsolete.

3) Energy efficiency due to simplified recovery and to load distribution: Painful recovery (Paint Point No. 2) is less painful if there is a well thought-through recovery algorithm in place, such that only the erroneous parts are recalculated. Since there is a much better control of the computational/aggregational flow, a better service-level and resource conflict management can be achieved by using continuous aggregation. It is true, that usually, batch jobs are performed during nighttime hours, when the workload on the computer is lower than during working hours. Unfortunately, due to computation errors or erroneous raw data, the batch aggregation has to be recomputed also during normal working hours. Hence, the computer capacity should support the extended load due to recomputing the batch jobs during working hours. On the contrary, by using continuous computation, the load is distributed uniformly over the whole duration of the data collection and as a result, peak loads remain manageable. Moreover, due to our aggregation strategy – such that calculation is performed during the collection phase as early as possible, best when the data is still in memory – reloading the persisted data into memory is reduced to a minimum. Besides, the small scale aggregation can be optimised by identifying the optimal size of the chunks, such that the time constraints are met with minimal computational effort. This way, smaller computers can be used, especially since the energy efficiency of the batch aggregation is in general significantly worse than the correspondent computation due to small scale aggregation.

B. Continuous aggregation versus batch jobs

1) Our fundamental computational strategy in a nutshell: According to the long time experience of the first author, the best performance in the field of Business Intelligence/-Data Warehouse is obtained if the data is processed/transformed/precalculated as soon as possible; best, *as soon as the data is known to the system*. This includes also multiple storage strategies of the same raw/transformed data. Sometimes, it is advantageous to pursuit a *dual strategy*. On the one hand try to follow the continuous computation strategy as long as possible i.e., as long as the implementation of the corresponding aggregation functions is possible with reasonable effort and run-time performance, and on the other hand, precalculate as much as possible by maintaining the batch jobs strategy.

2) Executions plans as the weak point of the batch jobs strategy: The main challenge of the batch jobs strategy, when using general purpose database management systems, is a technical one and it relates to the optimization through *execution plans*. In highly simplified terms, the execution plans attempt to establish the most efficient execution of statements (queries) out of a summary of pre-calculated statistics. Unfortunately, the execution plans do not always generate the optimal (fastest, most efficient) query; performance can also degrade if the execution plans are updated. Hence, if the streams are not steady, performance degradation of the batch jobs may occur. There are methods to overcome the automatic generation of the execution plans, but the problem in principle remains.

On the contrary, by using small scale aggregation, the size of data sets on which computation is performed is more or less constant and data is in memory, hence less prone to fluctuations due to the executions plans. It is therefore reasonable to assume some upper bounds, enabling real-time capabilities of the system.

C. Enhanced system modeling

One of the most important side benefits of the continuous information processing strategy is the straightforward system modeling. In this way, the design of the architecture, data flow, aggregation strategy, database schema design, etc., is given by the structure of the streaming data, the aggregation functions and the algorithms of their implementation. Thus, the more individualistic design, heavily based on the experience of the application developer is converted into a predefined set of well founded modeling strategies, sustaining a paradigm switch from more or less subjectively individualistic conceptions in software design and development towards objectively established optimal solutions. Quantitative estimations show that many Data Warehouse projects fail at a concerning rate, wasting all the time, money, and effort spent on them [40].

D. Performance advantages

1) Hardware upgrade vs. performance improvement: Next, two technical issues are addressed, which are decisive from technical point of view:

1) absence of Data Warehouse design methodology,
2) performance problems due to the high complexity, requirements on expandability and the low scalability of complex solutions.

According to the experience of the first author at Qimonda in the Business Intelligence and Data Warehouse environment, increasing the processing capabilities of the computers does not always lead to improved performance of the Data Warehouse application. By doubling the computing capacity, roughly 20% in performance improvement has been achieved. Using high performance racks produced the best results. In the end, when the effort for performance improvement is greater than the effort to redesign the Data Warehouse, appropriate measures should be taken. Furthermore, due to our modular straightforward design strategy, the flow of data can be much closely monitored, hence superior *data quality* can be achieved.

2) Broadening the tasks of the classical reporting strategy: The essence of the continuous information processing strategy is that it enables the calculation of the aggregation functions during the collection phase. For example, for reporting purposes, the data for a full day is collected. The classical batch jobs strategy envisaged the generation of the data pool for reporting only after the data has been fully collected. Hence, calculated/aggregated values for reporting were available on the next day, depending on the execution time of the batch jobs. Thus, the scope of classical reporting strategy was to capture, survey and review the production status of the previous day. On the contrary, based on the data already collected, the continuous aggregation strategy enables the calculation/generation of preliminary reports at various points in time. This way, for example, soon after 12:00, the daily reports show the production figures corresponding to the time frame [0:00, 12:00]. Therefore, if these figures are not optimal, corresponding measures to boost production can be taken. Thus, modern reporting based on our technology enables *production control*.

In some cases, optimisation can be substantial, saving time and costs. For example, in the semiconductor manufacturing, there are optional production steps, where the material is measured. The number of measurements can be in the range of hundreds and the measurement time can last for several hours. The common aggregation technology assumes that all measurement data is collected before starting the computation. By adopting our continuous computation technology, preliminary measurement results can be calculated. This way, faulty processed material can be identified earlier and the ramp-up time of a new product can be substantially reduced, thus giving the company decisive advantage over his competitors.

In conclusion, the price for achieving continuous aggregation may be high, the build in functions like standard deviation cannot be used any more, and as the case may be, new one-pass or similar algorithms for the aggregation functions have to be set up, hence algorithmic and programming effort may increase. The benefits are obvious, a straightforward design strategy, up-to-date aggregated values during data collection, a uniform computational effort over the data collection period and an efficient recalculation strategy, which lead in the end to a much efficient utilisation of computational resources. Improving the performance of batch jobs is tedious, if the redesign strategy is not an option, sophisticated data base technologies or costly rack high performance can help.

VI. Conclusion and Future Work

In the following, the advantages of the CIPM are summarized and the future work, we are concerned with, is sketched.

A. Conclusion

Satisfactory solutions to the problems caused by the nightly batch aggregation as pointed out by Cisco [8] are given, except for *Pain Point* No. 3. To ensure an accurate presentation of our methodology, a formal model has been set up and it has been shown that for a specific type of aggregation functions – including those that supports efficient one-pass implementation – the data aggregation can be performed continuously and thus allows real-time capabilities.

1) Advantages CIPM - Résumé: Continuous aggregation strategy supports:

1) *real-time capabilities*; if time constraints can be met,
2) *aggregated values corresponding to the captured data*; i.e., reporting capabilities at any point in time during data collection,
3) *enhanced production control* due to up-to-date aggregated data at any point in time during data collection,
4) *straightforward design strategies* due to clear, easy understandable architectural and implementation principles,
5) *easy maintenance* due to transparent and straightforward software development process,
6) *higher quality of aggregated data* due to the simplified architectural and implementation principles,
7) *uniform load of the underlying database system* due to the continuous aggregation principles,
8) *efficient recalculation of aggregated values*; in case erroneous data is collected, and last but not least:
9) *energy efficiency*; smaller computers can be used due to the fact that aggregation is performed during the whole data collection period.

We have not experienced major difficulties in implementing the CIPM approach in database application, implementation from the scratch is pretty straightforward, porting to CIPM an existing legacy database application using batch jobs, can be quite cumbersome. For sophisticated legacy applications, the most efficient method is to try to improve performance as long as possible by applying database technologies, by using high performance racks, etc.

2) Final considerations: The price of the advantages as above depends on the structure of the aggregation function. Most of the key performance indicators used in the industry permit an incremental representation, i.e., as functions of different representation of sum(), avg(), count(), similar to the the standard deviation, as presented in this article. The effort in this cases is manageable. Generally speaking, the aggregation function should permit efficient one-pass calculation, or in the case of holistic functions, an algorithm, such that the time constraints can be satisfied.

B. Future Work

The Pain Point No. 3 of Cisco's white paper [8]: "ad hoc reporting; managing unplanned reports in a plan-based environment", remains still unhandled and it is subject of future research. The question arise, as to what extent such unplanned reports can be meaningfully foreseen and set up. Furthermore, one asks oneself, what is the optimal strategy regarding volatile versus persistent aggregation, i.e., aggregation within a query set up by a visualisation tool versus aggregation persisted in a data storage. From an algorithmic perspective, persistent aggregation offers more advantages if the query is often invoked. Moreover, the results can be much better validated if the data is persisted. On the other hand, sporadic queries should remain volatile, i.e., the result of the queries should not be persisted for further reuse.

ACKNOWLEDGMENT

We acknowledge the assistance and helpful comments of the anonymous referees.

REFERENCES

[1] A. De Mauro, M. Greco, and M. Grimaldi, "A formal definition of big data based on its essential features," *Library Review*, 2016, Retrieved: September 2021. [Online]. Available: https://www.researchgate.net/publication/299379163_A_formal_definition_of_Big_Data_based_on_its_essential_features

[2] H. U. Buhl, M. Röglinger, F. Moser, and J. Heidemann, "Big Data," *Business & Information Systems Engineering*, vol. 5, no. 2, pp. 65–69, 2013, Retrieved: September 2021. [Online]. Available: https://doi.org/10.1007/s12599-013-0249-5

[3] Statista, "Volume of data/information created, captured, copied, and consumed worldwide from 2010 to 2025," 2021, Retrieved: September 2021. [Online]. Available: https://www.statista.com/statistics/871513/worldwide-data-created/

[4] R. Sousa, R. Miranda, A. Moreira, C. Alves, N. Lori, and J. Machado, "Software tools for conducting real-time information processing and visualization in industry: An up-to-date review," *Applied Sciences*, vol. 11, no. 11, p. 4800, 2021, Retrieved: September 2021. [Online]. Available: https://www.mdpi.com/2076-3417/11/11/4800

[5] K. Yasumoto, H. Yamaguchi, and H. Shigeno, "Survey of real-time processing technologies of iot data streams," *Journal of Information Processing*, vol. 24, no. 2, pp. 195–202, 2016, Retrieved: September 2021. [Online]. Available: https://doi.org/10.2197/ipsjjip.24.195

[6] I. Sommerville, "Software engineering 9th edition," *ISBN-10*, vol. 137035152, p. 18, 2011.

[7] Zinner *et al.*, "Real-time information systems and methodology based on continuous homomorphic processing in linear information spaces," 2015, Retrieved: September 2021. [Online]. Available: https://patentimages.storage.googleapis.com/ed/fa/37/6069417bdcc3eb/US20170032016A1.pdf

[8] Cisco, "BI and ETL Process Management Pain Points," *White Paper*, pp. 1–9, 2010, Retrieved: September 2021. [Online]. Available: https://www.cisco.com/c/dam/en/us/products/collateral/cloud-systems-management/tidal-enterprise-scheduler/whitepaper_c11-633329.pdf

[9] N. Schweikardt, "One-pass algorithm." 2009, Retrieved: September 2021. [Online]. Available: http://www.tks.informatik.uni-frankfurt.de/schweika/downloads/EncycDBS_OnePassAlgos.pdf

[10] P. E. O'Neil, "The sb-tree an index-sequential structure for high-performance sequential access," *Acta Informatica*, vol. 29, no. 3, pp. 241–265, 1992, Retrieved: September 2021. [Online]. Available: https://citeseerx.ist.psu.edu/viewdoc/download?doi=10.1.1.55.9482&rep=rep1&type=pdf

[11] J. Zhang, "Spatio-temporal aggregation over streaming geospatial data," in *Proceedings of the 10th International Conference on Extending Database Technology Ph. D. Workshop*. Citeseer, 2006, Retrieved: September 2021. [Online]. Available: https://citeseerx.ist.psu.edu/viewdoc/download?doi=10.1.1.84.8746&rep=rep1&type=pdf

[12] J. Yang and J. Widom, "Incremental computation and maintenance of temporal aggregates," *The VLDB Journal*, vol. 12, no. 3, pp. 262–283, 2003, Retrieved: September 2021. [Online]. Available: http://ilpubs.stanford.edu:8090/482/1/2000-6.pdf

[13] TU-Berlin-DIMA, "Scotty: Efficient window aggregation for out-of-order stream processing," *Generated by GitHub Pages*, 2021, Retrieved: September 2021. [Online]. Available: https:21:3103.09.202121:3103.09.202121:3103.09.202121:3103.09.202121:3103.09.2021//tu-berlin-dima.github.io/scotty-window-processor/

[14] J. Traub, P. M. Grulich, A. R. Cuellar, S. Breß, A. Katsifodimos, T. Rabl, and V. Markl, "Scotty: Efficient window aggregation for out-of-order stream processing," in *2018 IEEE 34th International Conference on Data Engineering (ICDE)*. IEEE, 2018, pp. 1300–1303, Retrieved: September 2021. [Online]. Available: https://hpi.de/fileadmin/user_upload/fachgebiete/rabl/publications/2018/ScottyICDE2018.pdf

[15] J. Traub, P. M. Grulich, A. R. Cuéllar, S. Breß, A. Katsifodimos, T. Rabl, and V. Markl, "Scotty: General and efficient open-source window aggregation for stream processing systems," *ACM Transactions on Database Systems (TODS)*, vol. 46, no. 1, pp. 1–46, 2021, Retrieved: September 2021. [Online]. Available: https://www.redaktion.tu-berlin.de/fileadmin/fg131/Publikation/Papers/Traub_TODS-21-Scotty_preprint.pdf

[16] K. Tangwongsan, M. Hirzel, and S. Schneider, "Sliding-window aggregation algorithms." 2019, Retrieved: September 2021. [Online]. Available: http://hirzels.com/martin/papers/encyc18-sliding-window.pdf

[17] ——, "Optimal and general out-of-order sliding-window aggregation," *Proceedings of the VLDB Endowment*, vol. 12, no. 10, pp. 1167–1180, 2019, Retrieved: September 2021. [Online]. Available: https://www.scott-a-s.com/files/vldb2019_fiba.pdf

[18] Z. Chen and A. Zhang, "A survey of approximate quantile computation on large-scale data," *IEEE Access*, vol. 8, pp. 34 585–34 597, 2020, Retrieved: September 2021. [Online]. Available: https://ieeexplore.ieee.org/stamp/stamp.jsp?arnumber=9001104

[19] P. P. Pebay, T. Terriberry, H. Kolla, and J. C. Bennett, "Formulas for robust, parallel computation of arbitrary-order, arbitrary-variate, statistical moments with arbitrary weights and compounding." Sandia National Lab.(SNL-CA), Livermore, CA (United States); The Xiph. Org , Tech. Rep., 2015, Retrieved: September 2021. [Online]. Available: https://www.osti.gov/servlets/purl/1504207

[20] P. Pébay, T. B. Terriberry, H. Kolla, and J. Bennett, "Numerically stable, scalable formulas for parallel and online computation of higher-order multivariate central moments with arbitrary weights," *Computational Statistics*, vol. 31, no. 4, pp. 1305–1325, 2016, Retrieved: September 2021. [Online]. Available: https://www.osti.gov/servlets/purl/1426900

[21] C. Labreuche, "A formal justification of a simple aggregation function based on criteria and rank weights," in *Proc. DA2PL2018, From Multiple Criteria Decis. Aid Preference Learn.*, 2018, pp. 1–1, Retrieved: September 2021. [Online]. Available: http://da2pl.cs.put.poznan.pl/programme/detailed-programme/da2pl2018-abstract-14.pdf

[22] R. Eccles and G. Serafeim, "Corporate and integrated reporting: A functional perspective,[w:] corporate stewardship: Achieving sustainable effectiveness, red," *E. Lawler, S. Mohrman, J. OToole, Greenleaf*, Posted: 2 Feb 2014 Last revised: 24 May 2018, Retrieved: September 2021. [Online]. Available: https://papers.ssrn.com/sol3/papers.cfm?abstract_id=2388716

[23] T. F. Chan, G. H. Golub, and R. J. LeVeque, "Algorithms for computing the sample variance: Analysis and recommendations," *The American Statistician*, vol. 37, no. 3, pp. 242–247, 1983, Retrieved: September 2021. [Online]. Available: http://www.cs.yale.edu/publications/techreports/tr222.pdf

[24] ——, "Updating formulae and a pairwise algorithm for computing sample variances," in *COMPSTAT 1982 5th Symposium held at Toulouse 1982*, 1982, pp. 30–41, Retrieved: September 2021. [Online]. Available: https://apps.dtic.mil/sti/pdfs/ADA083170.pdfP

[25] W. Hopp and M. Spearman, *Factory Physics: Third Edition*. Waveland Press, 2011.

[26] W. Hansch and T. Kubot, "Factory Dynamics Chapter 7 Lectures at the Universitaet der Bundeswehr Muenich," p. 68, Retrieved: September 2021. [Online]. Available: https://fac.ksu.edu.sa/sites/default/files/Factory%20Dynamics.pdf

[27] C.-F. Lindberg, S. Tan, J. Yan, and F. Starfelt, "Key performance indicators improve industrial performance," *Energy procedia*, vol. 75, pp. 1785–1790, 2015, Retrieved: September 2021. [Online]. Available: https://doi.org/10.1016/j.egypro.2015.07.474

[28] M. Zinner *et al.*, "Techniques and methodologies for measuring and increasing the quality of services: a case study based on data centers," *International Journal On Advances in Intelligent Systems, volume 13, numbers 1 and 2, 2020*, vol. 13, no. 1 & 2, pp. 19–35, 2020. [Online]. Available: http://www.thinkmind.org/articles/intsys_v13_n12_2020_2.pdf

[29] W. Kahan, "Pracniques: further remarks on reducing truncation errors," *Communications of the ACM*, vol. 8, no. 1, p. 40, 1965.

[30] T. Pham-Gia and T. Hung, "The mean and median absolute deviations," *Mathematical and Computer Modelling*, vol. 34, no. 7-8, pp. 921–936, 2001, Retrieved: September 2021. [Online]. Available: https://www.sciencedirect.com/science/article/pii/S0895717701001091

[31] R. C. Geary, "The ratio of the mean deviation to the standard deviation as a test of normality," *Biometrika*, vol. 27, no. 3/4, pp. 310–332, 1935.

[32] J. K. Patel and C. B. Read, *Handbook of the normal distribution*. CRC Press, 1996, vol. 150.

[33] J. L. Barlow, "Error analysis of a pairwise summation algorithm to compute the sample variance," *Numerische Mathematik*, vol. 58, no. 1, pp. 583–590, 1990, Retrieved: September 2021. [Online]. Available: https://de.booksc.eu/book/6543977/98912d

[34] J. Lewis and T. Disney, "Large limits to software estimation," *ACM Software Engineering Notes*, vol. 26, no. 4, pp. 54–59, 2001, Retrieved: September 2021. [Online]. Available: http://scribblethink.org/Work/Softestim/kcsest.pdf

[35] J. Lewis, "Mathematical limits to software estimation: Supplementary material," *Stanford University*, 2001, Retrieved: September 2021. [Online]. Available: http://scribblethink.org/Work/Softestim/softestim.html

[36] W. H. Roetzheim and R. A. Beasley, *Software project cost schedule estimating: best practices*. Prentice-Hall, Inc., 1998.

[37] B. Evgeniy, "Supercomputer beg with artificial intelligence of optimal resource use and management by continuous processing of large programs," *Glob Acad J Econ Buss*, vol. 1, pp. 21–26, 2019, Retrieved: September 2021. [Online]. Available: https://gajrc.com/media/articles/GAJEB_11_21-26_zOIbTWD.pdf

[38] E. A. Lee, "What is real time computing? a personal view." *IEEE Des. Test*, vol. 35, no. 2, pp. 64–72, 2018, Retrieved: September 2021. [Online]. Available: https://ptolemy.berkeley.edu/projects/chess/pubs/1192/Lee_WhatIsRealTime_Accepted.pdf

[39] TimeSys Corporation, "The concise handbook of real-time systems," *TimeSys Corporation Pittsburgh, PA, Version 1.3*, pp. 1–65, 2002, Retrieved: September 2021. [Online]. Available: https://course.ece.cmu.edu/~ece749/docs/RTSHandbook.pdf

[40] D. Asrani, R. Jain, and U. Saxena, "Data Warehouse Development Standardization Framework (DWDSF): A Way to Handle Data Warehouse Failure," *IOSR Journal of Computer Engineering (IOSR-JCE)*, vol. 19, pp. 29–38, 2017, Retrieved: September 2021. [Online]. Available: http://www.iosrjournals.org/iosr-jce/papers/Vol19-issue1/Version-2/E1901022938.pdf